Deep Song
The Dance Story of
Martha Graham

Deep Song
The Dance Story of
Martha Graham

Ernestine Stodelle

A Dance Horizons Book

SCHIRMER BOOKS
A Division of Macmillan, Inc.
NEW YORK

Collier Macmillan Publishers
LONDON

Schirmer Books
A Division of Macmillan, Inc.
866 Third Avenue, New York, N.Y. 10022

Collier Macmillan Canada, Inc.

Lines from "Every Soul Is a Circus" are reprinted with permission of Macmillan
Publishing Company from COLLECTED POEMS of Vachel Lindsay. Copyright 1929
by Macmillan Publishing Co., Inc., renewed 1957 by Nicholas C. Lindsay and Susan L.
Russell.

Excerpts from FOUR QUARTETS by T.S. Eliot are reprinted by permission of Faber
and Faber Ltd., and Harcourt Brace Jovanovich, Inc.; copyright 1943 by T.S. Eliot,
renewed 1971 by Esme Valerie Eliot.

Excerpt from THE FAMILY REUNION by T.S. Eliot is reprinted by permission of
Faber and Faber Ltd., and Harcourt Brace Jovanovich, Inc.; copyright 1939 by T.S. Eliot,
renewed 1967 by Esme Valerie Eliot.

Excerpts from WILDERNESS STAIR by Ben Belitt are reprinted by permission of Ben
Belitt and the Grove Press; copyright 1955 by Ben Belitt.

Excerpts from THE SELECTED POETRY OF ROBINSON JEFFERS are printed by
permission of Random House, Inc.; copyright 1927 by Robinson Jeffers, renewed 1959
by Robinson Jeffers.

The Berkshire Eagle (Pittsfield, MA) masthead used by permission.

Library of Congress Catalog Card Number: 84–1261

Printed in the United States of America

printing number
1   2   3   4   5   6   7   8   9   10

Library of Congress Cataloging in Publication Data

Stodelle, Ernestine.
    Deep song.

    "A Dance Horizons book."
    Bibliography: p.
    Includes index.
    1. Graham, Martha.   2. Choreographers—United States—
Biography.   3. Choreography.   I. Title.
GV1785.G7S86   1984   793.3'092'4 [B]   84–1261
ISBN 0-02-872520-4

For John, the beloved, and our Chamberlain-Komisarjevsky clan: Tanya, Liz, Margie, Christopher, Benedict, and John Jr.

Contents

List of Illustrations

Following page 74:

Martha Graham, age 2.

Martha Graham and Georgia Graham, c. 1900.

Ruth St. Denis in *Incense*, 1908.

Ruth St. Denis and Ted Shawn in duet from *Egyptian Ballet*, 1922.

Xochitl poster, Pantages Circuit season, 1920–21.

Martha Graham and Charles Weidman in *Danse Arabe*, c. 1921.

Martha Graham and Group in *Heretic*, 1929.

Martha Graham in *Two Primitive Canticles*, 1931.

Portrait, Martha Graham, c. 1930.

Martha Graham in *Lamentation*, 1935.

Louis Horst composes in his New York Studio, 1935.

Martha Graham and Dance Group in *Primitive Mysteries*, 1935.

Martha Graham and Dance Group in *Primitive Mysteries*, 1935.

Martha Graham in *Satyric Festival Song*, 1935.

Martha Graham in *Ekstasis*, 1935.

Martha Graham in *Frontier*, 1935.

Martha Hill, Ben Belitt, Bessie Schoenberg, Bennington School of the Dance, 1939, at Mills College, Oakland, California.

John Martin at Bennington School of the Dance, 1938.

Erick Hawkins, Doris Humphrey, Charles Weidman, Martha Graham, and Louis Horst at Bennington, 1941.

Following page 170:

Foreword

Since I have had the unusual good fortune of spending more than half of my life in contact with Martha Graham, her repertoire, and the technique that she evolved, even after leaving her company and working with my own, I deem it an honor, albeit a treacherous one, to try to "say" what I have been thinking and dancing for a good part of my life. Notwithstanding, I welcome the opportunity because it has forced me to look at what I have been involved in, from the distance of a spectator. The further back I step, the larger and more important looms the worth of the Graham contribution to dance technique, dance theater, the concept of theater, of human behavior, and of life itself.

Here is the largest, the most awe-inspiring, unique, and diverse repertoire by one choreographer ever to have been produced, comparable only to Shakespeare in dramaturgy and Picasso in painting. As if that in itself isn't wondrous enough, there is, in addition, a discipline of study to prepare the dancer to be able to perform these very special works built on the drives, rages, ecstasies, and passions of human experience. It is as if Martha tore open the center of the body and revealed those inner storms that Lorca calls the "dark root of the shriek," or those bright cascades of movement that churn upward in the body into a laugh or a leap.

Before Martha's way with dance, the front of the torso was immobile. Dancing involved the arms, the legs, the back, the hands, feet, and head. With laser-beam clarity she isolated and caught the passion of the contraction (which is an amplification of an involuntary physical reaction to a sob or laugh). She harnessed it into use as the visceral illumination of the hidden inner life of the dancer and it added a vitality as well as a vulnerability to the dance phrase, depending on the need of the theme. The contraction became the initiator of the beginning of movement that finds its way out from the center of the torso to the arms, legs, head, and finally into space. She disciplined it into a formalism lest a vestige of expressionism make it sentimental or soften or blur its impact. This formalism, no doubt, accounts for its durability over all of these years and throughout the facetious teeter-tottering changes in aesthetic fashions.

With the intuitiveness of genius and the perception of a seer who penetrates the timelessness of human behavior, Martha searches for and finds the crucial, telling movement needed for the choreography of the moment. It is at once visceral, ancient, and present, resonating in us a physical response that our bodies recall having experienced even before we were born. There is never a moment of beauty of line alone or a technical feat for itself, for the movement is always charged with dramatic or poetic imagery that makes it more than it is: urgent and moving as well as beautiful. Martha's involvement with the intricacies of human drives has forced her to find an element of dissonant and "distorted" movement, thereby extending the existing accepted dance vocabulary. The strangeness is never exploited as a gimmick, but is the organic result of dramatic need. She has changed the accepted image of dance and theater throughout the world. She has given the dancing body an additional concept: that of inner space, thus contributing *another* dimension to the language of dance.

Of course, the technique evolved from the treasures created by the repertoire. The dances that were built on the technique, those without dramatic scenario, such as *Diversion of Angels, Adorations,* and *"Acts of Light,"* are difficult, brilliant, and exciting. Their drama consists of the juxtaposition of contrasting movement within the choreography.

"'Tis the gift to be simple," the first line of the Shaker song that Aaron Copland used in *Appalachian Spring,* is very much a part of Martha's unique aesthetic. In her it is not only a gift but is a part of her genius *not* to begin by being simple but to become so, and in that act of becoming she discards all the tangential riches that have been explored in the time of making a dance until the core or seed movement emerges with profound and astounding simplicity.

To be able to perform this repertoire, one is forced to assume the size and weight and image of an array of personae who people the world's greatest myths and legends. One must become, as it were, archetypical of the time in civilization and specific dynamic of the role (or dance) in each work. How wonderful and challenging to have to research and find ways of becoming believable as the heroines Judith, St. Joan, or Ariadne, or the queens Elizabeth, Mary Stuart, Medea, Jocasta, or Clytemnestra—or to find one's way in movement with the sensibilities of Emily Dickinson or Mary as Virgin, Magdelene, and Mother.

The Graham repertoire cannot be performed merely by learning a sequence of movement, no matter how brilliantly the dancer masters the technical difficulties, and they are considerable. There must be a dramatic or poetic impulse that supplies a resonance of inner movement and breathes a specific dynamism of tension, weight, punctuation, delicacy, or transparency into a performance.

So vital and continually evolving an artist as Martha Graham defies summing up or classifying. Yet for me, nothing is quite so apt or prophetic of a career that has illuminated and celebrated the human condition in dance as the title of one of her earliest solos: *Ekstasis.*

Certainly there is no one more able to write about Martha Graham than Ernestine Stodelle. She has been part of the modern dance community most of her life, and has seen the Graham repertoire since 1929. As a dance critic, her reviews are written with insight and a sense of responsibility to the work and to the artist, and she possesses an intuitive perception that touches upon the reason behind the choreography and helps place it in the context of its social and cultural environment. Moreover, her rare esthetic sensibilities qualify her to write of Martha's unique theater of dance—which has vitalized half a century of dance activity and is still continuing to replenish and renew its thrust.

Pearl Lang
New York, November 11, 1983

Preface

"Before Yesterday," the title of the Prologue, was originally the title of the first installment in a series of articles on Martha Graham that began in the January 1962 issue of *Dance Observer*, a magazine founded and edited by Louis Horst.

That my highly ambitious effort—a chronicle of the creative achievements of Horst's "first pupil"—was even considered for publication by the man who was the supreme authority on Martha Graham is still a source of wonder to me. Only the largesse of thought that characterized Horst's attitude toward aspiring writers can account for his open-mindedness in accepting my fledgling manuscript. And only the subsequent experience of working under the eagle eye of an editor of the stature of Louis Horst could make it eventually possible for me to bring the dance story of Martha Graham to its current conclusion.

Although a mere six installments of my series had been written before Louis's death cut short his invaluable guidance, the benefit of his lucid thinking and, I might add, his generously proffered reminiscences of personal and professional associations over a period of nearly fifty years provided this writer with the perspective necessary to utilize the *Dance Observer* articles as basic research material for a book. To have *Deep Song: The Dance Story of Martha Graham* emerge in 1984, the year of nationwide celebrations of the Louis Horst Centennial, is especially gratifying to one of the last pupils—as far as dance reportage is concerned—of the acknowledged figurehead of early modern dance.

In retrospect, the original impulse behind the series was brazen. My adolescent writer's mind had envisioned no less than an entire history of American modern dance! Louis was ready to take it on, but almost immediately we were at a crossroad. Should we proceed laterally and focus the next installment on the achievements of Doris Humphrey and Charles Weidman, Graham's colleagues in the revolutionary thrust of the early modern dance? Or should we pursue our story vertically with Martha? To write of Doris and Charles would be natural for me, a former Humphrey-Weidman dancer who had had the honor of performing in the first season of the historic Dance Repertory Theatre, but a parallel recounting might make for confusion. Louis's decision was "to finish with Martha" and then "go back and pick up the others," including the German-born Hanya Holm and the disciples of the four pioneers.

The irony of this decision is that no chronicler of the modern dance is ever "finished" with Martha Graham. At age ninety, she still poses a threat to a critic's equilibrium—her creative adventures go on, accumulating laurels throughout the world. She still attracts the participation of contemporary artists of the performing caliber of ballet classicist Rudolph Nureyev, who has aligned himself repeatedly with the Graham Company, and of soprano Leontyne Price, whose regal voice enlarges the dimensions of Samuel Barber's stirring score for *Andromache's Lament*.

So the plan was laid from the beginning to write a critique of Martha Graham's performing and choreographing achievements, not a biography. The dance itself would be the protagonist in the drama of her artistic development. Yet, since the dance has been the very fabric of Martha Graham's life, a narrative line of *relevant* personal experience would have to be threaded through the story of this remarkable woman's career.

If the double focus of my tale serves to illuminate the reader's consciousness of the dynamic evolution of one of our century's most gifted artists, then my efforts have not been in vain.

Acknowledgments

My long sojourn in the labyrinthian groves of Martha Graham's aesthetic achievements can only be described as a reliving of memorable moments not only in my own and my subject's lives but also in the lives of those who shared their personal recollections with me.

Most emphatically, my gratitude for insights gleaned goes first to Martha Graham and then to two members of her immediate family: her sister, Georgia Graham Sargeant, whom I interviewed in the mid-1960s, and to the late Mary H. Bear, Martha's Auntie Re, whom I had the privilege of meeting in Santa Barbara when she was ninety-two. From them came an understanding of Martha's childhood and youth to complement the fascinating background supplied by the artist herself.

Next in line are the Graham dancers, and the choreographer's colleagues and collaborators, to all of whom I owe an immeasurable debt. There seems to be a bond between members of the arts professions to share worthwhile experiences. Far from being an exception, Graham associates reinforce the rule.

Among the names listed on page xx are those of May Forbes, Louis Horst's older sister, with whom I maintained a cherished friendship for more than ten years following Louis's death, and that of Anne Douglas, a former Denishawn dancer, who clarified—no less than May—details of Louis's nonprofessional life.

Nor could I ever have delivered a coherent manuscript without the valuable assistance over the years of personal associates who dedicated a considerable portion of their energies to the ferreting out of information essential for academically correct Notes. Without Jennifer White Seidler and Rochelle Davis of times past, and especially without Kay Woodard, whose indefatigable probing in recent years has miraculously uncovered long-forgotten sources of indispensable quotations, *Deep Song* may never have attained a scholastically publishable level. To Kay, and to Monica Ziermann, Lyndell Betzner, the late Margaret Mahoney, Cynthia Fiore, Lauren Shaw, Reina Wieland, and John Chamberlain, Jr., all of whom assisted me at strategic moments in the copying of almost unreadable manuscripts, I feel indebted.

Dance Associates, Colleagues, and Collaborators Interviewed:

Marguerite Andrus (Fuller)
Ben Belitt
Bonnie Bird
Dorothy Bird
Joseph Campbell
Anne Douglas (Doucet)
Jane Dudley
Jean Erdman
Vivian Fine
Nina Fonaroff
May Forbes
Natalie Harris (Wheatley)
Erick Hawkins
Martha Hill
Mary Hinkson
Linda Hodes
Sachiyo Ito
Ruth Jentzer (Gottdiener)

Pearl Lang
Eugene Lester
Evelyn Lohoefer
Sophie Maslow
Barbara Morgan
Ruth L. Murray
Isamu Noguchi
May O'Donnell
Bertram Ross
Winthrop Sargeant
Ted Shawn
Jane Sherman
Bessie Schoenberg
Gertrude Shurr
Robert Starer
Paul Taylor
Marnie Thomas (Wood)
Marian Van Tuyl

Charles Weidman, Sallie Wilson, Ethel Winter,
David Wood

As far as gratitude for critical estimates of my writing is concerned, I have only to remember the incisive analysis of Louis Horst, Ben Belitt, and of the late Rachel Baker to realize how far these three wise minds made me travel to see the light. The further questioning of longtime friends Jule Eisenbud and Richard Galligan helped me redefine the way. I began to stumble less, assisted in no small measure by the calm remedial suggestions of my own copy editor Edith White and by the practical tactics of a lovely Humphrey dancer-turned-secretary: Gail Corbin.

Compassion and understanding were, despite periods of suspended action, always within reach. There was Al Pischl of Dance Horizons, who made me pull my unfinished manuscript out of a file where it had lain for three or four years . . . but Pischl's request was complied with only after one of my granddaughters, Alexandra Metaksa, had read a chapter or two out of curiosity and had remarked with the candor of youthful certainty: "This should be published." More than anything else, a child's opinion put me back on Martha Graham's labyrinthian path.

Once I had returned in earnest, valued friends—Eleanor Powers, Pat Collins, Virginia Stuermer, Joan Targa, Sally and George Cohn, Dr. M. William Ziedman, and all six of my children—sustained me with their perception of what I was trying to do.

And then there were the stalwart, unruffled heroes and heroines of the Dance Collection of the New York Public Library at Lincoln Center who, under the all-knowing curatorship of Genevieve Oswald, removed obstacles along the way. I am particularly grateful for the kind assistance of Nancy Shawcross, Monica Moseley, Lacy McDearmon, and Henry Wisneski.

But the underlying propulsion was the consistently supportive attitude of my experienced writer-husband, John Chamberlain, and of Anne Morrow Lindbergh, who has encouraged me from the beginning of our thirty-five-year-old friendship to write about the art that has become for me a testament of faith and a form of deep emotional-intellectual-physical commitment. To these two superb craftsmen of the written word, I bow in gratitude.

Ernestine Stodelle
Cheshire, Connecticut
May 28, 1984

Prologue

Before Yesterday

A girl of fourteen brought up in a strict Irish–Scotch Presbyterian environment at the end of the nineteenth century might never have succumbed to the blandishments of tropical life in Spanish-influenced southern California. Or the reverse could have happened: a drastic disavowal of self-discipline in favor of self-indulgence.

The adolescent Martha Graham did not reject the color, warmth, and sensuousness of the atmosphere that greeted her when she and her family moved from a suburb of Pittsburgh, Pennsylvania, to Santa Barbara on California's golden coast; but neither did she give herself without reservations to the seductive new world she encountered. The moral rectitude in which she had been reared remained, to a great extent, inviolate. Straightness as a virtue—combined with straightness as bodily experience—were clearly seen in the growing girl's physique and personality. Even as a schoolchild walking down the streets of her native town of Allegheny, or of nearby Mars, where relatives on her mother's side lived, Martha Graham's stance revealed determination and individuality. A strong sense of form, engendered by disciplined family life, would continue to carve its path through her body and set the muscle tone for future behavior.

Then, too, there were external factors: the town that the young Martha Graham lived in had a self-consciousness of its own. The streets were neatly and conventionally planned; the churches, semi-religious societies, and clubs were many; the sturdy lines of two impressive government-built buildings—an arsenal and a penitentiary—could be pointed to as guardians of civic security and order; more pridefully, the townsfolk could take visitors up a hill at the city's northwest end to marvel at a newly constructed observatory, evidence of Allegheny's up-to-dateness in modern man's quest for scientific knowledge. God's universe was, clerically and secularly, presumed to be at their fingertips.

Compared to industrialized Pittsburgh, its rapidly growing, fiery,

1

smoke-spewing neighbor to the south, Allegheny was a small residential area. True, its busy waterfront at the confluence of three rivers—the Monongahela, the Allegheny, and the Ohio—kept Allegheny, like Pittsburgh, bustling with shipping commerce; but the town remained firmly separate in its social attitudes and urban policies until it was annexed by the affluent "city of steel" in 1907.

A like independence could be detected in Martha Graham's childhood personality. Deference to authority was instilled in her very bones. Her upbringing would not have had it otherwise. Yet, courteous or obedient as she was, she always retained a strong sense of her own self-worth. Quietly standing still when spoken to, she listened attentively. Adults were to be respected, their admonishments heeded, their orders followed. But there were circumstances when she *knew* what was right for her, and nothing could stop her; for example, that incident on the train when she was not more than four years old and her mother took her to visit some relatives. Martha had been on a train before, and had not liked it in the least. As soon as she perceived where she was and the train started to move, she began to protest. Mrs. Graham paid no attention. When the conductor walked into their carriage, the little girl saw her opportunity. "Man!" cried Martha, stamping her foot angrily, "I'm Dr. Graham's daughter, and I want out of here!"

One can see the little girl standing at attention, listening carefully to the words of her beloved father as if she were the one person chosen to be the recipient of his outpouring of knowledge. Her heart might be pounding with a tumultuous excitement (from something quite alien), but she would be maintaining an appearance of polite absorption in the words she was granted to hear. Her replies would be equally impressive, or so she thought, until one day she was shocked to hear the observant Dr. Graham suddenly remark, "Martha, you're not telling me the truth!"

Wide-eyed, she stammered, "How do you know?"

"I can tell by the way you are moving," was his candid retort.

That was Martha's first lesson in psychology—a notable one considering that her teacher was a specialist in nervous diseases. Dr. George Greenfield Graham had received his degree from the College of Physicians and Surgeons in Baltimore. Ten years before marrying Jane Beers, also a native of Pennsylvania, he had joined the staff of the Western Pennsylvania Hospital–Insane Department in the town of Dixmont, which was close to Allegheny. Appointed senior assistant physician after two years, he remained on the hospital staff until 1893 when he resigned to go into private practice. (Later, Martha liked to say that it was her father who gave her her first dancing lesson when he chided her about her lie.)

One can see the child dressing to go to church in the dark of a Pennsylvania winter morning: carefully smoothing out her Sunday dress, tying the sash just so, and slipping into her best warm coat; then the final touches, putting on her most becoming bonnet, buttoning her gloves, and when stepping through the front door with her mother, father, and sisters, lowering a little veil over her deep-set eyes, small, straight, aristocratic nose, and pleasantly generous mouth. Decorum was everywhere but in the eyes, mouth, and chin, the last so much an extension of the jawbone that the face could have appeared bottom-heavy had not the eyes overwhelmed the viewer first. Hers were a poet's eyes, both introspective and visionary; they would have tales to tell one day that the child could hardly suspect . . . though, surely, fantasies had already begun to assert themselves in her imagination.

Some fantasies are meant to be nourished in the privacy of a growing child's solitude; some fantasies are acted out with props, costumes, and a scenario. In spite of the strictness of their daily life, the acting out of homemade plays was a common occurrence in the household of Dr. George Graham and his wife, Jane, known more familiarly as Jennie. Such harmless indulgences had been introduced by Lizzie, the young Irish girl with whom Dr. Graham had first come into contact when he was an intern in a hospital which specialized in nervous diseases. He had personally supervised her case—the source of which was never discussed—and had been struck by the orphan girl's wild ways and warmhearted nature. Lizzie vowed that Dr. Graham had saved her life. With characteristic intensity she wanted to repay him with nothing less than total devotion to him and his family. The opportunity arose when she heard that Mrs. Graham had given birth to a baby girl, on May 11, 1894. A few weeks later, baggage in hand, Elizabeth Prendergast rang the doorbell of a large, comfortable-looking house at 1534 Fremont Street.

"I am Lizzie," she said shyly but resolutely to the maid who answered. "I've come to stay. I told Dr. Graham when he would get married and have children, I would come to take care of them."

Lizzie became "Sizzie" to Dr. Graham's new baby, whose name was Martha. All the affection that had been denied the orphan child

3

was showered on her little charge. Lizzie sang to Martha, played on the floor with Martha, and told fascinating stories right out of her head. Lizzie had never gone to school, but she was a good Roman Catholic. She went to church regularly, and church, for her, was a place full of enchantment. One lighted candles at altars, one knelt in prayer, one made the sign of the cross from forehead to chest and from shoulder to shoulder; and one bowed one's head in homage to saints carved in stone. The church was a kind of theater where one performed rituals with all sorts of elaborate, meaningful gestures. Lizzie simply transferred the theater of ecclesiastic rituals to whatever place she might be playing with the children: the kitchen, the nursery, or outdoors. To the impressionistic young Martha, playing with Lizzie was an escape into a dream world; perhaps, also, a redefinition of "real" life.

Later, real life and make-believe life would merge in Martha's consciousness, and the moral rectitude demanded in her behavior as a child would be transferred to equally stern aesthetic ideals adopted later:

"Out of emotion comes form."

"You are in competition with only one person and that is yourself."

"When the teacher enters the room, the students come to attention. . . . When the teacher gives a correction, there's no leaning at the barre. Their feet come together and their hands come down to their sides or behind them, and they listen. Now that is not for regimentation. That is for the glory of belonging to a very sacred art which you serve. . . . It's a religion."

The rituals of Lizzie's Roman Catholic inheritance were not as foreign to Dr. Graham as might have been presumed. There had been experiences in the physician's life as a boy when he, too, enacted rituals at a Roman Catholic church while visiting his grandmother on her plantation in Hannibal, Missouri. The chanting and processionals had held him spellbound. Something deep within him had been stirred. A hint of this side of his nature could be seen in a portrait that hung in a prominent place in the house on Fremont Street: A small boy with chestnut locks, sitting in a child's chair, looked out at you with clear blue eyes; he seemed to be frowning slightly, as though he disapproved of having to sit still for so long.

Fifteen years older than his dainty wife, whom Martha remembered him carrying upstairs in his arms one day, Dr. Graham took charge of every domestic and social situation in their first years of

4

marriage. To his family and his patients Dr. Graham was "a man of the world," sophisticated, efficient, charming in manner and dress. Because of his fair hair and blue eyes, his colleagues called him "Blondie Graham." Of the three daughters born to the Grahams, Mary, the second child, resembled her father most. She, too, was blonde and blue-eyed. "She had a remarkable mind . . . should have been a writer," said Auntie Re, after whom she was named (Mrs. Graham's sister, Mary, was affectionately called "Auntie Re"). Mary was born in 1896, and four years later came the auburn-haired Georgia, whom everyone called "Geordie." Sensitive and petite like her mother, Geordie won everybody's heart. But she was not very strong; at one time she was dangerously ill with scarlet fever.

Though disarmingly pretty with her dark curls (as Martha remembered her mother), Jane Beers Graham could be strict and forbidding at times. The Puritan in her (the Beers family dated back nine generations to New England's Miles Standish) would often emerge in sharp reaction to some minor provocation. Then she would gather herself up—all ninety-eight pounds of her—and strenuously object to what she termed frivolous behavior on the part of her daughters. Immediately, the girls would fall into line.

Being the oldest, Martha was considered the most responsible of the three girls. Perhaps she felt herself to be reprehensible when their behavior was criticized. She never did and she never would shirk her duties. Honor was bound up in the very act of being given a responsibility. Somewhere here one might find the kernel of that high sense of dedication which filled Martha's adult life and determined her attitude toward her art. She constantly averred that she did not choose to become a dancer but "was chosen." She was the recipient of an honor, and that honor was not merely an earthly award. It was a gesture from superior forces in the form of a blessing. "I was elected," she would say, and with these words she soared into a mystical realm, where the reality of hard work blended with the glory of being the "chosen" one.

Having resigned from the staff of the Western Pennsylvania Hospital the year he married, Dr. Graham set up private practice in his home. Called "The Surgery" by the children, his office contained the physician's library of medical books, a library which furnished Martha with her first introduction to human anatomy. One day, seated on the floor while her father was away and Lizzie was busy with her younger sisters, Martha was finally able to satisfy her curiosity about how babies are born. With her nose deep inside a much-illustrated tome, she suddenly found herself lifted up emphatically by Lizzie and sent flying out of the room. The book was closed behind her with a bang, the inference being that never again would the surgeon's oldest daughter have access to what was considered forbidden information.

Books were Martha's passion, and if it couldn't be a two-volume edition on human reproduction, then she would settle just as happily for one of Jules Verne's fantastic voyages to the moon or under the sea. And lacking stories, there would be the dictionary, her "favorite book." Words always intrigued her. It became a game to take long, many-syllabled nouns and break them up into shorter ones, and to discover the strange meaning of root words like "sophist," from which the word "philosophy" came.

Martha was nearly twelve years old when her brother William was born. The long-awaited coming of a son filled the house with joy. A boy on the Beers's side of the family was a rarity. There had been three sets of three daughters, the first set being Martha's mother and her two younger sisters, Anna and Mary. The second and third sets were Mary's three daughters and Jennie's trio.

In her delight at having a son, Mrs. Graham used to carry the baby around the house all day long. "Why don't you put that child down and let him walk?" her husband would ask; yet nothing could convince the doting mother to part with her son.

Before he was two years old, Billy contracted measles. When complications set in, Jennie was distraught. Gloom settled over the house. Curtains were drawn, blocking out what sunshine there might be. Colleagues of Dr. Graham came and went quietly. Lizzie and the children spoke in hushed voices. Then tragedy struck. On the afternoon of January 24, 1908, Billy died. He was one year, eight months, and twenty-eight days old. Jennie Graham withdrew to her room, and for weeks not one of the girls dared enter uninvited.

It was in the spring of 1908 that George Graham made the decision to move his family to the West Coast. His wife's despondency over the loss of their son and young Mary's recurring asthmatic attacks forced him to consider a change of climate and a change of atmosphere as the most beneficial remedies.

The quiet streets and quaint Spanish architecture of southern California's seacoast towns, which he and his wife had visited sometime previously, offered the kind of relaxed life that appealed to him. He decided to investigate the area again. A return trip reassured him. He and Jennie were particularly drawn to the town of Santa Barbara on the south side of California's bulging coast. Its sunny streets with their Spanish-style adobe houses were laid out neatly and unostentatiously between the protective inland Sierra Madre range and the sparkling blue Pacific. From its sandy beaches one could see the shadowy outlines of three lovely islands—San Miguel, Santa Rosa, and Santa Cruz—rising out of the sea like jewels. And looking down commandingly from its grassy hill at the north end of the town was the architecturally splendid Spanish mission. Glistening tiles covered the roofs of the church and the arcade of an attached monastery, while the imposing sandstone entrance to the mission, with its Renaissance pediment and twin bell-shaped towers, was approached through walkways lined with magnificent shrubbery.

To this lush country of leisurely living in a veritable garden of huge cacti plants and brilliantly colored flowers came the adolescent Martha Graham in 1908. The sturdy body of the fourteen-year-old girl reflected her family's Calvinistic attitudes. The serious look on her rather gaunt face spoke only of youthful determination to achieve one's goal, whatever it might be. But the dancer within her, as yet to be born, would be deeply affected by everything she would see, hear, and touch . . . and, most of all, by the surge of new sensations that would be evoked by the wildly beautiful new world around her.

The fragrance of orange and lemon blossoms, the curious sight of gray bark peeling off smoothly from tall eucalyptus trees, and flowers everywhere were endless surprises. Martha, Mary, and Geordie had never seen such an array of colors before, nor so much blueness in the sky. And every day lavishly sunny.

Upon occasion they had a special treat: a walk with their mother to a mesa that overlooked the ocean near the old Diblee estate. Once up on its broad surface with no one else around, the girls—especially Martha and Mary—seemed to lose all sense of decorum. Geordie, still somewhat timid at the age of ten, would look at them enviously. They would charge across the high plateau like bareback circus riders leaping through hoop after hoop. There was no stopping them. "Freedom! I ran. I fell down. I got up. I ran again," was Martha's description years later of what Santa Barbara's light and space meant to her.

Nearly two years of living on the West Coast, and Dr. Graham's daughters had lost the pinched look of eastern city-bred children. His wife, too, had benefited from the change. Unfortunately, it would be another two years before he could join them, being obliged to maintain his practice in Allegheny.

The doctor's decision to move his family west had been a wise one. Mimi, as he affectionately called Mary, had become noticeably sturdier. Her asthmatic attacks were less and less debilitating. Geordie was doing very well attending a private school. Martha was developing into a very presentable young lady of sixteen. Obviously she was not going to grow much taller than her present height of five feet two, but she had fine proportions—a strong, straight body and a slender neck that gave her an aristocratic look—and she moved with self-assurance. She wasn't pretty, but there was something arresting about her. At Santa Barbara High School, which she entered in August 1909, a year after the move west, her classmates spoke of her as a "shy, retiring girl," even though she occasionally attended dancing parties and helped to organize them. One of her school friends, Marguerite Andrus, obviously mistook Martha's serious demeanor for "modest girlishness." The serious expression on Martha's face hid an intensity that no one suspected. It also hid a determination that only her family knew about firsthand. There was no denying Martha when she had decided upon something.

By the time Jennie Graham's sister, Auntie Re, came from Freedom, Pennsylvania, to live with the Graham family in September 1910, it was clear to everyone that Martha "had a mind of her own." She took her eastern aunt somewhat aback one day by announcing, "Everyone is destined to become what he becomes." Suddenly aware that she was talking to an elder, she added deferentially, "Don't you think so?"

Obviously, Martha had decided that Destiny was as final as "God's Will."

There was no outward sign, however, of Martha's tryst with Destiny. She still remained a dutiful and conscientious daughter, a model for her younger sisters. Southern California's relaxed atmosphere did not drastically alter Jane Graham's opinions about child-rearing. Almost everything the girls did had to pass the judgmental eye of their kind but strict mother: for example, the way they dressed for school—hair tied back neatly in braids or with wide bows, scrubbed faces, long cotton stockings, middy-style blouses, and knee-covering pleated skirts. On Sundays and for special events they wore leghorn hats and pretty dresses with eyelet embroidery and ruffles. They were obliged to sit up properly at the dinner table, hands on lap when served, and, of course, whenever addressed by adults, they were expected to stand up and answer politely. When their handsome and loving father came to visit them at their spacious two-story Victorian wooden house at 1633 Garden Street, with its pillared porch and bay window, they would be agog with excitement. In the summer they could go with him to Alameda Park, only two blocks away, to the weekly music concerts; or there would be an excursion on the electric streetcar to Martha's favorite place, the Spanish mission.

Because her mother knew one of the priests at the Spanish mission, Martha was allowed to explore the wonders of the mission's beautiful grounds. Coral-red hibiscus, pink-petaled oleander, and delphiniums of all shades of blue grew profusely in exquisite gardens; while cacti plantings of many sizes and shapes fanned out stiffly alongside flowering acacias, tall palms, and delicate pepper trees. Martha learned with fascination about the Indians, for whom the mission had been established in the latter part of the eighteenth century. Within the mission's confines, the Indians had constructed a sacred, secret chamber known as the kivas. It contained a hole that supposedly descended to the center of the earth. The story went that after the Indians had participated in a service, they would go outside and perform their own dances. Martha's imagination lighted up as she pictured the secret ceremonies in the "skyhole" followed by the joyous dancing in the sunshine.

But only a soul-shaking experience could give the serious, high-minded adolescent girl the direction and spiritual meaning that her sensitive nature craved. Only a soul-shaking experience could stir into being the creative urges hidden deep within her. By chance—or was it Destiny?—such a cataclysmic experience would take place in the spring of the year in which Martha turned seventeen.

———— • • • ————

In the annals of dance history, it is recorded that the thirty-three-year-old Ruth St. Denis, an American dancer who had achieved fame on the European continent for her exotic interpretations of Oriental dance, gave a series of matinees during the Christmas season of 1910.

9

The adventurous Miss St. Denis performed in a lavish presentation of a self-choreographed dance-drama entitled *Egypta* at the New Amsterdam Theatre in New York City. Sponsored by an enterprising theater owner and producer, Henry B. Harris, the program was received enthusiastically, and the next step in the burgeoning career of the young artist, who was to share with Isadora Duncan the glory of fostering an American art of the dance, was to tour the United States from coast to coast in a program of solo dances, some of which would be drawn from *Egypta*.

In April 1911 Martha was casually passing a store in downtown Santa Barbara when she saw a poster in the window announcing an appearance of the dancer Ruth St. Denis in a series of eight performances at the Los Angeles Mason Opera House at the end of the month. An attached photograph revealed a beautiful woman sitting cross-legged in regal, mysterious splendor on a small, throne-like platform covered with cloth. She was wearing an elaborate costume consisting of a multi-jeweled yoke worn over a tight-fitting bodice and a dark skirt, over which were spread garlands of flowers, possibly marigolds. On her arms were glistening bracelets; a pointed diadem containing resplendent stones crowned her head; in her hands she carried a small bowl. Her eyes were closed and the expression on her face suggested spiritual ecstasy. (The photograph represented, as Martha discovered afterward, St. Denis's famous impersonation of Radha, the beloved of the Hindu god Krishna. *Radha* was a dance describing the five senses, and the bowl, presumably containing wine, represented the sense of taste.)

Transfixed by the photograph, Martha avidly studied the details of the dancer's costume, pose, and facial features. When she turned to go, her mind was made up. Whatever her parents might say, she must go to Los Angeles to see Ruth St. Denis "or be forever thwarted." (The fact that St. Denis was also going to perform in Santa Barbara the following month may not have been known as yet to the young girl; or, characteristically, she might have seized the earlier opportunity within the opera house's elaborate setting rather than the familiar, less-romantic atmosphere of Santa Barbara's Potter Theatre.)

To Martha's delight, her father, who was visiting them at the time, not only gave his consent but declared that he would take her to Los Angeles himself. And when, on the night that would eventually change his daughter's life, he pinned a corsage of violets on Martha's best dress, she felt that her world was complete.

When the curtain of the Mason Opera House rose, Dr. Graham's impressionable daughter lost consciousness of the fact that she was sitting in a darkened auditorium surrounded by hundreds of people. She seemed to be carried backward thousands of years as three dances from Ruth St. Denis's dance-drama *Egypta* unfolded: *The Tamboura* or *Palace Dance, The Veil of Isis,* and *The Dance of Day.*

A tall, willowy woman, wearing a red wig with long, gold-beaded braids, stood alone on a stage that seemed to represent a throne room in a sumptuous palace. A wide, jeweled collar with a halter embraced her neck, while an elaborate girdle held in place a dark blue transparent skirt that swung sinuously around her hips as she broke into a lively dance with a square tambourine. Her flashing eyes suggested that she was performing for the pleasure of an imaginary audience, whose reactions to her dancing were clearly discernible in her changing expressions. There was something utterly captivating about this young woman with her ingratiating glances and elusive ways.

In the second number, the dancer impersonated the goddess Isis. This time her movements were regally slow, each gesture succinctly defined. An ornate headdress with horns and a moon disk glistened on a short, straight-cut black wig, while her whole body seemed enwrapped in diaphanous veils decorated in gold. Fascinated, Martha watched the exquisitely costumed goddess deftly manipulate the veils in constantly shifting forms.

In the dance that followed, *Dance of Day,* St. Denis was first seen lying on a slab, as if asleep. She wore a coarse peasant dress, and her movements, mostly pantomimic, told the "tale of Egypt's rise and fall" in patterns that recalled the two-dimensional designs of Egyptian murals.

For Martha, every motion had mysterious significance. And when the dancer performed her most famous solos—*Incense, The Cobras, Nautch, Yogi,* and *Radha*—she felt that she was being initiated into the mystic rites of the Orient.

In *The Cobras,* the most dramatically effective dance, St. Denis represented a snake charmer. Dressed in ragged clothes, a turban wrapped around unkempt black hair, and seated on a small platform, she used her long, graceful arms as though they were two snakes winding around her neck and body. From the fingers of each hand two green rings shone menacingly like the serpents' eyes. The strange tunes of a snake charmer's flute accompanied the curious ritual. Suddenly, a hiss, the writhing snakes reared their heads and struck! In the stunned silence that followed the curtain descended.

By the time she and her father left the theater, there was no doubt in Martha's mind about her future. She had fallen under the spell of a performer who had opened her eyes to the magic of the theater. For weeks afterward, Ruth St. Denis would live in her mind as a being of hypnotic fascination.

To Martha's father, the profession of a dancer was unthinkable. Besides, there was her education to consider: two more years of high school and then college—possibly Vassar in the East or Mills College in northern California. The matter was closed—as far as Dr. Graham was concerned. As far as Martha was concerned, it would remain a submerged desire connected somehow with her premonition of faith in a personal Destiny.

Seeing Ruth St. Denis was a turning point in Martha's life. It seemed that Destiny had laid its hand on her shoulder. With the whole of her being, the sensitive girl responded to the artistry of the dancer-actress. In addition, there was the enveloping atmosphere of the theater itself with its mystery of illusion. Its call was imperative.

When an opportunity came during the following summer to appear in a local amateur production, she readily accepted; and though she was but one of thirty-seven geisha girls in a production entitled *A Night in Japan,* the excitement of being on the stage and wearing exotic makeup confirmed the seventeen-year-old girl's hidden sense of identification with the stage. And in her junior year, Destiny signaled her again. Now participating in dramatics in preference to sports activities, she was given the leading role in the class presentation of Virgil's *Dido, The Phoenician Queen.*

To Lizzie, such opportunities were further manifestations of fate. In her naive, adoring way, Lizzie was convinced that her favorite was endowed with extraordinary gifts, and she had no doubt that her genius would be recognized one day. "I'll be your maid backstage when you become a famous actress," she vowed, certain that Martha would rise to fame.

The college preparatory course in which Martha was enrolled at Santa Barbara High School included algebra, Latin, Spanish, music, English and history. Though history was Martha's best subject, her ability in English won her the job of editor during her sophomore year of the school publication, *Olive and Gold.* Interestingly, her first contribution to the magazine was a comedy, set in a girls' locker room. Her short story, "Music and Maid," won third prize in a contest held by the magazine. Minor successes, but pertinent indications of a literary bent.

A sewing course, which she took in addition to all her other subjects, yielded strange and wonderful results. Martha would bring material home to try out new ways of cutting and fitting her clothes with her mother's and Auntie Re's help. Her deftness with the needle was a constant surprise to both women, except on one occasion when Martha was making a slip. Dissatisfied that it wasn't tight enough, she worked on it late into the night, sewing and resewing the seams to make it fit perfectly. At last the image in the mirror was acceptable. But when Martha tried to take the slip off, it was impossible to get it over her head or past her hips. In the end, her mother had to come to her rescue and cut it away from her body! (Shades of a future time when Martha would change costume designs at the twelfth hour before performances.)

Certainly, Martha had no illusions about herself as possessing personal beauty. Her senior photograph in the *Olive and Gold* revealed a rather plain girl with pursed lips, large eyes, dark hair sweeping over her ears, and a determined look on her long, oval-shaped face. But after seeing Ruth St. Denis dance, her consciousness about stylishness took a theatrical turn.

On one occasion, when the family had decided to go to the center of town at carnival time, Martha lingered behind to arrange her hair in a special way. Her mother, Auntie Re, and their daughters were already boarding the State Street trolley that would take them to the mardi gras when Martha could be seen a good half-block away strolling down Valerio Street. Something about the way she was dressed—all in white with a bright red velvet ribbon in her hair—made the conductor wait patiently for her. Well aware of the effect she was making, Martha mounted the trolley steps slowly and settled in her seat with the air of a prima donna.

"There was something about her even then that made everyone stop and look," recalled Auntie Re more than fifty years later.

On the other hand, Martha's down-to-earth side, developed conscientiously by her parents, served her well in an emergency. There was an incident involving a fire that she started inadvertently with a stage set cut out of the local newspaper. Though she had propped the set up carefully on top of the dining room table, it didn't look realistic enough. It was sadly without atmosphere. So she lighted a small candle behind a fabricated window to suggest moonlight. This pleased her. But the next moment, the set was in flames. Without thinking of the danger to herself, Martha gathered up the burning papers and rushed to the open window. Why the flimsy lace curtains never went up in flames was a mystery to everyone in the family.

To all outward appearances, Martha was a contented young lady enjoying her senior year. Made editor-in-chief of the Commencement number of *Olive and Gold* (published by the senior class), she did a creditable job on the layout, which followed the usual format of senior-class books: photographs of each graduating member with descriptive couplets beneath.

When it came to finding the right word to describe the character of a classmate named Helen, Martha's editorial staff had a little trouble. Writing in the third person, Martha humorously related their predicament in a short anecdote entitled "A Note About Helen."

> In preparing the senior book, one of the girls asked what she should write about Helen.
> "Say she is a coquette," said Martha Graham.
> "How do you spell it?" asked the girl, addressing another editor.
> "K-o-q-u-e-t-t-e."
> A few minutes passed. The girl returned.
> "I looked it up in the dictionary and couldn't find it."
> "Try q-u-o-q-u-e-t-t-e," said Martha.
> The girl disappeared.
> "Sorry," she said, coming back almost immediately, "but that can't be the spelling."
> "Coquette is slang," said Martha, "and slang is never in the dictionary."

That seemed to settle the matter!
Martha's own caption read:

Capable, generous, willing to do—
To the noblest standards, faithful and true.

Obviously very willing "to do," Martha took charge of programs for the Track Dance at Pythian Hall the spring she graduated (1913), and had a good time herself in her home-designed clothes and fancy coiffures.

But within her, the longing to go on the stage remained undiminished. As far as her parents' attitude to the theater was concerned, Dr. and Mrs. Graham reverted to their Calvinistic prejudices. Such worldly pleasures were "sinful."

Anxious to know the exact meaning of "sinful," Martha consulted the dictionary, and found that one of the root meanings of the word was "to miss the mark." Evidently, in primitive times, failing to hit the target—whether animal or human—meant that one sinned . . . made a mistake, had to go hungry, or could have been killed oneself. Another explanation of the word "sin" was "transgression of religious law." The meaning of the word "transgression" was familiar to her from church and Sunday school. Transgression was like "trespass" in the Lord's Prayer, only more dreadful. Years of daily parental reading of the Bible, and of reading favorite chapters on her own, had made Martha clearly conscious of her "upright" Presbyterian heritage. Yet it was perplexing to try to understand how the theater—with its historical pageants, its operas, and its plays in verse (like Shakespeare's)—could be called "sinful." Her parents had even taken her when she was about four years old to a Punch and Judy show that was being performed in an Atlantic City hotel lobby. Certainly that wasn't "sinful." Confronted with the thought of "transgressing" if she became a dancer or an actress, Martha reasoned herself into guilt-free justification. Had not her father, whom she "idealized," relented somewhat when he said, "I am not interested in religion alone; I am only anxious that you become a cultured woman of the world and understand religion"? Certainly, when he said "cultured," he meant well-read and sophisticated.

In such a mood, Martha had dropped basketball and joined the Quorum, a literary and dramatic debating society. Then in her senior year she tried out for the class play, *Prunella*, by Lawrence Houseman and Granville Barker. The play was presented in Potter Theatre (as was *A Night in Japan*), and Martha played the role of "Privacy, Prunella's timid but loving aunt." (When shown the program fifty-three years later on the occasion of Santa Barbara's honoring her with "Martha Graham Day," Martha smiled and remarked, "I was anything but timid and loving at that time.")

Still nursing her desire to go on the stage, Martha did not apply to college as her parents had hoped, but enrolled for an extra year of postgraduate work at Santa Barbara High School. In a sense, she was treading water; but her courses in psychology, advanced algebra, chemistry, German, and English gave her some satisfaction.

The more determined Martha became about anything she wanted to do, the more she revealed the stubbornness she had inherited from her mother's side of the family. The Beerses always seemed to achieve their aims regardless of obstacles.

There was Great-grandmother Beers, who lived on a farm outside of Mars. Tired of waiting for news of the Civil War in which her husband and son were fighting, Grandmother Beers picked herself up one sunny day, put on her bonnet and shawl, and trudged off with her knitting bag toward Pittsburgh, over twenty-five miles away. Two days of vigorous walking, busily knitting as she traveled, and two nights of staying at farmhouses along the way, brought her to the place where the news she sought was to be found. Once informed to her satisfaction about the war's progress, she turned right around and started back home, knitting needles flashing all the way!

Meanwhile, her red-haired son, John, whose gifts for mimicry and folk dancing won him friends everywhere, attained what he had in his mind, though less openly. Captured by the enemy, he was taken to the infamous Andersonville Prison, noted for cruel treatment of Union soldiers. From there, he was transferred to Castle Thunder, equally formidable as a fortress. Observing that some of the guards were Irish like himself, and likewise bored with the prison's dull routine, John Beers pulled a few tricks out of his bag: a couple of Irish ballads, a few impersonations of shady personalities in broad Irish brogue, and a jolly Irish jig. He gave quite a show one night. The next morning, while sweeping the courtyard with a fellow prisoner, he took a swift look around. "Let's make a try for it," he muttered under his breath. His comrade didn't dare attempt a break, but John Beers simply dropped his broom and walked away. The guards conveniently looked in the other direction.

Like her grandfather, Martha bided her time. When the moment would come, she would be prepared. Marguerite Andrus had told her about a junior college in Los Angeles where young people who wanted to go on the stage could have instruction in acting and theater crafts. It was part of of a large institution called the Cumnock School of Expression.

———•••———

Then death struck again. Dr. Graham, after only two years of living with his family on the West Coast, succumbed to a heart ailment that had been troubling him for some time. On August 11, 1914, he was quietly buried in the Santa Barbara Cemetery.

It was a house of women now. The girls wandered disconsolately through the rooms; Lizzie cried openly like a child. Martha stored the hurt in a secret place where she could face it privately. But her sadness contained a powerful undertow. Destiny had spoken. A new strength rose up in her as she began to see her future more clearly. The sensitive, introspective girl was becoming aware of herself as an individual. The visceral and, most likely, the sexual elements in her nature were asserting themselves. She started planning her future. Now that she had finished her postgraduate course at Santa Barbara High School, she would enroll in the Cumnock School of Expression in Los Angeles.

"There is only one thing in the world and that is the individual," she would say years later with the conviction of experience, "and you are only an individual because you have accepted from your heritage that which has gone either into your bloodstream or that others have helped you to receive."

Chapter One

Denishawn

In the summer of 1916, a somewhat plump, dark-haired young woman of twenty-two walked into a Spanish-styled stucco house on a hilltop estate in Los Angeles and enrolled in the Ruth St. Denis School of Dancing and Related Arts, also known as Denishawn, which the famous dancer and her husband, Ted Shawn, had founded the previous year. To her future teachers and classmates, the girl seemed "exceedingly shy and quiet."

It was customary at Denishawn for "Miss Ruth," as the students called Ruth St. Denis, and Mr. Shawn to give "diagnosis lessons" to prospective pupils. The newly registered Martha Graham was no exception.

Ushered into a room no bigger than a typical living room, Martha waited anxiously for the appearance of the mysteriously entrancing creature who had captured her imagination on that memorable evening over five years ago. Blue-green curtains hung on the sides of casement windows. The only furniture in the otherwise bare room was a small bench, like a dais, on one side facing the windows, and a grand piano in the corner. The piano, to Martha's surprise, was painted white. Behind it sat a heavyset man in shirt-sleeves, smoking a cigarette from the corner of his mouth, and looking down toward the keyboard as though deep in the perusal of a musical score. Actually, he was reading a detective story. When she had entered the room, he had not seemed to notice her.

At the farthest end of the studio another blue-green curtain rustled, and a tall, slender woman with a halo of soft, fluffy white hair glided in. She wore a long, flowing garment which billowed around her as she walked toward Martha. Like a priestess about to participate in a ritual, she sat down regally, and, letting her skirt fall in pretty folds around her legs, said with a gracious smile, "Now dance for me."

"Excuse me," murmured the awestruck Martha Graham, "I have

never danced before. I don't know how. I've never had a lesson in my life."

Miss St. Denis sighed. "Well, my dear, you must know something. . . ." She turned to the pianist: "Louie, play a waltz."

The white piano came to life. Martha, at first petrified at the thought of revealing her lack of experience, found herself responding to the situation with a daring she never thought she possessed.

She began to move around the room. She had an audience now, and unconsciously her performing instincts took over. Certainly, what she did was unoriginal and probably the result of her acting lessons at the Cumnock School and whatever dance instruction she had received there (and obviously discredited); but she gave her "dance" the ring of truth in the way she flung herself spontaneously into the movements.

"That will do, thank you," said Miss St. Denis coolly with a graceful nod when the music came to an end. Unimpressed, she had privately decided to turn the new pupil over to her husband.

Louis Horst's thoughts did not return to the book. He had been watching the dark-haired girl while his fingers were running through the familiar music he had played for countless other "diagnosis lessons." He liked what he saw—not the mixture of gestures, kicks, and turns of the girl's improvised performing but the zeal behind them. Novice as she was, there was something special about this girl. Horst's clear blue eyes took in everything: Obviously, she was overweight for her height (she couldn't have been more than five feet two) but she carried her head well and had a strong, intelligent face (not pretty by any means). Unlike other prospective Denishawn students, who were tongue-tied in Miss Ruth's presence, the girl kept her dignity in a nice, respectful way.

Having formed a decisive opinion of the newcomer, Horst dismissed her from his mind, and stuffing the detective story into the pocket of his coat, left to resume his duties as accompanist for classes held in the outdoor pavilion.

Martha sat down at Miss Ruth's feet.

"You have a great deal to learn, my dear," said the lovely lady with a somewhat rueful sigh, and she proceeded to tell her future student about the aims and ideals of study at Denishawn.

"We seek by every possible means to discover the nature of the talent of each individual, the kind of dancing which each one does best, to which the whole personality of the pupil is suited. In the faculty of 'Denishawn' all schools of the dance are represented—purely classic ballet of the Italian, French, and Russian schools, national dancing of various sorts, Greek dancing which was first given to this generation by Isadora Duncan, and finally the entire gamut of East Indian, Egyptian, Japanese, and other oriental dances, which I myself have developed."

Mingled with Miss Ruth's description of classes and the "all-round practical education in all these matters related to the dance in its finished production" was her vision of what a dancer should become: not only a skilled technician who could perform dances of various styles, such as the East Indian, Japanese, or Spanish dances which she and Mr. Shawn presented on their programs, but also an "artist." To be an artist meant to be a *thinking* dancer—one who used physical means to express feelings, aspirations, and vital human ideas. In the hands of an artist, the dance could become a great spiritual force. For what was the body but a "temple of the holy spirit"? This temple was not only the habitat of the individual soul, but the symbolic dwelling-place of all spiritual consciousness.

As she spoke Miss St. Denis's pale blue eyes glowed and her gestures became increasingly expressive. "To me there is only one real drama: the drama of man's struggle to emerge from the limitations imposed by his own concept of time and space." Her subdued voice gathered force. "*Radha* was the symbol of realization that only by a complete denial of the attachments of sense does one experience the golden lotus of illumination."

Her face, now radiant, seemed to match her words. "My final use to art is impersonal, for when I dance I am really an abstraction, a creature set apart from time and space, unrelated to human things in the ordinary sense. I feel a certain limitless state of being, a curious unending movement not only of my dance, but of my very being. I could go on and on without cessation, subject only to the necessary limits of the body. This of course is more or less true of all dancing—that is its great symbolism and value to life. But I believe that with me another quality is added to the dancer. I feel when I dance before great audiences that I am delivering a wordless message of immortality."

Ruth St. Denis turned her eyes toward the opaque bands of sunlight streaming through the casement windows. Even in the bright daylight of the studio, she seemed a being of mystery and magic. Under her spell ever since she first saw her dance, the impres-

21

sionable young Martha Graham would never cease to emulate the statuesque dancer consciously or unconsciously in one facet or another of her own personality. Even when she began to perceive less godlike traits in her idol, Martha would retain a sense of humility toward the woman who was the prime inspiration of her life. And when Ruth St. Denis died in 1968, she wrote a deeply felt eulogy that concluded with, "We touch her feet."

Under the strict and thorough Mr. Shawn, Martha learned ballet fundamentals (performed barefoot), character dancing, and western forms of ethnic dance: American Indian and Spanish, in particular. Henrietta Russell Hovey taught a class devoted to dramatic gesture based on the theories of François Delsarte (a system of expression that Martha may possibly have been exposed to at the Cumnock School). Miss Ruth gave lessons in Oriental dance, including a class in yoga, which appropriately met at sunset in the outdoor studio, a former tennis court that was converted into a large dance area by means of a wooden platform and a practice barre. In yoga classes Martha had her first experience of bodily contact with the floor.

Denishawn technique consisted mostly of barefoot ballet exercises at the barre and arm and body work in the center of the room. Combinations of movements such as glissades, jetés and pirouettes were practiced as well, but the overall attack was softer. There were also certain floor exercises for stretching, some fairly strenuous. Martha worked hard and learned quickly. She found gratifications she had never dreamed of in the struggle to build her body into a strong and sensitive instrument capable of fulfilling her teachers' demands. The joy of working at a difficult assignment radiated from her, changing the serious young woman into a vital, more openly intense personality. These were the beginnings of Martha's awareness of what she later called "the frenzy which animates the dancer's body frame from within."

Martha came to Denishawn in the second summer of the school's existence prior to her last year of attending the Cumnock School. Already the institution founded by the renowned dancers had achieved a countrywide reputation. It was the only dance school in America to offer the professional performer a total program of study. In addition to the classes in free-style ballet and ethnic dance, there were lectures on the history and philosophy of the dance, discussions on Oriental art and Greek philosophy, and courses in music, lighting, makeup, and "anything else that seemed even remotely related to the dance."

One related subject involved sessions in the art of posing for photographs—a skill at which Miss Ruth became a virtuoso, and which she felt was essential to the would-be performer.

"We wanted the school to be a stream for ideas," wrote Ruth St. Denis in her autobiography, *An Unfinished Life*. "The whole articulation of the school—Ted's and my talents and experiences, the technical classes, the library, and the lectures—was intended as food either for the student who merely wanted a deepening and releasing experience of life or for the definitely avowed dancer with a career before her." (That "definitely avowed dancer" was definitely of the ilk of the intensely serious Martha Graham!)

Once more Ruth St. Denis was expressing herself idealistically, but this time as a reformer, one of the roles she assumed in her advance toward new aesthetic concepts in dance education. No longer the Ruthie Dennis who broke into the world of popular theatrical entertainment through dime museums* and variety halls, she now viewed dancing as an art form, a perspective that she could not always maintain in practice, being forced for financial reasons to turn back to vaudeville from time to time throughout her career.

In 1915 the Denishawn approach to dance education was revolutionary. Apparently, no other American institution of the dance had assumed the responsibility of developing its students' minds in tandem with their bodies. In Germany there was Isadora Duncan's school for children in Grünewald, a suburb of Berlin, where, under the guidance of Elizabeth Duncan, Isadora's sister, dance instruction was considered of "vital importance . . . for the purpose of character formation." Known as the Forest School, it was founded in 1904–1905, and from its ranks came the six disciples—Anna, Erica, Irma, Lisa, Margot, and Maria-Theresa—to whom Isadora was "legally" permitted to give the surname of Duncan (without formal adoption).

Typical American dancing schools of the period concentrated on the most elementary technical training: routine exercises in ballet vernacular with emphasis on acrobatic display rather than on style, and a repertory of stock dance steps prevalent in the entertainment forms of the day. Few educators existed like Mary Wood Hinman (Doris Humphrey's first dancing teacher), who was farsighted and broad-minded. The Denishawn idea of a school that would include

*Dime museums were prevalent in the 1890s and had tiny stages fit only for one performer.

"all the arts as an essential part of the dancer's training" was unheard of on this side of the Atlantic. Its philosophy, based partly on John Dewey's theories of modern education, was yet to find its way into the general world of dance instruction.

It must be remembered that in the early years of twentieth-century America, the principal form of dance entertainment was vaudeville with its mixture of all dance styles: clogging and soft-shoe, tap, acrobatics, ballet, and "character" dancing, which could be imitative of Russian, Rumanian, or other folk forms. Vaudeville or variety dance acts made no pretense of exhibiting anything beyond the nimble execution of intricate steps, contortionist feats, or fancy postcard tableaux. The most innovative dancer had been Loie Fuller of the swirling lighting effects; she undoubtedly contributed much to St. Denis's awareness of the theatricality implicit in yards of draped material.

While it is true that "the period in which St. Denis's dance material matured was the era of greatest expansion for American vaudeville," and that during the many years of their partnership St. Denis and Shawn resorted to accepting (separately or together) vaudeville engagements for purely financial reasons, it is also true that they always set their sights in the direction of concert programs, where their creative efforts would be judged by higher aesthetic standards.

When Ruth St. Denis broke into the concert field in 1906 with a special matinee at New York's Hudson Theatre, the vaudevillian style of her exotic offerings was still in evidence. But her subsequent European tours, where she attracted the attention of such eminent dramatists as Hugo von Hofmannsthal, Franz Wedekind, and Gerhart Hauptmann, were aimed at lifting the level of dance from that of superficial entertainment to that of art, as it is understood in the realm of concert programs. Likewise, Isadora Duncan's aims, even as early as her appearances in England in 1900, were to elevate dancing to the realm of serious art. An astute critic at that time was quoted as saying: "Until Isadora Duncan appeared and gave the dance a new form and life, helping us to realize that the dance be an art, it had no validity other than as mere diversion."

They were mountaintop people—Ruth St. Denis, Ted Shawn, and Isadora Duncan—envisioning the future from the heights of idealism. To them, dancing was not only—in the words of the Greek writer, Lucian—"grace and elegance . . . harmonious movement" but also "display of mind." To this end, they cultivated the spirit as well as the body. They were humanists of the dance, believing that all that concerned humanity—history, philosophy, religion, nature, and art—concerned the dancer. "We should regard dance disciplines of the future as an integral part of our moral unfolding as well as physical development," wrote Ruth St. Denis. "I believe that dance communicates man's deepest, highest and most truly spiritual thoughts and emotions far better than words," stated Ted Shawn in his *Credo*. "I see America dancing," was Isadora's prophecy, and she foresaw the "living leap of the child springing toward the heights, toward its future vision of life that would express America." Out of this threefold idealism came the modern dancers of the twentieth century.

Whereas Ruth St. Denis, Ted Shawn and Isadora Duncan anticipated the time when American dancers would emerge as independent creative artists, they themselves were important participants in a golden age of visionary discovery. In the pre–World War I period, tidal waves of change were being set in motion by giant personalities. In science there were Albert Einstein, Marie Curie; in aviation, the Wright brothers; in psychology, Sigmund Freud, Carl Jung; in philosophy, Bertrand Russell, Benedetto Croce, Alfred North Whitehead; in literature, James Joyce, W. B. Yeats, Robert Frost; in painting, Wassily Kandinsky, Edvard Munch, Pablo Picasso, Henri Matisse, Marc Chagall; in sculpture, Auguste Rodin, Aristide Maillol, Constantin Brancusi; in the theater, George Bernard Shaw, J. M. Synge, Henrik Ibsen, August Strindberg, Adolphe Appia, Gordon Craig, and in Russia, Anton Chekhov, Ivan Turgenev, Constantine Stanislavsky; in music, Igor Stravinsky, Sergei Prokofiev, Arnold Schoenberg; in acting, Eleanora Duse, Ellen Terry, Sarah Bernhardt, Vera Komisarjevsky; in opera, Fyodor Chaliapin, Enrico Caruso, Ernestine Schumann-Heink, Geraldine Farrar; and in the dance itself, there were St. Denis's and Isadora's European contemporaries, the leading figures of Sergei Diaghilev's first Parisian productions of Russian ballet, Anna Pavlova, Tamara Karsavina, Vaslav Nijinsky, Michel Fokine. Everywhere were signs of ferment, change, and achievement. Though late in catching up with twentieth-century trends in science, literature, and art, the dance was moving steadily to the front.

In this atmosphere of exploration and fantastic accomplishment, Martha began to absorb the far-reaching philosophy of her teachers while disciplining herself in the craft of the dance styles they taught.

It would not take her long to realize that though she was being trained for drama at the Cumnock School, the true outlet for her creative energies would ultimately lie in the visceral world of dance. Compared to acting, dancing yielded an indescribable exhilaration. Returning to Denishawn after her graduation from Cumnock in the spring of 1917, she would plunge full-force into movement as the direct expression of her energies.

For the moment, however, she was only a transient summer student. This meant taking classes out of doors, eating a boxed lunch under the feathery pepper trees, living, breathing dance in surroundings that included a menagerie of dogs and cats (once even a prize peacock!), for it was Ruth St. Denis's and Ted Shawn's idealistic aim that their students should live in harmony with nature and thereby cultivate the spiritual values that infused the dance as an art.

California—the birthplace of Isadora Duncan, the home of Denishawn, the environment of Martha's girlhood—was to play a major role in the emergence of American modern dance. A great state on the westernmost edge of a young, enterprising country, it would serve as the starting point of a new generation of dancers who would march eastward and, eventually, around the world, armed with an art of their own devising.

———— ··· ————

One day in the summer of 1917, Mr. Shawn decided to teach an entire dance in a single lesson to draw out the performing abilities of the students in Martha's class. The dance was Moorish in style, a combination of Arabian and Spanish characteristics of movement. Later it was entitled *Serenata Morisca*.

Given the assignment, the class went into action. With surprise, Mr. Shawn found himself watching one of his dancers as though mesmerized. It was Martha, the reticent girl with the usually quiet, studious look on her long, rather plain face. She was tearing across the room with a fervor he had never suspected she possessed. Her body had come to life with unexpected power; her eyes had a fire in them that he had never seen before.

When the lesson was finished, Mr. Shawn took Martha aside. "You seem to know instinctively how to project," he said. "Your movements were strong, clean-cut, and accurate. With faith and hard work, you will grow into a fine dramatic dancer. But, remember, you are not the willowy, fragile type, like Florence O'Denishawn.''* He nodded in the direction of a tall, slender, blonde girl who was leaving the studio. ''You are not a lyrical dancer. Your gift is like a mustard seed. It will grow into a sturdy oak with deep roots.''

That was the beginning of Ted Shawn's recognition of Martha's performing gifts. It would take a few years, however, before he would create a ballet specifically for her. In the meantime, he would find a way to utilize her gifts as a teacher, for Martha with her serious attitude had impressed both Ruth St. Denis and her husband as a devoted follower of Denishawn's principles. ''Most of the time in my class,'' recalled Miss Ruth, ''she sat very still and listened.'' With Martha's return to Denishawn after her graduation from Cumnock, she would be given the opportunity to teach some of Shawn's classes during and after the period of his enlistment in the war.

Great dancers are born, not made, so the saying goes. If this is true, then it is also true of great teachers. In any case, there is no doubt that Ruth St. Denis and Ted Shawn were great teachers. In spite of the fact that Miss Ruth took no interest in correcting technical problems, she gave her students the benefit of her rich, spiritual outlook on dance as an art. ''I was never a good teacher,'' she admitted frankly, then added wittily, ''But I can inspire like hell.'' On the other hand, Mr. Shawn was strict in respect to both technique and dance repertoire. He was systematic, articulate, and demanding, with the flavorsome spice of realistic humor thrown in to lighten the atmosphere. As a youth, Shawn had been studying for the ministry when a paralyzing illness cut short his intentions. He turned from religion to dance, and approached it just as fervently, albeit methodically. For the more mystic Miss Ruth, dance was always a form of expressing religious feeling; toward the end of her life, she devoted all her energies to creating ''temple'' services which were performed as ritualistic events.

A religious attitude implies vision and faith. It also implies unswerving dedication. Idealism, however, is not enough when dealing with untrained bodies and minds. In addition to being able to evoke a student's enthusiasm, a teacher of dance should have a thorough understanding of the concrete difficulties involved in the

---

*Florence Andrews assumed the surname ''O'Denishawn,'' under which she danced, according to Ruth St. Denis, ''for several years with great success.''

study of bodily movement. He must be able to detect anatomical problems, give the pertinent correction, and, at the same time, recognize where anatomy and psychology are intertwined in a student's personality and physique. In this sense, the would-be teacher must develop an awareness of the students' needs as well as of their aspirations.

The art of teaching, like the art of performing, is an art of communication. True teaching involves the same problem as choreographing, which Martha described in later years as bringing "the idea of one person into focus for the many." The one person, in this instance, must have the passion of an idealist, the sensitivity of a psychologist, the ear of a musician, the eye of a painter, and, last but not least, a golden tongue that cajoles, exhorts, inflames, and subdues, and also unravels all knots of doubt and confusion in the would-be dancer's mind!

It wasn't possible to be in the presence of the visionary Miss Ruth and not have her luminous thinking shed light on one's own philosophy of life. Nor could a student take classes with Ted Shawn and remain untouched by the sparkling clarity of his mind. It was inevitable that Denishawn would breed a new generation of dancers and teachers who would spread the radiant energy of their unique directors throughout the country.

In those years, Martha was learning how to teach. Only gradually would she discover herself and prove to others her capabilities as an instructor and director. In time to come, the steel of her aesthetic preferences would shine (and cut) like a sharpened, polished blade. Once in the mid-20s, annoyed at the loose fit of a student's tank suit, she grabbed the bulky part of the garment, and pulling it tight around the girl's waist forced her to study herself in the mirror with the command, "Now see how beautiful you look!"

One thing, however, was certain from the beginning. Her conscientiousness was infectious. Teaching her students what she herself had been taught (her own technique would come years later and at the price of great sacrifice), Martha would demand of her class the same efforts she demanded of herself. Working as hard as Martha meant working with the hammer and chisel of one's own strength of body and mind. Nothing less. If Martha wanted her students to glide smoothly and noiselessly across the hardwood floor, toes turned in Japanese style, they would do it, even if they had to hold their breath and grow purple in the face. A fan had to be opened and closed, just so. Martha would show them once or twice, and that was it. A scarf had to be caught and wound about the body with the look of pure abandon. Martha did it as though the scarf were part of her own body. Now came the students' turn. Beads of perspiration formed on foreheads already puckering with anxiety; fingers felt as though they were "all thumbs"; nothing held in place, nothing wound, nothing floated. Yards of material fell in shapeless mounds on the floor. But when, after hours of dogged working with sheets and old clothes at home, the miracle of "getting it" actually came to pass, Martha's approval and the flash of her smile brought indescribable satisfaction. Her students marched out of the studio aglow with the pride of hard-won accomplishment.

Not only Martha, but another remarkable disciple of Ruth St. Denis and Ted Shawn further developed her teaching skills while being trained as a Denishawn dancer. Her path, except for the fact that she started taking dancing lessons as a child and gave lessons at the age of eighteen, paralleled Martha's in many important ways: She came to Denishawn in the summer of 1917, one year after Martha; she started studying under the same happy conditions at the Los Angeles school; she joined the Denishawn faculty shortly afterward; she soon became a member of a small vaudeville touring company headed by Ruth St. Denis (1918–1919) and eventually performed in the large-scale Denishawn ballets. She was a dancer of great beauty and power, and a woman of rare intellect; and, also like Martha, she was destined to become a leading figure in modern dance. She, too, would found a school, establish a curriculum, and lead thousands of others in the direction of a new dance of her own making. And she would reach heights of choreographic accomplishment hitherto unknown in America. Pioneer and independent artist, Denishawn-bred Doris Humphrey was to create a technique and build theories of movement and composition, on a par with Graham technique and theory. Doris Humphrey would, like her renowned colleague, change the history of American dance.

Their common Denishawn background provided Doris Humphrey and Martha Graham with a solid foundation in theater crafts which would serve them throughout their artistic careers. Yet it is interesting to note that during their many years of performing with Denishawn, their appearances never coincided until the very end of Martha's last company tour. At the beginning, Martha was Ted Shawn's protégée, dancing principally with him, while

Humphrey performed with the Ruth St. Denis Concert Dancers, being Miss Ruth's protégée. Circumstances were such that when Shawn and St. Denis combined forces in 1921, Humphrey was off on her own vaudeville tour. By the time that Doris caught up with Denishawn, Martha was on the verge of leaving the company.

———————— ··· ————————

With her actress's temperament, naturally Martha thought of herself as a performer, not teacher. The stage was her goal. And she never lost sight of it. During the early years at Denishawn she had only a few performing opportunities, the first one coming almost immediately after she had enrolled. Invited to perform in the famous Greek Theatre on the campus of the University of California at Berkeley, Ruth St. Denis decided to utilize her entire school, plus nearly one hundred students from the university's summer session, in an ambitious spectacle entitled *A Dance Pageant of Egypt, Greece and India.* Though Martha was only one of the Dancers with Triangles, it was a great thrill for her to be involved in such a monumental production. Preparations for the pageant required constant rehearsing, the dyeing and sewing of nearly 450 costumes, and the removal of the entire school to Berkeley for the final rehearsals.

Other minor performing opportunities came Martha's way as time went on, but it was not until Shawn conceived a ballet with her in mind that her talents came to light. She was to dance the part of Xochitl (pronounced "Zochil"), a young Indian girl whose father discovers an intoxicating liquor brewed from a maguey plant. Inflamed by the liquor, the Tolchec emperor becomes enamored of Xochitl and forces his attentions upon her. A passionate fight takes place which is interrupted by the father's return, and his wrath is only assuaged by his daughter's fervent pleas to spare the life of the emperor. A happy ending takes place in which the repentant emperor makes Xochitl empress of the Tolchecs.

In Martha's hands, *Xochitl* was nothing short of spectacular.

The premiere took place in Long Beach, California, in June 1920. A few weeks later the ballet was booked for a Pantages circuit vaudeville tour of the western states. Before the opening, Martha was rigid with stage fright. On one hand, she was dying to show the world what she could do with such an exciting role; on the other, she was terrified of failing to do her best. In this state of limbo she managed to survive until the moment she stepped out on the stage and the curtain went up. Then everything fell into place. Suddenly aware of her audience, she became aware of herself in new ways. The stage now felt as if it were her natural domain. She moved through it with an intuitive sense of the effectiveness of each gesture. Within a short time, Martha's tempestuous characterization of the maiden Xochitl would almost eclipse Shawn's virile interpretation of the Emperor Tepancaltzin.

The vaudeville tour began in Tacoma, Washington, with a Denishawn dancer, Robert Gorham, taking over for Mr. Shawn as the emperor. Events, however, decided that a newcomer to Denishawn who was still in Los Angeles attending classes would be the third dancer to perform the leading male role. This young man was to be Martha Graham's partner for the two years that *Xochitl* would play throughout the West and Southwest of the United States; he would continue to dance with her in duets, such as *Danse Arabe,* and in the lyrical, romantic ballet, *The Princess and the Demon,* on subsequent tours. His name was Charles Weidman.

Tall, lithe, and strong, Weidman managed to hold the balance of dramatic effectiveness as Emperor Tepancaltzin with the fiery Xochitl, though at times Martha's "black-panther ferocity" nearly overcame him. He also played the part of Xochitl's father when Shawn danced the leading role. Pauline Lawrence, a former Denishawn dancer now turned musician, was the pianist for the vaudeville tour of the ballet, whose cast by this time included another talented Graham girl, Geordie, who had come to study at her sister's school during the war, and also Anne Douglas, who joined the company later in the tour when one of the dancers became ill. Subsequently, Geordie and Anne became roommates.

Xochitl was Martha's official debut as a performer of star stature. *Xochitl* marked, as well, her first experience of being in charge of a touring company. It was a task that involved, among other strenuous responsibilities, the handling of all the railroad tickets; these were bought at the onset of the tour by Pantages himself and then repaid by the members of the cast from their weekly salaries. (The system worked very well except on one occasion when Martha lost the tickets in Seattle!)

For Martha, responsibilities were nothing new. Ever since her father had died and she had graduated from the Cumnock School in

1917, the financial status of the Graham family became increasingly precarious. When she started teaching at Denishawn, she assumed more than her share of her mother's and Lizzie's support, a concern that would remain with her until her mother's remarriage in 1927 to Homer N. Duffy, a business man of some means.

It was the prolonged Pantages vaudeville tour of *Xochitl*—three performances a day on weekdays and four performances on Saturday and Sunday—that gave Martha the stage experience she craved. Still idealistic she was careful not to let the repetitiousness of the experience lower the company's standards. According to Anne Douglas, she "would take out easy steps and put in more interesting ones every so often. With several shows a day it kept us from getting stale." And then Douglas adds, "In all those months I can't remember her having any temper spells so she must have been learning and growing also."

In addition to its tough experiences, *Xochitl* gave Martha her first taste of fame. Impressed by her performance, the *Tacoma New Tribune* called her "a brilliant young dancer." When they played Santa Barbara at the beginning of October, the occasion of a former city resident's triumphant return warranted a special interview with a reporter from the *Santa Barbara News*. Martha's response to her first interviewer's queries was humble but not without a certain irony: "So far the only value of my work—if it has art value—is absolute sincerity. I would not do anything I could not feel. A dance must dominate me completely, until I lose sense of anything else. Later what I may do may be called art; but not yet."

The "art value" of Martha's dancing was unmistakably relegated to the future. And no one knew better than she how crucial it would be for her to gain mastery over her own explosive nature, onstage and offstage.

It would take years before Ted Shawn's protégée would gain the control she longed for in her search for perfection . . . years of absolute dedication, of relentless self-discipline, of doggedly hanging on when performing had almost lost its luster and personal gratification seemed to be ebbing away.

In the meantime, there would be Louie. Taskmaster, godfather, critic, sage, lover, he would guide her through the dangerous terrain that she must cross in her journey toward self-realization.

Chapter Two

The Immortal Blow

Louis Horst, the man who was to exert the greatest artistic influence on Martha's career, was originally contracted to serve as temporary musical director for Ruth St. Denis and Ted Shawn when circumstances deprived them of an accompanist at the end of a short engagement at the Alcazar Theatre in San Francisco in October 1915. Engaged for the first two weeks of a projected cross-country tour, Louis remained with Denishawn for a good ten years, endearing himself more and more through his fine musicianship, keen sense of humor, and rough honesty. On their part, the idealistic Miss Ruth and Mr. Shawn introduced Louis to the beauty and meaning of the dance as an art. As a result, he became that rare person, a musician who loved the dance more than his own profession.

Born in 1884 in Kansas City, Missouri (also Ted Shawn's birthplace), Louis was the second child of German parents; his mother came from Wiesbaden, his father from Giessen, outside of Frankfurt. When Louis was scarcely nine years old and his sister, May, was seven, his family moved to San Francisco, where Conrad Horst taught music theory at the conservatory and played the trumpet in the San Francisco Orchestra. Papa Horst took his children's musical training seriously. May learned how to play the trumpet and Louis was put to work on violin and piano. By the time Louis was twenty, he had a job playing the piano in a "highfalutin" German restaurant known as Tait Zincand's on Market Street. Zincand's, with its sparkling chandeliers and fancy décor, was the place for elegantly attired ladies and gentlemen to go on Saturday and Sunday afternoons after the races. And the small orchestra Louis played in was the best of its kind in town.

Music may have been Louis's profession, but baseball was his private passion. Almost every time the San Francisco Seals or the Oakland Oakies played in their hometown ball parks, Louis could be found in the bleachers, watching the game intently, scorecard in hand. He didn't miss a move then, just as he never missed a trick later when dancers occupied his attention. In the early days, his life was divided between baseball games in the afternoons and playing in a variety of "joints"—high class and low class—at night: dance halls, vaudeville theaters, restaurants, and even a "parlor house" in Nevada where they called him The Professor, and where he got his first taste of life's most basic realities.

Life in San Francisco was both comfortable and stimulating for Louis Horst, whose Germanic upbringing and musical talents had engendered in him a lusty appreciation of the cultural, gastronomic, and geographical resources at his disposal in northern California. With its mild climate and high, wide view of the Pacific, its theaters and concert halls, its variety of good restaurants, the city of hills offered many irresistible indulgences. By 1915 Louis had already been married for six years; he would have probably settled down permanently to his half-Bohemian, half-burgher existence were it not for the fact that his very pretty, delicately formed wife loved to dance. A student at Denishawn's first summer school courses, Betty Myrle Horst (née Cunningham) had been invited to join the newly organized company for its first large-scale concert and vaudeville tour. It was she who had recommended Louis for the temporary job that was to last a full decade and eventually make reverberating changes in the history of dance.

Louis had never played for dancers before; but he had achieved a minor reputation as an accompanist for Madame de Pasquali, a coloratura soprano. In accepting the temporary offer from Denishawn, he had no particular interest beyond the immediate replenishment of his rapidly emptying pockets and certainly no intention of leaving San Francisco for more than a few days. Taking his violin to a musician friend named Kissinger, Louis said, "Keep it under your bed. I'll be back for it next week," and departed on the first stage of a nationwide tour that would wind up at the Hudson Theatre in New York City on December 31. By that time he was not only playing the piano but also conducting an orchestra when circumstances permitted the Denishawn Company that luxury. Evidently, life with a dance company brought unexpected gratifications to the young man, whose professional experiences had been circumscribed by music alone. It also brought about changes in his personality. No longer the tentative fellow whose self-confidence was so meager that his wife "had to keep track of him before engagements because he might not appear" (though he always did), Louis Horst was discovering his own creative impulses. He found himself looking over musical scores with Miss Ruth's and Mr. Shawn's ideas in mind, suggesting changes that were more musically correct, and actually preparing for a future time when he would compose a dance score.

Like Ruth St. Denis, Louis Horst had prematurely white hair. Tall, broad-shouldered, and increasingly rotund as time went on, his step was as light as a dancer's and his gestures often as graceful. His sense of humor could be crude, even shocking; but he always managed to turn a subject into a fascinating discourse on broader issues. Louis had never finished high school, but he made up for it by reading voraciously all kinds of literature. He devoured detective stories by the pocketful, but Nietzsche, the exultant romanticist, and Schopenhauer, the dour realist, were his favorite authors; time and again, his companions would glimpse a volume of one or the other philosopher's books between piles of music scores in Louis's well-worn briefcase.

He liked to call himself an atheist ("There is no justice," he would say), but how could one believe him when he looked like a drawing of Jehovah and wielded the patriarchal power of a Moses? In many other ways as well, his personality was tantalizingly paradoxical. After he had become a dance critic in addition to being a teacher of dance composition, he would sit with tears coursing down his cheeks at a performance of a perfectly realized work, but woe to the dancer in his class who couldn't keep the beat! And pity was certainly not one of his attributes. "I know it hurts," he would say to a student trying to hold a difficult position. "You didn't think it was going to be fun, did you?"

Louis's affections were veiled in ironic allusions. He jokingly referred to dancers as "hoofers," but to him they were the most beautiful people in the world, and he could never think of loving a woman who wasn't a dancer and couldn't, in his opinion, dance well.

Out of the corner of his observant eye, Louis had watched Martha grow from the shy, untrained girl he had first played for into the sophisticated performer who was responsible for the spectacular success of *Xochitl*. Now Ted Shawn was planning a cross-country tour of his own, with Martha as his leading lady. A small company of dancers composed of two other women—Betty May and Dorothea Bowen—and Charles Weidman would perform a highly diversified program of Shawn's choreography, and Louis Horst would serve as their music director.

It was on this 1921 tour that Martha and Louis established what might be termed an unconventional relationship. Circumstances were propitious for a ripening of mutual interests accompanied by real affection. Betty Horst was no longer with Denishawn, having been forced because of illness to leave the cast of the vaudeville-touring *Julnar of the Sea*, a Shawn spectacle especially designed for an extensive Pantages circuit run that Louis had also gone on in 1919. Betty's illness was diagnosed as tuberculosis, and it was necessary for her to depart when the company was playing Texas. Though she had never been a leading dancer with the company, her presence was sorely missed. It was essential, of course, for Louis to maintain his position as music director of the production. Betty's and Louis's ten-year-old marriage, however, had become surprisingly "free-style," according to another member of the *Julnar* cast. A tacit understanding about personal freedom (possibly due to sexual indifference on Louis's part—a fact hinted at later) permitted them both to indulge in going out with companions of their own choice.

Though strangely ambiguous, Louis's marital relationship didn't seem to trouble him unduly, except for the fact that he always would feel a sense of responsibility about Betty. Whether it was due to her fragile health or to the practical Germanic side of his nature, it was obvious that his concern for his young wife's well-being precluded any thought of divorce throughout his life—a thorny fact that Martha would have to deal with as best she could in the years ahead.

As for Martha, Louis was becoming more and more important to her in a personal as well as professional way. It was comforting to be with a man who was her senior by nearly ten years and to be guided by the superior aesthetic judgment of a critical mind. He was not shocked by her tantrums, nor did he submit to them. On the contrary, he knew how to wait them out or how to cut them short with a few decisive words. But the deepest attraction between them seemed to lie in the realm of books and philosophical ideas. In retrospect, Horst once described their relationship as essentially "esoteric."

36

As the train bearing Ted Shawn's small company would be chugging eastward across Wyoming and South Dakota, Louis would slip one of his beloved editions of Nietzsche or Schopenhauer into Martha's hands. Their intellectual sharing turned out to be the main nourishment for Martha during those interminable cross-country train rides. Wherever they headed on the tour that was going to take them eventually to New York, she would forget the fatigue of one-night stands while she curled up on a dusty velour seat in the dimly lit coach and let the words of Louis's treasured thinkers roll over her. Come the next day, she and Louis would discuss what she had read, and other members of the company would cock their ears, picking up tidbits of their philosophical exchanges. Little did her colleagues realize that Ted Shawn's leading lady was going to put into immediate practice Schopenhauer's and Nietzsche's dynamic views of life.

With startling accuracy—as far as concerned a dancer's experience—the author of *The World as Will and Idea* described the complex functioning of the human personality: "The act of will and movement of the body are not two different things objectively known . . . they are one and the same. . . . The action of the body is nothing but of the will objectified." Equally confirming, anatomically as well as emotionally: "The whole nervous system constitutes the antennae of the will, which it stretches within and without." But lest one become a slave to the will, one must have directives from the intellect: "Philosophy purifies the will. But philosophy is to be understood as experience and thought, not as mere reading."

How big a role Martha's will had already played in her life! Had she not fought her way by sheer will? All those years of waiting to study, and then, having at last succeeded in discovering herself as a dancer, being shunted into teaching instead of performing. (From the perspective of decades later, Martha remembered those thwarted times with a touch of irony: "The classic remark made to me at Denishawn was 'Martha, you're really not creative.' They felt I didn't have the dignity for concert work and, besides, I wasn't concert material because I wasn't a blonde. Instead, musicals and the night club field were suggested.")

"With regard to the intellect," Schopenhauer further declared (when speaking of genius), "nature is highly aristocratic. The distinctions which it has established are greater than those which are made in any country by birth, rank, wealth, or caste."

On the other hand, Nietzsche, who understood creative compulsion, spoke of "the glorious power to *do* . . . for which eternal suffering is not too high a price to pay."

Here we can detect the same exalted sense of mission that would be voiced time and again by Martha in the words "I did not choose to become a dancer. I was chosen."

Inspired equally by Schopenhauer's analytical approach and Nietzsche's romantic fervor, Martha's will would always ride in tandem with her intellect. From now on she would take the steepest path she could find, recognizing that whatever sacrifices she would have to make would be part of a pact with Destiny. Self-appointed as her guide, Louis never doubted that hers was the caliber of genius.

Humility was never one of Martha's traits, except, of course, when linked to honesty. In one of her first interviews as a Denishawn dancer, she was reported as saying, "I owe all that I am to Nietzsche and Schopenhauer." A good forty years later, when all London was applauding her, she wrote to Louis, "I owe it all to you."

———•••———

The program presented by Ted Shawn and his dancers consisted of no less than twenty-one numbers, which included several solos for Martha and the entire second act of *Xochitl*. Louis provided two piano solos to permit the dancers to catch their breath as they dove in and out of wigs, hats, shoes, scarfs, bracelets, and earrings, to say nothing of authentic Spanish and Burmese costumes replete with fans, ankle bells, and finger cymbals. They danced in high school auditoriums, grand opera houses, convention halls, and theaters large and small for audiences of all kinds: clubs, societies, the general public. The experience, like the Pantages *Xochitl* tour, was relentless, but it provided Martha with invaluable firsthand knowledge of show business.

Their final engagement at the Apollo Theatre in New York in December 1921 brought about a much-prized opportunity: a three-and-a-half year contract beginning the following fall with the impresario Daniel Mayer. Impressed not only by the group's excellent dancing but also by the fact that Shawn had dedicated his program to his famous partner-wife, calling her "High Priestess of the Dance," Mayer suggested that St. Denis join the company.

Complicated negotiations ensued. The opportunity to be managed by Mayer, a kind of secondary Hurok who had arranged tours for Pavlova, Paderewski, and Caruso, was not lost on St. Denis, who had recently been performing on her own with some dissatisfaction. As was her wont, she insisted on top billing (much to Shawn's annoyance) and, demanding certain financial conditions, agreed to participate in a preliminary southeastern April tour planned by Shawn to be immediately followed by vaudeville engagements in Great Britain. The main attraction for both of them would be, of course, the proposed cross-country tours that would allow them to propagate their ideas throughout the United States.

Only eleven years after she had first seen Ruth St. Denis perform in Los Angeles, Martha Graham, now a full-fledged member of the Denishawn Company and a dance personality in her own right, set sail from Boston for England with the expanded Denishawn entourage. There was one flaw, however, in this dream of foreign conquest, as far as Martha was concerned. To her chagrin, because Louis had arranged it, Betty Horst, now recovered, had been invited to participate in the English tour.

At London's famous Coliseum, the "artistic" numbers staged by the resourceful American choreographers would often precede or follow circus-type acts in the Coliseum's vaudeville format of three shows a day. One such act was a fleet of trained pigeons called "Lady Alice's Pets," and Martha loved to watch them as she waited in the wings for her turn. Their nervous flutterings reminded her of her own trepidations before going on the stage. "That's the way I feel," she once whispered to Charles Weidman, vibrating her hands characteristically, "all fluttery!"

One night, costumed and ready to go on in her solo, *Valse Aragonaise,* Martha felt something soft nuzzling her shoulder. Indignant, she wheeled around, only to find a beautiful white horse trying to nibble the fringe of her Spanish shawl!

Despite the thrill of performing in a foreign country, Martha was beginning to feel a deep discontent. Not only was her relationship to Louis obviously jeopardized by the presence of his wife, but other unaccountable things were happening. Throughout the English tour

Miss Ruth insisted upon dancing the role of Xochitl; relegated to the ensemble, Martha had to live through every performance with fury and grief battling in her heart as she danced behind Ruth St. Denis and alongside Betty Horst. Almost as disturbing was St. Denis's taking over the *Malgueña*, the duet that Martha had performed with Shawn throughout their cross-country tour. Such untoward changes could only be explained by Miss Ruth's insistence on star billing.

Most likely, Martha's discontent was noticed by her observant employer, who was not above admitting her own egotistical failings in having assumed that she could dance *Xochitl* as well as its original interpreter. Or, perhaps, Shawn had dared to say that he could give a more convincing performance of the intoxicated Mexican emperor when faced with a passionately protesting Graham. At any rate, Martha was seemingly placated by the scheduling of an additional solo plus a new ballet, *The Princess and the Demon* (with Charles Weidman), for the forthcoming Mayer Tour, in which Betty Horst would not be performing, having returned to San Francisco to teach in her own school of dance.

Meanwhile, Louis began to feel discontented, too, but not because of his dual personal involvements. His dissatisfaction was for totally aesthetic reasons; it concerned the questionable rapport between the two arts—dance and music—that he dealt with as Denishawn's music director. In general, the musical level of the repertoire had clearly risen as a result of his influence, but there was still the inadequacy of a dance score that "consisted of . . . a bit of this and a bit of that . . . often the cuts amounted to chasms." No wonder that such lack of respect for music downgraded the dance in the eyes of musicians. On the other hand, Louis also objected to the fact that the dance was considered the handmaiden of music, inasmuch as the music's mood and style always dictated the movement.

It was not until Ruth St. Denis had been awakened to an understanding of musical structure through acquaintance with the theories of Émile Jaques-Dalcroze that she took a creative view toward dance composition in relation to music. The innovative Swiss educator had developed a method of analyzing and expressing musical structure through rhythmic motion. Called "eurythmics," it would be introduced many years later into the Denishawn school curriculum by the Dalcroze exponent Elsa Findlay, who had elicited St. Denis's admiration for her ability to bring about "a clear understanding of the theory of music." Whether it was the result of her contact with

Dalcroze's educational innovations or with Isadora Duncan's inspired use of music, St. Denis became interested in 1918 in rather literal musical interpretations that she called "music visualizations." As an experiment in composition, music visualization made an effort to transfer instrumental sounds and rhythmic punctuation into the language of motion: Low, heavy movements depicted the weighty chords of the bass viols; soft, rippling gestures represented the plucked strings of a harp; and precisely timed steps mirrored note values, just as dynamic emphasis was stressed according to the intensity of the musical phrasing. St. Denis's enthusiasm for Dalcrozean relationships generated—with the assistance of the budding choreographer Doris Humphrey and the dancer Claire Niles—a whole repertoire of music visualizations by the end of 1919.

From Louis's point of view, music visualization was another enslavement of the dance not far removed from the type of Duncanesque interpretative dancing that made an effort to reflect the music's mood while following its rhythmic patterns with corresponding timing. He considered Isadora Duncan to be an "isolated phenomenon—a performer of great genius, the originator of a short-lived intensely romantic kind of dance, and the victim of a mass of embarrassingly sentimental imitators." Inspired by Duncan's personally liberal approach to music but lacking her innate sense of phrasing, her imitators were inclined to produce what Louis called a "vague formlessness."

Why should the dance depend on music for its inspiration and form? With characteristic independence of mind, Louis Horst wanted to see the dance stand on its own two feet as an art.

Through artistic grapevines Louis had heard about a revolutionary German dancer, a former student of teacher-theorist Rudolph Laban named Mary Wigman, who was beginning to create dances that did not rely upon music. While she did not dispense with music altogether, she pared down her accompaniment to a restrained use of flutes, gongs, drums, and occasionally a piano—the prime purpose being to provide a background atmosphere that would enhance the dramatic or lyrical qualities of her dances. First and foremost for Wigman were her inwardly alive images and those spontaneous impulses that sparked her creativity.

The logic of this viewpoint and method appealed to Louis. Yet, in spite of the fact that Wigman had broken the Siamese twin mold of music-involved dance, her approach brought up other problems—

problems of dance composition. Louis's experience as accompanist and music director had shown him that regardless of how music was handled, a dance must exist in its own right as a work of art. Clearly, composition was a craft that had to be mastered.

These tantalizing considerations had to be put aside for the time being. Louis, too, was swept up in the 1922–1923 Mayer Tour, which took the Denishawn Company through the northeastern, midwestern, and southern states. They played Pittsburgh, Martha's birthplace, and St. Louis, the largest city in Louis's home state; and they had return engagements in Philadelphia, Boston, and New York. Their program again was one of great diversity, with music visualizations constituting the whole first section.

By the time they finished the seven-month tour, they were familiar with every accent east of the Mississippi: a southern drawl, a midwestern twang, a Bostonian *a*, and Brooklynese. They (meaning Louis, in particular) had memorized the names of the best restaurants and hotels in every good-sized city as provision against future one-night stands. But what was most important, they could pride themselves on the fact that they had brought dance as an art into the "sticks," where thousands of Americans had previously held the notion that dancing was a matter of eye-catching steps pulled off in fancy costumes. The only other comparable touring troupe known to regional Americans was Anna Pavlova's ballet company, which performed in the United States frequently during and after World War I.

Yet these considerations were not enough for Martha. Nor was the fact that the prolonged Denishawn tours had forged her into a professional artist. The discontent that had been ameliorated by the gift of new roles was growing into a consuming restlessness. And Martha was not one to put up long with fetters. Still, there was nothing to do but wait out the end of the tour, which was to come to a climax in New York with twelve performances at Town Hall and then terminate with three sets of one-night stands in nearby Massachusetts, Connecticut, and New Jersey.

For the Town Hall engagement an important former member of the Ruth St. Denis Concert Dancers, who had been touring on her own, would return to the company: Doris Humphrey. Lured back by Ruth St. Denis, who had always appreciated her dancing and choreographic skills, Doris Humphrey would be performing on the same program (though not in the same dances) as Martha. Humphrey was billed as Guest Artist (though in very small print) and was slated to dance her popular scarf dance, *Valse Caprice*, while Martha would be seen, among other numbers, in an exotic solo entitled *Moon of Love*. The paths of the two principal creators of the future modern dance would not coincide again until each one had broken out of the folds of matriarchal-patriarchal Denishawn and established herself as an independent artist.

Sitting in the audience at one of the Town Hall performances was John Murray Anderson, impresario-director of the *Greenwich Village Follies*. Responding to the strangely intense dark-haired Graham rather than to the lyrical, golden-haired Humphrey, he came backstage afterward to talk to Shawn about engaging Martha for his forthcoming edition of the *Follies*. A precedent for such an arrangement with Shawn had already been set for a former dancer, Ada Forman, inasmuch as the departing dancer was free to use Denishawn material as required by the new booking.

Her fetters loosened by an appealing offer to perform on her own, Martha accepted the job with alacrity. If, at this moment, she consulted Louis (a moot point, since she was obviously dissatisfied with the "other woman" role she was playing in his life), he might well have encouraged her, knowing that her future was limited in Denishawn.

Six months later, when the still-spectacular *Xochitl* was drawing applause in small and large cities across the country with Georgia Graham in her sister's role, Martha was already dancing on Broadway—a prophetic start in a career of more than one hundred and seventy-five New York premieres.

———•••———

Martha's participation in the *Greenwich Village Follies of 1923* could hardly be said to have struck a drastically new note in her theatrical experiences. Produced by The Bohemians at the Winter Garden, the production was a typical revue, not very different from those vaudeville programs in which Denishawn numbers had been inserted for "artistic reasons." Skits, travesties, renditions of popular songs (including *Mon Homme*, delivered by the Parisian Yvonne George), parodies of old ballads, and a lavish ballet based on the Oscar Wilde tale *The Nightingale and the Rose*, in which Martha did not dance, were presented. The staple of the 1923 edition, in which she did appear, was reported to have been the big production number *The Garden of Kama,* described in a program note as "A tragedy of India conceived and arranged by John Murray Anderson from the Indian Love Lyrics of Laurence Hope." Curiously, the poems of Laurence Hope had provided the inspiration of Ruth St. Denis's and Ted Shawn's first joint ballet, also entitled *The Garden of Kama;* but in this instance the Oriental dances had more of an authentic ring, being choreographed by Michio Ito, the Japanese dancer. (Ito endowed Martha's *Follies* experience with somewhat of an international flavor inasmuch as he had studied not only dance in Europe but philosophy in Egypt and when in England had made the acquaintance of Ezra Pound and William Butler Yeats.) As a second number, Martha simply performed her old *Serenata Morisca* in a Spanish fiesta scene typically Denishawn.

At first it seemed to Martha that her move from Denishawn was bearing fruit. She was billed as a soloist, was earning good money ($350 weekly), and was thought of as a dancer in her own right. But was the *Follies* experience so different from other show stints that she had done in the early Denishawn days when she took outside jobs? There was the time when she and Charles Weidman had agreed to stage their own vaudeville act at Grauman's Million Dollar Theatre in Los Angeles to earn some much-needed money. They concocted a Parisian apache dance in which Charles wore a rakish beret and she was costumed in a tight black Montmartre-style skirt. Seven times a day, seven days a week, Charles flung her to the floor, pulled her up roughly, and then, in a climactic finish, whirled her around while she clung to him, hands clasped about his neck, legs wheeling through the air. Those were the days when almost everything she earned was sent to her mother and Lizzie, and she couldn't afford to refuse a job. Now there were deeper considerations at stake, even though she was still sending money home as regularly as possible.

The second *Greenwich Village Follies* season rolled around, and the experience of dancing the same exotic numbers night after night began to manifest itself in a "divine dissatisfaction," a deep discontent that refused to sanction mediocre work by any rationale. Her spirit was crying for meaning, and time was rushing by—a fear always connected with the fact that she started dancing in Denishawn at the late age of twenty-two. Now she was thirty! The contrast between what she was doing and what she wanted to do was brought out radically when she went to matinee performances at the Century

Theatre, where the great Eleanora Duse was performing in Ibsen's *Ghosts* and other plays. Her acting and that of Maurice Schwartz at the Yiddish Art Theatre on Second Avenue could bring tears to Martha's eyes. Returning to the *Follies* now seemed a desecration of her own art.

"Divine dissatisfaction" had seized Louis, too. Having toured the length and breadth of the United States with the second and third Mayer Tours (1923–1925), he resigned from Denishawn during the summer of 1925 prior to the company's departure to the Orient. Feeling the need to rediscover his own musical talents, he left for Europe with Vienna as his destination. His plan was to study composition with the musicians Richard Stohr and Max Persin.

At about the same time, Martha was offered a teaching post at the Eastman School of Music in Rochester, New York. The artistic environment sounded promising. She would be provided with a studio, pupils to train, and, most of all, opportunities to choreograph. She decided to accept the offer from Rouben Mamoulian, the Russian-Armenian theater director who was in charge of the newly formed Eastman School of Dance and Dramatic Action.

A new wave of energy came over her as she planned her future. In September and October of 1925 she would establish herself in Rochester, then return to New York for the gala November opening of the John Murray Anderson–Robert Milton School (of theater arts), at which she and Michio Ito would perform (along with Noel Coward), and then start teaching there on a part-time basis, which would permit her to commute to Rochester every fortnight for three days.

The Eastman experience proved to have mixed blessings. On the one hand, she did have golden opportunities to work by herself and with some talented pupils, who became the first recipients of movement ideas along the lines of "contraction" and "release." But she was rankled by the school's insistence that she should create dances for the Eastman Theatre, which showed movies and wanted dance numbers to go with them. With sudden clairvoyance, Martha saw herself being duped into staging revue numbers, not unlike Denishawn's and those in the *Follies*. "So, when they wanted me to come back for a second year," recalled Martha later, "and I walked into that big room—it seemed to me it was a tremendous room [no doubt, because her feelings were more than life-size]—to sign my contract for ruining myself at a tremendous amount of money at that time—and today!—I picked up the pen and started to write, and I put down 'M—' and said, 'Excuse me, Mr. Hansen, I cannot do it.' And then I turned and walked out."

The experience, in reality, had been far from shallow. She had been able to work on elements of technique that would serve her later in the formulation of a still-to-be-discovered style. And she had developed a trio of dancers, whom she presented the following spring in her first New York concert. They were Evelyn Sabin, Thelma Biracree, and Betty MacDonald. That her pupils absorbed the first manifestations of Martha's pedagogical and choreographic gifts can be proved in an Eastman film of the May 1926 stage production, *Flute of Krishna*. Though obviously Denishawn-inspired as far as theme and style were concerned, the performing of Robert Ross as the god Krishna, of Evelyn Sabin as Radha, and of Thelma Biracree, Betty MacDonald, and Constance Finkel as the Three Apsarases (Dancing Girls) indicated an extraordinary ability on the part of the director to create dramatic verity through expressive movement.

In Viennese restaurants and cafes, they played Johann Strauss, Waldteufel, Lehár, and other nineteenth-century composers. Listening to Liszt, Louis was faintly amused. Hadn't he played *Liebestraum* for Ruth St. Denis innumerable times in almost every big American city? Now Liszt was entertaining him as he sat drinking beer at a sidewalk café not far from the magnificent buildings of the Austrian National Library. With him were Frances Steloff of the Gotham Book Mart in New York and her husband, David Moss. They were on a book-buying expedition. (The following year Frances Steloff would be instrumental in helping to finance Martha's concert debut.)

Though Louis was studying music composition, it was the dance that would be most enriched by his Viennese experiences. In less than two years after his return home he would set a precedent in America by reversing the roles of dance and its accompaniment. *Fragments*, a suite in two movements, *Tragedy* and *Comedy*, premiered in 1927, was choreographed by Martha first; then Louis, scaling the music to suit the dance's idea and material form, composed the score. From now on, music would be considered the "handmaiden" of dance, not vice-versa. From now on, a new breed of modern musicians would find stimulation for musical ideas in the changing dynamics and rhythmic nuances of movement itself. A unique musical repertoire would emerge that would take its cue from corresponding sources of energy that infuse motion and sound. Released from the bondage of conventional partnership, each art would discover fresh impulses and configurations. And in the process of its self-discovery, the new dance would develop its own techniques and its own theories of composition.

Such engrossing thoughts did not, however, occupy Louis's facile mind all the time. He certainly indulged in Vienna's visual and gastronomic delights, as well as pursuing arduous studies at the Akademie, which he felt were "dry, pedagogical, but like sowing seeds. I only hope there will be some harvest." In the same letter that he voiced these sentiments to Ruth St. Denis, he said revealingly, "I was not trying to follow your advice—to forget you all—after 10 years of such play and labor as ours—one can't forget." Then he admitted with uncharacteristic openness, "I have been painfully lonesome."

But who would have guessed in the early days of 1926 that the white-haired gentleman leaning over the rail of the incoming transatlantic steamer was destined to play the role of father of modern choreography? Possibly, only one person in the entire world. She stood there, waiting on the breezy westside dock, her eyes glistening with anticipation, the long strands of her black hair tied back in a neat but voluminous knot. As the boat settled alongside the wharf and the passengers filed down the gangplank, an amused expression passed over her face. The gentleman in question had put on untold pounds. Buttons stretching to the bursting point indicated a most impressive rotund waist. Carrying a steamer blanket with leather straps around it, and wearing a European hat instead of his familiar peaked cap, the American-born Louis Horst looked more German than any German possibly could!

"Hello, Martha," he said in a gruff, matter-of-fact voice. But the tenderness in his eyes spoke of other things.

Martha's Ninth Street studio served as a combination home, school and "laboratory." A bedroom and kitchen inconspicuously

47

located in the rear took care of her personal needs; the rest of the area was filled with space, not furniture. There was an inlaid parquet floor, elegant of design and glowing from the fine patina of its variegated woods. Warm and pliant, it was a pleasure to feel beneath one's bare feet. No draperies softened the lines of the windows; no pictures hung on walls painted an ascetic grayish-white. But there was Louis's piano in one corner and a drum with a mallet nearby.

Work never fazed Martha. She would sit on the floor for hours trying to discover the movement path that the simple act of breathing takes. She would work late at night and then rise at six in the morning to work again—even in the winter, when the floor was icy cold.

She would sit absolutely still, concentrating on the action of inhaling and exhaling. Inhaling gave her a sense of power, a feeling of the body renewing itself; exhaling was, basically, a letting go of the spirit as well as of the breath. But it wasn't passive. She tried to classify the movements muscularly by calling them "contraction" for the act of exhalation and "release" for the act of inhalation. But even the words had an emotional ring to them. And the movements of the body which coordinated with the breathing acts became more and more expressive as Martha built up the dimensions of the inhalation-exhalation rhythms.

Louis would find her on the floor when he would come to play for classes or rehearsals. (He was living up on West Fifty-seventh Street in the late twenties.) He would grunt something about her having been there all night. No remark from Martha. No change of position. But with the arrival of a student or group member, she would rise and work would begin. There was always a new dance in the making, a new idea to explore.

"My first original dances were terrible, but they were a beginning."

But what is a beginning? Sometimes it is a reckless leap into the unknown; sometimes it is the most tentative of steps in a journey—"to go I know not whither to fetch I know not what," as in the old Russian fairy tale of that title. There is only one pack to carry on one's back: faith in oneself. And even that wavers sometimes.

When Martha broke away from Ruth St. Denis and Ted Shawn, she found old ingrained habits clinging to her regardless of the fact that she no longer performed her directors' dances. Her first New York concert in April 1926 still contained romantic and exotic numbers reminiscent of her Denishawn days. While she was favorably received, it was not until she premiered *Revolt* a year and a half later and *Immigrant* in the spring of 1928 that it became obvious that she was developing a style of her own: straight-lined instead of curved, forceful instead of pretty. And with the premiere of the Greek-inspired *Fragments* to Louis's delicate score for flute and tam-tam (a shallow gong with a thin tone like a cymbal), Martha proved that she had a singular gift for both tragedy and comedy.

Tragedy, the first of the two dances in the *Fragments* suite, was gravely processional, pictorially like the draped terra-cotta figurines of Tanagra. Clad in sculptured folds of bright red jersey, she moved slowly with a sense of profound resignation. In the background the flute maintained a cool melodic line, suggestive of an Olympian remoteness, while the intermittent strokes on the metallic gong seemed to knell ominously for man, the victim of the gods' immutable decrees.

In *Comedy*, she was a tightly-wound spring of perpetual motion. Staccato runs, sudden stops, abrupt kicks in bas-relief profile called Pan to mind. Puck, archaic Pan's modern counterpart, was on stage too, at least in spirit. From the first moment of the dancer's appearance, the audience was reading mischief into every gesture. The timing of a jump, an impudent shrug of the shoulder, the way she suddenly cocked her head to one side, would be signals for merriment. In the middle of the dance, in the center of the stage, she dropped to the floor on one leg, sat precariously perched for a moment with the other leg stiffly extended, and then recovered swiftly in a single upward shift of weight . . . then off she went again on a merry chase that impishly led nowhere.

Undetected behind these brilliant beginnings was the slow, laborious forging of a style of movement indisputably her own.

Years later Martha was to call Ruth St. Denis and Isadora Duncan "a double matriarch" of the American dance. The description is significant. The matriarch is the dominating figure of creation. To achieve one's own identity, one must renounce the mother figure and strike out for oneself. As the double matriarch, Isadora Duncan and Ruth St. Denis bequeathed the inspiring vision of an American dance to their disciples. But its technique and choreographic form would have to be forged by the next generation of dancers.

Acutely aware of the disproportion between her choreographic abilities and her driving ambitions, Martha would lose faith and sink into an apathy from which only Louis could rescue her. This he did instinctively by becoming the stern master, the patriarch whose word was law. "Now you work!" he would say, and get up from the piano and start to walk out. The black Irish in Martha would flare up. Temper would meet temper. Tears, threats on Martha's part. But Louis always won. Pushed back into the studio, Martha would scream in protest, vowing she would give up dancing altogether.

"You can't give up, there is nothing else you know how to do!" Louis would retort, turning the key in the lock.

Only when the sound of his steps died away would she subside.

A couple of hours later he would be back.

"Let's see what you've done."

The shape of a dance would begin to emerge. The better it was, the stricter Louis became. His criticism was straight to the point.

"Why that movement?" he would ask roughly, "Can't you find something better?" Again Martha would fly off the handle. Jehovian in his pronouncements, Louis budged neither from his chair nor his settled opinion. Stalemate.

During one such impasse, Martha reached the breaking point. Infuriated, she looked wildly around. Before Louis knew it, a Japanese sandal came hurtling in his direction.

"If you do that again," he warned, "I'll slap you."

A drum mallet swept by his head.

Louis Horst rose—a good 240 pounds of wrath—and strode across the room.

Martha remained defiant. It was *her* dance, not his. If she wanted to, she could destroy it.

Not so, thought Louis, raising a threatening hand. It belongs to *posterity!*

And with that, he slapped her.

Chapter Three

Revolt in the Dance

Alone on an empty stage, with black velvet curtains as the only background, a young woman stood close to the footlights on a small, semicircular platform painted dead-white. She wore a long-sleeved, tightly fitted, ankle-length red chiffon-velvet dress. Straight black hair fell like a mane behind an oval face with high cheekbones, deep-set eyes, a finely molded nose, and a strong, angular jaw. There was intensity in this face, but only as part of a greater intensity that gripped the entire body as it stood poised on the brink of action.

A dissonant chord from an unseen piano broke the stillness. At the same instant, the taut body released its pent-up force . . . not in great swathes of motion, but in sudden, small shocks detonating from the torso. Hard and dry, involving very little action in the arms and legs, the thrusts functioned like depth-charges sending vibrations through the entire body and into the surrounding air. Vermilion circles, angles, intersecting lines all seemed to replace one another in vivid, rapid succession. Yet, not once did the dancer leave the platform where her feet, like sturdy springs, pulsated in widespread balance.

Called simply *Dance*, Martha's solo had mystified its audience when it was first performed in 1929. Even its subtitle—a quotation from Nietzsche, "strong free joyous action"—seemed misleading. Strong, yes, but free and joyous? The very restrictions of the narrow, tubular-shaped costume Martha wore would limit any exuberant impulses. Even more incongruous was the fact that the small two-step platform constituted the sole performing area! Rooted to its dimensions, Martha looked, as one of her dancers (Martha Hill) remarked, "as if she dared someone to come and move her feet."

Such impressions, however, were in perfect keeping with Martha's intention to open her audience's eyes to the new dynamics of the dance she was creating. Instead of extravagantly scattering energy in a stage-wide expression of freedom and joy, she concentrated on making the torso the center of vital action. There, where the spine, heart, and lungs hold dominion, she released prime forces of energy in an intense, but brief, sequence of percussive gestures. With each breath-propelled thrust she seemed to be saying, as she did indeed say later: "My dancing is just dancing. It is not an attempt to interpret life in a literary sense. It is the affirmation of life through movement. Its only aim is to impart the sensation of living, to energize the spectator into keener awareness of the vigor, of the mystery, the humor, and variety and the wonder of life."

Within a year of its premiere, Martha would choose *Dance* to launch her contribution to the opening night program of the newly formed Dance Repertory Theatre. Unique in its aim to establish a new form of American dance, the project was to present the work of four revolutionary-minded dancers in a series of joint and individual performances: Martha Graham, Helen Tamiris, and the partner-collaborators Doris Humphrey and Charles Weidman. With Louis Horst as their music director, they would rent the Maxine Elliott's Theatre, at Thirty-ninth Street near Broadway, for eight days beginning January 5, 1930.

It was a daring venture. None of the dancers could boast of an established reputation. Performing as infrequently as two or three concerts a year, their appeal, for the most part, had been limited to other avant-garde artists—writers, musicians, painters, sculptors—and, occasionally, intellectuals from the academic world. Nothing daunted, they divided the week's tenancy into nine performances: three to be shared, and two apiece for individual programs.

The choice of the Maxine Elliott's Theatre had symbolic overtones. To begin with, Maxine Elliott was a famous American actress of the early twentieth century who courageously introduced new techniques in acting. Secondly, the theater's location was just around the corner from the tradition-studded Metropolitan Opera House, where opera ballet, poorly directed and on the whole poorly danced, had become a relic of an outmoded form. To be sure, the diamond horseshoe of tiered boxes containing society's elite glittered as before and the resplendent chandeliers still vibrated with the high notes of coloratura vocalistics, but such lavish surroundings only served to heighten the modernists' disdain for traditional glamour.

Emphasizing even further the role of the Maxine Elliott's Theatre as an outpost of avant-gardism was the fact that only three blocks to the north, where the Great White Way began, dancing as sheer entertainment was flourishing spectacularly. In Keith's Palace Theatre, buck and wing, tap, soft-shoe, clog, acrobatic, skirt, and adagio dancing were brought to a fine art in vaudeville acts; at the Capitol Theatre, prior to a film showing, a lineup of Chester Hale Girls kicked their pretty legs in chorus-style fashion; and, at the newly built Roxy Theatre, lavish pageants were frequently presented under the aegis of the Russian, Diaghilev-trained Leonide Massine. Equally mesmerizing for the general public were the revues that featured the imported English craze called "precision dancing" and the musical comedies dominated by the chic, diaphanously costumed Albertina Rasch Dancers.

All around them was dancing, but to Martha Graham, Doris Humphrey, Helen Tamiris, and Charles Weidman the multitudinous styles of popular dance were mainly derived from other epochs and other cultures. The time was ripe, they believed, for the emergence of the dance as an American art expressive of their country as it exists geographically and as it functions socially. To them, America's jagged mountains, great lakes, sun-baked deserts, winding rivers, and wind-swept prairies suggested vigorous, freewheeling movement. Cities like New York, Pittsburgh, Los Angeles, Chicago, Boston, Dallas vibrated with industrial energy and social change; and they sought to define these forces and express these dynamics in a dance that had a rougher texture than the polished European ballet associated with the touring productions of the late Anna Pavlova or the imitative Oriental, Spanish, and other foreign styles that had formed the backbone of Denishawn's presentations.

They were pioneers, and proud of it—each one an individual artist with an individual technique and approach. And they had no doubts that they were creating an art worthy of twentieth-century America.

"A new vitality is possessing us," said Martha. "No art can live and pass untouched through such a vital period as we are now experiencing."

The Dance Repertory Theatre would offer no painted scenery, no fancy costumes, no symphonic orchestral accompaniments, no story ballets. Themes dealing with modern life, nature, social injustice, and psychological relationships between men and women would be explored in starkly expressive movement in the simplest of costumes on a bare stage. No more delicately curled fingers, no more the "look-how-easy-it-is" smile, no more the virtuoso leap or multiple spin. Hands firmly held would reflect the straightforward realism of the body's posture; facial expressions would be stern, concentrated; instead of soaring effortlessly through space, the dancer would shoot upward angularly, impulsively, or purposely submit to the force of gravity in earth-dominated motions.

And punctuating all would be, "America's great gift to the arts . . . rhythm: rich, full, unabashed, virile."

Their dances would seize that rhythm, fill the stage of the Maxine Elliott's Theatre with it, and, eventually, send it forth in powerful waves across the world.

Supported by a few visionary persons of note—among them, Otto Kahn, Mrs. W. K. Vanderbilt, Anne Morgan (sister of J. P. Morgan), Irvin S. Chanin, and Carlos Salzedo—the young revolutionists staged their campaign. And for want of a better name, they would be called "modern dancers."

———— ··· ————

Backstage on the night of January 5, the excitement surrounding a premiere could be felt in the prescient silence that invaded corridors and dressing rooms. Martha was to open the program dancing five solos and making an appearance in an ensemble work. Tamiris was to take the second section, after the first intermission. And Humphrey and Weidman with their Concert Group were to conclude the performance.

While Martha was still performing *Dance*, Tamiris and the Humphrey-Weidman contingent were putting the finishing touches on their makeup and slipping into costumes for the opening numbers of their particular sections. The dissonant rhythms of the Honegger music could be heard faintly in the upstairs corridors alongside the wall that separated the dressing quarters from the area high above the stage where backdrops and scenery parts were generally "flown."

Had anyone stepped out on the scaffolding used to support stage-hands while they focused lights or adjusted cycloramas, he would have witnessed a curious three-part spectacle from that great height. About fifty feet below was Martha, brightly lighted, dancing on her small white platform; offstage, behind the wings, could be seen the rounded back, flying fingers, and white shock of hair of Louis Horst playing the piano; and in some remote corner backstage, crowded together in semidarkness, ten girls, clad in long black rayon-jersey dresses with kerchiefs tightly wound around their heads, were silently "warming up." They were members of Martha's group, and they were getting ready to dance *Heretic*, her final offering.

Some of the girls were sitting on the floor, stretching and bending in insect-like positions; some, in deep knee-bends, were rising slowly, tilting obliquely backward; and others, standing with arms tautly held at their sides, would suddenly twist and drop all the way to the floor, landing on one shoulder noiselessly and smoothly in a back fall. A closer look would have discovered that the expressions on all of the girls' faces were the same: serious, intense.

These were no ordinary young women. All of them were Graham disciples in the truest sense of the word. They literally gave their lives to dancing. Daily classes in technique and evening-long rehearsals several times a week (and sometimes in the afternoon as well) were only part of their dedication. A Graham dancer believed in "the cultivation of the being." That meant seeing exhibitions of paintings and sculpture; attending concerts at Carnegie Hall and elsewhere to listen to Bach, Ravel, Scriabin, Poulenc, Satie, and all the modern composers recommended by Louis; reading books on philosophy and psychology; and talking, thinking, breathing dance.

Few of the dancers had enough money to exist on; most of them worked as stenographers or office clerks, efficient and businesslike from nine to five, or as part-time salesgirls in millinery shops and department stores. Some waited on tables in small restaurants or posed as artists' models, sitting like statues for seemingly endless periods of time and then dashing across town for another appointment of immobility elsewhere. But come rehearsal time, and they would all be on their way to the studio. And no job, however lucrative, would be accepted if it would interfere with the intensive rehearsals that preceded a performance.

For most of them, the dance would become a lifelong profession, as it would for the greater part of Martha's dancers throughout the years. From the early group (circa 1930–1933) would emerge the nationally known educators Martha Hill, Bessie Schoenberg, Bonnie Bird, and Gertrude Shurr; the choreographers Ethel Butler, Sophie Maslow, May O'Donnell, and Anna Sokolow; the dancers Dorothy Bird, and Lillian Shapero. And those who eventually left the field would carry with them the idealistic vision of dance as conceived and taught by Graham.

One of the dancers, Betty MacDonald, had danced with Martha at the Eastman School in Rochester, as had Evelyn Sabin, who had been in the premiere of *Heretic* the preceding spring. Later, others, hearing about an extraordinary dancer who was breaking away from tradition, came straggling into her private studio. Those who had seen her first independent performances had likewise fallen under her spell. They all came, as countless others would come in the years to follow, partly out of curiosity, but mostly out of a need to identify with something and someone greater than themselves. Their ignorance and their desire to learn made them humble—which was the only way to face Martha Graham. But in facing her, and in meeting her demands, they grew strong.

At first they stood like delicate reeds in front of her, listening with young minds and trying in vain to follow her commands. They scarcely understood what she was talking about when she said, "Movement in the modern dance is the product not of invention but of discovery—discovery of what the body will do, and what it can do in the expression of emotion." Her voice with its special timbre, husky and vibrant, seemed to coax and to threaten at one and the same time. They were not intimidated, but inspired. "Your training only gives you freedom." Freedom? Penance, rather! Discipline on Martha's terms was relentless. Sometimes they worked in a daze, blindly struggling with unyielding joints and muscles—but they kept working because Martha's exhortations could not be disregarded. They only knew that when she spoke of a dancer's body being "a dynamo of energy, exciting, courageous, powerful," they would subscribe to whatever she asked of them; and they continued like demons, never letting up until the class was over. Home at last, they would fall into a deep well of physical and emotional exhaustion with a wonderful sense of gratification.

As a teacher, Martha did not ask them to imitate her, but to feel the movement as their own. Nor did she ask for perfection of line as a ballet teacher would. In her search for the telling gesture, she was relentless with herself as well. Leading them, she demonstrated her theory of contraction and release: how movement springs from the body's center, the mid-torso, where the breath resides. With a letting out of breath, the diaphragm spasmodically contracts, forcing movement inward and backward in a concave curve of the spine. Breath indrawn is released in a ripple of motion, spiraling upward and outward through torso, neck, and arms. Total action involves the body at all times, seated, standing, or traveling through space.

The walk she evolved made deliberate contact with the floor. "Come down into the earth with your heels," she would say, and the word "into" supplied the key feeling. The run she evolved charged across the room—the way Martha, as a child, had raced across the mesa high above the sea at Santa Barbara—arms swinging oppositionally against the long, lithe stride of legs. The leap she evolved took off from the ground in one piece; full-fashioned, yet spontaneous, it had to contain what Martha called the "perfect timing to the Now."

Her exercises seemed forged with fire. Muscles the girls never knew existed began to pull and splice legs and torsos. Thigh muscles known as *quadriceps femoris* seemed to swell in pain after hours of work on falls and deep knee-bends. Many a time they had to walk backward down the steep outside steps of Martha's studio on Ninth Street!

But come the next day, there they were again, dressed in tank-suit practice attire, ready to submit to further "torture." Whatever their childhood background in dance training—ballet, interpretative, character—might have been, Martha stripped them of stylistic mannerisms, stripped them as she stripped herself down to the anatomy of her own body's feelings. The human being was her starting point, not the decorative gestures of a style that was merely assumed. For her, the aesthetic code that clung to established forms had to be flung aside, without doubt, without question.

Their bodies became hard, muscular. Reshaped into flexible, tensile instruments, they could coil and uncoil at a moment's notice. Their minds, acutely attentive, grew alert to the physicalities of their surroundings: the elasticity of space; the precise nearness or distance of another dancer and her proposed trajectory of movement across the stage; the springboard of the floor beneath their bare feet; the intoxicating spin of fast turns and the stillness that followed as the room "subsided." Nerves took hold of rhythm, shook it, beat it, punctuating time with body accents. And music ceased to be an external incentive, a thing apart from oneself that starts up the battery of motion. As Louis or Dini de Remer, Martha's other accompanist, played quiet chords at irregular intervals during the lessons, the sound of the strange harmonies seemed an integral part of their bodies' inflections.

———————

When the Honegger music ended, the girls heard a burst of applause, the rumbling descent of the curtain, then the swish of its ascent and more applause. A second later Martha swept by, flushed and breathless. It was quite dark and they quickly made a path for her, knowing that she would return in a few moments in the costume for *Deux Valses Sentimentales*, with its music by Maurice Ravel.

The small platform had already been removed and placed upended against the brick backstage wall. Now, instead of stark centrally focused lighting, the entire stage was diffused with a radiance in keeping with the spirit of the Ravel waltzes and the ensuing *Four Insincerities*, in which Martha satirized social behavior in dances entitled *Petulance, Remorse, Politeness* and *Vivacity*.

Then once more the platform was placed mid-stage and the lighting refocused to create a dark void around a small, centrally bright area. Wearing a simple three-quarter-length black dress with a pointed white collar and large white organdy cuffs, her hair caught up in a soft net, Martha seated herself on the platform, her legs bent to one side, her body partially facing the audience, her eyes scanning the darkness around her.

Half-dance, half-pantomime, *Adolescence* was the first of Martha Graham's probings into the netherworld of the psyche—in this instance, the complex emotions of a growing girl, whose ambivalent desires and fears kept her anchored to uncertainty. Tentatively, she would reach out toward the darkness surrounding her as if seeking to fathom the future. Then, fearful of committing herself to the unknown, she would quickly return to her nest of light and withdraw into herself. With the barest of movements—formal and self-contained—the dancer created a private world where adolescent curiosity, self-preoccupation, wonder, and dread mixed with erotic daydreams. And in the background, Hindemith's *Prelude and Song* wove its own web of harmonic fantasies.

One more solo, the Greek-inspired *Fragments: Tragedy, Comedy,* then Martha led her group onstage to take positions for *Heretic,* the final number of her section of the program.

When the curtain rose, a double wall of human forms dressed in black Puritan garb stood facing a slender figure in white with her back to the audience. With the first chords of the music, the lone woman advanced defiantly. Immediately the lines shifted, blocking her way with the simplest of formations. A bitter dialogue ensued in which each side remained obdurate. Then, abruptly, the music —*Old Breton Song*—stopped.

In the silence that followed, the group returned to its original position and resumed its intransigeant attitude. With the repeat of the music, the woman struck out again in an effort to break through the solid barrier. Stiffening at a new angle, the group formed another blockade; but the woman moved forward undaunted. It almost seemed that from sheer force of will she would succeed in liberating herself. Then the group split apart, re-formed, and created a fresh impasse.

Ominous silence, marked only by the grim return of the group and the woman to their first uncompromising stance. This time, with the reiteration of the music, the conflict was resumed with even greater intensity: a desperate lunging against her foes, another forced retreat, a reckless thrust, and then the final overthrow. . . . Trapped and broken, the heretic fell at the feet of her oppressors.

Fittingly, Martha brought her opening night contribution to a climax with a dance of individual rebellion. While this was partly a coincidence of programming and of Martha's growing preoccupation with the struggle of a single mind against dogmatic tradition, there were other telling factors connected with the Dance Repertory Theatre's first season's display of revolutionary ideas.

The New York City–born and bred Helen Tamiris, who was responsible for initiating and organizing the collective project,* had

*Tamiris's personal representatives assumed impresario responsibilities with the words, as printed on the program cover:

THE ACTORS-MANAGERS, INC.
HAS THE HONOR TO INTRODUCE TO NEW YORK

received her ballet training at the Metropolitan Opera School of Ballet and had consequently performed in the Metropolitan's corps de ballet and in operas in South America; but the limitations of opera-style ballet irked her. It was Tamiris who, it could be said, openly rebelled against the venerable institution around the corner from the Maxine Elliott's Theatre.

Christened Helen Becker, Tamiris was a tall, beautiful young woman with a shock of unruly reddish-brown hair. Even before her first concert in 1927, she had identified with trends in modern art through two brothers who were avant-garde painters. In one of her programs she wrote a Manifest, which asked, with characteristic zeal: "Will people never rebel against artificialities, pseudo-romanticism and affected sophistication? The dance of today must have a dynamic tempo and be valid, precise, spontaneous, free, normal, natural and human." Then, in a more reflective mood, she stated: "Art is international, but the artist is a product of nationality and his principal duty to himself is to express the spirit of his race."

At first it appeared that Tamiris was the one who most vividly (and obviously) described the America of their times. The protagonist of her solo entitled *Twentieth Century Bacchante* was unquestionably a hellion who reveled in Arcadias similar to Central Park or the rougher Hudson River Palisades. In *Dance of the City*, also performed on the Dance Repertory Theatre's opening night program, Tamiris used a siren accompaniment that was realistically suggestive of the screech of ambulances and police cars racing through the streets of Manhattan. She also may have been the first American modern dancer to use jazz in a serious vein, and, certainly, her eloquent interpretations in *Three Negro Spirituals*, a group of solos with which she concluded her section that night, revealed a remarkable empathy for black culture and a gift for transforming ethnic material into an art form.

The second of these solos, *Swing Low, Sweet Chariot*, epitomized the mournful, yearning, faith-filled piety of the Negro people. Behind the slow, extended gestures, one divined the hidden energies of a downtrodden race—energies capable of releasing great spiritual power.

Tamiris's point of view was, in essence, evangelical. She was the first to "spread the gospel" of the new American dance abroad, performing her *Negro Spirituals* in Austria as early as 1928. (More than two decades would pass before Graham would invade the European consciousness.) While not capable of matching the innovative brilliance of her Dance Repertory Theatre colleagues, the flamboyant, free-spirited, talented Tamiris nevertheless was a vital member of the early modern dance family, and later a choreographer of distinction for Broadway musicals.

When the curtain rose on the Humphrey-Weidman section of the opening night program, fourteen girls, clad in short, rust-colored straight-line tunics, were grouped upstage center, some upright in frieze-like formations, some in half-crouching positions. Tall screens flanked the action, giving the scene a monumental look. Close to the stage's edge, a huge red scarf covered a figure lying face downward.

An ominous rumble of the kettledrum, signaling the first statement by the piano—a loud chord followed by a descending passage interspersed with chords—and the covered figure drew herself up in one motion and dramatically flung off the scarf.

Edvard Grieg's *Concerto in A Minor* for piano and orchestra had begun, with Doris Humphrey performing the solo part with her Concert Group. In the dance that ensued, the use of the ensemble was unlike any previously seen. Small groups within the large group moved in counterpoint, until the soloist—at the helm, so to speak—brought them forcibly into unison. Even in this early work, Doris Humphrey proved herself to be a choreographer of uncommon skill. She handled the ensemble movement with a unique sense of the dynamic relationship of its component parts; her designs were broad-scaled, at times heroic; she used music as a background for action that was stirring and climactic without a story line. As a dancer, she was like a shaft of light, air-borne, shimmering, intense.

Endowed with a remarkable analytical mind, Doris Humphrey became interested early in her independent career in the "hard facts" of pure motion. Unlike Martha, who was building a technique out of her own body-feelings, Doris looked beyond herself to discover immemorial laws of the universe, as did Lucretius in his philosophical-poetic treatise, *Of the Nature of Things*.

With a passionate desire to understand reality objectively ("I believe in getting along with as few illusions as possible"), Doris Humphrey focused her attention on the interplay of natural forces outside the body as well as within it: the interaction of wave and wind (*Water Study*); biological growth (*Dances for Women*); and, most significantly, the omnipotence of gravity as seen in man's constant struggle to keep his equilibrium. Out of this struggle, she devised an entire technique based on natural movement—walking, running, leaping, falling, and recovering—all of which, she felt, could be theatrically exciting to see and to perform even without emotional implications, because pure movement contained its own dramatic potential.

"Moving the body stirs the emotions," wrote Doris Humphrey in defense of dance compositions without overt emotional expressiveness, such as her own *Drama of Motion.*

Compare this to Martha Graham's statement: "Out of emotion comes form."

But can one compare? The French say *Comparaison n'a pas raison,* which means, roughly translated, "Comparison has no sense." Yet, when two artists are born into the same epoch, when each contributes a mammoth share in the unfolding of a new form that eventually interpenetrates and transforms the medium itself, it is almost impossible not to compare their individual contributions.

To begin with, their American heritage had fascinating similarities. Miles Standish was Martha's ancestor on her mother's side. Though not a direct relation, Ralph Waldo Emerson figured in Doris Humphrey's family background. He could well have been a blood relative, for his philosophy of self-reliance was part and parcel of Doris's indomitable temperament. Like Standish, Emerson was instrumental in building a "new world." Like Martha, Doris was building a new world.

Ancestral strains are deep and complex. Mark how reverently Martha speaks of childhood scenes: "I remember being taken by my father into a beautiful kitchen in St. Louis and being presented to Aunt Chloe, who was dressed in white and sitting in a rocking chair." To the little girl of four or five, being "presented to Aunt Chloe" (notice the formality of the phrase) was an experience that would hover over her imagination all her life. As did the figure of Martha's grandmother, "who, for me as a child, was very beautiful and very unapproachable and very frightening. . . . She always wore black."

On the set of *Appalachian Spring,* there is a slender rocking chair;

in *Letter to the World,* one of the characters is entitled "Ancestress," and she is dressed in black.

With Doris, one could almost trace Emerson's sovereign thinking: "My dance is an art concerned with human values. It upholds only those values which make for harmony and opposes all forces inimical to those values."

Doris, the extrovert, for whom nature was a never-ending source of wonder; Martha, the introvert, fighting a personal battle with life.

———————

Until the moment Charles Weidman appeared onstage, the program at the Maxine Elliott's Theatre had been dominated by female choreographers whose various interpretations of drama, lyricism, or even comedy (as in Martha's *Fragments*) made negligible use of pantomimic gesture. Now, suddenly, the heretofore empty stage was filled with imaginary objects: houses, people, things, even flying pots and pans!

Pantomime, the art of making you see what really isn't there, was Weidman's special domain. By merely indicating with hand, head, or eyes the presence of an imaginary person or thing, Martha's former Denishawn dance partner could conjure up a world of his own making. No sooner did Weidman and two members of his male group— John Glenn and Eugene LeSieur—bounce into view in their troubadour costumes in *Minstrels,* then the whole theater seemed to vibrate with the merry sounds of their voiceless carolling and the melodic plucking of their invisible lutes. Boisterous without uttering a sound, pathetically humorous in a Chaplinesque way, *Minstrels* was a forerunner of a style of comedy created solely by Weidman. Drawn from daily gesture, saturated with rhythm, as broadly stroked as a cartoon or as subtle as a wink, it was called "kinetic pantomime."

At this early date, however, the Denishawn influence was still present in two of Weidman's solos: *Japanese Actor, Seventeenth-Century* (performed on the opening night program) and *Passion and Compassion,* a double portrait of Savonarola and St. Francis of Assisi. Transformed into the fiery Florentine prior or into the tranquil bird-loving monk, Weidman was equally convincing. Later, as his perspective widened and the control of his dramatic and comic gifts for movement deepened, he would produce works of extraordinary power: a remarkably sensitive *Portrait of Lincoln;* short episodic farces wrought out of his inimitable gestural vocabulary, the Thurber-based *Fables for Our Time;* and *Flickers,* fast-speed parodies of the melodramatic plots and ham acting of silent movie shorts.

Still associated with Martha through the Neighborhood Playhouse School of the Theatre productions, Weidman had performed opposite her in Richard Strauss's *Ein Heldenleben* the year before the opening of the Dance Repertory Theatre. As described by one critic, "the pantomime and dancing of Martha Graham and Charles Weidman were unforgettably beautiful." But this collaboration would end with the 1930 Neighborhood Playhouse presentation of Loeffler's *A Pagan Poem.* From then on, Weidman would dance exclusively with Doris Humphrey. Their partnership was to become almost as famous as that of Ruth St. Denis and Ted Shawn.

———— ••• ————

Enveloped in voluminous tentlike folds of gray jersey, the hooded figure sat on a low bench, knees projecting widely to each side, hands clenched together in the deep folds of the weblike material. Only her face, hands, and feet were visible. *Lamentation* was the title of the solo Martha had chosen to premiere on the night of January 8, her first individual concert in the Dance Repertory Theatre series. More sculptural than kinetic, *Lamentation* created its movement through the dynamically changing forms of the costume. Manipulated by the simplest of gestures, the material stretched and swelled, flattened and curved.

At times the hooded figure appeared to be as square and impersonal as a block of granite. Then, with a convulsive twist and a low sweep of the upper body, head down, across the pelvic center, the dancer swung to a high diagonal line. Another thrust upward to the opposite side culminated in a new cry of anguish. Now the face was almost lost to view as the figure rose to a triangular peak: hands clasped together far above the head while legs and feet formed a wide-spread base. Climactic, the movement struck a high-pitched note of sorrow and then subsided. Nothing existed now but the emptiness of completely spent emotion.

Lamentation . . . the embryo of *Deep Song.*

Chapter Four
"I Am a Dancer"

There is bone, there is muscle; there is mind, there is feeling. The "interior landscape" with its invisible awarenesses furnished the incentive for Martha's dances, but the physical materials of creation were no less important. To Martha, the body was a "thrilling wonder...a dynamo of energy." It was the spokesman for the psyche, or the soul.

Feeling this way, Martha was revolting against her Puritan ancestry and Victorian upbringing, which considered mind and body as separate units, often antagonistic to each other. On the contrary, Martha was to place all her faith in the body as an instrument to be "shaped, disciplined, honored and, in time, trusted." Being a dancer was an act of total commitment "costing not less than everything."

The song she sang was wordless, but its rhythms and harmonies were the body's articulations: the breath's pulsations, the earth-bound walk, the throbbing tensions of percussive accents, the jet-like jump and rebounding fall. Nothing escaped her awareness. "In a dancer there is a reverence for...the miracle of the small beautiful bones and their delicate strength." And she equated the movement that is "clean, precise" with that which is eloquent and truthful. In one of her notebooks she would write: "The answer is not control of gesture first—the technic of outer behavior—but rather the technic of inner behavior."

"I am a dancer," were the opening words of articles written, acceptance speeches, and unwritten, unspoken stances. "I am a dancer," was her attitude toward life. It was fire fighting fire; life fighting life—the weapon being the body, that citadel of energy and spirit, that instrument of faith incarnate.

In every dance the statement was made. Yet the words—in movement—did not come easily. A poet searches for the *mot juste,* the exact rendering of thought in rhythm or rhyme. A dancer searches in space and time for the right feeling and thought to take shape. Movement impulses are rejected by the score if they do not serve to tell the truth. "Movement never lies," Dr. Graham had said, and Martha repeated it to herself as she discarded phrase after phrase of purely invented design.

When the truth was made manifest, it happened like a flooding of sunlight. Such was the creation of *Heretic,* composed in one evening "out of whole cloth," as Bessie Schoenberg has related. Every movement held. Working intuitively, Martha knew exactly what she wanted to say and had no doubts about the functional form in which to say it. The music that Louis found for her, *Old Breton Song,* had the thrust and sparse melodic content that she needed; by repeating it several times with intervals of silence, she could restate her theme with the mounting crescendo of a pitched battle.

That night she worked like one possessed. Movement piled up on top of movement until *Heretic* burst forth, full-grown at the end of hours that seemed like seconds. It set a precedent for future dances cast in the concerto form, in which Martha would play the solo part against the group's orchestrated themes.

Other dances underwent prolonged turmoils of creation, some of them never reaching the stage. There was the low, infertile winter when Martha had her studio on the third floor of a condemned building on West Fifty-ninth Street, facing Central Park. From the windows the girls could see the small frozen lake where children and a few adults skated in colorful jackets, mittens, and knitted caps on sunless afternoons. The trees were bare and nubby, the paths seldom trod, and the few tall apartment houses on the west side of the park's now-brown rectangle made strangely ornate silhouettes against the wintry sky. Down at the Fifth Avenue corner entrance, opposite the sumptuous Plaza Hotel, a few shiny hansom cabs with drivers in top hats and long coats stood waiting for fares. To attract passengers and to protect their aging horses, the cabbies would throw bright red, green and blue plaid blankets over the beasts and decorate the side lanterns of their carriages with sprigs of holly that, come evening, glistened almost as brightly as the polished brass fittings on the horses' leather harnesses. Fifty-ninth Street had a crosstown trolley then, and the girls could hear its rhythmic clanging in the silence that seemed to hang like a pall over the studio whenever Martha sat in stony contemplation.

Rehearsals would be called, and everyone would come, giving up dinner invitations or getting off work early. In those days, because the studio was quite cold, Martha wore a long, warm practice dress (she usually wore a gray tank suit for work), and her hair fell in straight sheaths over her shoulders, nearly to her waist. To someone who had seen her on the stage, it didn't seem possible that it was the same person. In contrast to her imposing stature behind the footlights, she seemed tiny, almost bird-like in the studio. Her delicate bones, long neck, rounded thighs and bosom gave her a frail, feminine look; only her feet, solid and strong in their claw-like squareness, betrayed her relentless working habits. They gripped the floor as though they would never let go. They had a monumental look—like the sculptured feet of a Roman emperor.

When the rehearsal started, Martha seemed to become even smaller, wrapped tight, as it were, in the cocoon of thought. Seated on the floor, her back to the mirror, she faced the open center of the rectangular room. No one dared to cross her line of vision. Along the margins of that space, the girls would be stretching quietly on the floor, or staring patiently out of the window. Once in a while Martha would speak. One of the girls would be called into the "sacred" center. Instructions would be given in tentative tones. Suddenly coming to life, the girl would strike a pattern in the waiting space.

A despondent shake of the head from her director would stop her in her tracks.

"Sit down," would be muttered in a lifeless voice.

And silence would fall again.

How did it feel to be called to rehearsal and then used so little? This was hard, no doubt, and a far cry from the fast-action rehearsal of today when minutes count and choreographers, fully aware of the cost of production, are flaying their dancers' nerves with the rapid repairing of old movements and factory-swift inventions of new ones. Time is money (one of Martha's girls, Jane Dudley, composed a satiric dance with that title), but, as we know, clock time has little to do with creativity, which can take eons or split seconds to do its work.

After the explosive birth of *Heretic* in April 1929, Martha would have to wait until the muse would speak to her again in such crystal-clear language. So be it. She would not trifle with anything that she knew within herself to be contrived. The cost—"not less than everything"—was hers to pay, and if that involved waiting an eternity, she would wait it out until she found how to say what she wanted to say.

To the girls, the waiting might have been tedious at times, but it was never irritating. For them it was a great privilege to be members of Martha's group. Even during those bleak months when the frozen ground outside the studio seemed to have imprisoned their teacher's powers of inspiration, they felt that every moment, perhaps the fallow ones in particular, had significance. They never doubted that a new work, possibly greater than ever before, was in the making; and they wouldn't have missed an opportunity to share in the experience. Let Martha merely say "I have an idea" and they would come to rehearse Sundays, holidays, or whole weekends.

In a simple, straightforward way, they worshipped her. They never questioned her judgment; they believed every word she said, considering it to be the truth—Martha's truth. She was honest with herself. That was proof enough of her honesty with them. She was dominated by a vision of the highest order; it was an honor to be dominated by her.

Strange as it may have seemed to outsiders, it was perfectly natural for those who came into contact with Martha Graham to sense her importance and to pay homage to her. The habitually same audiences that attended her every concert soon came to be known as "the cult of Martha Graham." But something far deeper than a "cult" of a semireligious fanaticism was in the making. Religious feelings were present, but they stemmed from humanity's natural inclination to identify with an ideal.

"Then come with me," said the man in Grimm's fairy tale," and become a Stargazer. There is nothing better than that, for nothing is hidden from you."

In worshipping Martha, the girls were bowing before the creative act, which she as a dancer symbolized. Like a goddess of fertility she was bound up with nature's mysterious cycles. Her seemingly barren moments would eventually bear fruit—of that they had no doubts. And her own uncompromising nature, which held to its ideals, was certain proof of the abundance of her unseen resources.

The gratifications of working with her were always present: beauty, meaning, wisdom. When she instructed them, her words were extravagant but always convincing: "Grace is your relationship to the world, your attitude to the people with whom and for whom you are dancing." And what young person could resist the glorious vision of "My dancing . . . is an affirmation of life through movement"?

Compared to her "revelations," other people's pronouncements seemed pedestrian, dull-witted. Martha lived in a realm apart. To be there with her was to partake of the same rarified air.

———————

In the same bare Fifty-ninth Street studio, where the furnishings consisted of a chest of drawers, an army cot, a kitchen table, a couple of chairs, a victrola, and Louis's grand piano, Martha received Léonide Massine. He had come to discuss her role in his production of Stravinsky's *Le Sacre du Printemps*, which was to be presented by Leopold Stokowski under the auspices of the League of Composers in April 1930. It was a meeting of strangely diverse creative minds. Born a year apart, and resembling each other somewhat with their black hair, deep-set eyes, wiry bodies, and serious, intense expressions, Massine and Martha were, at this moment in their careers, at almost opposite stages of accomplishment in the eyes of the world.

The Russian-born choreographer had already achieved fame as one of Sergei Diaghilev's chief choreographers in the later years of the Ballets Russes. Besides dancing principal roles in the repertory, he had composed no less than seventeen ballets between 1915 and 1928, many of them strikingly effective. Now performing in New York City with his own company at the Roxy, Massine had been asked to restage his 1920 version of the famous Stravinsky work for its American premiere as a ballet (Stokowski had previously presented the music at one of his concerts). The setting and costumes would be those originally designed by Nicolas Roerich for the "scandalous" 1913 Parisian premiere choreographed by Nijinsky.

Martha, who was virtually at the beginning of her independent career, was not unaware of the honor of being approached by people of renown in musical and ballet circles. She was also aware of the fact that it was Stokowski and Roerich who had selected her for the role of The Chosen One in Stravinsky's reenactment of a pagan ritual in which a virgin of a tribal community, chosen for her beauty, dances herself to death to ensure the return of the earth's fertility at springtime.

To be invited to perform the leading role in a ballet of such historic importance was an indication that her talents were being noticed beyond the confines of the limited modern dance world. The glamour that had been attached to the names of Nijinsky, Diaghilev, and Stravinsky as *grands artistes* in prewar Paris was far from being diminished with time. On the contrary, the scandal that had taken place when *Le Sacre du Printemps* was unveiled May 29, 1913, still struck nostalgic chords in the memories of the artistic elite. Stravinsky's music with its irregular rhythms and constant changes of key and tempo had been hissed and shouted at during the entire first night performance; equally intolerable had been Nijinsky's antiballetic earthbound movements that attempted to follow every beat of the incomprehensible score. After seven performances the ballet was withdrawn. But to those in the forefront of twentieth-century innovations in music, ballet, and the theater, the original *Sacre* was an avant-garde landmark. For Martha it would be an opportunity and an association of no small proportions.

Massine's version, by contrast to Nijinsky's, was highly successful. By 1920 Stravinsky's epoch-making score had become recognized for its true worth. The new *Sacre,* in the words of Lydia Sokolova, who danced the role of The Chosen One, was "a typical Massine production, clear-cut and methodical, with each group counting like mad against the others, but each holding its own. In Massine's choreography nothing was ever left to chance." While this method of mathematical dissection served the choreographer to advantage in Paris at the onset of the twenties, it was bound to become thorny in America in the 1930s, when it came to superimposing movements on the instinctually propelled Martha Graham.

Rehearsals were held in the Dalton School gymnasium. It so happened that several members of Martha's own company were in the cast as well as four dancers from the Humphrey-Weidman group. According to Eleanor King of the latter ensemble, while Martha waited for her cue to appear in the second scene she sat in a corner with a shawl over head, obviously indifferent to the action around her. According to others who were present, Massine and Martha "crossed swords" when it came to the rehearsing of the sacrificial dance with its complicated counts and pulsations. The resulting deadlock grew more ominous as opening night drew nearer. Finally, Massine in desperation suggested that Martha resign.

"You will be a failure," he said testily.

"Did Stokowski say that?" asked Martha boldly.

When Massine answered yes, Martha went directly to the conductor, who not only told her that he wanted her to stay, but assured her that she need not wear the heavy stockings and laced footgear worn by the others in the cast, but could dance barefoot. He also told her (probably at her request) that she could dress her own hair as she liked instead of being obliged to wear the long, braided blonde wig designed by Roerich.

With Stokowski's support behind her, Martha made a volte-face, and, in her own words, did "exactly as Massine said" for the remainder of the rehearsals. With characteristic honesty, she admitted later, "Although I worked with Massine in 1930, when I appeared in his version of Stravinsky's *Sacre du Printemps,* this was *not* a collaboration—it was a question of take it or leave it."

As a result of her capitulation, Martha's opening night performance in Philadelphia on April 11, 1930, and her subsequent performances, including those at the Metropolitan Opera House in New York on April 22 and 23, were triumphant. Massine's intricately manipulated movement patterns for the sacrificial dance were infused with a pagan fervor of breathtaking power. The primitive drive of Stravinsky's relentless rhythms had found its perfect embodiment in Martha's galvanic leaps and frenzied vibrations.

Whatever might have been the emotional reason for the conflictual drama behind the scenes of *Le Sacre du Printemps,* years later Martha chose to remember her Massine-Stokowski collaboration as "a great turning point" in her life. True to her strong will and compulsive need to use all experience creatively, she interpreted the sacrificial dance in terms of a personal act of sacrifice. "*Sacre* is a ritual. When I danced it in 1930, I was so immersed in the ritual and the sacrifice of the Chosen One that I believed in it. . . . I think the Chosen One is the artist. The principal thing is that it has to do with the artist as his own doom-maker; he composes himself to death."

Louis, who had been the first to recognize the magnitude of Martha's talent, always seemed to know what to do in a crisis. Though he, too, was buffeted by the changing dynamics of her temperament—the hot and cold of her impulses and reactions—he could nonetheless steer her choreographic course with steadiness.

"You're putting out the fire," she once accused him, the Irish in her rising in indignation at a sharp criticism.

"Only to make a bigger one," he answered stolidly, the German in him again standing firm.

Another whole section of a dance would go down the throw-away chute.

Louis was the Rock of Gibraltar, a landmark to navigate by. His presence at the piano—his inlaid maple grand piano, which shone like a polished parquet floor—was reassuring to students and members of the group alike. At rehearsals his humor eased many a tense moment. "You have great talent," he would say to one of the girls, "but you have one problem: you can't stay on the beat!"

When doubts assailed Martha that he knew to be unwarranted, he would quietly stand by. Once, in a fit of dejection at a dress rehearsal the night before a concert, Martha told the girls to pack up and go home; the new dance would be taken off the program. Louis got hold of the company and told them all to stay. When the storm cleared, they were still there, and Martha went to work again putting the composition into final shape, readying it for a public that was to acclaim it a masterpiece. The almost-abandoned dance was *Primitive Mysteries,* that milestone in American dance history.

Louis knew it would be a masterful work, knew it from the start when Martha began to choreograph it in the Ninth-Street studio and he began to compose the music for it. What cause was there for him to doubt? He had acted instinctively, bringing together two elements that belonged together: Martha and the Southwest. The deeply responsive chord that was struck in the audience at the Craig Theatre on the night of February 2, 1931 only confirmed the rightness of his intuitive purposes. Thirteen months later, in March 1932, that confirmation would achieve national dimensions when the John Simon Guggenheim Memorial Foundation would bestow a Fellowship on Martha Graham, the first ever granted a dancer, for the express purpose of studying the culture of Mexico and Yucatan.

The germ of Louis's idea originated in the fall of 1930. Returning from California where Martha had visited her mother and Lizzie, an opportunity presented itself for a brief trip to the Indian desert country outside of Santa Fé, New Mexico. As in Mexico proper, Spanish invaders had superimposed Catholicism on the Indian tribes that inhabited the region that stretched north into the American Rockies. The converted Indians built adobe churches, sculpted sacred santos figurines, and observed holy days like good Christians, but not without infusing the rites with a fervor typically their own. The result was a blend of Spanish Christianity with Indian culture, a blend unique to Mexico and the American Southwest.

For Louis, whose appreciation of primitive forms had already reached a point of consuming interest, the visit to the Southwest was like a pilgrimage.

For Martha, the Southwest recalled childhood experiences that had secretly nourished her over the years: remembrances of the Spanish mission in Santa Barbara with its kivas, or "skyhole," which the Indians mystically supposed led to the center of the earth where "the Father" was to be found. Even deeper than these visual memories and legendary tales was Martha's identification with the "ritual" of play-enacting, an identification that had begun with Lizzie, whose sense of drama was closely bound up with her Roman Catholic background.

The mystic in Martha found its "skyhole" in the Southwest. Entering it with the full force of the awakened child within herself, she found "the Father"—the giver of life. Symbolically, the Father could be the sun, the source of all creative energy. After years of living in close quarters on the East Coast ("I abominate the murk and twilight of New York rooms," she once said in an interview), traveling to the Southwest, where light and space cleanse the eye and spirit, must have called forth Martha's first impressions of California after the dark of Pittsburgh. But in New Mexico the sun beat down with relentless heat. It penetrated the marrow of one's bones . . . it entered the skyhole of one's being.

Returning to California, as she tried to do every summer to see her mother, never did this for Martha. California was too bountiful in its endowments. The richness of mountain, sea, flower, and bush was overpowering. There was nothing to do but to succumb to California's charms and to luxuriate in them. But the Southwest's inscrutable past stimulated her profoundly.

Primitive Mysteries and *Primitive Canticles* were the desert flowers of this deep stimulation. About Martha's *Primitive Mysteries*, critic Winthrop Sargeant perceptively wrote: "A strong feeling for the ritualistic which had always been present in her approach received fresh impetus from the vast sage-brush deserts and the simple dark-skinned race of artists that inhabits them." No other work composed before or since that deals with pagan ritual, has so successfully captured the childlike spirit of adoration and unquestioning faith permeating *Primitive Mysteries*.

Then there was the movement itself: starkly simple, blunt, unadorned. Using the body as a total instrument was the main characteristic of the new dance. Louis called it a "back to the primitive urge." But he clearly differentiated between "a truly primitive approach [which] would be an affectation today" and the new aesthetic that emerged as a result of the modern artist's appreciation of primitive forms. Asymmetry, reflective of the naiveté of primitive art, was favored over sophisticated symmetry. The intensity of primitive experience, as evident in humanity's early preoccupation with nature and magic, becomes transformed in modern dance into another kind of intensity: the use of movement as elementary experience. Without imitating the customs or behavior of primitive life, the modern artist conveys—through formal adaptation of the elements involved—the essence of primitive characteristics: force, power, simplicity.

Whereas the primitive dancer stamped on the ground with the whole of the foot, or in lifting the knee flexed the ankle angularly at the joint, the modern dancer, without actually reproducing those movements per se, uses their rough textures and broken rhythms to express the vitality of the feeling behind such movements. An inner muscular awareness of weight and energy is manifest in every step, every lift of the leg, every turn of the body. Whereas tribal man moved in repetitious patterns without being conscious of movement as pure form, modern dancers use repetition knowingly, planting impressions like seeds so that their ideas will build cumulatively without recourse to overt or sequential gesture. The sheer power of repetition drove *Heretic*'s message of bigotry home. Repetition and purity of feeling also created the primitivistic ardor of *Primitive Mysteries*.

Not a direct translation, but a ritual about a ritual, *Primitive Mysteries* reenacted an annual Hispanic-Indian ceremony in honor of the Virgin Mary. It stated its themes in three luminous sections: *Hymn to the Virgin* (commemoration of the birth of Christ); *Crucifixus* (his death on the cross); and *Hosanna* (his Resurrection).

In silence, twelve dancers in long, dark-blue dresses enter from the wings with slow emphatic steps that are punctuated by a hesitant lift of each foot before it strikes the floor. They are symmetrically grouped in the form of a large square with one side open to the audi-

Martha Graham, age 2. COURTESY MARY ANTHONY.

Martha Graham and Georgia
Graham, c. 1900. ARTHUR TODD
COLLECTION.

Ruth St. Denis in *Incense*, 1908. COURTESY
DANCE COLLECTION, NEW YORK PUBLIC LIBRARY.

Ruth St. Denis and Ted Shawn in
duet from *Egyptian Ballet*, 1922.
COURTESY DANCE COLLECTION, NEW YORK
PUBLIC LIBRARY.

Xochitl poster, Pantages Circuit season, 1920-21. COURTESY DANCE COLLECTION, NEW YORK PUBLIC LIBRARY.

Martha Graham and Charles Weidman in *Danse Arabe,* c. 1921. Courtesy
Dance Collection, New York Public Library.

Martha Graham and Group
in *Heretic*, 1929. PHOTOGRAPH
BY SOICHI SUNAMI. COURTESY
DANCE COLLECTION, NEW YORK
PUBLIC LIBRARY.

Martha Graham in *Two
Primitive Canticles*, 1931.
PHOTOGRAPH BY SOICHI SUNAMI.
COURTESY DANCE COLLECTION,
NEW YORK PUBLIC LIBRARY.

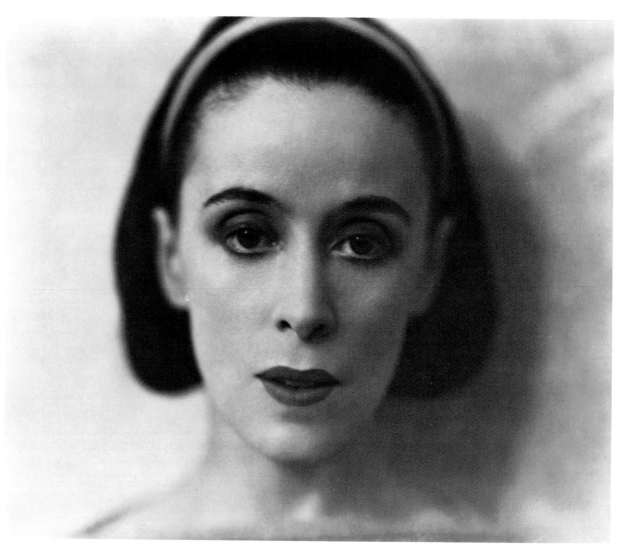

Portrait, Martha Graham, c. 1930. PHOTOGRAPH BY SOICHI SUNAMI. COURTESY DANCE
COLLECTION, NEW YORK PUBLIC LIBRARY.

Martha Graham in *Lamentation*, 1935. Photograph by Barbara Morgan.

Louis Horst composes in his New York Studio, 1935. PHOTOGRAPH BY BARBARA MORGAN.

Martha Graham and Dance Group in *Primitive Mysteries*, 1935. Photograph by Barbara Morgan.

Martha Graham and Dance Group in *Primitive Mysteries*, 1935. PHOTOGRAPH BY BARBARA MORGAN.

Martha Graham in *Satyric Festival Song*, 1935. PHOTOGRAPH BY BARBARA MORGAN.

Martha Graham in *Ekstasis*, 1935. PHOTOGRAPH BY BARBARA MORGAN.

Martha Graham in *Frontier*, 1935. Photograph by Barbara Morgan.

Martha Hill, Ben Belitt, and Bessie Schoenberg, Bennington School of the Dance, 1939, at Mills College, Oakland, California. PHOTOGRAPH COURTESY MARTHA HILL.

John Martin at Bennington School of the Dance, 1938. PHOTOGRAPH BY BARBARA MORGAN.

Erick Hawkins, Doris Humphrey, Charles Weidman, Martha Graham, and
Louis Horst at Bennington, 1941. Photograph by Pix, Inc. Louis Horst Collection.
Courtesy Dance Collection, New York Public Library.

ence. In the center, as if enclosed in a space of her own, is a figure in white. A chosen member of the village community, she enacts the role of the Virgin Mother, to whom they will pay homage, and whose grief and final exultation they will share.

Approaching the center of the stage, the women take their places ceremoniously. The four dancers at the rear sit on the floor with their knees propped up squarely before them; the two side groups close their respective ranks; the figure in white faces front, her long straight black hair falling behind her shoulders, her hands held formally by her sides.

With the first notes of the music played by flute, oboe, and piano, the dancers commence their ritual of adoration. A calm ecstasy pervades the scene as the Virgin skims across the stage, alternately joining one or the other of the two side groups. Each time she comes to a cluster of dancers, they reassemble themselves to frame her, sometimes swaying with her with cradling motions, sometimes circling around her with high leg lifts and extended arms, sometimes catching her tenderly as she drops backward, arms extended sideways.

The ceremony of homage proceeds like a series of mosaic tableaux, each scene clear and complete in itself, the monolithic movement serving to emphasize the childlike quality of the rite. At one moment, eight of the acolytes converge stage center to form a passageway for the Virgin. Two at a time drop on their knees, from opposite sides, and twisting sideways from the waist bend reverentially to acknowledge her as she advances slowly. Her body inclines formally toward them, while her gestures remain detached and madonna-like. The ritual reaches a high point as the twelve dancers circle around the Virgin in spirited homage, their backs taut, one arm bent sharply at the elbow, the other thrust downward percussively. Their staccato movements, sudden reversals of direction, and brief, plunging, straight-backed knee-bends create a rhythmic tension that comes to a climax in a formal bow from the waist down to the figure in white. At that point, the music stops.

In silence, the dancers group themselves as before and solemnly leave the stage in their original processional formation. The sound of their footsteps is like a swish of twigs against a drum skin; the tempo of their walk, slow-paced, even. In returning from whence they came, they seem to be setting the scene for the enactment of a second ritual.

An empty stage. Moments of silence. Again the sound of footsteps. Three dancers enter in profile, side by side. Then appears the Virgin flanked by two tall girls; finally, two more groups, all moving with "a feeling of suspension at the pause of each step."

The figure in white and her two attendants turn to face front up-stage center; the others take positions respectfully apart.

Dissonant chords are struck on the piano; the flute and oboe play sustained high notes. Seemingly locked together, the groups advance toward the center with weighted tread, their legs restrictively striking forward from the hip; then, retreating, they shift to form new positions at oblique angles. The Virgin and the two dancers flanking her inch downstage with the same earthbound motion. With their arms pointing diagonally high across her head toward the imagined figure on the cross, she moves almost rigidly, as if in a trance.

At the dreaded moment of Christ's death, they stop abruptly, and the grief-stricken Virgin, as though stifling a cry, covers the lower part of her face with tensely held hands. Collected in a group, the ten other dancers strike a position symbolizing the crown of thorns: with palms pressing hard against foreheads and fingers distended like spikes, they stand riveted in isolation. The Virgin stretches her arms outward in the sign of the cross, sharing the burden of sacrifice.

Taut shifting motions again bring the groups together to the downstage corner, where they crouch on the floor facing the Virgin. One by one, like arrows shot from a bow bound to the ground, they spring into arched, suspended leaps that encircle the figure in white. Gaining speed, the leaps change to runs, and within seconds the whirl of the anguished disciples has completely hidden the Virgin and her acolytes. Then stillness, silence, and a return to formality. The dancers take their places in the procession, and slowly, emphatically, file offstage.

Now eye and ear are washed clean of sight and sound. The stage is a light-filled desert casting a hypnotic spell. Twice have the dancers come and gone; the third time is at hand. An expectant hush comes over the audience. A sense of inevitability enters the specta-tor's consciousness. Imbedded in primitive and civilized man alike, the number three is the symbol of our primal experiences: the cyclical trio of birth, life, and death; the climax of every mystic rite; the trip-tych form of the Christian creed; the ultimate proof of human exis-tence—man, woman, and child.

The dancers reenter with their weighted, body-straight walk. A single dancer now escorts the Virgin. Again they take their places:

five girls across the rear of the stage toward the left; five girls in a frieze-like line downstage right. The *Hosanna* begins. The spirit is one of intense identification with the Virgin's sorrow and exaltation. We see the descent from the cross, symbolically performed by the single dancer with the Virgin. With broken falling movements she drops into the Virgin's lap to lie across her knees. Later, in similar fashion, the dancers drop backward to the floor, hips slantingly upraised; at this moment the Virgin is lying flat on the floor, arms extending upward, hands meeting in a spired point.

A tender, prescient moment emerges; standing behind the Virgin, her attendant strikes the form of a halo above the grieving Mother's head. Sudden silence. Then a change of mood. Motion fills the stage. Arms are lifted high in celebration, and bodies tilt backward exultantly. A double sign of the cross marks the climax: both the attendant's and the Virgin's arms are outstretched in parallel lines one above the other. The ritual is complete.

The flute, the oboe are silent. The resonant percussive tones of the piano have died out. Ceremoniously, the dancers resume their places in the squared-off lines, their profiles etched against the lighted backdrop. They wait for the Virgin to take her hallowed place among them. A pause; then, with the suspended lift of each foot anticipating the next step, the procession offstage begins.

When the last girl has disappeared into the wings, the curtain descends.

In the 1930s, 66 Fifth Avenue between Twelfth and Thirteenth Streets looked like a small uptown office building with its lobby entrance and elevator on the right. There was even a listing of its occupants on the side wall. At one time Ruth St. Denis and La Meri had studios there. A small moviehouse showing experimental films among others was housed on the ground floor; on the street front the long-established firm of Dauber & Pine ran a fine arts bookshop. Looking down Fifth Avenue one saw the imposing Judson Arch in Washington Square, while the view northward caught a glimpse of the triangular form of the Flatiron Building at Twenty-third Street's X-shaped intersection of Broadway and Fifth.

The daily occupants of Sixty-six were mostly college-age girls, students of Mills College for Women, which had floors of classrooms in the building. These were the girls who made the hallways ring with high-pitched chatter and noisy footsteps between classes and at the end of the day. During the late afternoon and evening, some less conventional-looking young women and men sped up and down the elevator on their way to the few dance studios located in the building. About the same age as the college students, they were obviously different: less carefree, less time-free, less chatty.

Occasionally a single figure would emerge from the elevator and stand waiting for someone in the vestibule near the outside door. She was generally dressed in dark clothes, and if one was standing next to her by chance, one was struck by the thoughtful, intense expression in her deep-set, amber-flecked eyes. Her straight back and sturdy legs, her pulled-tight long black hair twisted into a bun at the nape of the neck, and her trigger-ready awareness of what was going on around her fairly shouted her name. When she glanced at you, she seemed to know immediately who you were—nondescript, anonymous you—with the same sudden recognition that you had felt when you realized you were in the presence of the dancer who had sent you reeling home from her last concert, your life forever changed.

It was to 66 Fifth Avenue that Martha eventually moved in the early thirties, in her odyssey from a Carnegie Hall studio to West Fifty-ninth Street to East Ninth. No longer able to live where she worked, she took an apartment around the corner on Twelfth Street. The school was growing steadily, and Louis's role was not only that of accompanist but of teacher as well. It was at Sixty-six that Louis started teaching Martha's girls and other interested students the course in Pre-Classic Forms that he had inaugurated at the Neighborhood Playhouse School of the Theatre, where he and Martha had been teaching since 1928.

With his students sitting at his feet, Louis would analyze the diverse styles and forms of pre-classic music composed for dancing: pavanes, galliards, courantes, allemandes, gavottes, and so on. Using the musical tempo and phrase counts as rhythmic groundwork for dances to be composed individually by the students, he would proceed to teach "choreography." This was the first attempt to give formal instruction in modern dance composition. In fact, the word "choreography," which is constantly used today, was hardly known by dancers in the thirties. Martha declared that she didn't know what the word meant until Louis gave her Thoinot Arbeau's *Orchesography* (which had been published in 1588 and was one of the earliest detailed descriptions of fifteenth- and sixteenth-century dances).

Westward on Fourteenth Street were artists' studios and art supply shops. Other shops of all kinds—selling hardware, secondhand clothing, books, and stationery—lined both sides of the wide street. In particular, there was the Fourteenth Street Outlet, a mecca for materials of all sorts, where dancers could rummage for hours among remnants and bolts of inexpensive jerseys and crepes.

It was in such a shop, and in similar ones—the Regent's Fabric House in the East Fifties or a small fabric store on Orchard Street—that Martha found the rayon and wool jerseys of her "long woolens" period. Wool jersey and tubing revealed the torso's expressiveness and gave contour to leg action, which at that time was less important in a virtuosic sense. With the primitivistic approach, the aim was to convey the immediacy of emotional feeling. In the early thirties, Martha concentrated on "the subtle being . . . that lies beneath the grosser muscles." The central body was the spokesman. Arms moved outward and upward from the rib cage, legs struck their spatial patterns from deep inside the pelvis. "Fleshies," basic undergarments not unlike tank suits (the name came from Denishawn days), would be the starting point for a costume. Their jersey texture permitted feelings to announce themselves through other yielding fabrics with the same clarity and emphasis that Martha always sought.

Fourteenth Street, with its mixture of art, commerce, and politics (Union Square, where Broadway cut through on its diagonal march downtown, was the site of demonstrations against war and fascism), could be described as the northeast frontier of Greenwich Village. On Second Avenue in the colorful Jewish area known as the East Side was the Yiddish Art Theatre, where Maurice Schwartz—who mesmerized Martha with his fine acting—could be seen in such classics as Ansky's *The Dybbuk.*

Between Sixth and Seventh Avenues on Fourteenth Street the Civic Repertory Theatre presented Eva Le Gallienne's superbly interpreted productions of plays by Ibsen, Chekhov, Barrie, and Shaw. East of Union Square, near Klein's marked-down-dress store, the New York Band and Instrument Store, run by R. G. Darrell, the Bach enthusiast, offered dancers golden opportunities to listen for hours in small booths to their favorite composers; another such haven was the more elegant Gramophone Shop uptown. With their seemingly inexhaustible supply of classical and modern 78-rpm records, these music stores served as libraries from which dancers with choreographic urges could select the accompaniment for their next composition.

In Greenwich Village proper, there was e. e. cummings, writing his innovative poetry, and painting as well. Other serious artists living there in the twenties and thirties—who, like Martha, would contribute to the art and literature of the twentieth century—were Edna St. Vincent Millay, Edmund Wilson, Eugene O'Neill, Thomas Wolfe, Edward Hopper, Moses Soyer (who painted modern dancers; his wife, Ida, was in Tamiris's group), Raphael Soyer (his brother, also a painter), and many young musicians who would be composing scores for modern dancers: David Diamond, Lehman Engel, Norman Lloyd, and Alex North.

Life in the winding streets and mews was vastly stimulating then. Just around the corner from Martha's studio lived Max Eastman, whose foreword for Arnold Genthe's book of photographs of Isadora Duncan referred to the dancer as one of those "giants of mankind who not only . . . entertain the world, but . . . move it."

Further west were cold-water flats where struggling artists lived hand to mouth, earning a few dollars at odd jobs, then spending it on paint and canvas instead of solid food. Their top-floor studios were cluttered with books, secondhand furniture picked up around University Place, half-empty coffee mugs, life-size clay figures covered mysteriously with damp cloths, blocks of marble, and still-life arrangements of flowers or old fruit sitting untouched on tables for days. When the north light faded from skylight windows, the studios would become the meeting-places of artists-turned-sociologists, and the daylong murmur of brushes or the staccato sounds of hammer and chisel would give way to animated arguments about art, government, and the rights of the working people.

———— • • • ————

From the back windows of Martha's studio the girls could see the lights of her apartment. When the light would be turned off prior to an evening rehearsal, they could time her appearance at the studio.

The moment she arrived, she'd slip into her dressing room—a tiny compartment cut out of the small entrance hall with a couch and a chest of drawers in it. The women's dressing room was in a curtained area, and the men's changing room was merely a closet carved out of the same small lobby.

Martha's and Louis's classes kept the studio busy all day long; at night Martha often stayed to work by herself after rehearsals with the company had come to an end. New solos were in the making for New York premieres; and there were old works to be rehearsed for out-of-town dates. Requests for solo performances were multiplying. Martha had traveled as far west as Seattle, the city of her first success in *Xochitl* a decade earlier. Additional performances in Georgia, Alabama, Mississippi, and Chicago, being scattered dates, could hardly be called a "tour." But wherever Martha went she seemed to collect more devotees.

Trailing her back from the famous Cornish School in Seattle, where she had performed and taught, came Bonnie Bird and Dorothy Bird. No one who had ever taught them was anything like Martha. Standing in front of the class, small and straight, she would say defiantly, "It's not my job to look beautiful. It's my job to look interesting. We are not here to please the audience." Describing the body's relationship to the ground: "Grab the floor with your bare feet"; then, derisively, "Putting shoes on is like wearing white gloves to keep you away from the dirty earth!"

From Michigan came Marian Van Tuyl, who had the "life-changing" experience of seeing Martha dance at Ann Arbor. From Sacramento, California, came May O'Donnell; from Manhattan itself appeared Sophie Maslow. Their presence not only as dancers but as potential actress-dancers deepened the group's powers and made it possible for Martha to explore movement in terms of dramatic action.

Students came from almost everywhere. The books Louis kept of the studio's enrollment had many entries of names, but few aspiring dancers had money in those Depression days to pay for lessons. Scholarships were given freely to those of talent, while the struggle went on month after month to pay the studio rent. If it hadn't been for outside teaching jobs—at the Neighborhood Playhouse School of the Theatre and at Sarah Lawrence College in nearby Bronxville—Martha and Louis would have been hard put to maintain the studio in spite of Martha's growing reputation as an avant-garde figure of major importance.

Unable to pay for lessons, the members of the company decided that the least they could do was to clean the studio. The mirrors reflected shining images; the floor was smooth and spotless. A sign in the entrance hall forbade visitors to walk across the maple floor with shoes on—a Japanese custom that suited the simplicity of the studio's pictureless white walls and its stoic atmosphere.

The spirit of stoicism belonged to the Depression climate of the thirties. A nickel apple from a corner cart or a foamy milkshake drunk in haste at an open soda counter along Fourteenth Street would serve as lunch or supper if one was on the way to rehearsal. Martha ate frequently at the Automat, a noisy cafeteria where the patron chose his nourishment by inserting a few nickels and dimes into walled cabinets with small compartments covered by glass doors. Wearing the same camel's hair coat and beret-type hat winters on end, Martha could be spotted from afar. Even if she had had money, she wouldn't have spent it on street clothes. Costumes always came first.

For every New York concert, money had to be borrowed. It was a matter of course for Martha to go to the bank a couple of weeks prior to the performance and sign a loan for funds to finance the venture; then, funds in hand, fliers and posters would be printed and mailed to libraries, schools, dance studios, and any theatrical establishments that might be useful. The rest of the money, after a sum was put aside for the theater rental and for the musicians that Louis would hire, would go to buy costume material.

Martha's personal costumes, designed and sewn by her, were generally ankle-length. Sometimes the material fell in huge folds, as in *Lamentation,* or clung to her legs, as did the form-fitting knitted tubing of *Ekstasis.* She used all kinds of weaves, rough or smooth, shining or dull; she used all kinds of stripes, broad and narrow often mixed, as in her vertically striped black and white straight-lined sheath for *Primitive Canticles.* Under her hands, cloth behaved humanly. It moved with the body like its skin, or it stubbornly kept its own form, standing out rigidly with each bend of the knee or thrust of the hip until it had a regal stature, like the overskirt, stiff as a tapestry, in *Imperial Gesture.*

Color had significance: the Virgin's costume in *Primitive Mysteries* was the white of luminous purity. The material was organdy; it swung out layer upon layer, falling from the waist with a narrow overlap down the center of the skirt; it stood out from the shoulders in semidetached sleeves, leaving Martha's arms free to etch out their formal gestures. The girl's wool jersey dresses were a dark grayish blue, providing a weighted contrast. And each girl sewed her own costume, often far into the night after rehearsals had ended.

Martha had stripped costume down to the essentials of line, color, and texture. Yet certain tactics learned at Denishawn were still apparent: the use of yards and yards of material to create a dramatic effect (the materials would become more voluminous, the effects more spectacular, as her "woolen period" would be left behind); the manipulation of fabric to create extraordinary enveloping effects. All these maneuvers led to her own devices of employing a costume, or part of it, as a "prop." In the satiric two-part solo *Harlequinade*, the polka-dotted scarf that served as a huge handkerchief for Martha to weep in and then lug around with miserable mien in *Pessimism* became a flying emblem hung from her waist as she scampered about foolishly in *Optimism*.

In those days it was the Guild Theatre on West Fifty-second Street where modern dancers gave their two or three Sunday night dance concerts each year. At first there was a law against Sunday performances, but the dancers banded together and formed the Concert Dancers League of New York City. Headed by the fiery, outspoken Agnes de Mille, they fought the legislation and virtually pushed the Sabbath League out of the theater.

The Guild concerts represented the goal of an entire year's work. The approval of the attending public and favorable reviews in the *New York Times* and *Herald Tribune* by the perceptive John Martin and Mary F. Watkins were the plums to reach for. A new work was prepared for the Guild Theatre with fear and trembling, excitement and pride.

Early in the morning of a concert, Martha, Louis, and the group would move into the theater with costumes, music, and props. While the stagehands would be setting up the lights under Martha's direction, some of the girls would be covering specific areas onstage for the focusing of "specials": those spotlights that serve to dramatize a particularly important moment of the action. Everywhere backstage was feverish activity: unpacking and ironing costumes, sewing rips or making last-minute alterations, going over changes in the choreography of the new dances, being available to Martha for checking out the colors of the "gels" that had to be replaced between dances. Choreographers did their own lighting then—whoever heard of a "lighting designer" for the dance in the thirties? It was

Louis who suggested to Martha, "Why not try Jean?" That was Jean Rosenthal, a former student of theirs at the Neighborhood Playhouse School; the Jean Rosenthal who was to change concepts of lighting the dance—ballet and modern—for all time.

Rehearsals would begin as soon as the stage could be cleared, and then all those weeks and weeks of arduous work could be pulled together in one tremendous effort that needed only the presence of an audience to become incandescent. The dress rehearsal, with lights, music, and costumes, might take hours, with trying scenes of temperamental outbursts from technicians and Martha alike when something went wrong. Once, in the middle of a leaping sequence, the wrong light switch was pulled and the dancers found themselves in sudden darkness. Instinctively they landed in the right place, but the music stopped abruptly and Louis could be heard muttering furiously as the girls stood still, breathing hard. With the return of lights, the rehearsal resumed full force, and so did everyone's anxieties.

Tension mounted as the minutes grew shorter before curtain time. Small talk ceased in the dressing rooms. The mirrors, framed by brightly burning lamp bulbs, reflected the gradual transformation of tired, perspiring faces into exotically painted visages staring back at their owners with heavily lashed eyes and vermilion lips. Long hair would be combed severely back and caught with a strong barrette. Martha would be scooping up handfuls of Vaseline to smooth down her hair until it shone like patent leather in one long strip.

The corridors became as silent as the cloistered walks of a monastery. Louis would be under the stage close to the door leading to the orchestra pit or up in the wings going over a score for last-minute reminders with flutist Hugo Bergamasco. Martha's mood would be like a bowstring drawn tight. Anything could snap it. (Once, long before, when she was seized with stage fright, Louis had to push her onstage.) Silently the girls would file down the dressing room stairs to find places backstage to warm up. As white and taut as Martha, they moved like cats in a dark alley.

Suddenly, the performance would be on with Martha already out there dancing a solo, possibly *Satiric Festival Song*. Her impish capers and off-balance runs and the way she tossed her hair about with jerky motions of her head would be drawing gales of laughter. Another solo, and the suite, *Dance Songs*, would be concluded. Then they—her dancers—would be on in *Primitive Mysteries*. To enter walking in unison without music would take every ounce of control. . . .

"Audiences who come to be amused and entertained will go away disappointed," wrote John Martin in the *New York Times*, "for Miss Graham's programs are alive with passion and protest. . . . She does the unforgivable thing for a dancer to do—she makes you think."

A caption under a print of a painting of Martha by Edward Biberman in an issue of the magazine *Theatre Arts Monthly* read: "The cerebral, specialized and laboratorial studies of Martha Graham." The words were taken from an accompanying article written by Mary F. Watkins.

It was obvious that Martha was shaking people up everywhere! If she made people think, that was a mere by-product. Her motive was to communicate the intensity of living—living as a dancer lives, in "complete focus upon a given instant." At such a moment, one's awareness of oneself in relation to one's surroundings is acutely sensitive. Then, and only then, does the experience of dancing reveal itself to be the perfect fusion of the inner and outer person. "Dancing," Martha would say, is "movement made divinely significant." Its significance, though, was always in the realm of feeling. Intuition rather than intellect was the requisite key to understand Martha's kinetic language.

"I do not compose ideologically," she averred, "and I have never considered my dances in any way intellectual. Whatever theory may be read into them proceeds from the material and not vice-versa."

Her defenders were many—among them critics from newspapers throughout the country as well as from the New York metropolitan area. "Martha Graham demonstrated not only . . . freedom from convention or tradition, but also possession of creative artistic intellect," wrote the spokesman from the *Philadelphia Public Ledger* in November 1932.

Whether curiosity brought the uninitiated, or whether her reputation as a technician of extraordinary merit was attracting a wider public, there was no doubt that the radical nature of Martha's dancing elicited both "a thunder of bravos" and heated arguments.

Controversies were rampant. The erudite Lincoln Kirstein, dance historian and ballet entrepreneur, disliked Martha intensely at first; eventually he admitted that "the force of the personality of the woman magnetized me continually," and that after seeing her choreography for Katharine Cornell's production of *Romeo and Juliet* (1934) and for Archibald MacLeish's *Panic* (1934), he had a "nucleus of comprehension."

But the person who protested the most against Martha's unswerving modernism was none other than the ballet choreographer Michel Fokine.

The setting for the much publicized Fokine–Graham controversy was the downstairs studio of the recently built New School for Social Research on West Twelfth Street. A sunken circular performing area in the center of the studio permitted the audience—seated slightly higher on a narrow bordering strip—to view the movement from different perspectives. The atmosphere was intimate; speakers standing with their backs to the rear of the room (which was generally free of seats when such events took place) did not need to raise their voices unduly. Indirect overhead lighting bathed the center area with a naturalness that was in keeping with the informality of the dance presentations.

When John Martin inaugurated his initial series of modern dance lecture-demonstrations in 1931, he invited Doris Humphrey, Hanya Holm, and Martha Graham to describe their personal approaches to the aesthetics of dance on consecutive Friday evenings. In one of the audiences that attended Martha's demonstrations was—unknown to her—the renowned Fokine, whose *Les Sylphides, Petrouchka, Le Spectre de la Rose,* and other works had contributed to the Parisian successes of Diaghilev's Ballets Russes.

To Fokine, Martha looked like a "fanatical prophetess." To Martha, Fokine, whom she had never met and therefore did not recognize, was merely an inquisitive man on the sidelines whose name she did not know. As she explained her technique of contraction and release based on the natural rhythm of the breath, the girls demonstrated.

At that time Martha was at the height of her percussive period, when her movements, initiated by sudden, accented strokes, radiated upward, outward, or downward according to the inner drive of the dance. Sharp at first, then resonantly sustained, each movement would be replaced by fresh motion, some strokes short and tight as drumbeats, some long and extended with the increased intensity of a reverberating gong.

It was Martha's intensity that disturbed Fokine. He could not equate the impulses of her accented movements with the natural flow of breath or the joy of dancing, which he felt must be expressed in lighthearted aerial motion. But he carefully desisted from speaking until someone in the audience asked Martha what she thought of ballet during the question-and-answer period that followed the demonstration.

Speaking of the European ballet after being queried regarding her opinion of it, Martha mentioned Anna Pavlova's greatness as being apparent in even the least of her movements. "She bowed very well," said Martha, who believed that curtain calls should give the final flourish to the impression that a dancer has made throughout the performance.

Interpreting her remark as intended sarcasm, Fokine was shocked.

Then Martha went on to say, with complete conviction and characteristic honesty, "But when a ballet dancer performs a Grecian dance it becomes horrible!"

At this point Fokine, who had composed many ballets based on myths of ancient Greece and who was known for his revolutionary balletic reforms in pre-war Russia and France, spoke up. Sparks of temperament lighted up the room as the famous ballet master ridiculed the lecturer's use of the body in ways that he privately thought were "ugly in form and hateful in spirit."

Refusing to budge from her point of view, Martha simply took "fifth position" and asked coolly, "How can one dance a Greek dance in such a position?"

Fokine retorted by defending the fact that there existed Greek ballets built entirely along the lines of natural movement, and he concluded, "You criticize the ballet without knowing anything about it."

Martha bristled. Fokine kept heckling and Martha bristled even more. Finally, in desperation, Mr. Martin looked at his watch.

"Mr. Fokine," he said, "we cannot continue this argument. Ballet has had its chance of saying what it had to say during three centuries, so the modern dance has a right to talk for three weeks!"

Martha flushed. "I didn't know I was talking to Michel Fokine." Then, looking straight at him, she added firmly, "We shall never understand each other."

Ironically, neither Graham nor Fokine could recognize in the other the same revolutionary drive for artistic integrity that possessed each of them singly.

Chapter Five

The View From Vermont

The mile-long road that leads from Route 67A to the pulsating Commons Building of Bennington College in southern Vermont is lined with thick-trunked evergreens and sturdy elms. In 1934 the elms were more slender and the various accommodations on campus fewer, but the view from the three-storied white-columned Commons was the same: A wide sweep of lawn, neatly bordered on each side by small white-clapboard dormitories, dipped into acres of lush meadowland that seemed to drop off suddenly into an unseen valley. Beyond, to the south and west, rose a range of bluish-purple mountains. They lay in series, rather like musical sequences of well-modulated variations.

Splashed with gold in the early morning sunlight and outlined in scarlet at the end of a summer's day, these luminous mountains formed a symbolic barrier between New York City's tight, feverish existence and the state of Vermont's spacious calm. Metropolitan tensions would subside as one faced the graceful contours of peaks that did not scrape the sky as did the loftier, more austere range to the north known as the Green Mountains; less formidable but of geographical kinship, the kindly Berkshire Hills of western Massachusetts and northern Connecticut soothed the eye.

Bennington was indeed a haven to repair to after a strenuous New York season, and yet it was from the high tableland of the college's campus that Martha Graham and her colleagues—Doris Humphrey, Charles Weidman, and Hanya Holm—began to view all of America with fresh perspective. In the quietude of these rolling Vermont hills, new insights into their country's past, present

89

problems, and future possibilities would provide themes for dances that would change the face of that art on a national scale.

Once again, an enterprise of joint productivity would make its mark—like the Dance Repertory Theatre—on dance history. For five summers, beginning in 1934, the Bennington College School of the Dance would offer pioneer modern dancers the opportunity to work creatively in fields and on subjects of their own choice. Teaching and performing opportunities would be theirs in abundance, and all without the strain of financial burdens associated with the New York scene. It was, almost literally, a golden opportunity for the artists; for the students who would take their courses and for the audiences who would see the premieres of seminal works, it would be a memorable, fruitful experience. That the Bennington format would have the tremendous impact that it had on the artistic and academic worlds of American dance could not, of course, be foreseen, but one person—the author of its format—had the clear-sightedness to recognize its educational potential. That person was Martha Hill, a former member of Martha Graham's dance group who had been recommended by Graham to head Bennington's dance program when the college was founded in 1932.

Already an experienced teacher, Hill had been instrumental in introducing a graduate dance major into the curriculum of the physical education department of New York University, where she had been teaching since 1930. Under her aegis, the NYU dance major soon blossomed into an M.A. degree with specialization in dance, an academic innovation of no small consequence in the early thirties (only a handful of institutions in higher education had followed the pioneer establishment of accredited dance courses at the University of Wisconsin under the directive of Margaret H'Doubler). Now, as director of the new dance program at Bennington, a post she held simultaneously with her assistant professorship at NYU, Martha Hill became increasingly aware of the need to supplement the academic approach with leadership from professional artists. It was a sophisticated view, drawn obviously from her own enlightening experiences of performing in the Graham group. And it was far from practical, given Bennington's 194-mile distance from New York (a geographical problem that did not seem to trouble the metropolitan-based Miss Hill, who already had struck her students as the acme of sophistication).

In a most unexpected way, an opportunity soon arose to put Hill's unconventional academic ideas to the test. According to Bessie Schoenberg, who shared Hill's winter teaching assignments, Bennington's first president, Dr. Robert D. Leigh, "had a great talent for smelling out gifted young people and for taking long chances." One Sunday morning the adventurous Dr. Leigh, who had been advised by Bennington's trustees to find means of utilizing the college facilities during the summer to produce some much-needed income, was taking a walk around the campus with the intention of talking to the ever-inventive Martha Hill. At the moment of their encounter, Hill happened to be drying her hair outdoors.

Nothing fazed, Leigh spoke his mind. "We should do something here in the summer, and I was wondering if there was anything in the dance that you could think of."

That was encouragement enough for the dauntless educator to take off on a vision of her own. In no time, that vision would become a blueprint for changing the face of dance in America. And the central figure in the blueprint would be Martha Graham.

———————————

Enlisting the administrative assistance of Mary Josephine Shelly of Columbia University Teachers College and of Chicago University, Martha Hill made it possible for Bennington to offer summer workshops for dancers and dance teachers throughout the country —workshops designed to teach the new art of modern dance in the most comprehensive professional manner possible. The prime enticement, of course, was the opportunity to study personally with Martha Graham, Doris Humphrey, Charles Weidman, and the dancer-choreographer-teacher Hanya Holm.

A disciple of the great Mary Wigman, in whose company she had performed and at whose school in Dresden, Germany, she had taught, Hanya Holm had been brought to America in 1931 by the renowned impresario Sol Hurok, who had been responsible for bringing over Wigman for her first transcontinental tour the preceding year. His aim was to organize a New York branch of the Wigman school. A man of astute artistic judgment, Hurok had presented (among other renowned performers) Anna Pavlova, Isadora Duncan, and Loie Fuller in his celebrated tours. (Approximately fifteen years later Graham would be under his aegis.) Gradually adapting her very special talents to the American scene surrounding her, Holm took over the management of the Wigman school, gave it her name, and established her own reputation as a leading exponent of modern dance.

Once grouped together at Bennington, Martha, Doris, Hanya, and Charles became affectionately known as The Big Four. They should have been referred to as The Big Five, for Louis Horst was no less a leading figure, being a pioneer himself in the field of teaching dance composition and music composition for the dance.

In the beginning years, Bennington's summer school staff included (besides director-founder Martha Hill and her assistants Mary Jo Shelly and former Graham dancer Bessie Schoenberg) musician-composers Gregory Tucker and Norman Lloyd, and, as lecturer on dance criticism and history of dance, John Martin.

Between 1935 and 1941—during which time the School of the Dance was transformed into the School of the Arts—some of the finest modern dance works ever created were conceived and premiered in the Bennington Festival Series. There were even opportunities for the more talented students to perform in compositions that called for a larger cast than the resident choreographer's own company. One of these was Martha's ambitious *Panorama* (1935), which called for twenty-four workshop dancers in addition to her twelve group members.

But in spite of its excellent score by Norman Lloyd and its partial use of the first mobiles that Alexander Calder designed for the stage, the large-scale *Panorama* could not compare in lasting importance to Hanya Holm's symphonically conceived *Trend* (1937) or to Doris Humphrey's visionary, affirmative *Passacaglia in C Minor* (1938)—both of which have taken their place in history as masterworks of the Bennington period.

Within the span of two years fellowships were awarded to six choreographically gifted dancers who were deemed potential leaders for the modern dance: José Limón, Anna Sokolow, Esther Junger (1937); Eleanor King, Louise Kloepperer, Marian Van Tuyl (1938).

"The fellowship was a big honor," remarked Anna Sokolow in retrospect; "it gave me the strength to go on and to do what I believed in." Always conscious of the personal-social struggles of young people caught in the conflicts of contemporary urban life, Sokolow was to emerge as one of the twentieth century's most articulate choreographers.

Likewise, the recognition afforded by the Bennington fellowships provided significant stimulus to the other recipients: José Limón was to become one of the leading male dancer-choreographers of the next thirty years, creating dramatic works of enduring value; Esther Junger, formerly an independent soloist outside of the Bennington circle, turned her talents in the direction of ensemble pieces; Eleanor King, Louise Kloepperer, and Marian Van Tuyl were to enrich the western and midwestern environments with their choreographic and teaching ventures in the states of Washington, Wisconsin, and California, respectively. In addition, Van Tuyl became a spokesman for the literary world of dance by editing and publishing the annual magazine *Impulse,* which, in turn, published Louis Horst's second book on choreography, *Modern Dance Forms,* drawn from his classes in Bennington as well as in New York.

Not only did Louis teach dance composition but also music composition for the dance, a course inaugurated in 1936. In the latter, he advised his student-musicians to keep their scores "open and spacious, so the audience could see the dance through it." One of his most talented students, Evelyn Lohoefer, remembers how Norman Lloyd, his associate in the course, used to help her interpret Louis's directives when he was having an obstinate day and wouldn't bother to clarify his demands. Throughout both courses the maestro's credo was unequivocal: "To compose is not an inspirational experience."

Notwithstanding, Louis himself was an inspiration. In shirt sleeves, suspenders, a cigarette dangling from his lips, his sharp eyes following every move whether he was playing for the dancer or not, Louis had a formidable way of dominating the room. His caustic and sometimes crude sense of humor could cut a dancer's ego into shreds; but his insights into the subject of aesthetic productivity could stir a sensitive soul to fresh understanding of basic creative values. If the cost meant the breakdown of an inflated self-esteem, it was little enough payment for such enlightenment. Sitting on the floor at his feet, wide-eyed and dance-hungry, were young women destined to become the future educators of American dance. Prominent among them were Helen Alkire (Ohio State University), Ruth Bloomer (director of Connecticut College School of Dance when it eventually took over the Bennington summer program), Ruth Diamond (University of Nebraska), Margaret Erlanger (University of Illinois), Alma Hawkins (University of California at Los Angeles), Ruth Murray (Wayne State University), and Virginia Tanner (University of Utah). Also at Louis's feet (taking a lesson in obedience) would be his dachshund, Max.

The voice of the master would carry to the ends of the room, accompanied by a silence of devout attentiveness and the scratching of pens on paper. Composing was as hard work with Louis as dancing was with Martha. He insisted on "structuring" a dance as carefully as an architect would design a building. Some of the "phys ed" teachers, whose academic responsibilities other than calisthenics and sports included teaching folk dance forms or stimulating their students' self-expression with freestyle movement, found the going difficult. And Louis had his little fun at their expense.

"Don't behave as if you're dancing for Louis the Fourteenth. Just for plain Louis."

Then, to provoke them: "Do the impossible! Move with audacity into space!"

Louis liked puns and took pleasure in exploring the comic possibilities of such words as "terror." "Tear it to shreds," he would say with a mischievous gleam in his eye. "Tear-roar!"

Among his students was an aspiring young dancer whose agile mind would store away some of Louis's imperishable aesthetic truths. But she had a sense of humor, too, and could see, as she later reported, how Louis "used any and all methods to make his points. He would praise, scold, cajole, prod, castigate, flatter, or sniff that famous sound signifying that he was bored or upset." Her name was Gertrude Lippincott and she hailed from Minnesota, where she would return to maintain Bennington's high standards through her own work in the Midwest.

When the lesson was over, Louis would throw in a half-encouraging, half-skeptical, "Now bring in a *good* gigue tomorrow."

Come the next day, the students would file in hesitantly, trying not to catch his eagle eye.

"Come on in!" he'd say cheerfully. "I won't bite you."

But everybody knew better. Louis had a bark, and a bite. Yet laughter would tumble out on top of tears, and frankness, though it sometimes hurt, could lead a would-be choreographer out of the darkness of incompetence. No one knew better than Martha how Louis could fan the flames of creativity with "the magic of his imagination, his cruelty, his demonic will and his skill."

Louis was at Bennington the entire summer; weekly workshops were held on Saturdays, and at the end of the six-week session his students would give a demonstration of the summer's work. It was informally presented, but a special aura surrounded the event when Louis would have his assistant and one of Martha's outstanding dancers, May O'Donnell, perform her *Whole Tone Study*—a little gem of a work that displayed May's remarkable physical control and purity of style in "even spatial design," the movement counterpart of whole tones. From 1934 to 1936 May was Louis's assistant, as was also Anna Sokolow in 1935.

Martha's participation expanded from two weeks of teaching to full-time instruction and performances at the end of every season until 1941. "Without Martha Graham," writes Sali Ann Kriegsman in her book *Modern Dance in America: The Bennington Years*, "the project could not have succeeded; and it was Graham who gained most conspicuously from the Bennington Association. Of The Big Four, she alone was in residence each summer; after the school closed in 1942, only Graham was invited by Bennington College to return as artist-in-residence for three consecutive years." Often she came up to Bennington before the school opened if she wanted to work uninterruptedly on a new composition. On those occasions, as in other absences from the New York studio, her classes would usually be taken over by Gertrude Shurr. While Martha was up in Bennington during the season, Bonnie and Dorothy Bird, Ethel Butler, and later Gertrude would be her assistants.

Martha's arrival, like her leave-taking, was a sight to behold. In the old open Model-T Ford which she and Louis had bought second-hand when they spent their summers in New Canaan before the advent of Bennington, the luggage would be piled high. Since neither Martha nor Louis drove, at the wheel would be Bonnie Bird, the most practical member of the equipage. Up the winding road, under the leafy elms, the car would noisily chug its way until its royal occupants were in full campus view: Martha and Louis in the back seat, scarves and necktie flying, hats shielding faces from sun and wind, and in their arms, held protectively, the dachshunds Allah and Mädel.

Was it Martha's sense of theater that made everything she did seem spectacular? Or was it her psychic presence that operated offstage as effectively as onstage? Whatever it was, and wherever it came from, the sight of Martha Graham always created a stir, just as it had in the early days when she walked down the street in Santa Barbara while the conductor kept the trolley waiting for her.

At Bennington, the stage seemed to be set for her every day after lunch when all the students would throw themselves down on the soft grass of the quadrangle in front of Commons for a short period of relaxation. The air would be buzzing with small talk when the front door of Commons would open and Martha would emerge, attired in a silk Japanese *happi* coat slipped over her practice costume. The chatter would suddenly cease, and all heads turn in her direction. With the air of a queen passing among adoring subjects, she would pick her way through the half-reclining groups, nodding graciously to this one and that one. Some students would sit up stiffly, embarrassed at being caught off-guard; others would simply stare, curiosity mixing with admiration.

For Martha it was normal and natural to have people stop whatever they were doing when she appeared. This is the actress's reasoning: to be effective, an entrance should have an audience, and an audience deserves a performance that is stirring, captivating. She justified it all by saying that they were paying homage not to her but to the art she served. Nonetheless, she adored it and would have admitted as much. For those who watched in wonder as Martha made her way toward the little clapboard house that was hers at the bottom of the grassy hill, even the clouds seemed to stand still until the regal figure—becoming smaller and smaller and straighter and straighter—disappeared.

Approximately eight months after Martha's first summer at Bennington, the curtain of the Guild Theatre in New York rose on *Frontier*, the solo that would become the dancer's signature piece during the second decade of her career. Slight as it was, *Frontier* was Martha's all-encompassing view of the Midwest, for she subtitled her dance *American Perspective of the Plains*. Both the setting by Isamu Noguchi (the first of more than twenty décors the sculptor would design for Martha) and the nineteenth-century dress she wore evoked the spirit of pioneer life in a yet-to-be-cultivated landscape. Principally, it was Louis's music, written after the dance had been choreographed, that "caught the emotion behind the movement . . . and opened a vista of the American plains that the dancer was viewing," according to composer Norman Lloyd. He also commented: "At the beginning of Martha Graham's *Frontier*, she slowly raised her arm to a position over her head. The obvious solution would have been to write music that rose slowly. But . . . the music was active, quivering with excitement."

In front of a fence-like barrier of two horizontal bars suggesting a prairie outpost stood a young woman in a homespun pinkish-brown jumper worn over a white blouse with dolman sleeves. From behind the barrier, two ropes stretched diagonally outward and upward like cables looping off into regions unknown. Beyond and to the sides of the frail fence seemed to lie a wilderness of unconquerable vastness.

With bold, outflung gestures, the woman advanced toward the audience, as if her westward march lay in their direction. At moments she seemed air-sprung as she leaped joyously through space with head-high sideways kicks. At other times she seemed part of the earth as she spread her legs on the floor, hands clasped tightly together in a forward thrust. Every moment radiated confidence and determination.

A subtle change took place. As though a high prairie wind started to blow across the outpost's rectangular confines, the solitary figure wavered, moved skimmingly sideways, backward, and to the opposite side to the eerie intermingling of a flute and piano. With the tremulous moment's passing, she resumes her spirited advance, this time with a brief sideways motion again in which she suggestively holds her arms in a cradling position. Then backing up to the barrier, she strikes a last decisive gesture as the curtain descends.

Frontier broke through the restraints of formalized motion and trancelike facial expression as previously seen in Martha's primitivistic and puritanical works. Without overt emphasis, the dancer let her feelings "speak" through her face; her hands, now freed from the cupped triangular form of earlier dance gestures, would change according to the different feelings she was projecting.

Frontier was destined to become Martha's trademark, the dance that would be associated with her name across the continent. *Frontier* was pure Americana: forthright, free—the very spirit of an indomitable westward-moving people. Though *Frontier* had a place of honor on every program, including those she presented with her group, other solos, such as *Harlequinade* and *Ekstasis*, varied the evening's offerings with glints of humor and sculptural lyricism. An all-solo program, demanded the utmost in strength, but Martha's physical prowess was increasing yearly at such a rate that critics were beginning to call her technique "prodigious." Paul Love wrote in *Dance Observer:* "She has developed her body to the point where it can do impossible things with ease and nonchalance."

With Noguchi's sparse setting and Louis's vibrant score, *Frontier* traveled westward as Martha performed it over and over again on her first transcontinental solo tour the year following its premiere.

The long train rides with Louis recalled Denishawn touring days. As mileage piled up, and the experience of successful engagements in Michigan, Washington, and Oregon became gratifying memories, they found themselves in high spirits as they neared San Francisco, where Louis's sister, May, awaited them. They would go to her apartment on California Street, have an intimate supper with May and her husband, Ernest Forbes, the diplomat, and then prepare for the next date in Oakland, across the bay.

In Oakland, there was some trouble with the lighting and some minor difficulties with the floor cloth, the canvas that is stretched across the boards of the stage. Coming back on the old ferry that routinely crossed the bay, May, who hadn't noticed anything wrong, waxed enthusiastic about the performance. But Martha was silent. Louis looked on noncommittally.

"What's the matter, Martha?" May questioned. "You seem to be depressed."

"I am," she replied. "It was a terrible performance. I've never danced so badly in my life."

May gasped. Louis winked at his sister in the moonlight.

Martha continued. "The stage, the theater, the lights, my costumes—everything! Especially the way I danced." She sank into a pose of utter dejection. Standing at the rail's edge, she looked like a Greek statue expressing infinite despair.

A realist, May spoke up. "Well, I never! Now, listen here, Martha! If it wasn't perfect—that's no tragedy." Then, with the outspokenness of a Horstian, she added derisively, "Stop behaving like a spoiled prima donna!"

At that, Martha had to smile. Years later she loved to tell the story to friends in May's presence, adding amusing comments about her own unrelenting self-criticism.

From Oakland and San Francisco, Martha's tour took her southward to Santa Barbara, where her mother, Auntie Re, and Lizzie still lived. To Lizzie, Martha had become the "star" she had envisioned long ago. "Star" or not, Martha had indeed become a public figure. In January of the previous year she had been appointed to the

New York Municipal Art Committee by Mayor Fiorello La Guardia. The next year she would be dancing at the White House for President and Mrs. Roosevelt. For Martha, returning to Santa Barbara was less than triumphant. (Triumph would come thirty years later when the mayor of Santa Barbara would proclaim November 2, 1966, "Martha Graham Day.") Southern Californian audiences seemed unresponsive to new ideas compared to easterners. But then, she had to admit, California, the birthplace of the American dance, had been abandoned for New York and . . . Bennington. Yet, return she would, again and again, performance or not, if only to see her mother and Lizzie.

"Man's inhumanity to man makes countless thousands mourn," Grandfather Beers used to say, quoting Robert Burns, during the Civil War. Now, across the Atlantic another country, Spain, was being torn by fratricidal strife. Two young American writers, John Dos Passos and Ernest Hemingway, who had lived previously in Spain and felt close to the Spanish people, became involved in the ideological struggle. Hemingway became a war correspondent and Dos Passos was to help create a film, *The Spanish Earth*. Antoine de St. Exupéry, the French aviator and man of letters, who went himself to the front, told the tale of brother against brother in his book *Wind, Sand and Stars*. Another Frenchman, the philosopher and art critic André Malraux, flew for the Spanish Loyalists.

How could an artist stand by silently as man's inhumanity to man was beginning to encircle the world? Martha had already voiced her protests against violence in her refusal to accept the Nazi government's invitation to perform with her group when Germany was host to the 1936 Olympics. Now, recognizing the portentousness of European events, she created two solos dealing with the consequences of violence: *Immediate Tragedy* and *Deep Song*. The second dance was to take its place as one of her most powerful statements. Critic George Beiswanger's verdict revealed its double-edged protest: "The fierce, fighting anguish of *Deep Song* is as direct and as objective as a shout."

Its opening mood was one of quivering premonition. The parting curtains found the dancer seated on a long white bench, her glossy black hair tied tightly in a bun at the nape of her neck, her legs spreading her wide-striped paneled skirt to the far sides. With an intake of the breath, a dance of unspeakable sorrow began; it told the tale of not one woman but of all women who suffer when sons, brothers, and husbands go to war to kill other women's sons, brothers, and husbands.

Twisting sideways, the dancer arched high over the bench, her face dropping into the palm of a hand. Then, like a wounded animal, she threw herself forward to writhe and crawl in a frenzy of despair. A series of falls soon followed, some breaking backward, some half-suspended as though transfixed in the grip of tortured feelings.

The background of Henry Cowell's music, which made use of the plucked piano strings as well as of the percussive keyboard, echoed with guitar-like poignancy *Deep Song*'s tormented cry of modern Spain. "Every dance is . . . a kind of fever chart, a graph of the heart," Martha would say. *Deep Song* was that graph. It was *Lamentation* suddenly unbound—*Lamentation* released from its guttural anonymity into a pulsating cry of human despair.

Did *Deep Song* verge on propaganda? In the mid-thirties, the politically oriented trend against war and fascism gave birth to a rash of outspoken plays, poems, murals, and choreographic works concerned with "man's inhumanity to man." Martha was no exception to this trend. Along with other dancers, including Anna Sokolow, Helen Tamiris, Paul Draper, Hanya Holm's company, and Ballet Caravan, she performed in a special benefit concert to "aid Spanish democracy." This was in January 1938. Two years previously *Dance Observer*, a magazine that Louis had founded as a voice for modern dance, ran an essay by the composer-philosopher Dane Rudhyar entitled "Art and Propaganda." Rudhyar made an effort to differentiate between "art with vital content" based on the artist's personal experience and propaganda as "intellectually learned doctrine."

Without doubt, *Deep Song,* as well as the earlier *Chronicle* and *Immediate Tragedy,* was "art with vital content." But if propaganda, according to the dictionary, means the dissemination of ideas and principles, *Deep Song* could be called propagandistic too; for it was humanistically concerned with the fate of mankind. "The greater an artist of the theater is, the higher are the summits from which he sees life and the wider is his outlook on the world," wrote Theodore Komisarjevsky in his book *The Theatre and a Changing Civilization.* Martha's *Deep Song* was no less than a vision of mankind as brethren, regardless of differences in nationality.

Not until *Clytemnestra, Legend of Judith,* and *Cortege of Eagles* would Martha deal again with the consequences of "man's inhumanity to man" on this visionary level, and with that stab at one's conscience that was provoked by the single-mindedness of *Deep Song.* Seen in retrospect, *Deep Song* was to be the last of Martha's great solos. More and more would she turn her thoughts to large-scale ideas in which she would cast herself as a symbolic figurehead within the expanded ensemble she now had at her disposal. The sweep of her mind and the range of her talents drove her inevitably in this direction. First and foremost, she was actress as much as dancer. From the beginning she disclosed an imperative need to dramatize the very experience of being on the stage. Secondly, though Martha had been performing professionally for only sixteen years by 1936, she was already forty-two years old, an amazing fact when one considers her body's phenomenal powers at the time. Clearly, however, she could not concentrate on solos far into the future. From a practical viewpoint, choreography for the group should soon become the main focus of her energies. But to do this with *positive* purpose, and not as a *substitute* for loss of specific skills, Martha would have to draw upon psychological reserves far beneath the surface. She would have to revert to "the fundamental process of artistic production," which, as the psychologist Otto Rank tells us, amounts to a "constructive victory" over inhibiting factors. Throughout her life, Martha would be faced with the drawback of her late start in dancing. The way would be fraught with pain, and the price she would pay for her need to express her creative compulsions through her own body would almost cost her her life.

Deep Song, premiered in December 1937, pointed prophetically to change. The following year would be transitional, experimental. A more theatrical use of source material, settings, accompaniment, and costumes would establish a new choreographic formula, expandable yet unique; and the ensuing years would produce works that would justifiably contribute to the emergence of large-scale concepts to be known as "The Theatre of Martha Graham."

Each year brought more students and devotees of the new dance to Bennington from all over the country. As the student-dancers and student-teachers returned to their home states, curiosity about what was taking place in Vermont would be generated, and with it, a growing respect for the artists who directed the program. Subsequent enrollments would increase, while audiences with interests beyond the single art of the dance would fill the Armory in the town of Bennington, where, from 1935 until the war (with one year's exception), the annual summer Dance Festival was held: a series of performances with new works by faculty members that had been specially prepared on campus. After the war broke out and the Armory was being utilized solely for military purposes, productions would be presented in the College Theater on the third floor of the Commons Building. Ingeniously carved into the building's existing structure, the 40'-deep-by-20'-wide stage served to present the greater part of the summer's programs.

Criticisms of the Festival performances would appear in newspapers and periodicals that recognized the increasing importance of the burgeoning American modern dance. The *Christian Science Monitor* sent its new free-lance critic, Margaret Lloyd, who called herself a layman but whose keen perceptions of the structure and import of the new dance forms were to produce some of the finest prose ever to be written on that art. Along with the eminent John Martin of the *New York Times* came another critic, a young dancer-turned-writer from the *Boston Herald.* Destined to be contributing his opinions in reviews for the *New York Herald Tribune* under the byline of Walter Terry, he, too, would be influencing public opinion for years to come with his enlightened views.

Theatre Arts Magazine, which covered the English and European theater scene as well as the American, would be represented by editors Edith J. Isaacs and Stark Young, and dance critic George Beiswanger. And, of course, writers from Louis's *Dance Observer* would be on hand to expound their views on the works unfolding in the Vermont mountains. Even the *London Dancing Times* sent its American correspondent, Arthur Todd. And as for visual documentation of that history-making epoch, there was artist-photographer Thomas Bouchard shooting trenchant photographs of the intrepid modernists. Bearing the title of "official photographer" during the summers of 1936 and 1937, he recorded dance action wherever it might occur: in rehearsals, in classrooms, out of doors, under all circumstances and in all sorts of light. As a result, his lens captured the "sweat and strain of creation" that future dancers would never know when performing the self-same dances in revivals. Uniquely alive in their spontaneousness, Bouchard's shots are memorable proof of Bennington's untamed dancing fervor, a fervor that was recaptured with pictorial and literary distinction years later when *Dance Perspective* editors Selma Jeanne Cohen and A. J. Pischl brought out *Days of Divine Indiscipline* with equally vivid photographs by Thomas Bouchard and text by John Martin.

With her unique gift for matching and stimulating creative minds, Martha Hill had by 1938 begun to enlarge her faculty, drawing upon two exceptional artists from her winter program: Arch Lauterer, the lighting and stage designer, would teach stagecraft and collaborate on dance productions for Martha and Hanya Holm; the poet Ben Belitt, who would formally join the summer school in 1939 when it was temporarily transferred to Mills College in Oakland, California, was engaged to introduce the use of poetry and prose in creative dance. Lauterer had been responsible for the lighting of the two solos, *Opening Dance* and *Immediate Tragedy,* which were premiered in the Vermont State Armory the previous summer. His association with Martha would grow into a highly sensitive artistic relationship that would reach a climax with *Deaths and Entrances* and *Letter to the World*. In years to come Belitt's own poetry would inspire Martha's choices of no less than four titles for her dances.

Barbara Morgan, the photographer, was invited to explore the campus in search of provocative action and naturalistic settings for dance photographs. Drawn to the modern dance in the mid-thirties as an art that stood for life-affirming principles in a time when the other arts negatively reflected the misery of the Depression, Morgan had already started her magnificent studies of Martha's dances— studies that would eventually be gathered in a book which would serve as a testament of faith in the modern dance as envisioned by Martha. Morgan's *Martha Graham: Sixteen Dances in Photographs* would not be the first book about Graham; Merle Armitage, a multi-gifted theater producer, agent, and writer, struck by *Frontier*'s powerful evocation of the Midwest, would call upon a select group of writers and artists, including dance historian Lincoln Kirstein and composer Wallingford Riegger, to contribute articles for a book on Martha that he would edit. Entitled simply *Martha Graham,* it also contained reprints of philosophical statements by the dancer herself—statements that resounded with intellectual vitality. Barbara Morgan's book, a work of art in format and layout, would set a precedent in dance photography with the mounting of long shots and close-ups in sequences that impressionistically reconstruct the dynamic content of a dance. Except for Arnold Genthe's and Edward Steichen's superb studies of Isadora Duncan—and Soichi Sunami's portraits of Agnes de Mille, Ruth St. Denis, Ted Shawn, Tamiris, and early Graham—no other mid-twentieth-century photographer has limned the personal incandescence of a dancer as skillfully as Barbara Morgan.

From Germany came Curt Sachs, author of the book *World History of the Dance*, which by 1937 would be translated into English by Bessie Schoenberg. Like Martha Hill, Schoenberg would become a leading figure in the academic world, principally at Sarah Lawrence College, where she was to foster the talents of budding members of the future avant-garde. Alexander Calder, the sculptor, came up in the summer of 1935 to supervise the mobiles he had designed for Martha's experimental large-scale *Panorama*, which utilized a multi-level set by Arch Lauterer (the first of eight Graham-Lauterer collaborations) and an "avant-garde" score by Norman Lloyd. The whole atmosphere was avant-garde. No one was intimidated by tradition. Fearlessness was in the air. A visitor, the young Joseph Campbell, described Bennington as "a zone of inexhaustible life-abundance."

In the expanded workshop cast of *Panorama* was a young woman who could scarcely be described as a student, except that she was studying modern dance for the first time in her life. Muriel Stuart, formerly of Anna Pavlova's ballet company, and currently a teacher at George Balanchine's School of American Ballet, came to study with Martha and Louis at the suggestion of Lincoln Kirstein, founder of Ballet Caravan, the forerunner of Ballet Society, which in turn preceded the New York City Ballet. Though still antagonistic to Martha's severe creative style (a position he later reversed when he admitted that he had been "unequipped for her simplicity and self-blinded to her genuinely primitive expression"), Kirstein was particularly interested in the American emphasis of Bennington's summer sessions. His own aims to create an "American" ballet company (the main intention of Ballet Caravan) were most likely at the bottom of his curiosity. At any rate, despite Kirstein's adverse reactions to modern dance, Martha Hill generously opened the doors of Bennington College, and the modest third-floor College Theatre was host to Ballet Caravan's debut on July 17, 1936. Ironically, a former Humphrey–Weidman dancer, Charles Laskey, and a future Graham principal dancer, Erick Hawkins, were in the casts of the productions presented.

Martha welcomed Muriel Stuart warmly, and their artistic relationship had a natural basis, each woman recognizing the integrity of the other's professionalism. Unsuspectingly, their personal empathy and Bennington's openness to absorb a ballet performance sowed the seeds for the gradual growth of kinship between the two forms—a kinship that would have its first official showing approximately twenty years later when Martha would collaborate with George Balanchine on *Episodes*.

Never antagonistic to ballet in a personal way, Martha saw its limitations as a creative expression of individuals living in the contemporary environment of the New World; and in spite of her argument with Fokine over the stereotyped technicalities of balletic style, she respected ballet as an art and acknowledged its invaluable methods of training the body. Had she not herself received ballet training (though somewhat modified) at Denishawn? Had she not said in 1932 that "the physical principles of great dancing remain inherently the same"?

To her students at The Juilliard School of Music, where she taught many years later (again at the invitation of Martha Hill, who created the Juilliard dance department in 1951) Martha averred: "My quarrel has never been with the ballet, as some of you have found out when you have been studying with me. I haven't been interested in destroying anything. I'm too busy doing something else and besides you don't destroy something that has been ... an accumulation of many lives over three hundred years. You don't want to destroy it."

The most important link with ballet, however, was provided in 1938 by Erick Hawkins, whom Martha had seen dance in Ballet Caravan's premiere, and who, in the meantime, had been studying Graham technique with Muriel Stuart. With more than a passing interest in modern dance, Hawkins pursued the possibility of working with Martha, first by taking her June course at the New York studio, then by requesting that she use him in some modest capacity at Bennington. Not adverse to the idea of a male addition to her company, she decided to include the ballet dancer in *American Document*, the composition slated for production that very summer.

The inclusion of a male dancer inevitably changed the character of the dance as a whole; but since *American Document*, visualized as a panoramic view of America from the times of the Indians to the present day, was cast in the loose form of a minstrel show, the insertion of additional numbers merely expanded the basic music-hall format. In more ways than one, *American Document* broke new ground for Martha. Not only was she dancing with a male partner for the first time since she had appeared with Charles Weidman in the Neighborhood Playhouse 1930 production of Charles Martin Loeffler's *A Pagan Poem,* but she was also dealing with a theme in a much freer choreographic style than ever before. Whereas her approach had always been—from the time she had hewn her own path of creativity—direct, taut, and above all sparse in its theatricality, now she was introducing a variety of colorful effects.

To begin with, there were often two men onstage: Hawkins as her partner or alone, and a male interlocutor, Housley Stevens, Jr., who introduced and closed the ballet, and quoted from Lincoln's Gettysburg Address, the Declaration of Independence, Jonathan Edward's sermons, the Song of Songs, Walt Whitman's poems, and other significant documents. Stevens's presence and the words he uttered served to give a focus to the action of the dance, while the score by composer Ray Green, a tuneful weaving of American folk rhythms with original themes, provided a background of familiar reference.

For Martha, the use of a spoken text was as revolutionary as the use of a male partner. Both innovations worked their magic. The words made Martha's newest work instantly intelligible, while the male–female relationship introduced elements of an exotic nature. Of the three duets Martha composed for herself and Hawkins, by far the most effective one was *Puritan Episode,* which played with a theme that had obviously fascinated her: the social castigation of natural love. It had appeared first in 1934 in *American Provincials,* and it would reappear in 1977 in *The Scarlet Letter* (the more straight-line narrative of the two works inspired by Hawthorne's famous novel). In *Puritan Episode* the Protestant taboo against sensual love, as spoken in excerpts for Jonathan Edwards's sermons, was counterpointed with readings from the Song of Songs, which in turn were visually reflected in Martha's and Erick's sexually suggestive movements. In its preview performance in Bennington in July 1938, and its subsequent New York premiere and transcontinental tour the following winter, *American Document* provided Martha's audiences with a fresh look at their country's history as seen through the creative lens of a dancer whose unusual style was becoming more and more comprehensible.

No longer could it be said that Martha Graham was one of those "modernists who have long held entrenched positions in arty lofts and studios, [who] have expressed sexless conceptions of revolt and starvation to the tootling of oboes and the thumping of drums," as a *Time* magazine article of that period reported with its customary satirical tone, no doubt hinting at Martha's concerts and her staunch followers when it added: "In Broadway theaters on Sunday nights these restless grim-eyed chorines illustrate the serious things of life before cool-black backdrops, attract audiences of starry-eyed worshippers at $2.50 top (standees 50¢)."

Martha might still be dancing on Sunday nights and charging $2.50 for tickets, but she was far from grim-eyed now. *American Document* had its share of optimism, especially in the *Emancipation Episode*, which spoke hopefully of freedom from slavery. And it certainly did *not* express "sexless conceptions," what with Martha and Erick dancing a duet that was high, wide, and handsome, and all about love's passions forcibly restrained by Puritan ethics.

Nor could Martha's intense way of moving be considered humorless anymore. Her next composition would veer wildly into comedy, throwing barbs of satire at the female's need to play the star performer in every love affair. As luck would have it—and luck was decidedly looking over Martha's shoulders in the late thirties—another male dancer would enter the Graham ranks: an exceedingly talented young man by the name of Merce (Mercier) Cunningham, who had been a student of Bonnie Bird in Seattle at the Cornish School before enrolling in the Bennington program at Mills College in 1939.

The luxury of having two splendid male dancers in her previously all-woman company touched off the dramatist (or should we say, the comedienne?) in Martha. Now she was ready to embark on her own version of the eternal triangle. Inspired by Vachel Lindsay's poem

Every soul is a Circus
Every mind is a tent
Every heart is a sawdust ring
Where the circling race is spent

she staged a circus of her own with tricks and props a-plenty. Her role would be that of the Empress of the Arena (a lady who was "her own most appreciative spectator"), who was held at whip's end by a

Ringmaster (Erick); nevertheless, she indulged in flirtations of the frothiest kind with an Acrobat (Merce), whose aerial antics swept her off her feet. While love incidents wavered and fluttered, an Ideal Spectator observed the silly proceedings. (This elegant figure with the self-conscious airs might possibly be considered another aspect of the Empress herself as she watched that lady perform her "star" turns.) Less personal renderings of circus acts consisted of humorous statuesque posings, scarf-waving, and lighthearted interludes danced by five Arenic Performers.

According to Margaret Lloyd, *Every Soul Is a Circus* inaugurated "the Theatre of Martha Graham," a title that has clung to Martha's rich use of deep songs that have soared into symphonic theatrical forms. Assuredly, the format Martha used in *Every Soul Is a Circus*, though somewhat episodic in comparison to the format she established later, contained the seeds from which would flower future masterworks. Her multiple gifts were to provide her with the necessary resources. The chief performer of her own conceptions, she would portray characters from classic and modern literature; as choreographer, she would devise movements that would evolve with the flow and logic of plays and epic poems; as playwright—a new role (one obviously hers from the beginning, as seen in the vein of such miniature dramatic sequences in dance form as *Heretic, American Provincials,* and *Chronicle*)—she would rewrite in the dynamic language of motion the scenarios of other playwrights and poets. And her choices of such sources would lead her instinctively toward the expression of these triple endowments. With increasing skill she would construct edifice after edifice based on her voracious reading of the world's finest dramas, novels, and psychological probings. Her own dictum would supply the working format of the Theatre of Martha Graham:

> True theatricality . . . does not depend on cheap tricks either of movement, costume or audience appeal. Primarily, it is a means employed to bring the idea of one person into focus for the many.

———————

While *American Document* had heralded a new era for Martha, Erick's increasingly important role in redefining her creative ideas had sown seeds of dissension among certain older members of the group, who missed working directly with Martha. Unwisely she would often permit her new leading man to conduct rehearsals in her stead. An unfortunate exodus took place in 1938. Four dancers left the group: May O'Donnell, Gertrude Shurr, Kathleen Slagle, and Anna Sokolow. O'Donnell and Shurr would, however, return to work with Martha from time to time after a period of pioneer experience on the West Coast, notably with the San Francisco Dance Theatre, which they organized with Ray Green, composer of the score for *American Document*.

Despite the loss of four valuable dancers, the group was by no means deprived of talent. There were the longstanding members—Ethel Butler, Sophie Maslow, Jane Dudley, Nina Fonaroff, Marie Marchowsky, and Marjorie Mazia—who would, with additional reinforcement in the persons of Jean Erdman, Nelle Fisher, and Natalie Harris, maintain the repertory at the high level of Martha's demands. Erdman, a Sarah Lawrence student at the time of her first studies with Martha, was also capable as an actress. She portrayed The Ideal Spectator in *Every Soul Is a Circus*.

One did not sever ties with Martha easily. The bond was too deep. The uncompromising passion that possessed Martha was reflected in her dancers' own dedication. If audiences at a Graham performance were considered "starry-eyed," how would *Time* magazine have described the selflessly devoted Graham dancers? To many of them Martha was more than a goddess, as Ruth St. Denis had been for her; she was a Mother Figure who embodied the greatest mystery of all: creativity. No less powerful as a source of inspiration, she dominated their lives with the intensity of her personality. Just as May O'Donnell and Gertrude Shurr would return, so would Jane Dudley, who later left for approximately one year and then came back to take over principal roles in Martha's dance-dramas.

Only under extreme conditions would a member of the company withdraw: because of a sudden deep dissatisfaction similar to that provoked by Erick's intrusion; an injury; or when the compulsion to expand one's own creative talents asserted itself, as with the choreographically gifted Anna Sokolow or with Nina Fonaroff, who remained eight years and then pursued a double career as teacher and choreographer. But even the thought of withdrawing from the totally absorbing life associated with Martha involved many moments of indecision and anguish for the more sensitive girls.

Once the decision was made, however, the greatest difficulty would be to confront Martha. Sometimes there would be scenes leading to hysterics and recriminations; at other times she would understand immediately and say, with sudden, unexpected generosity, "You must follow your destiny." Curiously, such a philosophical attitude could make the leavetaking harder, for though both individuals might agree that a parting was inevitable, the pain was still there. Then a fresh conflict would take place between the young dancer's sense of loyalty to Martha and the urgency of finding herself as a dancer in her own right.

Once having left the fold, unanticipated reactions were bound to surface. The initial joy of feeling free and independent could change into a darkening sense of isolation. Gone forever were the stimulating demands of Martha's classes and rehearsals; the day's end-goal that had given the rest of life focus and purpose for so many years. In spite of new assignments, weeks and months might unravel meaninglessly without the underlying tensions of Martha's vitality, Martha's personal magnetism, and Martha's exorbitant demands upon one's energies. The stringent form under which one had worked continually for so long, and against which rebellion had struck the hardest, suddenly seemed to be replaced by a directionless existence. At night dreams of being late for rehearsals or performances, of missing trains when on tour, would plague the guilt-stricken one . . . until such time as the pain and sense of identification with the mother or idol image of the teacher would wear away.

It might take months; it might take years. And even when one had put down the monster of Regret, attendance at a Bennington or Guild Theatre concert was enough to make the whole thing sweep over one all over again. Seeing Martha onstage dancing movements so familiar as to seem to be part of one's own body literally made one tremble. Then, going backstage afterward (impossible not to!) and approaching her, in spite of everything one might have become in the meantime (teacher in one's own school, choreographer, wife, mother), all the old feelings of adoration would return as greetings, seemingly lighthearted, would be interchanged. What was it one heard in Martha's voice? A tinge of reproach, an invitation to return? Or saw in her eyes? A look of hurt as though in seeing you again the pain of loss returned full force? She stood there on the strangely transformed stage surrounded by admirers, while electricians and stagehands shouted boisterously to one another as they took down

110

lights and struck sets: a small straight figure, her eyes still heavily made up, her final costume exchanged for a black embroidered Chinese robe, and every fiber in her muscular frame still tense from the "wonderful, wonderful performance." Yet, mixed with all the unspoken thoughts was the knowing look in her eyes that only through mutual agony is growth achieved. For Martha now was the Matriarch. She had taken her place in the honored line of succession. But she still remembered what it was to try to stand alone.

———— • • • ————

Hidden, as it were, from the surface immediacies of life were traits that alternately baffled and thrilled Martha's closest associates. The high-strung outbursts which took place when the net grew tight around her would seem to leave no one untouched; and the seeming callousness of her compulsion to work out a choreographic idea regardless of the strain on those involved was clearly the manifestation of egoistical indifference. Both could be explained by the fact that her volatile temperament neither gave her peace nor could it be trusted by others to deal equably with difficult situations. On the other hand, Martha's response to suffering was genuine and deep. At those moments one caught a glimpse of a richly veined empathy that moved her fearlessly into the thick of someone else's pain. It was proof of her capacity to respond with real commitment.

Such an experience came to Natalie Harris, a member of Martha's group in the late thirties. Natalie had been a Bennington student in the summer before Martha had premiered *American Document* in the "sleepy" hills of Vermont. When she came to New York in the fall to continue her studies and was invited to join the group, Martha spoke very seriously to her and to her parents, who accompanied her. "You cannot lead a double life," she warned; "you must choose what you really want to do." There was no pressure, but the young girl and her parents were deeply touched by Martha's wisdom as well as by her frankness.

Choosing to devote herself to dancing, Natalie left Sweetbriar College before she graduated and went to live in New York and work her way into the company. A year and a half later, when the company was on its third transcontinental tour, she received a telegram with the news that her father had died.

111

Encountering Natalie in the office of the hotel in Provo, Utah, near the university where they were to give a performance that evening, Martha called the young girl aside and said softly, "Come to my room if you want to see me."

An hour or two later, Natalie appeared.

"Sit down with me, here," said Martha gently, and drew her to the sofa.

In a few minutes, Natalie was speaking of her father and crying. Before she knew what had happened, Martha had gathered her up in her arms, shifted her to her own lap, and was rocking her tenderly, as one would a small child. In silence, the older woman shared the young girl's grief.

———•••———

The world premiere of *Letter to the World* took place on August 11, 1940, in the Commons Building's third-floor College Theatre.

Significantly, 1940 was the summer when the Bennington School of the Dance was converted into the Bennington School of the Arts. "As the School of the Dance was a cross-section of that art," wrote Mary Jo Shelly in *Dance Observer,* describing the changeover, "so the School of the Arts is a cross-section of the three performing arts (dance, drama and music) and theatre design."

With the inclusion of drama, music, and theater design departments in its summer curriculum, Bennington made a decisive step in the direction of "total" theater, to which goal Martha had been instinctively moving since *American Document.*

To some minds, such as Margaret Lloyd's, the transformations undermined Bennington's position as the summer citadel of American modern dance. In many respects the *Christian Science Monitor* dance critic was correct. The intensity that had first shot the school into national prominence as an educational institution was no longer operating at the same level after the summer at Mills College, where a decision had been made to forego the Festival performances. The return to Vermont found a fundamentally disturbing change in the curriculum: Students would no longer have the opportunity to study simultaneously under the personal instruction of The Big Four, but would have to choose one of the major techniques for intensive study with a Graham, a Holm, a Humphrey, or a Weidman associate teacher. In 1940 Doris and Charles were on leave, Martha did not teach at all but concentrated on her choreographic preparations for the Festival, which was resumed, and Holm had only a master course in dance for a small number of advanced students.

But for Martha Graham, a new era of creativity began that very summer. The programmatic shift of emphasis from only dance to the broader aspects of the art as related to music, drama, and theater design was distinctly to her advantage. The abundance of musical, literary, and stagecraft talent surrounding her in 1940 provided her with the chairlift, so to speak, for the first stage of her climb to the summit of achievement where she would remain for decades to come.

Striding the campus like a superfluity of royalty, resident practitioners of the various arts conferred with dancers, actors, and vocalists. Among them were Hunter Johnson, twice winner of the Prix de Rome, who was writing the score for Martha's forthcoming *Letter to the World;* Otto Luening, future pioneer in tape and electronic music, but presently director of the Music Division; Lincoln Kirstein, visiting lecturer; the Rhodes scholar Francis Fergusson, who was director of drama; and Arch Lauterer, Ben Belitt, and Ruth and Norman Lloyd, who remained, as before, integrally bound up with the creative functions of theater design, poetry, and music, respectively.

Engaged in vociferous counterpoint, drums, woodblocks, cymbals, and gongs echoed in otherwise silent study rooms; through open windows vocalists and instrumentalists could be heard struggling with the unique dissonances and intricate rhythms of Charles Ives's and Samuel Barber's latest works. The quietest activity of all was Helen Priest's course in dance notation, based on Rudolph von Laban's theories, which six of Martha's girls were studying. Almost everywhere else there was the buzzing excitement of preparing new projects for class demonstrations or for the Festival performances, of which each division—drama, dance, and music—had four.

Martha was working with a small company of nine women and five men (including Erick and Merce) on the most ambitious idea of her career to date: the tying together of the real and imaginary lives of the New England poetess Emily Dickinson. With utmost sensitivity, she set out to describe the private world of the nineteenth-century woman who lived most of the fifty-six years of her existence in the seclusion of her father's home in Amherst, Massachusetts. There, in a cloistered atmosphere, Emily Dickinson wrote hundreds upon hundreds of exquisite poems dealing symbolically with love (which brushed by her), with nature (with whose tender and vehement forces she felt a deep identification), and with death (which she both feared and welcomed as a fulfillment of her destiny).

To translate the delicate nuances of such a complex personality into the language of dance was Martha's self-chosen task. Though *Letter to the World* was not immediately successful in accomplishing what it set out to do, its significance as the cornerstone of the future Theatre of Martha Graham can be determined retrospectively. Surrounded as she was by the resident artists of the newly organized Bennington School of the Arts, Martha could realize the valuable benefits of gifted collaborators. Most important was Arch Lauterer, a highly perceptive scenic designer, whose imaginative sets for *Letter to the World* were "in themselves a form of dance"; and though Martha had always been her own superlative costume designer, she chose Edythe Gilfond, with whom she had worked in *American Document,* the solo *Columbiad,* and *Every Soul Is a Circus,* to take charge of the designs and execution of the new project.

At first showing, *Letter to the World* seemed too episodic and fragmented, with its five acts and thirteen scenes held tenuously together by the silken threads of Emily Dickinson's lyrical verses. Martha had chosen, quite rightly, a poetic form to express the poetic content of a story that sought to portray the dualistic nature of the poetess in simultaneous counterpart. It was the first of her big efforts to split a single personality into two images; in this instance, one image was expressed through the rhythmic logic of pure dance, and the other through the rhythmic cadence of the spoken word. She was still tossing about, as it were, in her desire to discover the right technique for conveying a story line without resorting to conventional means. No "found" way would suit her—just as no found way would have suited Emily Dickinson. By working at a feverish pitch, she managed to bring the production to the point of premiere; but its birth caused more bafflement than enthusiasm.

"Better let it sleep in the Vermont hills," was the sum of John Martin's review in the *New York Times.*

On the other hand, wholehearted praise went to *El Penitente,* not only from Martin but also from other critics, including Walter Terry, who had assumed the dance critic's post at the *New York Herald Tribune,* following Mary F. Watkins's withdrawal. A trio in the form of a Mexican-Spanish folk ritual, *El Penitente* was enacted as a miniature mystery play based on episodes from the Bible. The title refers to the sect of Penitents of the American Southwest who practice penance as a means of self-purification of sin.

Like cameos, each character in the ritual emerged with chiseled clarity: the self-flagellating Penitent (Erick), the Christ figure (Merce), and the threefold vision of Mary as Virgin, Magdalene, and Mother (Martha). Lauterer's delightful portable scenery and props (a cart, a pair of hanging curtains on a crossbar) and Edythe Gilfond's simple costume effects (a stunning mask for the Christ figure was designed by Noguchi for later productions) added charm to the stylized proceedings; while the movement, formalistically expressive of the religious rites of the dedicated sect, kept the trio of scenes within the bounds of a presentation performed by a group of strolling players. Louis's score, the last of those he would compose for Martha, had a sparseness and eloquence that matched the choreography. John Martin called the music "rich and lovely."

Though it was gratifying to have one of her premieres meet with such success, Martha's pride in her most ambitious effort, *Letter to the World,* was piqued. A good decade later, she was able to speak philosophically about her initial dissatisfaction and disappointment. "Sometimes a dance takes two years, two years of brooding, of thinking. You put it away, you forget about it. It comes back. It was that way with *Letter to the World.*"

We do not know how long Martha "brooded" on her Dickinson images, but we do know that only four months after its Bennington premiere *Letter to the World* was presented in New York, in January 1941, and John Martin, voicing the opinion of the dance world as well as his own, was willing to concede that Martha's latest creative effort was "a great part of the time . . . extraordinarily successful capturing the flavor of some of the poet's most radiant lines and making them unimaginably poignant."

In the original production Martha had called the Emily whose part she danced the One in White, and the "hidden" Emily of the poetry the One in Red. The latter was represented by the actress Margaret Meredith, who scarcely moved as she read the lines. In the New York premiere Jean Erdman, who took over the speaking role, not only read the poems with poetic feeling but moved with a dancer's eloquence. Commensurate with the new casting, Martha called her own part the One Who Dances, and the other self the One Who Speaks. These changes, plus a clarification and a deepening of the narrative action, gave the work fresh coherence and intelligibility. As a result, the granitic dancing of Jane Dudley as the Ancestress and of Merce Cunningham as March took on new luster.

The ballet began with Dickinson's own twin statement as both counterparts of Emily appeared in a trellised doorway.

I'm Nobody! Who are you?
Are you—Nobody—too?
Then there's a pair of us!

From that moment, the two women—shadow and substance—painted a double portrait of the poet whose outwardly uneventful life was intersected by two searing experiences: death and unrequited love. Death assumed the guise of fate in the form of an Ancestress (Jane Dudley), black-garmented and foreboding.

It's Coming—the postponeless Creature—
It gains the Block—and now—it gains the Door— . . .
And Carries one—out of it—to God—

Symbol of death, the postponeless Creature lifts the fear-stricken Emily in her arms and cradles her.

Looking at Death, is Dying

Phantom processions cross the stage, carrying a girl's body aloft. It is hers! The images clash, and panic assumes an ashen face.

Gay, Ghastly, Holiday!

But life returns, and all that Emily Dickinson loved—flowers, insects, birds, sky—spurt forth in bursts of movement, vivid and free.

Inebriate of Air—am I—
And Debauchee of Dew—
Reeling—thro endless summer days—
From inns of Molten Blue—

Consumed by the nectar of living, the "Little Tippler" dances and revels in life as a "spell."

Love enters, and Hope:

. . . the thing with feathers—
That perches in the soul—

It carries her into the certainty of her secret role.

I'm "wife"—I've finished that—
That other state—. . .

But love, longingly reached for and momentarily attained, slips silently away.

Of Course—I prayed—
And did God Care?
He cared as much as on the Air
A Bird—had stamped her foot—
And cried "Give me"—

Now words give out, and Emily dances alone with her torment. It is a seizure of grief, from which there is no release—only a return to the decorum of New England maidenhood.

Quietly, the poet takes her place on a small white bench, hands folded pensively in her lap, an expression of luminous resignation in her eyes.

This is my letter to the World

———— •••• ————

Not for two years, but for nearly ten years, Martha had brooded on Emily Dickinson's dual nature as expressed in her dance. After performing *Letter to the World* season after season, across the country and back, there was no doubt in any critic's mind—or in

117

Martha's—that she had "split the lark" and found the secret of Emily Dickinson's lyric gift, so perfectly described in the poet's own words:

> Split the Lark—and you'll find the Music—
> Bulb after Bulb, in Silver rolled—
> Scantily dealt to the Summer Morning
> Saved for your Ear when Lutes be old.
>
> Loose the Flood—you shall find it patent—
> Gush after Gush, reserved for you—
> Scarlet Experiment! Sceptic Thomas!
> Now, do you doubt that your Bird was true?

Chapter Six

The View From Within

"You do not realize how the headlines that make daily history affect the muscles of the human body," said Martha one day during the months of crises prior to the outbreak of World War II.

She saw the tension building up in her girls, whose boyfriends or husbands were next in line should America be drawn into the war. She saw it in the young men who came to her studio to take lessons. They were throwing themselves into the work with undue animation, as though the long-sought opportunity of working with her might suddenly be snatched away. Wariness, the first symptom of fear, was in the air, and though no one spoke openly about private dread, Martha could read nervous tension in her dancers' bodies as her father had once observed it in hers, when he had told her that feelings reveal themselves in movements, not words.

Then came December 7, 1941. Martha, Louis, and the company were on the train going to Miami to embark for Havana, where two performances had been scheduled under the auspices of Pro Arte, an organization headed by ballerina Alicia Alonso's mother. Incoming passengers brought in the startling news of America's entry into the war.

Mingled with the fears of what the involvement meant on a large scale were trivial concerns: Would the company be allowed to reenter the United States after the Cuban engagement? Would the Cubans' attitude run counter to that of the Allies? Would the return voyage across the Straits of Florida be dangerous? Like a mother hen, Martha grew worried about the fate of her children.

But no trouble ensued. Embarkation was smooth, and once the company was on Cuban soil they were warmly greeted by Alicia Alonso and her husband, Fernando. The Cuban mood seemed gay, almost carnival-like—curiously unreal compared to their own somber feelings regarding the war their country faced. Yet the dances they performed, among them *Frontier* and *Every Soul Is a Circus,* never seemed unreal in spite of their subject matter being worlds apart from international events, for neither Martha nor her dancers could visualize their art as being irrelevant.

A dancer was an "image-maker," fashioning images out of the very fabric of life. The trivialities of behavior that were mocked in *Every Soul Is a Circus* and the domestic squabbles that ran rampant in *Punch and The Judy* (the farcical ballet premiered the previous summer in Bennington) were all part of the human scene—just as were *Deep Song* and the humanistically motivated *Chronicle* (a reminder of the grim consequences of World War I violence). Martha's solo entitled *Spectre 1914 (Drums—Red Shroud—Lament)* opened *Chronicle* under the heading of *Dances Before Catastrophe.*

A vision more real than spectral, the dance evoked the terrors of past destructions at the same time it was pointing an accusing finger at the then ongoing Spanish Civil War. Costumed in a voluminously draped red dress, Martha moved with ominous import. The resounding drum rolls written in Wallingford Riegger's suggestively threatening score seemed to vibrate through her body while the yards and yards of gathered material spread about her made it appear at one moment that she was being strangled in a monstrous noose.

Yet *Chronicle* never had the impact of *Deep Song.* As its title suggests, the work—mainly in the form of ensemble passages—was a strangely impersonal rendering of war's horrors; on the other hand, the solo *Deep Song* transcended any suggestion of propagandistic doctrine in its personal grief-stricken cry against untimely death.

The great nations of the world were in combat. With heavy feelings of premonition Martha was to see many young dancers and friends go off to the war: the talented Daniel Nagrin, who had become Tamiris's partner; José Limón, the most promising male dancer to emerge from the Humphrey—Weidman company; and Ben Belitt, the poet, who was to figure prominently in her creative life when the war was over. From her own company, David Campbell and David Zellmer were gone. But Erick and Merce were still with her, and two new dancers—John Butler and Robert Horan—would soon join the group.

Once again, Martha was invited to be artist-in-residence at Bennington. Though there would be no festival in 1942, several exceedingly promising young dancers who were attached to Martha would be making their choreographic debuts that summer: Jean Erdman, Merce Cunningham, Jane Dudley, Sophie Maslow, and the Humphrey–Weidman company member Bill Bales. The work of all five dancers was a credit to Martha, Louis, and their Bennington colleagues. Even a hint of avant-gardism might have been detected in the Erdman–Cunningham *Credo in Us,* with its percussion quartet, including piano, by John Cage. And the fact that two Graham dancers teamed up with a Humphrey–Weidman dancer was adequate proof that the American modern dance could coordinate successfully within its own ranks.

Back in New York with a reduced touring schedule that winter and no Broadway performances, Martha turned to her books, her never-ending source of stimulation. A new work began to take hold of her. Her first impulse was to approach Arch Lauterer, whose innovative settings for *Letter to the World* had dovetailed perfectly with her sensitive interpretation of Emily Dickinson's personality. A master of stage design, his trellis-like décor suggesting the interior and exterior of the Dickinson home in Amherst, Massachusetts, conveyed the airiness of the poet's imagination while it opened countless channels of dance space for Martha. Lauterer, who "made his light dance with the dancers," would comprehend the subtleties of the theme that was absorbing her more and more. Together they would create—with the musical assistance of Hunter Johnson of *Letter to the World*—a darkly suggestive ballet based on the subconscious fears, desires, loves, and hates of another Emily: Emily Brontë. Its title taken from a poem by Dylan Thomas, *Deaths and Entrances* would once again deal with the theme of introspection that Martha had begun to explore, first in lighthearted satirical fashion in *Every Soul Is a Circus* and then in the poetical vein of *Letter to the World.*

A clue to the depth of penetration present in *Deaths and Entrances* can be ascertained in a quotation from Sir Francis Bacon that Martha entered in one of her notebooks: "For he who recollects or remembers, thinks; he who imagines, thinks; he who reasons, thinks; and in a word the spirit of man, whether prompted by sense or left to itself, whether in the functions of the intellect, or of the will and affections, dances to the tune of the tho'ts."

For the person who "recollects or remembers," time is seen through the telescopic lens of memory, where personal experience is reproduced with searing vividness. To look back is to look inward.

"In a dancer's body," wrote Martha, "we as audience must see ourselves."

To see ourselves—introspectively—that was the task that Martha set herself in 1943, when, stirred by the somber story of the Brontë sisters, she composed *Deaths and Entrances*. Not that *Deaths and Entrances* would become a straight narrative of the life of Emily Brontë, or a recital of emotional occurrences in the House of Haworth. No, such inspiration served mainly as a springboard for Martha's imagination. Off on a trajectory of her own, she would intuitively redesign the scenario suggested by a poem, a play, a novel, or even by history in the colorful terms of her private store of symbolic imagery.

Introspection would dominate the landscape of most of her creations for four solid years; then it would close its inward-searching eye for nearly a decade while she pursued lyrical impulses until 1958, when it would awaken refreshed, ready to penetrate the complexities of the "darkest" lady Martha would ever try to portray: Clytemnestra, the Greek queen, wife of Agamemnon and twin sister of Helen of Troy.

"The complex inner world of the emotions that depth psychology has disclosed, suggests a new realm for the artist's inspiration and consideration, and new areas and new definitions of beauty," wrote Louis Horst in his book, *Modern Dance Forms in Relation to the Other Modern Arts*, which grew out of his course Modern Dance Forms; and when discussing introspection as used by Martha in her dance dramas, Horst added: "Martha Graham's typical dramatic scene is laid within the mind or heart of a woman faced with an urgency of decision or action, and with the dramatis personae of the group performing as symbols of her complex emotional reactions."

Not only did the dancers surrounding Martha perform as symbols of personal recall, but inanimate objects served as symbols that represented whole segments of past experiences. "A symbol," we are told by the philosopher Suzanne Langer, "is any device whereby we are enabled to make an abstraction." In *Deaths and Entrances*, symbolic significance would be invested in what might outwardly be considered trifles: a shell, a goblet, a chess-piece. To the leading character, however, another world would be conjured up by their very presence. That world, in its turn, would become real for the audience as the dancer's vision materialized into dramatic reality.

The Brontë sisters—Emily, Charlotte, and Anne—wove their famous novels of sinister threads: *Wuthering Heights, Jane Eyre,* and

Agnes Gray being the respective sisters' harrowing descriptions of life on the bleak moors of nineteenth-century England. Martha called the three women "doom-eager," an Icelandic term meaning willing to face one's destiny no matter what the cost; death and despair penetrated their individual and joint lives, yet they triumphed spiritually. The choreography for *Deaths and Entrances* was inspired by the stream-of-consciousness technique of writers such as James Joyce, Marcel Proust, William Faulkner, and Virginia Woolf, whose novels dealt with the secret life of the psyche.

In the hands of a lesser artist, the use of such an ambiguous technique when applied to the dance could easily have resulted in failure. The stream of consciousness is a mighty subterranean river winding through emotional thickets that can never be fully cleared to reveal concrete meaning. Fantasies and realities change place before the wandering inner eye; fears assume the shapes of monsters; love lures and leers around the next corner; and the stream, instead of coming out at last on a peaceful clearing, returns to its source: the primeval world of god-images wearing the masks of our ancestors. Trying to follow its circuitous path, the dancer's creative imagination can be left stranded, helplessly confused within the jungle of the personal unconscious; and the resultant dance movements can become grotesquely incomprehensible.

But in Martha's hands, the journey into the depths of an individual—namely, the emotions of Emily Brontë, whose stream of consciousness dominated the action—became a drama of epic proportions. Fraught with unspeakable tension, the scenario of *Deaths and Entrances* was as irrational and as weird as the ghostly happenings in a tale by Edgar Allen Poe; and while its setting was as eerie as that of Emily's own "still as death" *Wuthering Heights,* the emotional line—a weaving together of the diverse passions of the sisters—held fast.

Three women—one in black, one in gray, one in brown—sit on one side of the stage around a low table strangely resembling a sliced-off tree trunk. They move with jerky, nervous, angular gestures. The One in Brown (Charlotte) seems to be possessed by a brooding misery; the One in Gray (Anne), by a sense of frustration as though she is seized by the feeling that her young life is being wasted away; the One in Black (Emily), the oldest, implacably bitter, seems to have claws of steel.

"Tonight in *Deaths and Entrances,*" wrote Martha in one of her notebooks, "while standing, I suddenly knew what witchcraft is—in microcosm—It is the being within each of us—sometimes the witch, sometimes the real being of good—of creative energy—no matter what area or direction of that activity."

Three children enter; they are the remembered selves of the three sisters' childhoods. One carries a large conch-shell. She places it on one of two small altar-like constructions on the opposite side of the stage. The sight of the shell nostalgically evokes scenes of carefree play. The children dance with a strange, compulsive abandon. Then the vision fades, and the One in Black is overwhelmed with morbid longing.

Another object—a goblet—stirs up memories of early love. Through the lens of Recall, three young men, elegantly attired as if for a ball, enter, sweep the sisters off their feet, and airily embrace them. Releasing their partners with a formal gesture, the young men disappear. But for the One in Black, the vision is a searing reminder of lost love identified with a fourth man, The Poetic Beloved, and she plunges into a succession of backward falls spanning the width of the stage. Drawn together again from sheer loneliness, the sisters sit once more around the truncated table, on which is a single red chess-piece. Isolation closes in around them as they begin to play their final game with Destiny.

Hidden antagonisms begin to surface. Seemingly erratic gestures building to a fearful climax send the One in Black into a paroxysm of fury. The red chess-piece, now in her hand, foretells a future dark with death . . . her own. Trembling with madness, she breaks into a dance wracked with despair. Footbeats stamp out angry protests; swinging arm and leg movements whip through the air as if attacking unseen foes. At the peak of insensate motion, she suddenly comes to a standstill, regaining control of herself. Her body straightens; her face becomes calm. She quietly picks up the goblet—a symbolic Cup of Life—and sets it down on the table in one decisive move, thus ending the game. Peace is restored; not the peace of passive resignation, but the vibrant acceptance of one's destiny.

———— ···· ————

Then, like a cry of release, came *Appalachian Spring*.

"Nothing Martha Graham has done before has had such deep joy about it," wrote John Martin after its premiere in Washington, D.C. in 1944.

In the midst of world turmoil, Martha chose to dance about the potential joys of domestic bliss. The most lyrical of her ballets to date, *Appalachian Spring* sang of nineteenth-century rustic life in the mountains of Pennsylvania. Its characters—a bride, her husband, a pioneer woman, a minister, and four girls who served as his admiring congregation—danced the simplest of narratives: the taking possession of a newly built house by a young married couple. The sunlit morning on which the action takes place could have represented any time of the year, but Martha chose spring for reasons deep in her own and her country's past. "My brother died in the winter [remembrances of the dark veil of Pittsburgh].... When spring came it was a release from terror ... a sense of resurrection, a sense of recovery of some beautiful and magical time." The "poignant stories" of early American settlers were part of her reasoning, too: the end of a New England winter's hardships and "the coming of their first spring" bringing the Puritans the same sense of resurrection.

In contrast to *Frontier* with its suggestion of a vast western wilderness to be conquered, the eastern environment of *Appalachian Spring* called for a domesticated interpretation of Americana. Its theme was, basically, the vision of what marriage could and should be, with Martha dancing the role of the Bride and Erick that of the Husbandman. Tillable fields and pastureland seemed to lie beyond the stage confines, while the dominant presence of the Pioneer Woman conveyed the spirit of nineteenth-century family resourcefulness. The spirit of American community life was there, too. Four little girls, suggesting the feminine contingent of townsfolk, fluttered around a stark, sincere, but overbearing revivalist Preacher (Merce Cunningham), whose sermon, full of fire and brimstone, was delivered shortly after his benediction of the marriage vows. Uncomplicated by inner emotional tensions, the bride and her groom sought nothing more than to dig their roots into a tiny portion of the earth.

Aaron Copland wrote the score, weaving nineteenth-century American folk tunes together in one continuous melodic tapestry. Noguchi designed the set with a sculptor's feeling for organic form: a sliced-off frame of a house, a cross-section view of a porch containing a lean, sparingly carved rocking chair, a fence not more than six feet wide, and a raked tree stump that served as a preacher's pulpit. Said Martha: "The scenery for this dance is the framework of a house.... It's the structure on which the house is built and behind the structure is the emotion that builds the house which is love."

125

Marriage did not enter the stage of Martha's personal life for approximately four years to come, but she was in love with her leading man, Erick Hawkins, and *Appalachian Spring* with its radiant positivism seemed to indicate that domestic bliss was around the corner. But such was not the case. The personal relationship between the two artists did not parallel their smoothly running working relationship, which, now that Erick had taken over the management of their business affairs—much in the manner of Ted Shawn in relation to his and Ruth St. Denis's careers—was beginning to reap practical advantages. Showing impressive business acumen, Hawkins had been able to obtain sufficient funds for presenting the New York premiere of *Deaths and Entrances,* which had had only a Bennington preview, with fresh sets and costumes by Lauterer and an orchestral version of Hunter Johnson's piano score.

Admittedly Martha needed close personal ties (her relationship of several decades with Louis was proof of that), but the unevenness of her private life with Erick was to carry its burden of high and low emotional experiences. Martha's Irish willfulness made her unpredictable and difficult to deal with, while Erick's desire for peace ("I never have hysterics") only accentuated the disparity of their temperaments. Feeling that Martha's anxieties were "anti-life," Hawkins would try to counteract their effect in his own way: "When one is quiet, lovely fresh ideas come up from the unconscious." Martha's needs were to stir up those around her to the same point of tension she felt, and thereby create the ambience for subconscious impulses to rise productively. Yet her basic clarity of thinking, her sense of humor and honesty with herself ("It's just that I've been willful"), could restore her perspective.

As far as creativity was concerned, no tantrums, no depressions would interfere with its steady productivity. Within the next four years (1943–1947) she would compose no fewer than six major works, and embark upon a period that heralded significant changes in her own dancing. Still at the peak of her performing powers, she would be drawing more and more upon her innate acting gifts, in preparation, perhaps, for the less active years ahead. Instinctively she chose roles that explored the female persona in its most dramatic aspects: a young bride, trusting and loving (*Appalachian Spring*); a complex woman coming to terms with reality through self-analysis (*Herodiade*); a mystical figure seeking understanding of the archetypal past where pleasure, pain, sex, and religion intermingle mysteriously

(*Dark Meadow*); the jealousy-driven Medea (*Cave of the Heart*); a modern Ariadne, lost in a labyrinth of fear (*Errand into the Maze*); and finally, a queen who accepts the moral responsibility of a crime not wholly hers (*Night Journey*).

With an actress's instinct for dramatic involvement, Martha was able to identify with every trait, subtle and obvious, of her highly differentiated characters. "A role must fit one as one's skin," she declared. With a dancer's compulsion to turn feelings into action, she utilized the staples of her technique: the convulsive breath flow of contraction and release; the rapidly skimming footwork composed of tiny sideways steps; the serpentine figure-eight of the leg swinging from the hip in double circles back to front; the swirling head-down arabesque turn that tilts the upper body close to the floor—a gesture only climaxed by that ultimate Graham statement, the instantaneous back fall. The staples would be seen time and again (much as a composer's tonal predilections), only the import of the movement would differ. A specific emotional drive determined the attack. "You transform yourself into the character," Martha said in an interview. It is both a conversion and "a trusting of one's nature." The nervous energy of that particular person experiencing that particular event takes over, and the interpretation regardless of recognizable technical means becomes uniquely associated with the character on hand.

The inspiration behind the roles that Martha created would come from American history, French imagist poetry, ancient rites suggestive of Celtic cults and Jungian philosophy, Greek mythology, and classic Greek drama.

"I am a thief," Martha would say humorously with pride in her variegated sources of inspiration, "but I give it all back . . . as I see it.'"

As a "thief," Martha had joined the best of brigands. Shakespeare "cribbed" most of his plots from identifiable sources; George Bernard Shaw scooped tidbits of history for *Caesar and Cleopatra*, not to mention his deft purloining of the Greek legend of Pygmalion and Galatea, which he redressed, English fashion, replete with Cockney accent, to serve as the delectable comedy *Pygmalion* (which was stolen in turn to make *My Fair Lady*); and Eugene O'Neill broke new ground for American drama with his *Mourning Becomes Electra*—a wholesale spiriting away of Aeschylus's *Oresteia*.

Learning a trick or two from fellow-thieves, Martha turned playwright as well. Her lifelong passion for reading, her intuitive powers of logic and analysis, and her natural gift for words as the carriers of more-than-life-sized feelings gave her the rich background and the practical tools of the playwright's craft. And permeating everything was her unerring sense of the incandescent reality of onstage experience, when imagination assumes visible form and every pore is open to receive energy from spectators and other performers alike. The dramas she read, the dramas she conceived, turned into dances, and vice-versa. To pinpoint the action, she would choose a moment of extreme emotional crisis as the core of her story. This she called "the instant," that sudden, blinding realization of one's true role in life . . . and death. It was, in effect, a rediscovery of the self with fresh insight.

Such a rediscovery took place in *Herodiade,* the second of three works that were premiered at the Coolidge Auditorium of the Library of Congress in October 1944, the first being *Appalachian Spring.*

In a subtle way, the performance at the prestigious Coolidge Auditorium was the direct result of an effort on Hawkins's part to attract the attention of Elizabeth Sprague Coolidge, a woman of astute musical judgment who was regarded as the founding patron of twentieth-century chamber music in America. At Erick's invitation, she attended one of Graham's concerts and was decidedly impressed. Spurred by her enthusiasm, Hawkins wrote to her from Bennington in the summer of 1943 with the suggestion that she consider commissioning scores for Martha from Aaron Copland and Paul Hindemith. A week later he received her gracious reply: "Yes. Come to see me in Washington." At that meeting Mrs. Coolidge further announced, "I want to commission a work from Carlos Chavez as well. You can have that, too."

In approaching Elizabeth Sprague Coolidge, whose prime interest was music, Hawkins was not only concerned with Martha's and the company's performing opportunities but also with the need for accompaniment of high originality to match the dances in their repertoire. In this respect he shared Louis Horst's view that the modern dance required freshly written music by a modern composer to create a theatrical whole. Hawkins was to maintain this attitude in regard to his own choreography after leaving Martha, in particular in his collaboration with the sensitive composer/accompanist Lucia Dlugoszewski. "I would compose the dance first," he stated in 1965, "complete to the last rhythmic subdivision of a pulse, as I have done in all choreography since 1951. Then I would commission the musical score."

And Louis, as Martha's musical director of twenty-two years, had pridefully noted in Barbara Morgan's book of photographs of Martha's dances published in 1941 that since the end of 1934, Martha "has not produced a single work for which the music was not especially composed."

Now, with Mrs. Coolidge's beneficence, Martha would be able to tap the vein of creativity that had opened up so impressively with *Deaths and Entrances*, namely the theme of introspection. Absorbing her more and more, introspection as a choreographic device would provide the structure of five of the six ensuing works that would mark the mid-forties as a period of rich invention. Continuing with *Herodiade*, which drew its inspiration from the imagist poem of the same title by the French symbolist Stéphane Mallarmé, introspection would reach its climax in *Night Journey*, also commissioned by the Coolidge Foundation.

In spite of the fact that the Coolidge commission was stimulating so many new ideas and that 1944 had gotten off to a fine start with a highly successful spring season at the National Theatre on Broadway (also made possible by Hawkins's fund-raising efforts), there were disappointments to face. Prime among these was the refusal of Arch Lauterer to collaborate with the designs for the projected Coolidge program. Piqued by the fact that his settings were relegated to a secondary place in Martha's productions and that they had either been disregarded or criticized adversely by the New York press, Lauterer considered further collaboration impossible. Distressed but resourceful, Martha called upon Noguchi, thereby reestablishing a collaboration that would eventually seal itself with glory in the Greek cycle that was yet to come.

Then Chavez, whose music she had danced to in 1932 (*Prelude*), informed her that his score could not be delivered in time. With Erick's persuasion once more, Mrs. Coolidge came to the rescue, offering to replace the Chavez work with one by Darius Milhaud, a composer whom Martha had also used previously (*Danza*, 1929). Agreeing, but finding herself deeply involved in the Copland and Hindemith works, she was forced to relegate the less evocative Milhaud score to the last minute, a maneuver to its disadvantage, for *Imagined Wing* (the dance title of Milhaud's proffered *Jeu de Prin-*

temps) was far from successful. It disappeared from the repertory after the first performance.

Her concentration on the Copland and Hindemith scores paid off magnificently. *Appalachian Spring,* originally visualized as a lyrical rendering of the Dance episode in Hart Crane's *The Bridge,* supplied a much-needed light touch for Martha's repertoire. Placed at the end of an evening's program, it proved to be entertaining in a much-appreciated exhilarating way. Audiences left the theater in a state of euphoria. Copland's Americana-based score, which later earned him a Pulitzer prize, was delightfully hummable. As a bride, Martha conveyed all the natural feelings of a young woman on the verge of a domestically fulfilling life; her husband, portrayed by the handsome Hawkins, was reassuringly capable and protective; and the members of the quaint community that surrounded the attractive couple had irresistible Victorian charm. Most important of all, Martha danced with consummate grace. In speaking of her fluttering, birdlike solo midway in the ballet, John Martin went so far as to exclaim: "Nowhere in her entire repertoire is there a more enchanting passage."

Dark where *Appalachian Spring* had been bright, inhibited where the other had been free, *Herodiade,* too, was enthusiastically received—proof once more of Martha's dual gifts for lyricism and drama. Following to some degree the scenario implied in the elaborate, abstruse poem, *Herodiade* is concerned with the thoughts of "a Woman" (so named on the program) who prepares herself for her destiny by scrutinizing her innermost feelings. A mirror and the presence of a Woman Attendant assist her in the painful act of self-confrontation. The illusion in the mirror has to be shattered step by step, or recognized for its potential power to reflect one's true personality, as in the Japanese poem:

> *I do not see myself*
> *Reflected in the mirror,*
> *Myself, reflected in the mirror,*
> *Sees me.*

Originally entitled *Mirror Before Me* (changed later at Hindemith's request), the dance is cast in ritualistic form, reminiscent of Martha's early primitive works. A few pantomimic gestures suffice to convey the tense atmosphere of an emotional ordeal. Primary movements of walking, jumping, squatting, sitting, falling suggest a certain compulsiveness in the very act of self-investigation. A prescient, almost eerie moment occurs when the Woman stands in front of the mirror and confronts the Attendant as her own reflection! Now we realize that *Herodiade* is a soliloquy, not a duet, and that the servant is a projection of the Woman's alterego.

Introspection, here, takes a strange detour. The view *from* within becomes the view *within*. In contrast to its use as recall in *Deaths and Entrances,* introspection *itself* serves as the choreographic weapon in *Herodiade*.

Because of its impacted emotional tension, the dance is charged with mystery. Clues are few, and Martha had no intention of spelling them out. Wisely so, for the fascination that engulfs one when watching *Herodiade* lies in the very complexity of its inward look.

Even the title, *Herodiade,* has its mysteries. Herodiade could be either Herod's wife or his daughter Salome, either of whom was called Herodias. They were both desperate, demanding women—traits that seem to be written into the very fabric of Mallarmé's and Martha's characters.

But there, similarities between Mallarmé's imagist poem and Martha's introspective dance go their individually fascinating ways. The action of the poem takes place in the boudoir of a neurotic, middle-aged society woman, who regards herself narcissistically in a mirror. Images of leaves frozen beneath the cold, still water of a pool coincide with the mirror's reflections of a beautiful woman as icy as her "solitary sister," the moon. Self-enamored, she sees "Herodias of the lucid glance of diamond" and delights in the "horror" of her own virginity. When the nurse asks, "For whom, devoured by anguish, do you keep the hidden splendor and vain enigma of yourself?" she answers, "For me." It is the answer of one who has withdrawn from life.

In contrast, Martha's dance exists in a kind of laboratory of the soul, where a woman dares to face the reality of her personality in an effort to live more fully.

"When you look in a mirror," said Martha, "what do you see? Do you see only what you want to see? Sometimes you do, sometimes, you don't . . . a mirror is an instrument in an endeavor to arrive at the truth. That is how it is used in *Herodiade*."

Noguchi's set bore the stunning imprint of his preoccupation with gravity "as a metaphor to define our precarious and pendulous existence." Three chalk-white constructions symmetrically placed to the sides and in front of a wide, dark center screen uncannily suggested at one and the same time fragments of furniture and isolated parts of the human anatomy: an empty standing frame spiked with bony extensions not unlike hip joints and ribs; a skeleton-like clothes rack with arms upraised in torment and the form of one foot at its base; a centrally placed stool attached to a flat post, at the summit of which was a small scooped-out form.

At the dress rehearsal, Hindemith was baffled. "Where is the mirror, where are the legends?"

Martha replied, ". . . but I'm dealing with the magic of the mind, not the actuality."

Sensing the necessity of a strong partner, Martha asked one of her former dancers, May O'Donnell, to perform the role of the Attendant. May had danced with the company in the thirties (1932–1938) and in the intervening years had pursued her own choreographic interests. She was also cast in the role of the Pioneer Woman in *Appalachian Spring,* a part she was admirably suited for with her statuesque build and heroic quality of motion. Compared to other members of Martha's company, May had maintained an unusual independence of spirit. To begin with, she had studied dancing previously in her native California and in New York as well (with Fe Alf) and had come to Martha not as a follower professing the faith, but more objectively, as a student seeking new stimulating experiences in the dance. Her own choreographic gifts first came into evidence in the studio concerts that Martha and Louis encouraged and arranged for company members to give in the mid-thirties. Particularly memorable was a solo that May performed in a simple white costume. Converting the rigorously disciplined Graham movement into more fluently lyrical gestures, the young golden-haired dancer resembled a Greek goddess as she lifted a sharply bent knee high in front of her, firmly curved her arm around it, and raised her eyes to some far-off Olympian height.

This Amazonian quality appealed to Martha. For the New York premieres the forthcoming spring (1945) of *Herodiade* and *Appalachian Spring* Martha would invite May to perform with her. Later she would bill May as "Guest Artist"—an unprecedented gesture on her part. It implied confidence in and need of O'Donnell's special gifts. Another gesture was the sharing of certain choreographic responsibilities by permitting May to work out many of her movement phrases, a practice begun already in *Deaths and Entrances* with Jane Dudley and Sophie Maslow, as the original interpreters of the respective roles of Charlotte and Anne Brontë.

To call *Herodiade* a soliloquy is to give credence to the fact that the full weight of the emotional line is carried by the main character. The presence of the Attendant suggests that she is but a facet of the Woman's personality, being both witness and collaborator in the act of self-purification. The psychological climax comes when the Attendant ritualistically circles three times around the Woman, each time releasing another part of her mistress's dress until she is revealed in a silver-white sheath, its color symbolically suggestive of the radiance of self-acceptance. From this psychological peak the Woman will move onward. Wrapping herself with one swift gesture in a voluminous black scarf that the Attendant has prepared for her, she advances with statuesque dignity into "the unknown" as the lights dim.

Beneath the many layers of meaning in *Herodiade* (one of which clearly suggests a woman's fear of aging) can be detected the spiritually affirmative philosophy of the great psychoanalyst Carl Jung, whose disciple, Dr. Frances Wickes, had become a bulwark of strength for Martha during the prolonged emotional crises of those overwrought years.

While the life Martha led had little time for relationships outside of the studio, among her few personal acquaintances was one whose creative insights struck deep chords of response in her. A former colleague at Bennington, the poet Ben Belitt was to reenter Martha's life after the war and stimulate her in the direction of another soliloquy as powerful as *Herodiade*. Invited by Martha Hill, who had a sixth sense for matching personalities, to a luncheon with Ben Belitt, Martha discovered the poet anew.

It was a particularly sensitive moment in both their lives. Following an assignment with the military police in the swamps of Louisiana, Belitt had been engaged in a depressing postwar job: editing films taken in combat. Considering that such work amounted to a prolongation of his disagreeable war experiences, he felt at odds and very much alone. A mutual sense of struggling against pressures of an overwhelming kind activated an exchange of letters—letters in which Martha would speak freely of her ideas for dances and encourage Belitt to draw upon his own rare gifts, for which she avowed admiration and respect.

Belitt's poems, first published in a slender volume entitled *Five-Fold Mesh,* had stirred Martha deeply. His metaphorical images were not distant from hers, dealing as they did with pain, beauty, and an intense awareness of the meaning of a single moment's experience. She whose impulse was to isolate those instants that suddenly reveal the panorama of an entire life felt a natural kinship with a literary mind of Belitt's caliber. It is even conceivable that intellectually Martha could have become a poet, as indeed she was in her dances. Words, like movement, could have become the articulation of those intuitions that consumed her at moments of peak awareness. Belitt himself has said: "She works blindly, as a poet might in the writing of a poem, and invites those breaks with rational procedure and intuitional collisions."

Martha's often-stated description of work as an obsessive ritual from which escape seems impossible could certainly describe any artist's compulsion to express thoughts and feelings; but it also must be acknowledged that the current of Martha's nervous energy ran like lightning through her bones and sinews, and therefore only raw physical action—albeit tamed into stylized gesture—could provide the completely gratifying answer.

In one of his replies to her letters, Belitt saw fit to enclose a poem he had dedicated to Martha and published years before in *The Nation.* Curiously, she had never seen it. Martha put a copy of the poem over her dressing table in the studio and another one on her bedside table. She even read the lines to her students at 66 Fifth Avenue and at the Neighborhood Playhouse School of the Theatre. The poem was Belitt's "Dance Piece" (later published in his book of poems *Wilderness Stair*). It began:

> The errand into the maze,
> Emblem, the heel's blow upon space,
> Speak of the need and order the dancer's will
> But the dance is still.

Drawn to the imagery of Belitt's line, "The errand into the maze," Martha viewed it as a haunting description of the labyrinthian experience of creative work. Inspired by the phrase, she decided to call a dance that was still to be composed, *The Errand into the Maze*. So strong was her identification with the poem that she had already commissioned a score from Gian-Carlo Menotti, the young Italian composer of the successful opera *The Consul*. And Noguchi would design the set.

To Belitt, Martha's need to dramatize experience made her an epic figure not only in the dance world but in personal life. Her generous nature, her passion for big feelings, big titles ("the big sound," said Belitt), and her extreme sensitivity toward those who suffered—all this, in his opinion, made Martha a formidable, more than life-size figure. Then, there was the other side, the "deceptively accessible and flirtatious Irish colleen," who took delight in uprooting others with her Irish humor, of which she was so proud. "It was this kind of laughing provocation," said Belitt, "that finally loosened me to regard her as a very great colleague with whom I could talk myself into stillness."

Inspired by Belitt's poem, Martha composed one of her most emotionally charged dances. Another literary souce contributed the basic framework: the Greek myth of Theseus's successful penetration of the labyrinth to kill the Minotaur with the help of the Cretan princess, Ariadne. Characteristically, Martha converted the myth to her own ends: she was a female Theseus (or Ariadne herself); the bull, a projection of her fears; and the journey through the labyrinth a ritual with cataclysmic psychological meaning.

From the moment the curtain rises, drumbeats, like palpitations, send tremors through the dancer's body. Standing close to an angled post upstage with her arms interlocked across her pelvis, the taut figure seems to be possessed by an indescribable anxiety. At her feet, a white-taped path zigzags downstage and comes to an end at the base of a sculptured form resembling a forked tree trunk. The path, which winds its way down a sloping platform the width of the stage, has double meaning. In one sense, it suggests that it represents the thread that Adriadne gave Theseus to guide him throught the labyrinth so that he could slay the mythological bull and return safely; in another sense, it symbolically traces the route one must take through the interior landscape of one's most fearsome imaginings to achieve spiritual release.

The dancer's first efforts to traverse the path are interrupted by the emergence of a bull-like creature wearing a wooden yoke, a mask, and stubby horns. Turning and twisting frenziedly, she succeeds in eluding his grip and the animal disappears into the shadows. Left alone, she seizes the loose end of the taped path and frantically loops it around the forked tree trunk in an effort to make a protective barrier for herself should he return. But his reentry catches her off guard and there ensues a physical struggle which is desperate but inconclusive. Falsely elated as she sees him roll away, she dances a lighthearted waltz that is cut short by his reemergence from the dark a third time. A decisive confrontation is now inevitable. They wrestle savagely, legs and arms locking in tight holds; then, with a sudden rush of strength, she climbs astride him and slowly, forcibly, brings him to the ground. As he slinks away, she resumes her advance with intensified purpose, slips behind the tree, and swiftly untying the tape, steps between the two forks of the trunks as if through a doorway, upright and free.

In Noguchi's notes, he likens the "doorway" to "suppliant hands, like pelvic bones, from which [and he quotes Martha] 'the child I never had comes forth, but the only child that comes forth is myself.'"

———————

A striking twinship can be discerned between *Errand into the Maze* and *Herodiade*. In both dances hidden fears and desires are ruthlessly examined and brought to light. Both compositions are essentially soliloquies in that the secondary characters merely reinforce the interior drama. In *Herodiade* the Woman Attendant is the contributor and witness to the inner event; in *Errand* the beast is a self-destructive element that has to be overcome.

Coming at an approximately midway point in Martha's independent performing career (1926–1969), these semi-solos can be seen as the forerunners of the self-judgmental *Night Journey* and *Clytemnestra*. They also can be seen as transitional points between dances that dealt directly with emotional situations and those in which Martha would portray specific characters within a given narrative: Medea (which just preceded *Errand*), Jocasta, Judith, St. Joan, Clytemnestra, Mary, Queen of Scots, Alcestis, Phaedra, Héloise. Did this mean that she would cease to dance out her private compulsions? That the legendary historic or literary figures whose personalities she would assume would take her further from herself?

To agree with this supposition one would have to assume that Martha's excursions into introspection, particularly her soliloquies, were autobiographical—an erroneous point of view. Tempting as it might be to describe *Herodiade* and *Errand into the Maze* as personal statements of periods of emotional unrest, there is no doubt that the artist in Martha always took precedence over the woman. At no point can she be accused of self-expression in the ordinary sense. Irrespective of her tendency to magnify personal experience on an epic scale, as Ben Belitt cogently remarked, all of Martha's dances were objectifications of emotional crisis. No matter how closely she related to the character she portrayed, Martha was primarily concerned with its theatrical projection.

The objectification of an emotional theme, however, does not deprive it of natural causes. *Errand into the Maze* came at a time in Martha's life when uncertainty must have been stalking her day and night. Her relationship with Erick still vacillated between extremes of feeling; and Louis, whose daily presence had always been a steadying factor, was no longer at her beck and call. Since Erick's entry into the company Louis's role as muscial director had been formally maintained, but intimacy was a thing of the past.

The argument here lies in the fact that Martha's personality was always in flux. The one thing that kept her on her course was her phenomenal inner drive. Her dancing was not just a reflection of it but the vibrational result of it. It accounted for the magnetism of her stage presence.

By 1947, Martha's reputation was fully stabilized. She had been under the famous Sol Hurok's management for over a year, and she had already premiered *Dark Meadow* and *Night Journey*. Hurok was so deeply impressed with her as an artist that he felt committed to write in 1953: "Martha Graham completed my triptych of modern dancers, commencing with Isadora Duncan and continuing with Mary Wigman as its center piece. Martha Graham is by far the greatest of the three." But he conceded that "she has chosen the road of the solitary and lonely experimenter . . . single-purposed, the most fanatical in her devotion to an idea and an ideal. About her and everything she does is an extraordinary integrity, a consummate honesty." The price of Martha's integrity was paid from within.

Circumstances seemed always to stand in the way of easy solutions. Time and again she would have to draw upon increasingly less available reserves to deal with the continual crises that faced her with the company. In the second Hurok season, the exceedingly valuable Merce Cunningham had to be replaced, and for programming considerations, it became necessary for Martha to turn over two of her roles—a most painful experience—to two of her leading dancers: Pearl Lang and Ethel Winter. Pearl was to dance the role of Mary Magdalene in *El Penitente;* Ethel, the solo, *Salem Shore,* a charming light-touch New England portrait of, presumably, a nineteenth-century sea captain's wife. Giving up these roles for the first time, even at the age of fifty-three, seemed to presage a future when her dancing powers would be diminished—a prospect that was unthinkable.

(Years later, when Ethel Winter was to dance her role in *Herodiade* in a performance at Juilliard, Martha could hardly watch it at the dress rehearsal. Sitting next to Louis in the darkened auditorium, she spoke of the strange sensation of witnessing the dance as an outsider—an experience that tore her apart.)

Then, as if to rescue her, philosophy and the ritual of practice would provide a way out: "There are times of complete frustration, there are daily small deaths. Then I need all the comfort that practice has stored in my memory."

Practice for a dancer is that daily act of obedience to the demands of art: the building up of physical reserves—strength, flexibility, endurance, and the readiness to respond to the overwhelming impulse to move. Practice is the dialogue between body and brain, when action meets reaction, force summons force, effort begets feeling, and movement, sure as an arrow in flight, takes off into space. The ritual of practice is like the ritual of prayer, profoundly connected with dawn or dusk; one cannot forget or neglect it, for it is bound up with the diurnal turn of the earth. "If you do two hours of technique today," says Martha, "you can't skip tomorrow and then do four hours the next day and expect it to work. You are one day behind what you can be."

Practice is the talisman to ward off the evil eye of injury. Once swiftness, lightness, and all the magic of intricate body coordinations have been mastered and absorbed into the physical mechanism, practice becomes even more urgent. Then, there is the obligation to keep the trained body in condition; should its disciplined resources lie unused, it might fail to fulfill the exorbitant demands made upon it when the moment of performance is at hand. Freedom is obtained only through what Graham calls "complete focus upon a given instant," which is nothing but perfect coordination, which is perfect timing. One misstep, one poor landing after a thrilling leap, and the result can be disastrous. So complex is the interweaving of muscle, bone, nerves, and the human will that a single fleeting moment of fear can send vibrations through the body that deflect it from its course and then the dancer, instead of moving effortlessly, is reduced to a faltering thing.

"Practice," says Martha, "means to perform, over and over in the face of all obstacles, some act of vision, of faith."

———— ··· ————

Dark Meadow is that act of vision, not of the future but of the far past when pagan rites set the pattern of psychic growth. There is no overt scenario, rather the subtle unfolding of a woman's conscious-ness in terms of quasi-religious imagery: an all-enveloping black cloth that serves as a death symbol; a small, folded towel that is of-fered ceremoniously from a bowl of presumably sacred water; a crudely made cross; bird feathers and arrows stuck like darts into the surface of a slanted form that supports the protagonist in moments of withdrawal.*

Characters of mythological stature dominate a landscape that is once again the interior domain of a central personality named One Who Seeks (Graham). Surrounding her are two archetypal figures: an earth-mother, She of the Ground (May O'Donnell), and a guru-like leader, He Who Summons (Erick Hawkins). Enacting their own ritu-als are Those Who Dance Together (Pearl Lang, Natanya Neumann, Marjorie Mazia, Ethel Winter, Yuriko, Mark Ryder, Douglas Watson, David Zellmer).

Isolated from the chorus, and subject only to the demands of the summoner and the earth-mother, the One Who Seeks struggles with invisible forces, spiritual and sexual, as she wanders symbolically through "The Dark Meadow of Ate." (The Goddess Ate has been described multifariously as fate, as sin, and as a malevolent divinity who prompts human beings to perform irresponsible acts.) The stage is strewn with rock-like forms and phallic posts. Reminiscently Cel-

---

*The original program note for *Dark Meadow* read: "*Dark Meadow* is a re-enactment of the Mys-teries which attend the eternal adventure of seeking" (January 1946).

tic, the rocks serve as altars, and the posts, like trees, sprout leaves at the climax of the dance. Close to the end, She of the Ground encloses one of the posts in the folds of a voluminous green cape that she wears. The gesture, sexually suggestive, becomes a metaphor for the cyclical process in nature and mankind.

Inspired by Plato's mythological references to the dark meadow of Ate and by Empedocles' fragment, "I have been ere now a boy and girl, a bush, a bird, a dumb fish in the sea," the theme of *Dark Meadow* embraces the eschatological doctrines of preexistence, penance, reincarnation, and final purification of the soul. The action, therefore, has veiled significance.

But while *Dark Meadow* takes introspection to philosophical heights, its choreography is rooted in the visceral world of bodily sensation. Movement bursts forth as though the choreographer had suddenly touched subterranean springs of compulsive-impulsive gesture: angular, slicing motions, asymmetrical jumps, rapid shifts in rhythms, and wild careenings through space. In contrast to the emotional fervor that seizes the chief characters is the cool, detached lyrical movement of the ensemble as the men and women perform slow, intricate, mesmerizing love duets. And in the background, Carlos Chavez's hauntingly melodious quartet, with its additional wind sections at the beginning and at the end, contributes atmospherically to the mysterious rites. Were it not for Martha's ability to convert her intellectual perceptions into the sensuous language of movement, *Dark Meadow* would remain cryptically aloof, tantalizingly inaccessible.

Chapter Seven

The View From Olympus

Errand into the Maze, with its subtle interweaving of legend with psychological drama, was not the first of Martha Graham's dramatic works to be inspired by Greek mythology. Nine months previously, in a spring program at Columbia University's McMillin Theater, she had premiered *Serpent Heart,* a chilling reenactment of the Jason-Medea myth. Revised and retitled *Cave of the Heart* for a Broadway premiere in the same season as *Errand,* the ballet took its narrative line almost directly from Euripides' *Medea,* in some minds the most harrowing of Greek tragedies. The last great Attic dramatist had given his audiences no glimpse of redemption as he drew the dark outlines of Medea's remorseless revenge.

It is fascinating to speculate on the origin of the ballet's first title: *Serpent Heart.* In the adventure of Jason and the Golden Fleece, there was a serpent who guarded the priceless golden mane of a ram sacrificed by a young Greek prince in the foreign kingdom of Colchis over which an unfriendly King Aeëtes ruled. Jason's successful attempt to procure the fleece was made possible only through the sorcery of King Aeëtes' daughter, Medea, who succeeded in lulling the serpent to sleep. Note that she did not kill the serpent but simply bewitched it.

But the story goes back further. It concerns the family of the gods whose residence was on the paradisical heights of Mount Olympus. What a hierarchy of power resided up there! The fate of all humankind in the ancient world lay in their hands. This lofty view of the gods' omnipotence was maintained in all Greek myths and plays despite the fact that the inhabitants of Mount Olympus were credited with the same trivial rivalries and ambitions that were typical of the

141

Greeks themselves. But this is perfectly understandable, for when the primitive Greeks turned from the worship of nature to the worship of the gods, it was natural that these gods would "reflect not only man's human form but also his human relations."

First and foremost, there was Zeus, the patriarchal figurehead. Vainglorious in his pride, he warned the members of his clan that even if they fastened a rope of gold to heaven and tried to drag him down, they could not. "But if I wished to drag you down," said he, "then I would. The rope I would bind to a pinnacle of Olympus and all would hang in air, yes, the very earth and the sea, too."

It was an enraged Zeus who sent those frightful creatures, the Harpies, to an aged truth-teller who had been given the gift of prophecy by Apollo. In Zeus's opinion, the future was entirely in *his* hands and to be divulged only at his discretion. Defending the soothsayer from the Harpies was the first act of valor committed by Jason and his sailors, the Argonauts, and though this kind deed did not anger Zeus outright, the prospect of the Argonauts encountering more formidable difficulties on their mission did worry Hera, Zeus's wife, who was on Jason's side.

Disturbed by the possibility of Jason's failing to procure the Golden Fleece, Hera sought the help of Aphrodite, and together (though they could scarcely be considered bosom friends) they plotted that Medea, who knew how to concoct magic potions, should fall in love with Jason. Thus was Cupid, Aphrodite's son, lured by a lovely ball of shining gold and blue enamel offered him by his mother as a bribe, drawn into the opening scene of the myth of Jason and Medea long before Euripides' tragedy began. Though Hera does not reappear in the ghastly dénouement of the Medea legend, it is very likely that she was chagrined at Jason for his ungrateful treatment of the woman who had saved his life. To abandon the mother of his children in order to marry the daughter of a king was unbefitting to a hero. It was at this point, most likely, that the serpent Medea had lulled to sleep on behalf of Jason reawakened and took up its abode in her breast.

The very nature of the choreography devised by Martha for her role of Medea metaphorically suggested the earthbound motions of a serpent. Lying flat on her stomach inside an elongated sculptured form with copper wires raying outward, she plotted her revenge during the love scenes between Jason and King Creon's daughter. With its wiry branches swirling over it, and almost enclosing her, the low-lying form resembled a cage, while her body, stretched out face forward, seemed almost reptilian. Later, when she was center-stage and erect, vibrations seized her, and in a frenzy of jealousy she slowly drew out of her mouth a fang-like red scarf. This was her "snake solo," which was preceded by "hip crawls" and "knee crawls" to Jason; it did not end until the scarf (called "snake" in one of Martha's notebooks) was "eaten," then "spit . . . out," wrapped around her arm, and finally coiled on the floor with a corresponding coiling (contraction) of her body over it. The program note for the first performances of *Serpent Heart* read in part: "This is a dance of possessive and destroying love, a love which feeds upon itself like the serpent heart, and when it is overthrown is fulfilled only in revenge."

Martha portrayed Medea as Euripides had presented her: the embodiment of evil. "Thou living hate," cried Jason, ". . . thou incarnate curse!"

When *Serpent Heart* was renamed *Cave of the Heart,* and the titles of three of the four characters who made up the cast were changed, the true nature of the choreographic concept became clear. Noguchi's functional sculptural forms and Samuel Barber's incisive, dissonant score remained the same, of course, but they now seemed an organic part of an underlying savagery. For with the titular transformation of "One like Medea" to "Sorceress," "One like Jason" to "Adventurer," and "Daughter of the King" to "Victim," the ballet began to reveal itself as a primitive dance in which the supernatural played a dominant role.

It was primitive in the sense that it dealt with primal feelings— love, hate, jealousy, vengeance—as related to primal forces in nature, such as fire, earth, sun (Medea's grandsire was the sun), and the animal world, as represented by the snake. Magic, more menacing than mysterious, filled the stage with diabolical insinuations. Now it became apparent why the "branches" that constituted Medea's cage-like habitat were rigidly twisted coils suggestive of hardened pathways to her heart rather than flowering branches of blossom-bearing trees or plants—those symbols of spiritual or terrestrial rebirth that Martha would use time and again in future works. In *Cave of the Heart* there would be no rebirth. All the characters were doomed, save the impersonal Chorus.

How much more to the point was the renaming of Jason as Adventurer. Now the title had twofold meaning. As the "hero-adventurer" who had fulfilled his mission in capturing the Golden Fleece, he was blessed by the gods. But his success was short-lived upon his return to his kingdom in Thessaly. During his absence his uncle had usurped the throne, and despite additional witchery on Medea's part, they had to flee and settle in Corinth. There his adventurous spirit, now chained to his ego, sought new laurels through marriage to the aging king of Corinth's daughter. Vainly trying to explain himself to Medea, whom he could not marry (legal union being outlawed between a Greek and a Colchian barbarian), he justified his treason as a shrewd move performed in her and their children's interest.

As the innocent Victim, the daughter of the king (who never appears in Euripides' play) seems to be without personality or character of her own. Nameless, she serves mainly as the target of Medea's demonic jealousy.

Of the original titles only Chorus remained: a single figure that represented the collective unconscious of Euripides' chorus of Corinthian women, who shared Medea's agony yet knew the ways of the gods and the frailty of man. Danced by May O'Donnell, her first gesture expressed a presentiment of disaster. Lying face downward on a sculptured base that had five heavy stubs like severed tree-trunks around its edges, she raised her head and, opening wide her mouth, let out a soundless shriek. It was the cry of one who is seized with terrible foreknowledge but is condemned to silence. If there was a truly tragic character in *Cave of the Heart,* it was not Jason, nor Medea, nor the Victim, but the Chorus, who was forced to play the painful role of witness to unbearable events.

In assuming the title of Sorceress, Martha was able to justify the high theatricality of her Medea image. Since jealousy violates natural feelings, the very texture of her choreography took on distortions of an erratic nature: Sinuous hip thrusts were interspersed with sensual writhings; curious motions of a spasmodic, lurching character appeared, including a strange off-balance spin (later called "Cave turn"), all of which would gradually be incorporated into the greater Graham vocabulary.

The primitive image was borne out in her costume as well. Medea's headdress was a web of stylized coils rooted inside the blue-black mound of her hair. At one time, a gold ribbon was wound from front to back ending in the high-piled chignon, from which the coils seemed to spring. (Later, when Helen McGehee danced the role, the gold ribbon was threaded through her tightly braided hair as it fell to one side of her head.) Martha's long black dress had one shoulder

144

bare except for roped straps, and again gold ribbon served as symbolic decoration swirling across the front of the costume in a serpentine pattern.

Yet nowhere was the supernatural splendor of the enchantress brought out more vividly than in Medea's final act of vengeance. Having poisoned the princess and inflicted the worst punishment of all on Jason by the murder of their children, she literally encloses herself in the copper "cage," which she has separated from its base. Moving across the stage with her "armor" of shining wings wrapped around her, she climbs onto the sculptured pedestal at the rear of the stage and ascends to her grandsire's fiery realm in the skies, as if mounted on her mythological dragon-chariot.

For whatever psychological reasons Martha chose to delve into the spiky web of Medea's powerful passions at that moment in her professional life, it is just as well not to try to piece together the few fragments that we know. One clear thing, however, emerges. Erick Hawkins had been a student of Greek literature while matriculating at Harvard. The rumor was that Erick's enthusiasm for Greek drama led him to talk about it to Martha hour after hour; perhaps his own desire to mount a work on the Oedipus legend—something he tried to do years later—was at the back of it.

We do not imply that Martha's spectacular use of Erick's open-minded sharing of his own ideas was a choice example of her self-admitted "thievery"; but credit should be given to Hawkin's role in stimulating Martha's interest in the stirring myths of the pre-Christian Hellenic world. Not that Erick introduced her to Greek literature —avid reader that she was and student of drama at the Cumnock School, she certainly knew the classics. But assuredly Erick awakened her to the dance potential of Greek tragedy. Once embarked on her own Hellenic journey, she was to enter her Greek period and create theater works that matched those of the great poets for character analysis and majesty of vision. The very next composition after the intermediary *Errand into the Maze* would be the most penetrating, and the most radical to date: *Night Journey*.

———— ∙∙∙ ————

But did Martha embark on her personal Hellenic journey all alone? Scarcely so. Far from traveling light, she traveled richly, like the Queen of Sheba. Her ship was laden not only with a cargo of ideas culled from a wealth of philosophical, psychological, and poetic sources, but also with a crew of carefully selected collaborators. So impressive was the galleon she commanded that surely the inhabitants of Mount Olympus were stirred out of their centuries-old apathy when they took to peering over their marble walls.

The sight that greeted them must have made them blink their eyes. Emblazoned on the ship's prow in gold lettering for all to see was a name—Greek, to be sure, but scarcely one to be tossed about: "Jocasta." At the helm was Martha, of course, but next to her, pointing out the dangers to be encountered as they made for port, was none other than their own revered Sophocles. Clad in his toga, he maintained a classic dignity that made everyone up on Mount Olympus sit up with pride. Next to him, tie flying in the morning breeze, was one of the world's most eminent scientists, a man whose psychological probings undoubtedly appealed to the patriarchal Zeus: Sigmund Freud. Behind him stood three distinguished gentlemen, without whom Martha would not have dared to make the voyage: the white-haired Louis Horst, the scholarly composer William Schuman, and the indispensable sculptor-designer Isamu Noguchi.

Then a strange thing happened . . . an event by no means decreed by the gods. Just as they landed at Piraeus, night descended and nothing more could be seen. The Greek world seemed to be suddenly engulfed by a black despair.

"Tragedy's one essential," wrote Edith Hamilton in *The Greek Way*, "is a soul that can feel greatly."

Not one, but two souls "feel greatly" in Sophocles' *Oedipus Rex*, the drama on which Martha based her *Night Journey*. Shoulder to shoulder, King Oedipus and Queen Jocasta stand condemned by the gods for their joint misdeeds. Yet the double tragedy in Sophocles' great play is not readily apparent inasmuch as the dramatic emphasis lies on the son, not on the mother. Oedipus dominates the action. Jocasta's role is limited to three sparse scenes. Her words are few but deeply revealing. She, even more than Oedipus, bears the burden of sin. When she and King Laius had tried to circumvent the oracle at Delphi which warned them that their son, Oedipus, would slay his father, they committed the greatest crime: disbelief in the power of Apollo, god of truth. Their punishment was ruthless: all the predictions of the oracle came to pass. Thus was their inordinate pride penalized.

But even so, were it not for the power of Jocasta and Oedipus to feel that such punishment was their due, there would be no tragedy in *Oedipus Rex*—only a pathetic tale of moral castigation. In openly acknowledging their sins—Jocasta by her suicide, Oedipus by his self-torture—the leading characters in Sophocles' play rose above the minor moral issues of the ancient myth from which the poet drew his inspiration. Tragedy, which implies heroism on a grand scale, "is enthroned," wrote Hamilton, "and to her realm those alone are admitted who belong to the only true aristocracy, that of all passionate souls."

Intuitively, Martha seized upon the role of Jocasta, not only for her performing needs as the protagonist of the ballets she conceived but also for those remarkable insights that Jocasta's character afforded. By shifting the focal point of the action from Oedipus to Jocasta, Martha was able to fill the role of the queen with a meaning far beyond the conventional Greek theme of man's powerlessness to alter fate's decrees. Jocasta's personality, seen in the light of twentieth-century scientific knowledge set in motion by Freud, took on new dimensions. Here was a woman who lived out (albeit unwittingly) the libidinous urge of every woman to become mother to her husband and wife to her son. Here was a woman who recognized the reciprocal instinct in men. In the ancient play, when Oedipus asked, "Must I not fear my mother's marriage bed?" she replied in a speech prophetically Freudian,

> This wedlock with thy mother fear not thou.
> How oft it chances that in dreams a man
> Has wed his mother! He who least regards
> Such brainsick phantasies lives most at ease.

And here was a woman whose sense of personal guilt, far from being neurotic, took on a heroic hue. Quick to perceive the truth as it was being disclosed, she had the nobility of mind to face her guilt and the courage to inflict upon herself her own punishment. Bidding farewell to Oedipus, she departed the stage with majestic calm: "O woe is thee, poor wretch! With that last word I leave thee, henceforth silent evermore." With Jocasta's suicide we hear the first knelling of the bell that never ceases its clamorous dirge until Oedipus, self-blinded and exiled, dies in Colonus, and their four children, the last of the royal family of Thebes, perish one by one.

Portraiture of such stature required a radical rebalancing of the original drama. Whereas the action of Sophocles' play takes place during the progression of an entire day, the whole of *Night Journey* is condensed into a flashback, in which Jocasta relives her role in the irretrievable chain of events that she had no right to try to alter. Calling the flashback an "instant of agony," Martha chose again the choreographic device of presenting a climactic moment in individual experience when an emotional crisis could reveal the depths to which a human being could sink or the heights to which he could rise.

In keeping with the refocusing of time sequences came other significant changes. Five secondary characters in the play were dropped. The chorus, no longer composed of Theban elders whose rambling discourses reveal lack of intimate knowledge concerning the action ("why stung with passionate grief hath the Queen thus departed?" they ask), is now comprised of six young women who dance in a frenzy of knowing the inevitable path of the tragic events they witness. They are the Daughters of the Night, participants in the never-ending dark of the unconscious. And instead of a gradual dénouement of the complex plot, the curtain rises at the moment Jocasta is holding aloft the cord with which she will strangle herself.

Thus begins *Night Journey*, the journey that Jocasta takes in her mind's eye backward into her past, where she will confront herself with her sins. In the blackness of her despair, says the program note, she "sees with double insight the triumphal entry of Oedipus, their meeting, courtship, marriage, their years of intimacy which were darkly crossed by the blind seer Tiresias." Symbolically speaking, the principal character in *Night Journey* is not Jocasta but Tiresias, who represents Truth. But blindness here is double-edged. In Sophocles' play, when Oedipus, blinded by anger, called Tiresias a "tricksy beggar-priest . . . in his proper art stone-blind," the prophet returned the insult with "Thou hast eyes, yet see'st not." Truth, then, is the main protagonist in this interior journey set in motion by pride, self-deceit, and guilt.

Once again, as in *Deaths and Entrances*, Martha would deal with introspection; only this time, the shaping of the drama would be on a symbolic, heroic scale equal to that of its inspiration. Its concern, as in Greek tragedy, would be to express the secret conflicts of the psyche under the greatest stresses imaginable.

From the very first, the action is pitched at an almost unbearable level of tension. Jocasta's double insight—seeing and reliving past experiences simultaneously—penetrates every scene. She now comprehends the ominous tapping of the aged Tiresias's staff, not a knotted stick but a huge pole that he swings himself forward on, crossing the stage with terrifying speed, as though hastening to cut short events before they take place. With pitiless clarity she recalls how the young, handsome Oedipus victoriously entered her widowed realm; how, having solved the riddle of the Sphinx, he was acclaimed by all (including herself) as the savior of Thebes. Onstage he is seen clad in a brown and gold toga, with a wreath of olive leaves encircling his dark hair, as he presents her with flowering branches (pagan symbols of vitality and fertility). But he is the conqueror as much as the suitor. When she sits on a small pedestal downstage left, he stands behind her arrogantly; his bare legs and gold-braided trunks catch the light as he flaunts propriety, throwing one leg over Jocasta's shoulder and locking her in an embrace. She plays the startled female, gasping in admiration and yielding step by step to the bold youth.

Behind them are a series of isolated pedestals shaped strangely like huge hourglasses. Placed strategically across the rear of the stage, they seem to mount in graded heights toward a sloping structure, oblong in shape and symbolically sculptured to resemble both a stylized bed and a macabre anatomical vise for the human body. To its side, hanging stiffly from the rafters, is a twisted strip of a curtain; it, too, has a symbolic character, as though it is but a fragment of a partition unsuccessfully dividing Jocasta's bedroom from the peering world beyond.

The courtship comes to an end as Jocasta rises with the branches and performs a dance of acceptance, and with Oedipus's cape wrapped around her shoulders the lovers move toward the connubial bed. There, by means of a long rope, symbolic of the umbilical cord, they bind themselves together in the web of incestuous love. It is a duet of terrible import, a cat's cradle of self-deception where every move adds to the further entanglement. Horror-stricken, the Daughters of the Night tear across the stage with jagged leaps and outthrust hands. Their gestures and body motions are stylized to the point of tautness. Archaically suggestive of Greek vase figures brought suddenly to life, they move stridently, attacking the space around them with desperation. They are the unforgiving witnesses of the double sin and must bear their pain in silence. Their backward falls, expressive of shock and indignation, hit the ground percussively; but in an instant they are up again as musical chords in rhythmically sawing counterpoint drive them onward. They run off in twisted, angular positions, and the action of the play moves on to its bitter end.

The seer's return, this time to pronounce the dreadful truth, interrupts the connubial scene. With his staff he ruthlessly severs the marriage cord, throws Oedipus's cape to the side, and leaves the mother and son, now wife and husband, to face their own evil. Almost at once Oedipus stiffens and backs away from the reclining Jocasta. Reaching for the large pin she wears across the front of her dress, he thrusts it into his eyes. In rigid blindness, he staggers sideways offstage.

Slowly Jocasta prepares herself. With utmost formality, she takes off her dress, revealing a simple sheath beneath. She picks up the cord, which lies in a heap at her feet. Raising it far above her head, she pulls it tightly around her neck, and falls limply backward. Once more Tiresias crosses the stage, his staff striking the ground with a hollow thud as the curtain descends.

"The very dreams that blister sleep, boil up from the basic, magic ring of myth," wrote Joseph Campbell in his penetrating examination of ancient hero-myths, *The Hero with a Thousand Faces*. A scholar of cosmic folklore and religion, Campbell, who was Martha's colleague at Sarah Lawrence College in the thirties, could be called her "unseen collaborator" on those dances that dealt with the dark quests of the soul through the mythological world.

To Campbell, the hero is one who responds to "the Call to Adventure" and dares to pass through the "dangerous crises of self-development" to achieve his goal. He is one of "the world's symbolic carriers of the destiny of Everyman."

Most of Martha's characters, whether they inhabited the mythological world or not, were hero-adventurers: Emily Dickinson, Emily Brontë, Joan of Arc, and all the Greek and Biblical figures who struggled with the mysterious forces of their own nature. Her instinctual use of introspection and ritual revealed a deep need, described so well by Ben Belitt, to identify with suspenseful situations of a heroic nature—situations that could dramatize a character's personal experience within the structure of the larger adventures of the soul.

The quest for self-discovery in the ritualistic *Herodiade* is that of every older woman who dares to face the closing circle of her life; in *Errand into the Maze*, the same quest demands the ruthless slaying of inner fears before one can experience spiritual rebirth. The passions underlying *Cave of the Heart* and *Night Journey* are but extreme examples of those that lie hidden in everyone whose desires are thwarted or who harbors, wittingly or unwittingly, sexual fantasies toward a parent or child.

Whereas Martha speaks of a dance as a "graph of the heart," Campbell writes of the "labyrinth without and within the heart." In both instances, the psyche traces a serpentine path that winds in and around itself; easy exits are avoided; only the hard-won egress representing ultimate effort can bring gratification.

More than a creator of heroines who sought their own salvation, Martha was herself a hero-adventurer. From the very first, she realized that the cost of self-realization would be "not less than everything." Uncompromising in her standards, relentless in her drive toward achievement, she could reject all proffered substitutes. Money, comfort, and fame were minor considerations. Endowing her intense dedication with a supernatural aura, she repeatedly avowed, "I did not choose to be a dancer. I was chosen." It was a pact with Fate.

Her path was not only labyrinthian but crowded with obstacles. Singleminded in her pursuit, she always found the way to circumvent or climb over each fresh obstacle. Only one obstacle remained persistently obdurate: her age. Time was her private Minotaur. Never doubting that she would emerge the victor, she planned to fight him with every means at her disposal. She seemed to be making a veiled allusion to her intended longevity as a dancer when she wrote: "Contrary to opinion, the dancer's body is nearer to the norm of what the body should be than any other. It has been brought to this possible norm by discipline, for the dancer, is, of necessity, a realist. Pavlova, Argentina, and Ruth St. Denis all practiced their art past the age of fifty." When these words were published, Martha was already forty-seven. She was to dance until the age of seventy-five!

"The hero is the man of self-achieved submission," writes Campbell. Submission would not be as easy for Martha as for her heroines.

Resignation on the stage can vibrate with promise, such as the closing scene of *Letter to the World* when the poet sits in expectant stillness, hands folded, eyes aflame; or the moment in *Deaths and Entrances* when the One in Black places the goblet on the table with a gesture of luminous acceptance of her destiny. Resignation in life has concealed heroics: no histrionic gestures, no resounding chords to bring the curtain down; nor one last chance to take a final bow. Yet for the hero-adventurer there are successive acts of spiritual growth involving death and resignation, "the everlastingly recurrent themes of . . . the soul's high adventure." These would come to Martha, too, but not without their corresponding payment: renunciation and acceptance.

Just as Campbell sees the hero as "the man or woman who has been able to battle past his personal and local historical limitations" to be reborn psychologically, so Martha perceives her heroines as embodiments of the will to survive. Such a transfiguration would, one day, take place within the dynamics of her private life.

Of the "seen" collaborators, the most important would always be the Japanese-American sculptor Isamu Noguchi. His presence on the ship that Sophocles helped steer to Piraeus practically guaranteed the success of Martha's nocturnal voyage deep into the soul of Jocasta. When he was a child Noguchi's American mother used to read to him the myths of ancient Greece. "As a result I believed in Apollo and all the gods of Olympus long before I knew of any other." Well initiated into the world that Martha was now recreating in her highly original fashion, the resourceful sculptor was one of the first to step ashore when the Jocasta docked in Piraeus.

From 1944 to 1967, Noguchi would be Martha's closest partner in the realization of her major works. Their intuitive aesthetic rapport was nothing short of miraculous. No one else in Martha's professional life outside of Louis Horst was to contribute so much of his own genius in the service of hers.

Years before the eventful beginning of their collaboration, Martha had met the sculptor when she had a studio in Carnegie Hall and he had a studio in Sherman Square. At that time Noguchi looked more Italian than Japanese with his curly black hair and piercing gaze. But it was his eastern quality that made him first appeal to Martha, who later admitted, "I am deeply Asian in all of my interests." (Although this statement is somewhat exaggerated, there is no doubt that Martha responded to the culture of the Far East with the same fervor of appreciation that possessed Ruth St. Denis.)

In 1929 Noguchi did two heads of Martha. The first was such a frankly anatomical rendering of her gaunt physiognomy at this particular time that the sculptor consented to do a second portrait-head which would be "more complimentary." Cast in bronze, the second head remains the most concrete proof of a collaboration based on intuitive understanding.

According to Noguchi, he met Martha through the Japanese dancer Michio Ito, when the latter was also teaching dancing at the John Murray Anderson–Robert Milton Studio. This was after Martha had left the Eastman School in Rochester and was just beginning her independent career in New York. Noguchi used to go and watch her "evolving her new and fundamental approach to the dance," as he describes the dancer's early experimental work at the Anderson–Milton School, where he first saw Martha teach.

With the years, their relationship grew into one of firm trust and affection. "I respected and loved him," said Martha. "We worked together without problems," said the sculptor. "I felt that I was an extension of Martha, and that she was an extension of me."

How deep the intuitive bonds were between them can be detected in *Frontier*, their first joint enterprise. The very fact that Martha called upon a sculptor and not a painter was the first telling gesture. Until *Frontier*, stage designers for the dance were, for the most part, painters, whose scenery—ostentatious or discreet—was placed at the back or close to the sides of the stage to permit the greatest possible freedom for the performer. Such décors succeeded more in decorating space (in the art nouveau style of Denishawn, for example) than in emphasizing the atmosphere suggested by the dance. Having no need of a visual illusion other than that created by the movement of her body, Martha always danced on a bare stage. Indeed, what kind of a backdrop other than velvet curtains or a lighted cyclorama could serve dances that were stripped to the kinetic elements of impulse, rhythm, and dynamic stress?

Frontier, however, required a vista—a perspective that would immediately extend the viewer's imagination in the direction of the boundless plains of the Midwest. Inconceivable would be a pictorial depiction of those plains—inconceivable in terms of the dynamics of the dance itself, which refused to capitulate to literal references, either in the costume or in the articulation of the performer's feelings. Symbolic imagery was needed: vigorous forms to match the vigor of the movement, spatial openness to match the wide-sweeping gestures of exploration suggested in the original title, *Perspectives*, which at the onset embraced two dances: the first being the solo, *Frontier*; the second, a trio called *Marching Song*, which Martha dropped shortly after its premiere.

Noguchi responded to Martha's needs with a radical concept, as fresh and new for the dance as the innovative scenery devised by the Swiss stage designer Adolphe Appia had been for opera and drama at the turn of the century. As with Appia, Noguchi saw the stage as an arena in which abstract forms could create the necessary theatrical illusion. While the set for *Frontier* had specific references to locale and time, it provided an atmosphere of boundless spaciousness. The upper half of the stage was given as much importance as the dancing area; the two cables rising obliquely in opposite directions from a tethered point behind the short section of a log fence at the rear of the scene seemed to travel onward and upward timelessly through infinity; the fence itself, a little wider than it was high, served to indicate a limited barrier of protection from unknown dangers . . . just enough to safeguard a human being while establishing a look-out toward conquerable domains.

"*Frontier* was my first set," writes Noguchi. "It was for me the genesis of an idea—to wed the total void of theater space to form and action." The clean lines of the cables with their illusion of endless distance echoed Martha's broad-stroked, high-flung movements. Space belonged to her, was part of her, and yet it retained its own identity as she moved through it boldly, defiantly.

Noguchi's set for *Appalachian Spring* with its linear concept of framed space likewise evoked a vista of America's great distances; but this time Martha's intention was not to conquer the wilderness but to establish a protective niche within its vastness. The pure lines of slender wooden poles served to indicate the outline of a simple country dwelling. Extending horizontally and vertically across the left side of the stage (as seen by the audience), they continued the roof line of a small white clapboard wall that had a bench in front of it, presumably the front entrance of the homestead. At the downstage end of the structure was an open area resembling a porch where a rocking chair faced outward. A log fence, similar to the barrier in *Frontier,* only shorter, stood on the opposite side of the stage, providing a place where the Husbandman could pause and scan his pastureland with pride. And the "pulpit," from which the Jonathan Edwards-like minister descended to make his prophetic pronouncements was simply a stylized tree-stump. Nothing could have been more sparse and yet more suggestive of rural Appalachia.

Again and again Noguchi's stage would provide a realm of fascinating geometric or organic forms that dovetailed imaginatively with Martha's themes. The climax of the sculptor's identification with Martha's creativity would come in 1958 with *Clytemnestra.* Yet the Noguchi setting that has no peer in the world of dance for sheer beauty of line and clarity of form is that of *Seraphic Dialogue,* premiered twenty years after *Frontier.* The shining brass tubing that constitutes the towering Chartres-like edifice seems to hold within its airy interior a radiance like that of Joan of Arc herself, the work's protagonist. Here, with the imagery of a constructivist, the sculptor fulfilled his scenic intention to depict "the life of Joan of Arc as a cathedral that fills her consciousness entirely." The soaring, gleaming hoops, triangles, and bars that intersect each other as they climb toward the theater rafters resplendently symbolize the medieval saint's celestial divinations.

It was a total sharing: Martha's prodigious creativity with Noguchi's fecund, responsive imagination. When obsessed by a new idea, Martha would elaborate on every aspect of it: the theme that was germinating within her, the myth or the legend of its inspiration, her special needs onstage. Listening intently to her (sometimes over the telephone), Noguchi absorbed its import and then went to work.

"I do my sculpture for myself, of course," he says frankly; but, somehow, Martha's use of it made it seem as if everything he designed had been made expressly for her—a strange truth, since her actual choreographic manipulation of the forms he devised came after the set was constructed. Then Noguchi's art came alive as though the inert forms had been awaiting Martha's touch. Embracing them as though they were living counterparts of herself, she adapted them to her movements and conversely adapted her movements to their unique contours.

In *Night Journey* she sat on the hourglass stool with such straightness that her body's natural curves seemed but a restatement of the stool's own pinched waist. She used the wide space the sculptor provided for the dancing in *Appalachian Spring* to fling movements energetically across the stage; then springing back onto the porch where Noguchi's lean, straight-backed rocking chair faced the fields, she swung it around joyously and planted herself in it, not to rock, but to kick spiritedly, thus emphasizing the tilt of its angled back. Similarly, she identified with the forked tree at the climax of *Errand into the Maze*, fitting herself into its forms as into a doorway. "The 'doorway' is like suppliant hands, like pelvic bones 'from which the child I never had comes forth, but the only child that comes forth is myself,'" said Martha, according to Noguchi.

And the wire dress in *Cave of the Heart*? Who but Noguchi could have created such an extraordinary combination of prop and costume? "The visual conception was entirely Noguchi's," writes Martin Friedman, "but Graham was specific about an important detail. 'There was one request I made of Isamu at that time. I said I would love to have a dress which shows the spiritual, half-goddess quality of Medea, but I don't want to wear it all the time. I wanted to walk in and out of it. I said I wanted the dress transparent if possible, but I didn't put any limitations on him.'"

Of course, there were limitations, but these only nourished Noguchi's creativity. The dress—to be worn and danced in—had to be portable; to be "walked in and out of" it had to be accessible; and that meant that it had to have its place onstage within the framework of the total theater space. Therefore, it had to be sculpture, too, and of a compatible shape, size, color, and texture. The shining wire dress consists of delicate brass stems or branches radiating from two central bands forming a bodice. When the curtain rises, the dress is seen spread out over the serpentine base where Medea lies crouched as she plots her vengeance. It stands there throughout the action like a scorched, leafless tree. When the moment comes to don it, Martha simply steps into it, but not before she raises it high above her head in a gesture of triumph, for now she has completed her revenge and has only to escape, and the dress, once donned, will become her golden chariot as she ascends to her grandsire's realm in the sun. The sight of a human form caught within the brassy spikes of its wiry branches makes the moment of her ascension a chilling thing to behold.

Such miraculous blendings of ideas and things, of shapes and intentions, developed embryonically, so to speak, between the dancer and the sculptor. When Martha commissioned Noguchi to do a work, his first step, after the deep, identifying listening and absorbing period, would be to make a scale-model based on everything she had said. Then he would invite Martha to his studio.

Walking around the forms and feeling somewhat unsure, Martha would say, "I'd like to think about it overnight."

Come the next day, the sculptor would inform her that he had already changed his designs, realizing that the first models did not fit in with her conception.

Yet, in spite of their miraculous aesthetic rapport, Noguchi's and Martha's philosophical perspectives actually came from opposite directions. Martha was humanistically concerned with man's fate in terms of his psychological awareness. Noguchi, especially at the beginning of his career, was "seeking identity with some primal matter beyond personalities and possessions." Certainly the materials of their mediums could not have been more dissimilar: one, the live, pulsating human body with its transient high-voltage feelings; the other, mathematically conceived or earth-related forms, plus multi-integrated constructions using such diverse materials as metal, stone, marble, ebony, travertine, and paper—the last, closest to the fluency and immateriality of human movement. Still they shared from the beginning a mutual need for utter simplicity of expression.

"In my work I wanted something irreducible, an absence of the gimmicky and clever." This is Noguchi speaking of his aims in 1931, the year that Martha created the clean, sparse, concentrated linear forms of *Primitive Mysteries*. In 1933 he turned more toward communication, "to find a way of sculpture that was humanly meaningful without being realistic, at once abstract and socially relevant." Martha's dances, tantalizingly abstract at first, gradually became more comprehensible through direct emotional relevance, in itself a social act.

But the most interesting philosophical-aesthetic attitude on Noguchi's part is his positive-negative statement "Art should disappear." Disappear?!! Yes, he assures one, it should disappear into its surroundings; should not be looked at as being separate, but should be part of the environment. Once this revolutionary concept settles in the mind, one sees how Noguchi's theatrical designs fulfill their basic intention, as do his outdoor architecturally related settings. Then one remembers the sculptor's own garden within the confines of his block-long studio in Long Island City. Mysterious shapes in stone and metal standing alongside of slender, recently planted trees fill an asymmetrically shaped enclosure. Manhattan is only across the river, but it does not intrude. The vertical lines of the sculptured and natural forms lead the eye upward—very much as the angled cables in *Frontier* illusionistically swung one's attention upward and outward into the vast reaches of space.

———————

When Martha's ship put to port at Piraeus, the fact that Jean Rosenthal, another valuable collaborator, was not on board probably seemed strange to those Olympians who had been following Martha's career out of curiosity or out of concern for their own part in it. For well over a decade, ever since Louis had suggested that Jean take over the lighting during one of Martha's dress rehearsals at the Guild Theatre in the thirties, the petite young woman with the uncanny ability to suffuse the stage with almost palpable luminosity had been Martha's treasured lighting designer. But there were valid reasons for Rosenthal's absence.

Already in January 1947, she had become responsible for the lighting of two new Balanchine works for Ballet Society, whose general director, Lincoln Kirstein, had also discovered Jean's gift for working "magic with . . . electrical equipment." Directors John Houseman and Orson Welles had likewise recognized her special talents. By February Rosenthal had created the designs for the premiere of *Errand into the Maze,* and shortly afterward she was hard at work on the lighting plot for *Night Journey* which once done permitted her to resume work with Ballet Society. In spirit, of course, Jean was on board the "Jocasta," for she and Martha "had one particular bond in common, which was a passion for Greek myths."

No Graham collaborator was more devoted than Jean Rosenthal. As a young girl she had learned the particulars of her craft when a student at the Neighborhood Playhouse School of the Theatre, where she soon became technical assistant to Martha. Struck by Martha's "intense sensuality and . . . equally intense spirituality," Jean threw herself into an association that was to last thirty-seven years. Their relationship became one of mutual respect, balanced, so to speak, on a beam of intuitive light. Jean referred to Martha's "silent collaboration . . . her silence a recognition of the dignity of another person's talent." Martha spoke of Jean's "dedication to as near perfection as possible"—and of her belief that "the theatre is a place to project the interior landscape, which is man's soul." It was a professional relationship that spawned fifty-three productions, many of them masterpieces.

Into Jean's sensitive, capable hands Martha placed her entire Greek cycle. The nervous tension that enveloped Martha's Ariadne at the beginning of *Errand into the Maze* seemed to vibrate in the starkly lighted stage. Medea's final ascent in *Cave of the Heart* became a shimmering, terrifying thing in the golden aura of Jean's lighting. And the glow that fell on Jocasta's upturned face when she was being wooed by Oedipus made the womanly queen seem but a young girl experiencing her first love. "The lighting came from Martha, the interior of Martha," wrote Jean. "The changes were keyed to the physical impulse, the human body, not to the music or the forms." Doubtlessly true, but the lighting also came from Jean, whose innate awareness of how to create a Hellenic atmosphere of sunlight crossed by dark despair rendered Martha's interpretations of Greek tragedy more vivid. Her precisely formulated lighting plots became the final, decisive means of conveying the true meaning of the work as a whole, once the set, costumes, props, accompaniment, and movement came together on the stage. Intangible and evanescent, Jean's lighting made Martha's visions a theatrical reality.

"Designing for the dance has been my most constant love," declared the woman whose technical skill not only illuminated the stage poetically but also enabled one to perceive the import of a dance movement as originally conceived by the choreographer. When she designed a set for Martha (she did three), Jean wove space and décor together. In *Plain of Prayer* the narrow, softly hanging high silk panels across the rear of the stage permitted movement to flow as naturally between them as did the changing patterns of light on the backdrop behind them. Her wide-spread set of obliquely slanted frames placed centerstage provided the simplest of visual effects for *One More Gaudy Night*, Martha's Antony–Cleopatra escapade with Paul Taylor and Ethel Winter as the irrepressible lovers.

So close was Rosenthal to the dramatic, comic, or lyric verity of Martha's dances that her lighting seemed inseparable from the movement itself. Until her death in 1969, she was both collaborator and friend to Martha. The nourishment she felt on her part was

Chapter Eight
A Lyrical Lull on Olympus

It must have been with mixed feelings of regret and relief that the gods on Mount Olympus saw Martha's ship depart for the premiere of *Night Journey*, which was not to be in Athens, but in Cambridge, Massachusetts. Only the research, deep and extensive, had been carried out during Martha's metaphorical sojourn with her retinue of collaborators on Hellenic shores.

The gods' own association with Martha could well be called a collaboration, too. It had begun long, long ago without fanfare or deliberate involvement on either side when she composed the sculpturesque *Fragments: Tragedy* and *Comedy* in 1928. By 1931 her inspirational source for the ensemble work *Bacchanale* and her ten-minute solo *Dithyrambic* could be traced directly to the liveliest god of them all: Dionysus. But these were isolated instances. During the fifteen years that elapsed between *Dithyrambic* and *Cave of the Heart* Martha had been content to delve into the rich resources of her native land or into the equally rich resources of her own personality to develop themes that reflected America's "monstrous vital rhythms, crude glowing colors, dynamic economy of gesture" and "the intensity of self-penetration." So it was not until 1946, the official beginning of what came to be known as Martha's Greek Cycle, that the divine family as a whole could be said to have participated in Martha's mythological explorations.

We already know how Aphrodite's and Hera's connivings prepared the groundwork for Medea's revenge in *Cave of the Heart*; and that if it hadn't been for Poseidon, god of the sea, who gave King Minos a remarkably beautiful bull that was irresistible to his wife, Pasiphaë, the Minotaur would never have been born. Without him there would have been no labyrinth for Martha's *Errand into the Maze*.

When it came to *Night Journey,* only the most subtle of collaborations marked the participation of the Olympian divinities. The roles that Apollo and Zeus played were magisterial, as usual; but they were hidden beneath the surface of the action. Apollo's severe punishment of the king and queen of Thebes was a strike from within the royal couple's conscience; and Zeus's blessing of Tiresias with the gift of prophecy, though remaining the backbone of the drama, never disclosed the fact that Zeus had acted out of pity for the young Tiresias, who had incensed Hera with his bold statement that woman's enjoyment in love was ninefold that of a man—a most truthful declaration, since Tiresias had been changed for a short time into a woman. Furious that her secret was divulged, Zeus's shrewish wife had blinded the fellow.

Yet, even for the mighty Zeus, Martha staged a surprise. Contrary to the Sophoclean retelling of the ancient myth, *Night Journey* re-created the ominous story of personal guilt from within the interior of a woman's mind—an absolutely novel approach for Zeus, who was a patriarch in the most rigid sense of the word. In his splendid habitat on Mount Olympus, the subject of feminism had never been discussed. *Night Journey* not only caught the omnipotent Zeus short on his blindness to women's rights, but it set in motion other thoughts that had—as all thoughts do when lying unquestioned —become prejudicial certainties. But rather than wrestle with the discomfort of such conscience-pricking concerns, Zeus returned to the peaceful pleasures of following his chauvinistic principles now that the "Jocasta" had left Hellenic shores. The turbulence engendered by the onslaught of Martha's Greek Cycle would be aerially suspended for a full decade. Not until the monumental *Clytemnestra,* as far ahead as 1958, would the Olympic clan be called into action on Martha's stage. Then Apollo himself and the glorious Athena would be called upon to dance out their royal judgments alongside of King Hades, who would rule the proceedings from his kingdom in the netherworld, where the murdered Clytemnestra would be exiled. The pause was exceedingly welcome.

For Martha, too, a new era was at hand. Sheer lyricism would put its mark on seven out of nine works to be born in the interim decade between the self-condemning Jocasta and the soul-searching Clytemnestra. Two solos would be transformed into group compositions:

Judith and *The Triumph of St. Joan* becoming respectively *Legend of Judith* and *Seraphic Dialogue*. Three of the remaining works were to be company dances: *Canticle for Innocent Comedians, Ardent Song,* and *Wilderness Stair (Diversion of Angels),* the most lyrical of all.

Ironically, *Wilderness Stair* was born in the summer of 1948, the summer that would contain the scars of Louis's departure—a double irony in that the dance was about adoration and young love, and if there had ever been adoration on Martha's part in her youth it was directed toward Louis Horst, who opened her mind to its own creative potential.

Twenty-two years of a relationship that went far beyond mere professional collaboration cannot be severed in a matter of minutes, as it seemed to be on the night of the dress rehearsal for *Wilderness Stair.* Tempers did flare up, but beneath the outbursts there were both deep and superficial reasons. On the surface, the quarrel between Martha and Louis had something to do with the way Louis, who was conducting, took the tempo of Dello Joio's score. The fact that Martha criticized him in front of his musicians irritated Louis, and angry words flew back and forth from the stage to the orchestra pit—a sign that both parties had reached a point of extreme touchiness.

For some time already, an undercurrent of estrangement had been creeping into their relationship. The conjecture is that Louis might have resented the fact that Hawkins had entered Martha's life with such deliberate self-assurance, an attitude that Martha seemed to encourage from the start. That Erick was a splendid dancer and a marvelous partner could only have drawn positive reactions from Louis, whose professional opinions were always clear of personal prejudices. But there was the matter of Martha's new thematic choices necessarily related to the personnel of her enlarged company. Still attached to his love of primitive and archaic forms, Louis could not help but consider her recent works less radical as creations; though he had to concede that she was redirecting her multiple gifts of acting, dancing, choreographing, and scriptwriting into a more comprehensive theatrical form, one that would certainly extend her performing range in the years to come. (Little did he guess that the epic *Clytemnestra* would re-create the primitive-archaic style with a vitality that would lift him off his feet!)

On Martha's part, her most urgent need now seemed to be to use her body to the fullest in whatever style would spring forth from her fertile imagination. Her horizon was expanding. Nothing could hold her back.

The meshing of great personalities is as mysterious as the creative intermingling of art and life. Both Louis and Martha were to go their separate ways after 1948 with no loss to their artistic powers. Louis continued to compose music for dancers (mainly Yuriko and Gertrude Lippincott) and scores for Julian Bryan's documentary films. He would maintain his classes in preclassic and modern dance forms at the Neighborhood Playhouse School of the Theatre and the Connecticut College School of Dance, and would become a member of the Juilliard dance faculty when Martha Hill instituted the dance program there in 1951. In addition there was the monthly issue of *Dance Observer*, over which he presided as editor-in-chief, but he always signed his name in alphabetical order with those of others on the editorial board. His ability to lure fine writers, including Winthrop Sargeant, Paul Love, Robert Sabin, Walter Sorell, Jennie Schulman, Nik Krevitsky, Harry Bernstein, and Arthur Todd, into serving the aims of *Dance Observer* would continue undiminished—as did his choreographic influence over young dancers of the caliber of Pearl Lang, Helen McGehee, Jean Erdman, Paul Taylor, Jennifer Muller, Jack Moore, and others, who recognized the supreme value of his authoritative criticism.

When the shock of parting had subsided, the relationship was resumed with no loss of deep feelings on either side. Always concerned about Louis personally, Martha would telephone him regularly and invite him to watch rehearsals, which meant, of course, that he would give his opinion in the old shotgun manner. No mincing words for Louis. (Once asked by a *Dance Observer* contributor who hadn't seen *Ardent Song* what it was like, Louis answered candidly: "Saw it once, and tried to forget it as soon as possible.")* In many ways, he was still Martha's Rock of Gibraltar. She knew in her heart that no one but Louis could point out the flaws in a new work.

Notwithstanding its personal turmoil, the summer of *Wilderness Stair*'s premiere was eventful on a broad national scale. It marked the birth of the Connecticut College School of Dance. Patterned after, and considered to be an outgrowth of, the Bennington School of Dance

---

*How critical opinions may differ can be seen in John Martin's comment that *Ardent Song* "may well be the richest and the most consistently beautiful of all her rituals."

now that the European war had ended and the educational world could rebalance itself with a more equalized enrollment of men and women, the new summer institution in New London, Connecticut, was dedicated to the same educational ideals as those established by the visionary founders of the Vermont project. Significantly, Martha Hill, who was still teaching concurrently at Bennington and New York University, would act as co-chairman with Connecticut College's dance educator, Ruth Bloomer. Enthusiastically endorsed by President Rosemary Parker, the summer school would sponsor an American Dance Festival on the final weekends of instruction, thereby offering—much in the same manner as Bennington—its resident artists opportunities to present new works.

The vista, of course, was not the same. No rolling mountains stretched southward, but rather an eastern-angled shoreline that looked upon the Atlantic, while a wide river, suitably called the Thames, carved a line parallel to the college campus. Nor did the eye follow the sun each evening conjuring up dramas and spirited dances that evoked the atmosphere of rural America with its historic adventures as well as repressions. Instead, the choreographers' imaginations turned to themes of universal import inspired by the Bible, by Shakespearean tragedy, by poetry, by music, and by the ever-expanding possibilities of mixed media. Among the many fine works presented during the first decade of the American Dance Festival series were José Limón's *The Moor's Pavane, The Exiles,* and *The Traitor;* Doris Humphrey's *Night Spell,* and *Ruins and Visions;* Pauline Koner's *Concertino* and *The Shining Dark;* Ruth Currier's *The Antagonists;* Daniel Nagrin's *Indeterminate Figure;* Sophie Maslow's *The Village I Knew;* and Alwin Nikolais's *Kaleidoscope*—all compositions of stature that would enrich the art of modern dance.

The crown jewel of the first season's premieres would be *Wilderness Stair.* But in Martha's eyes, as rehearsals proceeded, the new piece was not going smoothly. One of the reasons could have been that she was not dancing in it herself and somehow felt removed from the urgency of the commitment. Another reason could have been that Norman Dello Joio's music was, in his own words, "gay and outward . . . not at all the sort of thing she was accustomed to." As Martha did not hear the score until it was finished (a not unusual situation when she commissioned music), it is possible, as Dello Joio presumed, that "she may have been startled," a reaction that he might well have intended since he averred later that he "wanted to see the modern dance get away from its attachment to the umbilical cord." (This was, obviously, a thrust at *Night Journey,* which had had its New York premiere a few months previously.)

At any rate, Martha was experiencing one of those moments of self-doubt that would occasionally seize her, and knowing that her friend Ben Belitt would look at her work with fresh, sensitive eyes, she invited him to a rehearsal. In some mysterious way, the profundity of his poetic images would reinforce her creative perspective.

Rehearsals were being held at Knowlton, one of the older buildings that looked eastward across the college quadrangle. Chandeliers and French windows facing the broad stretch of campus green gave the cleared room the air of an elegant private salon. When Belitt entered, the dancers were in the process of warming up. Attired in practice clothes, they were bending and stretching by themselves in isolated areas of the room and did not seem to take notice of his arrival. Skirting the edges of the dance space, the poet joined Martha near the piano, where Dello Joio's score was spread out on the music rack.

In one corner of the room was Pearl Lang, who looked startlingly like Martha from a distance, only smaller-boned. Her body had the same extraordinary elasticity at the joints, and the movements of her long torso, slender arms, and legs had a similar percussive attack; but in Pearl, there was a lyricism of a special kind. It was evident from the beginning when she came to study with Martha while still enrolled at the University of Chicago, to which she returned after an initial June course. Impressed with her abilities, Martha asked Louis to look her up when he was touring the Midwest as accompanist–music director for Agnes de Mille and to invite her east to become a member of the company. Now Pearl was to make memorable what she called "the ecstasy of the contraction" as the Girl in Red, the later title of the role she created in *Wilderness Stair (Diversion of Angels).*

Not far removed from Lang were Helen McGehee and Natanya Neumann, who were to dance the corresponding leads in the new work (later known respectively as the Girl in Yellow and the Girl in White, though Neumann's costume was originally blue).

A member of the Graham company since 1944, McGehee had a knifelike edge to her movements when performing a dramatic role. Today, however, she was to dance as dartingly as a faun with her partner, Stuart Hodes, one of the composition's four men, including

Mark Ryder, Robert Cohan, and Dale Sehnert. The trio of women who made up the remainder of the cast—Dorothea Douglas, Joan Skinner, and Dorothy Berea—were practicing nearby.

Natanya took her place upstage center. Behind her, slightly to one side, stood Mark Ryder. With the music's first chords, he raised his hand high above her and with fingers outstretched struck the image of a halo behind her head. Then he repeated the gesture, moving around her as if performing a ritual of adoration. One by one the three other men leaped in from the wings, and circling around Natanya, paid homage to her with Ryder joining them.

From the "downstage right wing," quietly moving toward the center, came Lang. Pausing every few steps to strike a tilted position—right leg extending obliquely into the air, arms likewise extended sideways—she looked like a butterfly impaled upon a pin. A sharp contraction of the torso, another quiet step across the room, another high sideways extension, another contraction, then she disappeared behind "the proscenium arch." The mood changed as other dancers filled the room, turning it into a place of revelry where boys and girls danced exuberantly together.

In the middle of a playful duet, two dancers stopped, gazed at each other rapturously, and then resumed their joyous camaraderie in a whirl of excitement. The mood was now one of amorous interminglings, but suddenly it all stopped. Dello Joio's music trailed off, and the dancers faced Martha in silence. She had yet to devise the ending. Unable to commit herself at the moment, Martha said nothing. Just before the premiere she would have that flash of inspiration which would yield one of the most effective endings of any of her compositions: a sudden return to the dance's opening statement—the ritual of the halo—following Pearl Lang's last spirited diagonal cross-stage run to the final passage of music.

Watching intently, Belitt seemed to share the dancers' many-hued feelings. A kaleidoscope of images filled his mind. Later he sifted them through, writing them down for Martha:

It is the place of the Rock and the Ladder, the raven, the blessing, the tempter, the rose. It is the wish of the single-hearted, the undivided: play after the spirit's labor: games, flights, fancies, configurations of the lover's intention: the believed Possibility, at once strenuous and tender: humors of innocence, garlands, evangels, Joy on the Wilderness Stair, diversion of angels.

So, at first, Martha's new dance was called *Wilderness Stair,* the title of a book of poems that Belitt was to publish at a later date. By the second performance, Martha had changed *Wilderness Stair* to *Diversion of Angels.*

----·-·-·----

On the surface, at least in the beginning, Martha's and Erick's marriage and professional life seemed to be meshing successfully. With his strong business sense, Erick had become more and more preoccupied with the booking and management of the Graham company. No premieres were slated for 1949; but on January 4, 1950, Martha appeared with the Louisville Symphony Orchestra in an ambitious twenty-five-minute solo, *Judith,* to a commissioned score by William Schuman. With the orchestra onstage with her but somewhat hidden behind a translucent curtain, the dancer sought to depict the complex emotions of the legendary Biblical character prior to and following her murder of Holofernes, the chief general of the warring king of Assyria. As told in the Apocryphal Book of Judith, the young widow took off her mourning garments and dressed herself in seductive finery to penetrate the Assyrian camp in order to save her people from defeat in 350 B.C. Described by Graham as "a woman who does not want to leave the area of her sorrow to go out to face her Destiny," the introspective Judith would be the second of Martha's heroines to be transformed (like Medea) into a militant personality for the accomplishment of a specific malice. Judith's motivations, however, were self-sacrificial in contrast to Medea's bitterly contrived revenge.

A theme of such massive proportions would hardly seem manageable by a single dancer. But Martha's sheer artistry in the manipulation of the narrative made the solo dance-drama not only credible but stirring. With its score by William Schuman and its original setting by Charles Hyman and William Sherman, *Judith* was greeted enthusiastically at its Louisville premiere. By the time it was presented later in the year at Carnegie Hall, Noguchi had been called in to redesign the set with his typical semi-abstract forms.

Martha's relationship to music in general, and to Schuman's score in particular, was succinctly described two years later when she spoke of her compositional approach to a commissioned score: "I gave

William Schuman the idea for Judith—a script. I also gave him the Apocryphal quotations." The enlistment of the composer was the first act. "I never work away from the music. I never start to compose until I get the music. You are completely caught and held in the form of the music. You must accept all the limitations as well . . . Isadora Duncan was essentially moved by the music. Very often, however, I have been moved by the idea of the dance almost beyond being moved by the music."

John Martin had perceived this tendency previously when he wrote of Graham: "Her essential quality of movement is neither spatial nor musical but dramatic."

As far as *Judith* was concerned, the spatial as well as the musical limitations served Martha well. With her acute sense of timing, she chose not to dance to the music's opening and closing sections, but condensed the action into tightly packed narrative sequences to fit the space in which she performed: a restricted area between the orchestra and the stage's edge. Noguchi's symbolic but highly practical set and wealth of props made such pared-down choices possible. A standing support of crossed spears terminating in an upward-jutting phallic form, and a horizontal wooden beam covered with a draped cloth, had the royal appearance of Holofernes's tent. Opposite the tent was a huge balsa-wood lyre that served also as Judith's loom.

Martha said of the performance:

> I dressed myself on the stage. All the jewelry hung on the back of the lyre, and piece by piece, I put it on. It was a belt, a very big necklace, a snake armband, a headdress and a veil, and it took absolute concentration, because I had no mirror in front of me.
>
> The fabric over the animal in the tent was a very deep purple [designed by Martha, as was her sheath-like costume]—not blue purple, but Tyrian purple. It hung in folds, and I went to it, and then there was a moment when the stage was empty of action. Slowly, slowly I pulled down the curtain until Judith stood there alone and in her hands she had two branches of white flowers and the dance ended by her crossing the stage with those flowers.

How strongly Martha identified with her characters can be seen in the mixture of "she" and "I."

Such intermingling of oneself with a character is a natural attribute of a fine actor. Martha could be just as convincing when playing the role of a superficial woman as that of a Biblical heroine. Frivolous as was the scenario of *Gospel of Eve* (the solo created for the season that followed *Judith*), a fascinating point of philosophical reference was hidden in the depth of the characterization. Heart-shaped mirrors were used as props in *Gospel of Eve*—a miniature but clear echo of *Herodiade* with its theme of aging. "When a woman looks in a mirror . . . and if she's approaching the time when she's no longer young, she sees her skeleton, she sees her bones. . . . With *Herodiade*, it is a moment of decision when she faces the fact that she is no longer young—she is no longer a radiant young thing."

The success of the late January season at the 46th Street Theatre seemed to bode well for Martha and Erick artistically. The fact that Martha had felt inspired to create a ballet specifically for Erick would seem to represent a deposit of faith in his artistry, as well as in her own vision of a permanent relationship. Fascinated by the character of King Lear, Martha considered that the real meaning of Shakespeare's play was to be found in "Lear's mind." In one of her notebooks she wrote: "Storm and madness—tremendously real, but we are never allowed to forget the moral disorders of which they are both symbols." Casting Erick in the leading role, she set about interpreting the tragedy after studying Coleridge, Granville Barker, and Joseph Campbell on the subject.

Eye of Anguish, subtitled *A Purgatorial History of King Lear*, was received warmly in January 1950, but strangely enough, the work was not scheduled for the company's much-anticipated European tour—a tour that was planned with the financial help of the Baroness Bethsabée de Rothschild, who had offered to contribute to major costs of spring and summer seasons in Paris and London, respectively. The European tour was to be the beginning of the baroness's strong support of Martha, of whom she had expressed her deep admiration in a book entitled *La Dance Artistique aux États-Unis d'Amérique*, published in 1949.

Unfortunately, the tour—the first prolonged foreign tour in Martha's career—was to mark the end of Martha's and Erick's relationship. A severe knee injury on opening night in Paris made it impossible for Martha to continue performing, and after one performance in which the company danced unsuccessfully without her the season was canceled. The London season likewise had to be canceled—a situation intolerable to the already disappointed and disgruntled dancer. And, as if it were not enough to be incapacitated

Martha Graham in *Deep Song* (seated), 1937. Photograph by Barbara Morgan.

Martha Graham in *Deep Song* (on floor), 1937. Photograph by Barbara Morgan.

Martha Graham in *Deep Song* (standing), 1937. PHOTOGRAPH BY BARBARA MORGAN.

Martha Graham and Erick Hawkins in Puritan Love Duet from *American Document*, 1940. PHOTOGRAPH BY BARBARA MORGAN.

Martha Graham in *El Penitente*, 1940. Photograph by Barbara Morgan.

Martha Graham and Erick Hawkins in *Letter to the World*, 1940. Photograph by Barbara Morgan.

Martha Graham, Erick Hawkins, and Jean Erdman in *Letter to the World*, 1940.
PHOTOGRAPH BY BARBARA MORGAN.

Martha Graham in *Letter to the World*, 1940. PHOTOGRAPH BY BARBARA MORGAN.

Erick Hawkins, Martha Graham, and Merce Cunningham in *Deaths and Entrances*, 1945.
Photograph by Barbara Morgan.

Double image: Martha Graham, plus John Butler, Martha Graham, Jane Dudley, Erick Hawkins, Merce Cunningham, and Sophie Maslow in *Deaths and Entrances*, 1945. PHOTOGRAPH BY BARBARA MORGAN.

Martha Graham and Erick
Hawkins in *Dark Meadow*.
PHOTOGRAPH BY PHILIPPE
HALSMAN. COURTESY DANCE
COLLECTION, NEW YORK
PUBLIC LIBRARY.

Martha Graham in *Cave of
the Heart*. COURTESY DANCE
COLLECTION, NEW YORK
PUBLIC LIBRARY.

Martha Graham and Bertram Ross in *Night Journey*. Photograph by Martha Swope.

with an injury, Erick left her to her own devices in her London hotel and went off with friends for hours on end. Reproachful feelings on both sides led to vituperative exchanges, which in turn led to a separation, the inevitable result of deep-seated conflicts between two strong-willed personalities. The pain of that separation would take its toll on Martha's emotional life for many years to come.

It was a defeat for the company, as well. Disconsolate, they returned home without having had the gratification of really performing abroad. Their director went to the Southwest to recover.

Once back in her apartment, Martha took to reading omnivorously, as was her natural wont. On her night table was a weighty book of Aeschylus's plays containing *Agamemnon, The Libation Bearers,* and *The Eumenides;* alongside of it lay a volume of Robinson Jeffers's poetry. In the latter, a bookmark was slipped between the pages of a play entitled *The Tower Beyond Tragedy.* A peek inside would have informed the reader that Jeffers's play was also about Clytemnestra, Agamemnon's queen.

For the moment, however, any compulsions to create further dance dramas based on Greek mythology were to be swept aside. A few months after the European debacle, Martha was on the stage in the Carnegie Hall performance of *Judith.* There were, however, physical and emotional difficulties: her knee was not fully healed, and the struggle to live alone was often agonizing.

It would take almost a year before she could dance at her usual high performing level. Once more commissioned by the Louisville Symphony Orchestra, she would choose Norman Dello Joio as her music collaborator. Whatever theme Martha might have been conjuring up in the recesses of her creative imagination, it was obviously relegated to some future point or dropped completely during the course of her initial meeting with Dello Joio, when the composer began describing the work he was currently writing: a symphonic rendering of the life of Joan of Arc as maid, warrior, and saint. Like a match struck in darkness, the idea instantly took hold of Graham. Another lyrical dance to Dello Joio's melodious music would come into being; this time, a solo of grandiose proportions.

In *The Triumph of Saint Joan* Martha tried to carry the entire weight of the legend of France's savior, from the first time she heard the voices of St. Catherine, St. Michael, and St. Margaret through the war with England, and finally, to her martyrdom at the stake at the hands of the English in Rouen.

171

Love, with its quickened pulse and bounty of feeling, had been the theme of *Diversion of Angels*. Now, faith—purest of human passions—was to take possession of Martha's imagination. Joan of Arc was essentially a lyrical figure, despite the tragic circumstances of her conflict with the church and her martyrdom at the stake. In contrast to Emily Brontë, Medea, and Jocasta (whom Martha called her "dark ladies") Joan was a simple woman whose purpose in life was to fulfill the spiritual commandments of the three saints who spoke to her in her parents' garden in Domrémy. The young girl's personality was unclouded by the complex feelings of thwarted ambition, jealousy, revenge, or guilt that plagued the other characters. A glorious spiritual light, guided by faith, was to spread over Martha's newest work, making it possible for her to forget temporarily the pain of private loss.

She steeped herself in the fifteenth-century world of the Maid of Orléans; the pastoral life of the peasant folk of Joan's background; the religious fervor of the girl, her innocence of international politics, her resoluteness as a soldier, her fears, and her final victory over her enemies.

> It was Norman Dello Joio's idea and he wrote it in three sections and I took his suggestions. He gave it to me complete . . . this dance is not her actual life in any sense. It is what one imagines might have passed through her mind at various times. Because of the title, it had to be treated not from the point of view of her life but from the point of the possible condition of ecstasy which led her to do what she did. In that sense, I had no grounds to go on except what I imagined went on in her heart. These are *interior landscapes* and not the episodes of her life.

But *The Triumph of Saint Joan* failed as a solo work. Too much had to be said about the inner circumstances of Joan's life, and the solo form with its slender scaffolding could not support the telling of such big experiences as the battle scene and the saint's final spiritual triumph at the stake. Martha worked on it valiantly between the Louisville performance in 1951 and its Juilliard premiere sixteen months later, but the dance was overpowered by its script.

> I was not happy about St. Joan. I felt that I had missed. I was on the train going to California. Suddenly, out of nowhere, I wasn't thinking about anything. . . . "Of course, that's where you failed . . . in the last dance." I had stepped out of the last dance and portrayed a mood.

Joseph Wiseman [the actor] discovered what it was that I missed. "You must plant the lance . . . use it as a stake." The relationship to an object can be very intense and can change everything.

Wiseman was referring to the twelve-foot lance Martha used in the battle scene.

Four years later, Martha's conception of St. Joan would be reborn as a large-scale composition danced by seven characters. Norman Dello Joio's score remained intact, but a whole new production met the eye when the curtain rose on *Seraphic Dialogue* in May 1955. Noguchi's gleaming cathedral-like construction and Martha's Florentine-colored costumes transformed the stage into a radiant medieval setting. As if enthroned upon an altar sat St. Michael in brilliant blue; on each side of him, in niches of their own, were the violet-clad St. Margaret and St. Catherine; at St. Michael's feet was Joan, dressed in bright red. "Joan of Arc was aflame with passion. Like a Buddhist monk, she burned herself up."

As in *Letter to the World,* Martha split the personality of the leading character into component parts. The central Joan, who would be canonized as a saint, embodied three other Joans: the Maid, the Warrior, and the Martyr. The action took place at "the instant" of an encounter with Destiny—reminiscent of *Deaths and Entrances,* of *Herodiade,* of *Night Journey*—when Joan looked back upon her life at her moment of supreme exaltation and relived it through the lens of memory.

Clearly, Martha had reincarnated her original Joan into a figure of transcendent beauty, giving her celestial proportions under the title of *Seraphic Dialogue.*

A copper-skinned young man, naked except for a loincloth, was reclining face-downward on a narrow sloping platform that was only slightly wider and higher than himself. An amber spotlight shone down upon him, leaving the rest of the stage in darkness. Clinging all the while to the sculptured surface, the dancer began to stretch slowly, sensuously, like a huge lizard half-asleep on a golden embankment.

The curtain had just risen on *Canticle for Innocent Comedians,* a dance "in praise of the Earth as it turns." Rendered allegorically was the generating power of all life: the Sun.

Six lovely girls appeared. They were the mortals, the innocent comedians,

Who bear belief, like coronal,
And tender tokenings. . . .

With cheerful mien they moved the Sun and his platform offstage and prepared for the entrance of Earth, whose movements were richly expressive of the lushness of autumn's harvest. Then came the Wind, sweeping wildly across the scene; and Water and Fire in mock battle.

Once more the stage was reset, and the six girls lingered to see their handiwork while leaning against portable frames that served as part of the changing décor. The scaffolding of a double window was then placed in the center, and a white-robed figure, serene of face, round of gesture, slipped into view; watching spellbound on an adjacent windowsill was a Pierrot-like figure, a bewitched observer of the eternally fascinating Moon.

The landscape changed. A fragile frame of a structure with steps leading from it was moved into place upstage right. Enveloped in black, Death appeared, beautiful and cruel. A chill ran through the audience as she wound her way forward with movements that were strangely menacing. But now the doors of the framed structure opened, and within the silhouette of the doorway stood Earth, dressed in pale green. In each hand she carried a flowering branch, symbol of spring and rebirth. Quietly taking possession of the stage as Death withdrew, she seemed to anoint the ground with fresh life.

Was this the choreographer who had said, "I did not wish to be a tree, a flower, or a wave"? Ah, but that was eleven years previously. Though Martha would always honor "the miracle that is a human being," by 1952 she was drawing fresh inspiration from her surrounding world. Nature with its myriad, often undecipherable, forces was luring her into its own grand choreographic plan.

Martha's dance "in praise of the Earth as it turns" was indeed prophetic. *Canticle for Innocent Comedians* would soon be turning with the earth it praised. In February 1954 the Graham company would perform *Canticle for Innocent Comedians* in London, Holland, Sweden, Denmark, Belgium, and Paris. London had mixed reviews until the critic Richard Buckle turned the tide by calling attention to Martha's "life-enhancing qualities" and declaring that Graham "is one of the great creators of our time." The company tasted fame as Europe, when enchanted, can give it, freely, enthusiastically. In Paris, where they gave six performances at the Théâtre des Champs Elysées, Martha was honored with a medal from the city, a tribute that glowed with national pride in having such a distinguished guest.

Writing to Louis from Antwerp, Martha stated proudly that one member of the audience had ridden a motorbike from Hanover to Amsterdam; and that another had done the same from the Polar Circle to Stockholm. Proud of Louis's role in her success, she assured him that all her press conferences contained references to him; and going one step further in her appreciation of her mentor's influence on her own career, she spoke of his invaluable gift for stimulating individual creativity in the modern dance world at large.

By late May the company had played Italy, where Martha had experienced the emotional extremes of being utterly enchanted by Florence and of having to share her program with an opera company in Florence's 3,000-seat Communale. Not only did the pre-performance backstage furor of more than forty vociferous stagehands, plus policemen, firemen, and wardrobe personnel, make Martha's hands tremble as she applied her makeup, but on one occasion the audience itself became nearly uncontrollable during a performance of *Night Journey*. Only by advancing to the stage's edge with unmistakable warning gestures did Martha succeed in quieting the obstreperous public.

In writing from Turin to her friend Arthur Todd, prior to leaving for Zurich and Venice, Martha admitted that the tour's diverse experiences yielded fresh perspectives on her own personal as well as artistic growth. As was her wont, she visualized a time of rebirth . . . a premonition, perhaps, of the vital creative investment that would produce a major new work four years hence: *Clytemnestra*.

Two days after her arrival back home, Martha started teaching her usual June course. Actually she felt triumphant, not exhausted; the sense of having established an aesthetic rapport with Europe revitalized her. It completely wiped out the black remembrances of her disastrous 1950 tour.

Then came the most triumphant tour of all. From late October 1955 to early March 1956 the ancient countries of Japan, the Philippines, Thailand, Indonesia, Burma, India, Iran, and Israel, where dancing has been revered and practiced as an art since antiquity, were host to Martha and her company. With her were her musical director, Eugene Lester, her manager, Leroy Leatherman, her press representative, Craig Barton—a man of great sensitivity and understanding—and her good friend the Baroness de Rothschild, who had sponsored the preceding spring season in New York when *Seraphic Dialogue* had premiered. For Martha, it was a time of identification with a part of the world that had always bewitched her.

The State Department–sponsored Asian and Mideast tour (known as ANTA), which opened in Tokyo on November 1, was to engender overwhelming response from all countries visited, including those that had never before been exposed to the new art of modern dance.

Eugene Lester had left for Tokyo approximately three weeks ahead of the company to work with the orchestra. The Japanese musicians' reaction to the thoroughly Western music of the Graham repertoire was highly enthusiastic. (After Tokyo, tapes would be used throughout the tour.) By the time the company arrived, what with advance publicity and a lecture-demonstration prior to the opening night's performance of *Diversion of Angels, Night Journey,* and *Appalachian Spring,* excitement was running high on both sides of the footlights. Certainly Martha was rising to the enormous challenge of conquering the Orient, as had her predecessors, Ruth St. Denis and Ted Shawn, on their historic 1925–1927 Oriental tour. And conquer she did, everywhere, beginning with the Japanese public, the Tokyo dance elite, the press, and even the royalty of the Land of the Rising Sun. By the end of four performances in a 2,000-seat theater "packed with standees" the audience was wildly throwing flowers and confetti on the stage, and setting off fireworks, Japanese style, in a closing night party.

In Manila the company danced on an elevated platform encircled by thousands of spectators, an experience similar in scope to performances given in Rangoon, Burma, on an especially constructed teakwood stage for audiences of nearly five thousand people. The *Manila Evening News* described the dancing as celebrating "the beauty and reality of the human body, even as it claws deep into the human heart." In Jakarta, Indonesia, where restrictions involved additional visa requirements and special inspections, performances were sold out in advance and a special matinee for students (also sold out) had to be added.

The climax of the tour (now fully two months old) came in India, where, despite having endured the many discomforts that plague Westerners in the Far East—stomach disorders, uncomfortable dressing and washing conditions, and unfamiliar food—Martha and the company blazed through performance after performance in such remotely connected places as Calcutta, Madras, Bombay, New Delhi, and finally Karachi. In Madras the publication *The Hindu* reported that "Martha Graham, through her art, was helping to bring people together and cure them of narrow prejudice."

By February they were in Israel, having played Teheran with similar success. In the words of the cashier of the Habimah Theater in Tel-Aviv, there was a "massive and unrestrained" fever to obtain tickets to a Graham performance. The poor man was stampeded "in the streets, in the buses, wherever I happened to be or to pass, days and nights alike!"

The accumulated excitement was certainly wearing, but Martha, characteristically, was nourished by it. Rest after the tour's end on March 4 in the homeland of the baroness completely restored her; and before much time elapsed she flew over to Greece for a fortnight of wonderful impressions. She went to Delphi, where Apollo's oracle had foretold Laius's murder by his son, Oedipus; and with bated breath she walked the Sacred Way in Eleusir. She had the deeply moving experience of passing through the Lion Gateway to Agamemnon's palace at Mycenae—an act that presaged, no doubt, her future role as Clytemnestra.

Greece was quietly restorative after weeks of being feted by royalty and populace alike. In Tokyo there had been visits from Prince Chichibu, brother of the emperor, and also from the great Japanese classical dancer O-Han-San; in Thailand the company had been invited to give a special performance on the lawn of one of the Prince's estates; and in Iran the shah had requested a command performance in his palace. Quoted in *Dance Observer*, Martha remarked, "I do not know how we can do it, but we will try to work something out."

Greece was the Western world, full of clarity, logic, and common sense, in contrast to the mystic philosophy of the East. Greece represented the rational mind with its "insight that the world is system, is organic, therefore both orderly and alive." To fall under its sway again was intoxicating, a kind of contradication of impulses that seized her; yet, as with everything in life, opposites make an entity. From the metaphysical Far East to the clear-cut West is but a short step . . . when reality leads the way.

Side by side with the mystic, the realist in Martha absorbed the wonders of Greece, stored them in a secret place, and then turned to practical matters of the moment.

Such a moment was waiting for her when she returned to her own shores at the end of April: a film project, commissioned by WQED of Pittsburgh. To be titled *A Dancer's World,* the film would afford her an opportunity to present her personal philosophy (that marvelous mixture of East and West), her dance technique, and excerpts from the company's repertoire. Producer Nathan Kroll, a former concert violinist and conductor, conceived the idea of Martha narrating the film as if she were preparing herself backstage in her dressing room for a performance of *Night Journey.*

Wearing a Japanese *happi* coat, she is seen sitting in front of a large mirror making herself up. Her opening words are: "The theatre dressing room is a very special place. It is where the act of theatre begins—and make-up is a kind of magic." We see her transform herself into the character of Queen Jocasta. "You make up your face as you think she might have looked; you dress your hair as you think she might have dressed hers." With a deft touch of the hands, she readies her high-piled chignon into place for the large decorative pin that will be worn crosswise in front of it."And then, there comes a moment when she looks at you in the mirror, and you realize that she is looking at you and recognizing you as herself. It is through you, her love, her hope, her fear, her terror, is to be expressed."

The scene changes to the studio, where eleven dancers enter one by one in phrased sequences of individualized movement. In that sacred practicing space, seven women and four men —Yuriko, Helen McGehee, Gene McDonald, Ellen Siegel, Robert Cohan, Miriam Cole, David Wood, Lillian Biersteker, Bertram Ross, Ethel Winter, and Mary Hinkson—move ritualistically through a choreographed series of Martha's exercises. "It is here in the studio that the dancer learns his craft, the mastery of his instrument, which is the human body.... This required discipline ... not drill ... not something imposed from without ... but discipline imposed by you yourself upon yourself."

The harmonious rhythms of Cameron McCosh's score resound as the dancers spiral into falls, perform contractions while seated on the floor, rise smoothly and still dancing cross to the barre, where they continue their technical studies. With lyrical abandon, three sets of couples dance duets from *Diversion of Angels;* a fourth couple dances the Sarabande from *Dark Meadow*. Breath-filled turns and intricate lifts create an aura of absolute physical control. "When a dancer is at the peak of his power he has two lovely, fragile, perishable things —one is spontaneity—but it is something arrived at over years and years of training; . . . the other is simplicity—but it is also a different simplicity; it is the state of complete simplicity 'costing no less than everything' of which Mr. T. S. Eliot speaks."

Jocasta's gown is brought in by the dresser. And when Martha had donned it and put into place at the base of the V-neckline the brooch that Oedipus will tear off in his desperate act of self-blinding, the personality of Queen Jocasta becomes complete. She is ready to live once more that "instant when she recognizes the ultimate terms of her destiny."

Once completed, the film would travel back to Europe to win prizes at film festivals in Czechoslovakia, Venice, Edinburgh, and Carlsbad.

The dazzling light of lyricism was still in Martha's eyes when she received, along with her friend Agnes de Mille, the 1957 *Dance Magazine* Award at the Plaza Hotel. Agnes de Mille was honored for "bringing the art of dance to new millions" with two Omnibus television productions the preceding year; while Martha was praised by Paul Grey Hoffman, director of the United Nations Special Fund, as being "the greatest single ambassador we have ever sent to Asia."

Though she accepted the tribute with *grande dame* graciousness, Martha had private reservations. *Single* ambassador? That was a bit too much of a compliment. When a statesman like Paul Hoffman spoke of Martha's achievements as though they were accomplished singlehandedly, she felt she should protest. Her works could not exist without the dancers who made them live! Of all her collaborators they were the most essential. The very plot or mood of a piece, even the setting in which it was visualized, could only come to life through the individual efforts of her company members. Their individual characteristics peopled her imagination. In addition to those who appeared in the film there were Linda Hodes, Paul Taylor, Matt Turney, Stuart Hodes, and others coming up like Akiko Kanda, Richard Gain, Richard Kuch, Ellen Graff, and Dan Wagoner, to mention the most promising of the new recruits. Without her company dancers the ambassadorship would have been impossible! Then there was her friend the Baroness de Rothschild, whose generosity contributed to the spreading of good will to foreign lands.

Something else, too, was beginning to annoy Martha. She was tired of being looked upon as a phenomenon. One radio interviewer who had gushed about her amazing contributions to the world and about her having found "her own way" was instantly put down when Martha replied in the coolest tones she could command, "But I didn't find my own way. My own way was visited upon me."

Then, to the lady's surprise, Martha came up with one of her typical non-sequitors and uttered the not-unfamiliar names of Anna Pavlova, Isadora Duncan, Ruth St. Denis, and Mary Wigman. She then went on to say, "You make the reverence to the great dancer not out of slavery, but because you serve some deep, deep thing together."

One could almost hear the interviewer gasp as she made an effort to understand her guest's remarks. Hoping to ameliorate the situation, she murmured something about Miss Graham's extraordinary "creativity." At that, one could almost see Martha's amber-flecked eyes turn dark with fury. Had not the word creativity, used superficially, irked her countless times? Had she not clearly, emphatically, spoken at length on the subject?

"I do not make a vision of creativity," she had been heard to say, "I never use the word. I live and work out of Necessity . . . as deeply and commitally as an animal. There is no choice. As an animal lives, eating, drinking, begetting one's young without pretense or ambition. It is the water of life!"

And in one of those rapid, mysterious shifts of thought that would flutter the ears of those around her, Martha, almost inaudibly, mentioned something about a "deep sense of family tragedy" and the ominous words "Greece is not so different from New England" were heard.

What did she mean? That tragedy is the same the world over?

Incomprehensible as Martha's impassioned utterances might seem to simple mortals, up on Mount Olympus Athena trembled. Intuitively grasping her meaning, the goddess of wisdom suddenly saw visions of the House of Atreus—Agamemnon, Electra, Iphigenia, Orestes, Clytemnestra—a family doomed by its own misdeeds.

Quite obviously, Martha's mind was set: Noguchi had been summoned; the Egyptian composer Halim El-Dabh was already hard at work; Jean Rosenthal was happily scheming a light plot; and company members, headed by Helen McGehee, a scholar of Greek drama, were avidly rereading Aeschylus's *The Oresteia.*

180

Summoning Apollo, Athena vowed she would make amends for her unseemly display of vanity over the apple that started the Trojan War. Together she and the god of light would stand as a tribunal, judging the final crime of the House of Atreus. They alone would be able to lift the burden of guilt borne from an ancient curse.

She buckled on her armor. (Besides being goddess of wisdom, Athena was goddess of war.) Martha's conception called for nothing less than a retrospective view of Trojan battlefields and Greek homecomings.

The lyrical lull that lasted ten peaceful years on Mount Olympus had come to an end.

Chapter Nine
The Darkest Lady

The barbaric splendor of war-embroiled Greece provided the background. It was matched by taut, archaic movement starkly evocative of pagan times. But the action did not follow a chronological unfolding of events; instead it obeyed the same irrational logic of emotional flashbacks as in *Deaths and Entrances* and *Night Journey*. Far from being a straight-lined reenactment of Aeschylus's *The Oresteia*, Martha Graham's *Clytemnestra* took the form of a panoramic procession of remembered experiences witnessed from the depths of the murdered queen's mind. Introspection would again supply the choreographic impulse and framework.

Choosing Noguchi once more as her scenic collaborator, and adventurously inviting the Egyptian composer Halim El-Dabh to write the score—one of the most brilliant in her entire repertory—Martha dared the impossible: an evening-long ballet based on moral values encountered in the psyche.

Ten years and ten dances after *Night Journey*, her last Greek work, Martha would choose to think once more, and on an even grander scale, in terms of that climactic moment in individual experience when an emotional crisis would reveal the depths or the heights to which a human being could fall or rise. She had probed these moments in *Cave of the Heart* and *Night Journey*, respectively, using Medea's venomous hatred as the motif for destruction, and Jocasta's suicide as evidence of supreme nobility of character.

Unlike Medea, Clytemnestra was no enchantress endowed with supernatural powers. Nor was she a beauty over whom a war would be fought.

You'd never have thought the Queen was Helen's sister—
Troy's burning-flower from Sparta, the beautiful seaflower
Cut in clear stone, crowned with the fragrant golden mane,
she the ageless, the uncontaminable—
This Clytemnestra was her sister, low-statured, fierce-
lipped, not dark nor blonde, greenish-gray-eyed,
Sinewed with strength, you saw, under the purple folds
of the queen-cloak, but craftier than queenly. . . .

So begins Robinson Jeffers's long poem *The Tower Beyond Trage-dy*, which doubtless added another dimension to Martha's thoughts as she studied it alongside of Aeschylus's *Agamemnon, The Libation Bearers,* and *The Eumenides.*

Unlike Medea, Clytemnestra was a woman of natural capacities, but her instinct for revenge was similarly destructive; it also verged on the abnormal. She, too, harbored a serpent in her heart, nursing it for ten long years while Agamemnon was at war . . . nursing it for eventual retaliation for his killing of their youngest daughter, Iphigenia. In Martha's words, Clytemnestra was an "angry, wild, wicked woman," for she was not only a murderess and an adulteress but a person of inordinate pride and spitefulness. Even after death she exudes hate, this time for her son, who killed her in revenge for the death of his father. In the meanness of her spirit, she sends the Furies to torment Orestes. When he stands triumphant over her body—and that of her lover, Aegisthus—he suddenly sees (in Aeschylus's words): "Gorgon shapes throng up/Dusky their robes and all their hair enwound/Snakes coiled with snakes. . . ." The vision comes not from a sense of matricidal guilt but from the unrelenting consciousness of Clytemnestra's spirit, whose malevo-lent emanations will pursue him until he is finally acquitted by Athena and Apollo.

Unlike Jocasta, Clytemnestra refuses to acknowledge the evil of her misdeeds. She is the darkest of the Greek characters who have submitted to the machinations of their fate. Aeschylus himself leaves her groping and egotistically miserable in the final play of his trilogy. He is more concerned with the expiation of the blood-curse from the House of Atreus. But in Martha's *Clytemnestra,* the queen will even-tually come to terms with her soul and understand the significance of her life. Like a searchlight beam turned backward, the inverted eye of Clytemnestra's memory will probe the dark corners of her emotional experience as wife, mother, mistress, queen. It will rout out the eternal questions of fate and free will, of guilt and forgiveness, and reassess them in the courtroom of her inner self-judgment. There, in the speech of movement, each personality whose life was bound up with hers comes to the witness stand: Agamemnon, her unfaithful husband; Iphigenia ("my flower of pain"); Electra, her unforgiving child; Orestes, her avenging son; Helen, her sister; Paris, Helen's seducer; Aegisthus, Agamemnon's cousin, her lover; and Cassandra, prophetess of doom.

By dispensing with chronological sequence except when necessary to her purposes, by concentrating on the character of Clytemnestra, and by running off the entire sequence as if projected from within the queen's consciousness, Martha was able to build a psychological superstructure over the original Greek myth. Its theme was the resolution of personal conflict through acceptance and self-forgiveness.

"Modern literature," wrote Joseph Campbell, "is devoted in great measure to a courageous open-eyed observation of the sickeningly broken figurations that abound before us, around us and within."

In terms of the dance, *Clytemnestra* is such an observation. Its twentieth-century characteristics are atmospherically set when, before the Prologue begins, a man and a woman in modern evening clothes take their places on each side of the proscenium arch. They will constitute a chorus of two voices, bass and soprano. Their singing, which is like eerie chanting, will introduce the characters and illumine significant moments in the action. The first of these moments is the ominous appearance of the Messenger of Death, bald-skulled and naked to the waist; he wears a purple skirt that reaches to the floor. His slow crossing of the stage with a giant staff, around which a golden serpent is coiled, prepares us for the shattered majesty of the last queen of the House of Atreus.

The Prologue is set in the Underworld after Clytemnestra's death at the hand of Orestes. The Underworld is used here in a double sense. It represents the pit into which Clytemnestra's spirit has sunk, and "that most deep and subterranean end of wandering" described in Greek mythology. But for Clytemnestra the Underworld is not an end but a beginning of wandering; there is no peace for her in this Hades of her mind and heart where she stands stripped of her dignity, dishonored—a lone, tense figure, bitterly proud, bitterly resentful, half-hidden behind a cascade of golden streamers that symbolize the net of Hades. On her right is the King of Hades, his legs planted widely across a small platform with a sculptured throne-like form; he is holding two black-lacquered branches in his upraised hands. On her left stand the golden-garbed Apollo and Athena, deities of light and "wisdom and ultimate human insight." They will see her first as an unrepentant figure who refuses to accept her guilt. And in the end they will see her as one who has come to terms with the bitterness in her soul.

From the depths of a human throat a guttural cry is heard, and a woman's voice keens forth the words: *Cly-tem-nes-tra . . . Why . . . dishonored among the dead?* The *Why* is repeated in Clytemnestra's body as she moves tautly forward, thrusting one arm, then the other downward angrily in protest.

At first it seems that her fury is directed against the King of Hades. She sees him as her jailor, her foe, her judge. He is, in truth, her savior, for he forces her to turn her eyes inward and examine the moral issues of her life. As they dance a conflictual duet, he holds the glistening black branches high above her. Are the branches symbols of punishment? Are they the scourge of an irredeemable past or the promise of salvation? (The use of branches in pre-Greek culture was both expulsive and impulsive: expulsion of evil and induction of new life.) Only through suffering that leads to understanding will Clytemnestra know.

"As though by the will of Apollo and Athena," says the program note, "Clytemnestra begins the supreme effort to understand the past and her fate." Thus begins Clytemnestra's journey into the past.

It is a journey that no Greek poet ever took—a self-analytical journey into the tangled net of one's own compulsive actions; a journey that only twentieth-century man, reaching out desperately for understanding, dares take.

The procession begins. One by one each of the giant figures who peopled Clytemnestra's life moves across the stage, led by the King of Hades.

In her mind's eye, she confronts Helen of Troy, her sister. Does Helen, as the consort of Paris, bear the full guilt of the Trojan War? Or are the gods—masters of man's fate—to blame? This question must be answered in the depths of Clytemnestra's consciousness, for there, too, she must face final judgment on her own avenging role. In placing the tragedy of the Trojan War and its consequences at the gate of the gods, both sisters would be exonerated from blame: Helen from being the initial cause, Clytemnestra from seeking revenge. Then, where will the search for meaning lead? If the gods are in supreme command, freedom of individual will is canceled out. No, the gods are only *symbols* of forces that seem to shape man's destiny; the choice of action and the burden of responsibility are indubitably one's own. There lies the meaning of experience as seen in twentieth-century terms.

Helen, led off by Apollo and Athena, recedes into the background, a beautiful but shadowy figure embracing her private guilt. And almost immediately, there are visions of the war itself: the rape of Troy. Arrogant and cruel, the Greek warriors strike rigid two-dimensional positions—torso facing front, legs turned in profile, elbows sharply bent—reminiscent of the flat perspective of painted vases and sculptured friezes. With the consummate ease of javelin and discus throwers at Olympic games, they hurl the women to the floor and tower sensually above them while the women stiffen in tortured submission.

Was not Helen's wrong greater than Clytemnestra's? Or was Clytemnestra's a double guilt because it was intentional? While the war was being fought for Helen, Clytemnestra stayed at home, dark and brooding, plotting revenge against a husband who had craftily lured their youngest child to Aulis only to kill her there to appease the gods. Again, the indelible memory of Agamemnon's deception returns and she sees the sacrifice of Iphigenia in all its primitive horror: the terror of the girl as she beseeches the King of Hades to spare her; her own helplessness as her daughter pleads, reaching desperately toward her; and then the ghastly vision of the girl's body lying tensely across the intersection of two enormous spears, being borne away to the altar of fire instead of to an altar of love and marriage, as Agamemnon had promised when he sent for the child. The desire to kill seizes Clytemnestra as before. *Rejoicing I killed,* chants the voice, driving more deeply inward the queen's growing awareness of her implacable hate against her child's father.

She sees Electra and Orestes meeting in tense recognition of each other as bereaved sister and brother: Electra, quivering with mother-hate; Orestes, tormented by his mission. They plot their mother's death, and almost immediately the Furies appear, the future instruments of Clytemnestra's retaliation. Thus, the ancient blood-curse of the House of Atreus will pass successively from father to son.

In a scene entitled "The Chorus Summons the Characters," each character in the inexorable sweep of events makes an impassioned statement. Using two narrow sculptured forms with irregularly notched inner sides as a partially revealing screen, the cast announces itself: Helen, Paris, Electra, Aegisthus, Iphigenia, Agamemnon, and the prophetess Cassandra, Agamemnon's mistress, whose appearance rekindles Clytemnestra's lust for vengeance. The Prologue ends with Clytemnestra snatching the axe from its hiding place at the base of the throne, and holding it ominously and vaingloriously above her head.

A strange half-light, as of dawn, rests over the opening scene of Act I, where the Watchman of the House of Atreus, kneeling alongside a large shield, guards Mycenae. Tall and thin, scantily clothed in a gray loincloth, he seems to blend with the misty morning as if emphasizing the grayness of life when it harbors nothing but oncoming sorrow. The muted beat of the music has a metallic tone reminiscent of the clink of military armor. This is the day when the news of the fall of Troy will be flashed from beacons telling all Mycenae of the victorious Agamemnon's return. But there is an eerie quietude about the Watchman's slow, precise movements as he lifts, turns, and slides his shield ceremoniously from place to place. A spear-like point in the center of the shield enables it to be propped at oblique angles; it also serves to symbolize a death-dealing spike when, toward the end of his curious ritual, the Watchman bends over it, face downward, heart seemingly pierced, and slowly, laboriously pushes himself offstage.

Clytemnestra appears, wearing a voluminous transparent purple veil that falls over her hair and shoulders like an enveloping cape. She has resumed the role of the queen who ruthlessly ruled Mycenae in Agamemnon's absence—the queen who took the crafty Aegisthus for her paramour. The lovers dance together, and at the climax of an embrace Aegisthus slyly and forcibly twists Clytemnestra's arm backward toward the axe at the foot of the throne. Fearful at first, she pushes him away, but he pursues her, drawing her back with lavish endearments. Once the axe is in her hands, she senses the joy of revenge and the desire to slay Agamemnon now becomes a compulsion.

Sure of the fulfillment of their complicity, Aegisthus carefully puts the axe back in its place, and, lifting his future queen into the air, swirls her offstage.

When the time comes, everything plays into their hands. Returning from the war in an aura of triumph, Agamemnon brings with him his slave mistress, Cassandra, daughter of Priam and Hecuba, "a piece of goods out of the snatch of Asia." The moment of his arrival is gloriously depicted. Brought in on a chariot-like structure formed by criss-crossed spears carried by four attendants, he looks like a god in his shining chieftain's costume. Cassandra has preceded him, gravely anticipating the fateful meeting that she had already envisioned through her gift for prophecy.

Electra enters first, greeting her father and Cassandra with strained, ejaculatory gestures that seem to convey a message of warning. She withdraws to the far edge of the throne.

From the other side of the stage Clytemnestra appears. Around her shoulders and trailing to the floor is an enormous blood-red scarf with curved steel-supported ends held by two of her women. She crosses to her throne to await the king's first greeting.

He descends in splendor, holding his javelin upright. It symbolically separates them as they dance formally together.

As if parading his triumph, he resumes his pose on the chariot, leaving his javelin with Clytemnestra. She gives it back to him with mock humility before returning to the throne. Again he descends. This time he throws his sumptuous velvet cape across her lap, and then, contemptuously, sweeps it off so that it lands at Cassandra's feet. The shock of his insolence adds further incentive to her plan, but she hides her jealousy under a mask of feigned composure.

He proceeds to display his military prowess. Averting her face, Clytemnestra laughs convulsively when he throws his javelin into the air and catches it exhibitionistically with one hand and cockily continues to parade his virility. Pleased with himself, he returns to the chariot.

Ceremoniously, Clytemnestra's attendants unfold the scarf, laying it crosswise along the full width of the stage. Approaching Agamemnon, Clytemnestra kneels and places her hand under his foot to assist him in his descent. He kicks her hand away, then pulls her up roughly. She suffers to dance with him again, but with a rigidity that turns their duet into a caricature of a court dance. It is also a caricature of a marriage, presenting it as something both pompous and hypocritical.

The duet ends with her being carried in his arms like a doll and then being lowered onto the scarf. Before returning upstage, Agamemnon steps over her prone body, and once again kicks her proffered hand.

Incensed, she gathers up the scarf, wrapping it around herself like a death-shroud. Unwound, it will become the pathway to Agamemnon's bath.

Unconsciously doomed, the king awaits her next subservient act. She now advances toward him, takes his javelin, and gives it to one of his slaves. An ominous atmosphere surrounds them as they perform one last duet, moving slowly toward the throne, where Agamemnon will sit briefly . . .

At this instant, Electra breaks into an hysterical run. She circles madly around the entire stage and then disappears bat-like into the wings. Her outburst, like a silent scream, is unheeded by her father.

For Clytemnestra, the long-anticipated moment has arrived. Approaching the carpet, Agamemnon raises his foot to step on it. Then he pauses, leg suspended midair, as though suddenly and strangely aware of impending danger. In an agony of suspense Clytemnestra waits, holding out her hand invitingly. But the pause is momentary, and Agamemnon starts his fatal walk. Behind him stalks the King of Hades, holding aloft the two lacquered branches. The music has died down to only stealthy, percussive beats. An unearthly calm pervades the scene as Agamemnon disappears behind the now-raised steel-supported ends of the scarf, which, drawn together, will serve as curtains to conceal his disrobing for his bath. Clytemnestra goes over to the throne, picks up the axe, and, hiding it behind her back, slips between the curtains. They open briefly, and we see her brandish the axe over Agamemnon's head.

With sudden desperation, the stonelike Cassandra breaks into a dance. Horror at the deed to be committed and dread of her own death create a fabric of wild, impassioned gestures, which end with a sweeping flight toward the dying Agamemnon. We last see her lying over his dead body as the curtains are momentarily parted again and Clytemnestra raises the axe for a final blow. Then the fallen bodies are slowly transported offstage by Agamemnon's slaves on the bed of crossed spears.

With an air of triumph, Clytemnestra resumes her regal bearing. But when Helen of Troy appears, she checks herself. The two sisters confront each other, recognizing at last the terrible vengeance that each has set in motion. It is a moment of profound meaning, a presaging of eventual expiation of personal sin. Cool, beautiful, still seemingly unblemished, Helen watches her sister warily, from the opposite corner of the stage. The "fierce-lipped" Clytemnestra maintains her own distance. Instead of crossing on the diagonal path taken by all the characters in the play during the Prologue, the two women circle the stage, staying clear of each other. Between them lies the giant web of evil woven by one as a prelude to the Trojan War and tied into a deathknot by the other at its conclusion. Yet, even in retrospect, Clytemnestra is not fully convinced of her own guilt, and as Helen withdraws a smug sense of victory comes over her with the reappearance of Aegisthus. Another duet filled with pomp and hypocrisy takes place—this time, a celebration of a revenge already achieved. With mincing steps and self-satisfied mien, Clytemnestra dances alongside Aegisthus, who drunkenly preens himself as though he already wears a monarch's crown.

Behind them, unseen, appears the Messenger of Death. Sensing danger, Aegisthus leaves the stage. When Clytemnestra attempts to follow him, the Messenger of Death plants his staff on the train of Agamemnon's cloak, which she had flagrantly thrown across her shoulders. The edge of the cloak is caught. Startled, she turns around, and leaps behind the throne, terror-stricken. The curtain descends.

The action of Act II moves toward a second climax: Orestes' return and the slaying of Clytemnestra.

Partial darkness finds Clytemnestra sleeping at the foot of a slanted platform. Aegisthus, also asleep, is sprawled behind her across a tilted horizontal form like a bier. A sound as of wind rustling through the ill-fated house adds further gloom. At the far back stands a nightmarish vision: an incredibly tall, half-naked figure wearing a crown of leaves and holding a spear. At first it looks like the King of Hades, but as he rises and wearily moves downstage we know it to be the Ghost of Agamemnon. He wears thick platformed shoes that seem to anchor him to the earth. Once more we are witnessing a ritual, a trancelike ritual, in which the Ghost and Orestes play matching roles.

The Ghost's heavy steps seem to walk across Clytemnestra's heart. She shudders as if tormented by her dreams, and an anguished high-pitched cry rises above the stealthy beat of the music. Aegisthus merely stirs in his slumber.

Electra appears attended by Mourners. This heart-bitter girl seems forged of hate. Her dance of mourning contains as much anger as grief: her movements razor-sharp, her expression relentlessly set. Her one aim is to avenge her father's death and to enlist in her plot Orestes, whom she had saved as a child from their mother's wrath. Clytemnestra is roused, and together the four descendents of the House of Atreus dance a family portrait. They face each other, stepping sideways in a formal circle; like Agamemnon's Ghost they seem rooted to the earth as they shift weightily from position to position. Then, forming a totemic column—the Ghost at the apex, Electra below and in front of him, and Orestes on his knees—the trio inches forward with fixed look at Clytemnestra, who crouches in dread. When they break apart, the drama rapidly accelerates. Clytemnestra now begins to plead for her life. But Orestes, filled with Electra's venom, pursues and strikes her. When Aegisthus flees in terror, he throws the axe after him, killing him too.

Guilt now swirls over Orestes, and we see him engulfed by the horror of his deed. The Furies reappear, sent by the slain Clytemnestra, whose ghost "works like a sort of bacillus of madness." Torment is multiplied, and it seems that it will last forever.

There is no formal break between the end of Act II and the Epilogue which, like the Prologue, takes place in the Underworld; but a prescient interlude occurs in front of the drawn curtain in the form of a procession which Clytemnestra joins as she crosses the final threshold of her perilous journey toward self-discovery.

Helen, Iphigenia, Electra, and Cassandra enter first, moving in identical frieze-like patterns of tense gestures. As though enacting a dark ritual they cross the full width of the stage. Virtually passing them as they exit, Clytemnestra emerges swathed in the voluminous red veil that serves as a symbol of her opaque past . . . a past that only the deepest insight can penetrate. In a moment she is gone, and the gauze curtain begins to roll back, disclosing once more the Underworld with the golden streamers of the Net of Hades falling cylindrically from a great height. Within it is seen the queen, perched on a steep platform.

On each side of the stage, in statuesque radiance, Apollo and Athena stand as a tribunal, prepared to judge Orestes in the crime of matricide. The golden-garbed god and goddess dance their decisions, bringing the stage to life with the classic beauty of later Greece—the Greece of Phidias, Praxiteles, Pericles. Their gestures are noble, pure, symmetrical. Their chiseled leaps trace golden patterns in the air, signatures of the classic ideal. It is their benign verdict that changes the Furies into the Eumenides—the Well-Wishers—and, according to the program note, "puts an end to evil and the things of terror. She [Athena] ripped apart the terrible net of murder and vengeance, of love-in-hate and hate-in-love, the weaving of which had begun in the ancestral past and which Clytemnestra and Helen and Agamemnon had themselves woven to such a length that it snared all of Greece and Troy and virtually destroyed both."

The Eumenides enter resplendent with crimson scarves draped over their black dresses. Their presence is the embodiment of Athena's blessing. But Apollo's and Athena's judgment is an impersonal one. They have stopped the compounding of evil, but they have not exonerated the sinners, who must still come to terms with their private consciences.

But for Clytemnestra, the long journey has ended. The most secret point has been reached. There in the aching center of her mind the *Why* has at last been answered. The judge who pronounced her dishonored was not the King of Hades but the castigator of her soul—her inmost conscience. No longer proud and rebellious, Clytemnestra has received the verdict. Yes, said the Judging Self, she was a murderess; yes, she had avenged herself upon her son . . . but her greatest sin was against life itself. For had she not *misused* her life? They stood there in the darkest recesses of her soul, the Judging Self and the Willful Self confronting each other without mercy—like a face hating its own reflection.

Then a wondrous thing happened. The two selves became one, receiving in mystic rite the blessing of forgiveness through repentance and understanding.

Ceremoniously, the King of Hades hands Clytemnestra the branches. The gauze curtain that first hid the Underworld from view slowly starts to roll in front of it once more. With soft, lifted steps Clytemnestra begins to run. She circles behind the golden "net of

Hades" and advances toward the audience. Just as the curtain is about to close off the Underworld completely, she slips through, and holding the branches high above her head crosses the entire width of the stage as the chorus chants *Rebirth! . . . Rebirth!*

———— ··· ————

When the illusion of Grecian splendor had been stripped from the stage of the 54th St. Theatre at the close of *Clytemnestra* on April 25, 1960, and Martha, now attired in her black embroidered Chinese coat, was standing in the wings talking with admiring friends, it was apparent to all those who had seen that evening's performance that they had witnessed once more, two years to the month after its premiere in 1958, a "miracle of greatness," as John Martin would be attesting the next day in the *New York Times.*

Martha's circle of followers had grown considerably in the fifties. Not only did dancers, musicians, painters, writers, sculptors, and educators in all fields make it a point never to miss a Graham season, but businessmen and scientists were increasingly drawn to her visions. Among the latter were the distinguished Jungian psychoanalysts Drs. Erlo and Ann Van Waren, and Dr. Mary Roberts, who were familiar with most of her repertoire.

Always attentive to after-performance comments, Martha listened carefully to the many expressions of enthusiasm voiced by her admirers, including two dear friends, the dance critic Arthur Todd and Barbara Morgan, but when their praises were directed mainly at the remarkable innovativeness of her choreography, she objected.

"*Clytemnestra* would not have been possible without my dancers. You know"—and here her voice dropped to a serious, low tone—"Helen, Ethel, Bert, Yuriko, and Linda* have been with me nearly twenty years." The look in Martha's eyes implied a collaboration of inestimable value. She did not wish to be considered totally responsible for every choreographic detail; with characteristic honesty she wanted to give her dancers their due. Even though the program read "Choreography by Martha Graham," many of the movements that made the ballet's masterful conception come alive were

*Helen McGehee (Electra), Ethel Winter (Helen of Troy), Bertram Ross (Orestes and Agamemnon), Yuriko Kikuchi (Iphigenia), Linda Hodes (Cassandra, after Matt Turney's interpretation in the premiere).

conceived by those principal dancers whom Martha had named, plus others who had more recently joined the company: Paul Taylor, David Wood, Gene McDonald, Matt Turney. In almost all the works of this period, the leading dancers choreographed phrases of their own based on Martha's dramatic directives. This procedure was an accepted fact, as well as Martha's authoritative manipulation of their choreographic material. The creative relationship between Martha and her leading dancers was a collaboration in the best sense of the word, not basically different from the aesthetic rapport consistently achieved by Martha with her scenic and lighting designers, whom she would often refer to as her "artistic collaborators."

In these terms, the jointly created choreography in *Clytemnestra* heralded more emphatically than ever before the collaborative technique that would become an accepted procedure of future Graham compositions. Such deeply interwoven working methods were only possible, as Martha implied, after years of mutual aesthetic experiences, or, as in the case of Taylor, as immediate intuitive rapport.

Nowhere were these subtle interrelationships more clearly in evidence than when Martha shared the stage with her dancers. Certain scenes were never acted the same way twice—the result, to be sure, of Martha's acute sensitivity to the scene's dramatic potential. Intimate moments, such as the meaningful encounter between Helen of Troy and Clytemnestra after Agamemnon's murder demanded an awareness of an extraordinary kind on the part of Ethel Winter as Helen. To keep the emotional balance intact,Winter found that she spontaneously pitched her own performance to the intensity of Martha's current mood in that highly charged scene. Due to the younger artist's exquisite sense of timing, the drama inherent in that encounter was invariably held at a point of extreme tension.

Such sensitivity was characteristic of Winter, who was essentially a lyric dancer. Though her first experience with Martha had been at Bennington in 1944 as an undergraduate, only one year afterward she had become a member of the company. Martha chose her to take over the solo *Salem Shore* when it was revived for the 1947 New York season. A special luminosity suffused Winter's dancing, so much so that when she made her final entrance in *Seraphic Dialogue* as the canonized Joan of Arc, Agnes de Mille felt the need of asking Martha, "How did you get Ethel to walk like that? It always brings tears to my eyes." To which Martha replied with characteristic directness, "I never helped her."

If Martha cast her dancers with a sixth sense of their performing potential, surely her selection of Paul Taylor to play the role of Aegisthus was uncannily prescient. Taylor's bounding rubbery style of movement with its synchronous curves and angles became the perfect counterpart to Martha's implosive percussiveness. Aegisthus was always an outsider, a misfit, and Taylor played him that way. What could this coltish, sensual fellow possibly have in common with his cousin, the tyrannical Agamemnon who could command armies? With the compulsive overconscientious Orestes or his singleminded, embittered sister? Did Martha explain these telling details when assigning roles? Did she analyse for Taylor the character of the juvenile-tempered Aegisthus? To be sure she did, but never explicitly. Her metaphoric references would light up her dancers' minds and provide inspiration that would nourish ready-to-act muscular impulses.

With Taylor, one word sufficed to set in motion his unique creativity. Looking at him with a sly glint in her amber-flecked eyes and dropping her voice meaningfully on the last word, Martha proffered a single clue: "Aegisthus in *bad*." Only details had to be fleshed out. A naturally instinctive theatrical sense brought the young man to the fully rounded portrait of the deceitful Aegisthus; a portrait that has remained the most physically alive of any that have been painted since.

That Taylor's portrayal blended felicitously with Martha's interpretation of the doomed queen was most apparent in their duets, when the rhythmic play between them demanded subtle timing. No problem here, for in Taylor's own words, Graham movement "fit me like my skin"—a fact that he had known since the time he had combined study at Juilliard with additional classes at the Graham school.

An interesting response on Martha's part occurred in the Aegisthus–Clytemnestra "dance of triumph" when Taylor brought mock humor into play. Picking up the satire instantly, Martha glanced at him as if to say "I catch what you are doing," and thereupon played up the comedy until it was bristling with irony.

On the other hand, when Clytemnestra was dancing with the axe prior to the killing of Agamemnon, and Aegisthus was sitting on the throne watching her, Taylor was exceedingly careful not to deflect the audience's attention from Martha to himself. Holding in his hand the long purple veil that she had been wearing, he watched her dancing as if fascinated, but at the same time he was slowly and unobtrusively passing the material through a large safety pin that marked the point at which the veil would have to be handed back to Martha at the climax of the dance, when she would take it from him and wind it dramatically around her arm, as though symbolically ready to strangle Agamemnon. (In contrast, one recalls Rudolph Nureyev's flamboyant acting of Aegisthus years later when he used the scarf erotically, turning all eyes upon himself. But then, Martha was not onstage to deter him!)

Taylor's tactful recognition of his subsidiary role, which contained only scattered appearances throughout the ballet, was seen again at the beginning of Act II. As the recumbent Aegisthus in halfshadow he hardly moved during the dramatic scenes between the Ghost, Clytemnestra, Orestes, and Electra. Yet his immobility was not unnatural, for every now and then with a drowsy gesture he would flick his hand as though warding off an insect from his sleeping form. (Less concerned with the action around him, Nureyev insisted that a spotlight be focused on him throughout this scene.)

Entrusted with the dual portrayal of the roles of Orestes and Agamemnon, Bertram Ross, the most versatile dancer in the company, succeeded in creating two completely convincing characterizations. An actor-dancer of the stature to balance Martha, he shifted easily from the revengeful son to the overbearing husband, a feat that became all the more impressive at the end of the ballet, when, as Orestes, he became the terror-stricken victim of the Furies.

As Graham's leading man, Ross was for years an exemplar of strength and subtle support. She would often consult him on changes she had in mind, telephoning early in the morning or late at night to say, "I think I've worked this out." Then they would meet in the studio to solve the problem together. After one such session, Martha turned to Helen Lanfer, their accompanist, with the remark, "You see what I mean. . . . He is my skin!"

The multigifted Helen McGehee, for whom Aeschylus's *The Oresteia* was "the most completely engrossing of the tragedies," drew the character of Electra with swift, sharp strokes as clear and emphatic as the delineations of her pencil drawings of the many cities, European and Oriental, she had visited with the company. Together, Ross and McGehee provided Martha with the greater part of the intuitive bond she needed in the structural creation of *Clytemnestra* as a collaborative work of art.

McGehee's other important contribution was the designing of the women's costumes. Utilizing the silky sweep of black jersey—on which she had painted ancient Greek patterns in vivid greens, yellows, and reds—McGehee created a dress that adroitly combined a scarf (hanging from one shoulder) and a softly draped skirt that wrapped around the legs so as to permit the greatest freedom and yet reveal their contour. In conjunction with Martha's own designs for the men's costumes, McGehee's costumes, Noguchi's settings, and Rosenthal's lighting contributed significantly to the visual interpretation of *Clytemnestra*'s epic theme.

Curiously, the role of the Messenger of Death was the only one that was not creatively tied into the ballet from the beginning. Nor was it a spontaneous collaborative effort between David Wood, who danced the role, and Martha. Most of *Clytemnestra* had been choreographed before Wood came to Martha with an ultimatum. Profoundly moved by what he had seen in rehearsal and deeply disappointed that he had not been asked to dance in it, he demanded that she put him in it; otherwise he threatened to leave the company. Such a request could not be disregarded. Wood was most necessary to Martha for the proposed 1958 season, not only because he was in several other works but also because he was indispensable at rehearsals (two years later he would become rehearsal director for the company and actually assume that role in the satirical *Acrobats of God*).

Contrary to what might be expected—when faced with opposition Martha would be inclined to fight back—she agreed to Wood's demands. But the task of fitting him in demanded utmost ingenuity. All the roles had been cast, and the work was progressing at full pace, if not smoothly then with the normal anxieties that attended every Graham premiere.

Anxious to comply, yet undecided what to do, Martha gave David some costume material and a makeshift headpiece, and sent him to an upstairs room in the school building to start working out some movements of his own. Wood's extensive theatrical experience before coming to Martha served him well. Formerly a member of Hanya Holm's and José Limón's dance companies, he had also appeared with the New York City Opera Company, dancing in Charles Weidman's choreography for Komisarjevsky's production of Prokofiev's *The Love for Three Oranges*. His own choreographic instincts came to his aid as well. The movements he came up with had an eerie quality that stimulated Martha. She reshaped some of the phrases and gave him a tall staff to use with dramatic emphasis; a skullcap was substituted for the nondescript headgear; and leaving his chest bare, she deftly draped the material around his hips, allowing a long, snakelike train to trail behind him as he performed a sequence of slow, portentous movements across the full width of the stage before the curtain went up on the Prologue. By the time of the dress rehearsal, Wood's makeup would be set: sweeping upward and outward from the sockets of the eyes were wide, darkly painted patches reaching to the temple; the lower part of the cheeks as well as the jaw were shaded to give the face and skull a cadaverous, menacing look.

Now the Prologue for *Clytemnestra* was complete. Since death itself was to be the co-protagonist of the tragedy to be unveiled, it was only fitting that the scene in the Underworld should be heralded by the King of Hades' emissary. Accompanied by the eerie falsetto keening of the male singer, the Messenger of Death would announce the arrival in Hades of the darkest lady, whose tormented, self-searching journey would end in the redemptive ecstasy of rebirth.

Chapter Ten
Back to Brightness

The preparation for *Clytemnestra* had been long and intense, working its way from the depths of Martha's consciousness to the surface of a committed gesture. In spite of copious notes, including quotations gathered over the years and imagined scenarios, once she was engaged in the immediacy of rehearsals with El-Dabh's music and Noguchi's sculptural forms, Martha applied the full power of her rich intuitive reasoning to every detail of the production.

"I do not theorize," she averred later, "I don't talk about my dances from a theoretical point of view nor do I describe them beforehand. I could analyze now who Clytemnestra is—afterwards—and why I did it this way, but even as I work with the dancers I never describe beforehand the ideas. I proceed. Only with the composer, do I expose the structure so that he may proceed to work with the idea." She might have added that with her set designer she also shares her mystical and, occasionally, practical ideas.

No doubt, the reason for Martha's reticence to expose her choreographic concepts was simply that she didn't wish to commit herself; she wanted to leave all options available for that flash of intuition that could spring to her aid at given moments of creativity. In a sense, she was keeping her dancers in the dark because she herself was still in the dark. Only the broad outline was hers to give to her collaborators, and even this changed according to new discoveries —as we shall see when dealing with *Alcestis*.

Keeping her dancers in the same state of unknowingness as herself had a twofold advantage. It kept their and her own nervous energy at a high pitch. The tension that was created gave her the necessary emotional drive to battle her way through the thicket of her imagination. Marnie Thomas, David Wood's wife, describes the atmosphere in the company: "We were all superconscious of how she was reacting." In crisis after crisis they stood by, ready to follow in whatever direction she chose. As soon as the path became evident, their own creativity went into high gear, and with the machetes of their superbly trained bodies they helped her clear the way.

For those who were her students and not the intimate personnel of her company, Martha's changeable intensity created a theatrical aura in the classroom. But underneath was the steady drive that she inspired in all her students: to achieve perfection. Thus the ambitions that had prompted the young Denishawn student to declare (and to realize in her own way) "I want to become the greatest dancer in the world!" were passed on to her own pupils, and "nothing less than everything" was the payment of every Graham class. With her entry into the room, the spell was immediately cast. Martha had but to pronounce one of her visionary "truths" and the awed students would rise to the same level of idealistic dedication.

A characteristic statement was: "Posture . . . is a self-portrait of being. It is psychological as well as physiological." And then, like a revelation to those who listened: "There is only one law of posture that I have been able to discover—the perpendicular line connecting heaven and earth."

Visibly, spines would become straighter, heads would be lifted regally, and everyone would go to work, combining pleasure with pain. Masochism is not an unknown experience among dancers.

Whether pursued by doubts or in pursuit of dreams, Martha followed—as did Clytemnestra—a queenly path. A halo of awesomeness surrounded her. She was worshipped, she was feared. Ultimately invincible, she had the power to draw from the wellsprings of life immeasurable beauty, which carried for those who worked with her immeasurable meaning.

The creative miracle of the Graham season at the Adelphi Theatre in April 1958 lay not only in the premiere of the monumental *Clytemnestra* but also in the amazing switch that Martha was able to pull off when, two nights later, *Embattled Garden* was given its first performance. Compared to *Clytemnestra*, Martha's picturesque, fast-paced interpretation of what went on in civilization's first paradise was almost frivolous, except for one searing moment. While *Clytemnestra* made uncompromising demands upon the audience's knowledge of mythology and their instinctive psychological response to the action,

Embattled Garden catered to their sense of adventure in the raciest manner possible.

The garden was Eden, thousands of centuries old at the time of the Trojan War. But far from being the peaceful, idyllic, Biblical heaven-on-earth between the Euphrates and the Tigris, it was a battlefield where elemental passions initiated ferocious sallies and where innocence was strangely absent. Represented by Noguchi's square platform with sunken areas and flexible poles suggesting barren tree-trunks, Martha's garden was curiously lacking in nature's amenities. Nor was the relationship between the four characters who inhabited the garden—Adam, Eve, Lilith (Adam's first wife), and the serpent, called The Stranger—of ancient vintage. They were twentieth century to their fingertips.

One could read *Embattled Garden* a hundred different ways. For some, it was just flamenco-styled fireworks: slashing gestures performed with unrelenting pulse to Carlos Surinach's flamboyant Iberian-flavored score, with Martha's brilliant pink, black, and red costumes contrasting vividly with Noguchi's wavering green poles and gaudily painted platforms. The breakneck speed of the action matched the garish colors. Walter Terry called it "a wonderfully satiric glimpse of Eden." For others, *Embattled Garden* was one of the most seductive dances they had ever seen. Every move had sexual implications, from the opening and closing scenes of Eve's languorous hair-brushing as she crouched among the spiky trees to the cool, seemingly indifferent twist of Lilith's wrist as she slowly fanned herself under the stiff-limbed branch where The Stranger was coiled.

And for a chosen few, the climax came at one breathless moment when Adam, standing with tautly outstretched arms as though hanging on a cross, collapsed onto Eve's wide-spread knees. The vision of a Pietà was distinctly drawn, as if the Old and New Testaments suddenly coalesced into one blinding revelation that associated Adam's fall from grace with Christ's descent from the Cross—both figures being heroic embodiments of their Father's will: the first to people the earth in His name; the second, to bring His word unto the erring race of man.

Whatever reading one might wish to give *Embattled Garden*, superficial or profound, the ballet remains a marvelous example of sheer, uninhibited movement. Set to, indeed *sprung from* Carlos Surinach's infectious Spanish rhythms and tantalizing dissonances,

Martha's own version of misbehavior in the Book of Genesis might have been disturbingly risqué; but who could deny that it was first-rate theater?

———— ··· ————

Just as *Clytemnestra* and *Embattled Garden* represented extremes in Martha's creative output, the year 1958 contained personal experiences of an extreme nature. In July Martha's mother, Jane Beers Duffy, died. Returning to Santa Barbara and taking charge of her mother's effects, Martha had to face the past, an experience that involved painful confrontation with her own life, its ambitions and failures, the latter always seeming to outweigh the former in times of stress. Her self-judgment must have been relentless, for she burned all her letters to her mother—more than thirty years of devoted correspondence.

The personal blow of her mother's death was severe. In spite of Martha's absorbing professional life, family ties had remained tightly knit over the years. Jane Duffy had always gloried in her two dancing daughters' achievements. Geordie, as well as Martha, had made a name for herself as a leading Denishawn dancer. Staying on after Martha left, and performing many of her sister's roles with notable success in the Orient and on countrywide tours, she seemed to be well on her way to establishing a career of her own. Small like Martha and very much a Graham in her physiognomy—large eyes, oval face, small, straight nose—she had curly auburn hair falling softly to her shoulders and a femininity of her own. After she left Denishawn in the late twenties, she married music and dance critic Winthrop Sargeant, and later officiated in an administrative capacity in Martha's school. Besides sparing her sister much of the business trivia, she became indispensable in personal ways. But this submission to Martha's needs meant a complete neglect of her own talents; to Louis Horst, who was an integral part of the school during those years, Geordie's dedication had "tragic" implications. Had she not been overshadowed by her sister's personality and genius, Geordie would have, in his estimation, fulfilled her potential as a dancer.

From time to time Jane Duffy would visit her daughers on the East Coast, and Martha would make special trips to Santa Barbara. Besides her deep affection for her mother, there was an underlying sense of responsibility, as there always would be for Geordie, too. Responsibility gives one roots, and death tears them up. In that low period of loss followed by self-reassessment, there was nothing to do but to tread heavy-footed along the course she had charted for herself, finding solace in her reading and in her work. With Louis no longer alongside of her and Erick gone, the future held a premonition of bleakness. Four years previously, Martha had written: "We have all walked the high wire of circumstance at times." And like the acrobat who "does not choose to fall," she threw herself more compulsively than ever into her dances.

The insistent need to plunge again and again into ideas that possessed her would not condone any recession. Nor would she accept her growing limitations in regard to speed, leverage, and pure dance skills. She would continue to seek the all-too-necessary gratifications of performing, even when her colleagues and her public would become critical of her lessening powers, as would happen in a few years. Not yet was she ready to relinquish her roles to the more gifted dancers in her company. Not yet would she accept the restrictions of her sixty-three years—a thorn for those others, a cross for herself. As long as she could hold the stage with the power that was hers and hers alone, she would "not give up" (a statement she clung to even at the age of eighty-six).

Collaboration was really not the term. I was a guest and deeply honored to be a guest. Balanchine chose the music for me to use [Anton von Webern's symphonic compositions]. I could not agree to it until I found the idea. Neither of us started this with the idea of collaboration in the intrinsic meaning. He presented me with the *Passacaglia* and *Six Pieces for Orchestra*.* The original idea was for my choreography to begin and conclude the choreography for *Episodes*—it was to be an enclosure. However, it did not work out practically or theatrically and so we changed our minds.

Such was Martha's version of her contribution to *Episodes*, which had its premiere within the framework of a New York City Ballet program on May 14, 1959. Billed as a collaborative venture between the

*The *Six Pieces* were added when the *Passacaglia* proved insufficient for Graham's dramatic needs.

205

first lady of American modern dance and the Americanized czar of classic ballet, the news of the joint enterprise astonished the dance world. Curiously, the title, *Episodes,* did not refer to the intermittent nature of the combined offerings; rather, it came from an idea of the Russian painter Pavel Tchelitchev, who had suggested to Graham, Balanchine, and Lincoln Kirstein in December 1935 that they do together "an evening's spectacle involving three archetypes: Don Juan, Don Quixote, Hamlet." (Martha was to play a corresponding "feminine archetype.") The proposed ballet had never been realized.

When Kirstein brought up the subject of *Episodes* in January 1959, he spoke of "key characters of feminine distinction" for Martha to dance, having in mind an interpretation of *Alice in Wonderland* which seemed to Kirstein to carry the "essence of Martha's spirit." Unable to respond to this suggestion, but still interested in the project, Martha decided on Mary, Queen of Scots.

The brilliant, adventurous-minded Tchelitchev, who by this time was no longer alive, had made a strong impression on Martha. One of her favorite quotes was his facetious, rather terrorizing "It is five minutes to twelve." It seemed to carry a threat, a strange urgency that appealed to Martha's sense of danger. Could its dramatic implications have coincidentally suggested the fate of Mary Stuart, who was doomed to die at a fixed time?

"Anti-collaboration" might have been the better description of *Episodes I* and *Episodes II.* "The work as a whole jolts apart at the couplings more than once," wrote John Martin. "Miss Graham's section alone is costumed (also in several styles), while Balanchine works in practice clothes." In addition, Martha had chosen a character for whom "Fate had decreed from the outset that the great happenings of her life were to be concentrated in swift, short episodes," according to Stefan Zweig, whose masterful biography was her chief source of historical reference. Even the score, which consisted of Webern's only symphonic compositions, was not of one piece. Martha's share included the early, lush, and brooding *Passacaglia* (Opus 1) and *Six Pieces* (Opus 6), both composed in 1909 before the Austrian musician's use of the Schoenberg twelve-tone scale; whereas Balanchine's selections identified in style with Webern's late orchestral pieces, which the Russian choreographer described as "active and lean" and filling "air like molecules." His use of the fractured rhythms of the composer's atonal music was likewise fragmented and distorted in design, causing Martin to speak of a "super-mechanical nonhumanity" which moves the body "without the impulsion of human motive." Wisps of sound were visualized as splintered grotesque movement, albeit classical in texture.

To gain insight into the *Passacaglia*, Martha shut herself up in her third-floor studio and "played it and moved to it day after day after day," even though at the time she had no idea of dancing the role of the Scottish queen with her company, believing that one of the NYCB dancers would perform it. (Actually, the remarkably sensitive, adaptable Sallie Wilson would perform the part of Queen Elizabeth, while Paul Nickel, Kenneth Peterson, and William Carter played minor roles.) "But I moved myself into a state of mind," she added. That state of mind was nourished by two of Martha's revered poets, T. S. Eliot and Rainer Maria Rilke, the last a favorite, as she knew, of Webern's also. "It was from these two that I found my articulation."

"Inspiration" would have been the more precise word. For Martha had found in Eliot's "East Coker" (from *Four Quartets*) the line "In my beginning is my end," an inversion of Mary Stuart's famous "In my end is my beginning." Later on in the poem there is a similar paradoxical phrase, also applicable to Mary Stuart: "In order to possess what you do not possess/You must go by the way of dispossession." According to another book Martha studied—Raymond Preston's *Four Quartets Rehearsed*—Eliot indeed had Mary Stuart in mind, for "East Coker" ends with a literal translation of the words the queen had embroidered in French with uncanny premonition years before her execution: *En ma fin est mon commencement.*

The drama was there, vividly Grahamesque in its appeal: a queen who walked to her death majestically; a woman whose passionate nature had led her to experience lust, jealousy, revenge; a devout Catholic whose belief in her God-anointed right to rule never for a moment wavered. Zweig's description of Mary was of the stuff to ring in Martha's ears: "This daughter of the Stuarts would preserve even in her darkest hours, as the priceless heritage of her royal blood and courtly training, an exalted but nowise theatrical demeanor which will for all time endow her with a halo of romance." The queen's ordinary demeanor may not have seemed theatrical in Renaissance times when theatrics were commonplace, but her intuitive use of all the elements of drama was clearly evident in the way she staged her own execution. According to Zweig, "Mary prepared for her exit from life as one prepares for a festival, a triumph, a grand ceremony. Nothing was to be improvised, nothing was to be left to chance. Every effect was to be calculated; all was to be regal, splendid, and imposing." What a scenario for Martha! Webern's *Passacaglia* merely fed the flames of her creative use of the queen's martyrdom, with its opening passages of "dark turbulence and tearing anguish [that] seemed to indicate a kindred anguish to Mary, Queen of Scotland."

So it came about that another queen who met a violent death began to obsess Martha. So it came about that more than two thousand years after Homer had woven the legend of the ill-fated House of Atreus, a descendent of the ill-fated House of Stuart would become the subject of Martha's one hundred and thirty-eighth work. Like Clytemnestra, Mary Stuart wove a murderous plot around a husband she had come to despise. Like Clytemnestra, she allowed hate to overthrow reason in her quest for power and personal gratification. But there was one glaring difference. Whereas Clytemnestra died ignominiously, both morally and physically, and, in Martha's script, made atonement for her sins only *after* she had expired, Mary Stuart came to terms with her past *before* she mounted the steps leading to the executioner's block. Hers was no Freudian–Jungian retrospection—rather, a vision reversed. Life *after* death was the sole remaining hope of the luckless Scottish queen. A prisoner in a country that she considered her appointed right to rule, checkmated in every possible diplomatic move to free herself from Queen Elizabeth's enforced captivity, Mary had already been sacrificed on the block of Elizabeth's political intrigues. Dark as her deeds had been, Mary Stuart moved toward everlasting light on that fatal day when she was struck down, not by her weak-willed son, James VI, who refrained from protesting the English death decree, but by her "dear cousin's" personal fear and gnawing jealousy.

February 8, 1587, Fotheringay Castle. Ostensibly the action takes place at the time of the execution of Mary, Queen of Scotland and The Isles. But as soon as the curtain rises on a bare structure, seemingly etched in iron, of a wide platform approached by sets of steps on either side, with Martha as Mary standing stock-still beneath the scaffolding, we know that time is encapsulated into the instant before the queen's demise in which she will relive her past—an instant which, as for other heroines in Martha's roster of great figures, is a prelude to her tryst with "destiny."

Directly above her on the platform, a wooden high-backed chair faces the rear of the stage. Its boxlike form makes it look like an upended coffin. To the side of it is a high-standing halberd with a fretwork crest fanning out sideways like wings or teeth. On a half-landing leading to the platform stands the executioner, guarding, as it were, the throne of England. Later the massive chair will pivot around to disclose its royal occupant, the Virgin Queen, resplendently attired. When the time comes, she will rise and arrogantly descend to confront the pretender to her throne, not directly but in a veiled match of wits disguised as a game of court tennis.

Divesting herself of her queenly outer garment—a stiff, black, self-standing farthingale and over-bodice—Mary, as woman, is revealed in a symbolically pure white underdress, in which she will relive her encounters with the principal men in her life: Chastelard, Darnley, Riccio, and Bothwell. They constitute a ghostly procession of memories that gradually fade before the blinding reality of her commitment to her destiny.

The Four Marys, who were her childhood playmates and her loyal friends, prepare her for her death. With utmost ceremony they attire her in the blood-red garment she has chosen for the final event of her life. But first she must face the woman who has signed the decree for her execution—the woman whose right to rule she has dared to question. Gravely, Mary takes her place downstage opposite the imposing figure of the English queen. Their decisive match—the outcome of which she already knows—is about to begin.

With macabre formality, the executioner places in each opponent's hand a triangular racquet, to which is attached a short cord with a tiny tennis ball at the end. Facing the audience—not each other—the two sovereigns raise their racquets, but the ball never traverses space. In mock earnestness the game proceeds.

Elizabeth's serve has the resonance of a gong stroke; Mary's return has the ping of a plucked string. Like the diplomatically couched correspondence between the two queens, who conducted a personal war of words for nearly thirty years without a single face-to-face encounter, the invisible ball crosses and recrosses the stage. Terse, concentrated, with a sting of venom behind each stroke, the volley is sustained for approximately five exchanges until, outmaneuvered, the Scottish queen lets the unseen ball fly past her.

But Elizabeth's triumph is short-lived, for now Mary is the center of the world-stage. Proudly mounting the steps to the scaffold, her small, intense figure taut with dignity, Mary Stuart is now possessed by the white flame of her faith. Even Elizabeth's throne is no longer of importance. Overturned, it will become the executioner's block—the monument on which the Scottish queen's immortality will rest.

As Mary kneels before it, the towering halberd above her is lowered in the form of an axe. . . .

And what you own is what you do not own
And where you are is where you are not.

The building was empty of students, and it seemed that Martha was alone that Sunday afternoon in the early spring of 1959 when she opened the door to Sallie Wilson's ring. Dressed in her black mandarin coat with its long panels covering her black tights, she looked darkly mysterious as she said in a low voice, "Come with me." Then she disappeared down a shadowy corridor toward the rear studio, the New York City Ballet dancer following with an acute sense of excitement and trepidation. It was to be her first rehearsal with Martha on *Episodes*.

When the two women sat down on small Japanese supports and faced each other, Martha quietly, albeit dramatically, said, "I must tell you, I'm terrified of you." The ballet dancer merely smiled. That smile, which had an engaging intelligence of its own, acted as an immediate breakthrough to what would become a fine working rapport between the two artists.

Before proceeding with the rehearsal, Martha described the dramatic action of *Episodes* as she visualized it, a preliminary device she seldom resorted to with her own company. Then she began to show Wilson the choreography for the role of Queen Elizabeth. Obviously, she was making concessions to Sallie's classical training, for she had carefully substituted ballet's firm, upright use of the torso for her own stylistically flexible vocabulary. At this point, Sallie Wilson remonstrated. There was no need, she explained, to shape Elizabeth's part in balletic terms for her sake; she was most eager to try to perform the role exactly as Martha required; would she kindly teach her the precise movements she had in mind?

From that moment on, the rehearsal moved swiftly. Details would be clarified later in special sessions with Bertram Ross, who would help Wilson absorb the subtleties of the Graham movement. Responding to the choreographic material as well as to the dramatic implications of Elizabeth's imperious role, the ballet dancer won Martha's confidence. A month after the premiere of *Episodes*, Martha declared, "Sallie Wilson is a beautiful technician. She was utterly and absolutely cooperative, generous, curious and avid to learn all she could."

For Sallie, the experience of performing with Martha was revelatory. "Each movement had significance. Nothing was for nothing. Every gesture had a symbolic meaning...even before the tennis match, when we met briefly there was a formal gesture in which the right arm was sharply bent as if in salute. Yet we never faced each other. It was as though a pocket of air separated us. Then the game ...I hit the ball with a big, slow lyrical motion; Martha responded with a short, sharp stroke. The tension between us was total."

Nor was the ballet dancer's admiration restricted to Martha's staging or her onstage presence. There were other instances of the choreographer's adroit inventiveness, such as her delicate manipulation of the problem with Karinska's costumes. The situation could easily have swelled into a major crisis had not Martha used her own gift for costume designing as well as her sly sense of diplomacy.

The first costume fitting found Sallie on the verge of tears. She was being pinned by Karinska into the famous Russian costumer's splendid but too authentically designed reproduction of an elaborate sixteenth-century court gown that looked exactly as though it had stepped out of a portrait of the English queen. With its stiff-boned stomacher (the front part of a tight V-shaped bodice), its weighty farthingale hoop, its high, wired, upstanding collar, and long, puffed sleeves, the dress would be suitable only for acting the Queen Mother role in *The Sleeping Beauty*! Seeing her reflection in the mirror, Sallie felt her heart sink. By itself the costume was a masterpiece of design, but its weight and voluminousness would make it impossible to dance in. She looked appealingly at Martha, who was calmly (so it seemed) watching the fitting.

Without changing her expression, Martha issued Sallie a subtle command: "Now do some of the movements."

In her effort to comply, the dancer found it impossible to bend at the waist.

Feigning mild perplexity as they left, the two women went over to the Graham school, where the rest of the cast was assembled for rehearsal. After explaining the situation, Martha asked dramatically, "What shall we do?" No one dared offer a suggestion, much less Sallie Wilson, who stood in awe of her director's chameleon personality. Then Martha lowered her head and murmured with increased dramatic emphasis, "Let's pray." The brief silence that followed contained not prayers but a rush of ideas mainly in Martha's head, for her next move was to summon Helen McGehee to follow her into another room, and together they came up with some drastic revisions.

While keeping Karinska's original ornateness, Sallie's costume was completely redesigned. A long-sleeved bodice of form-fitting gold jersey with a "14-carat sheen" replaced the stiff-boned stomacher; the large hooped farthingale was removed and small, padded hip rolls emphasizing the womanly line of the pelvis took its place. On top of the heavy gold skirt, a secondary lightweight brocaded one was softly gathered. Its gold-threaded designs added further luster to the English queen's already glistening costume. Instead of an elaborate upstanding collar, a lacy wire one "as delicate as air" was substituted, and, similarly, a feather-light crown nestled in Sallie's hair.

But the main innovative change lay in the complex design of the skirt, which, like Helen McGehee's costumes for the women and the Furies in *Clytemnestra*, had trouser-like tights inserted beneath its folds. Getting into the costume meant first stepping into the tights and then fastening oneself into the gown as a whole. The dual coverage would enable a dancer to kick and perform other large-scale motions without exposing her legs. Since some of Queen Elizabeth's movements were high, sweeping *renversés* with simultaneous backbends, the costume retained its majestic attributes under all circumstances.

Though far from being minor changes, the alterations requested by Martha were immediately accepted. So willingly and skillfully did Karinska rework the costume that she was led to think that the final design was her own invention. Variations in other costumes were handled with similar skill. As Martha quite sincerely but also diplomatically remarked to the press, "Karinska was so generous and so wonderful in her understanding of the physical problems which are different from the essential ballet problems. Anatomically, artistically and creatively, she was so sensitive and so inspiring. In my first black dress, with its abstraction of the ruched collar, I had the security of feeling beautiful every time I appeared in it on stage."

From a historical point of view, was the Graham–Balanchine collaboration reciprocally important? From an aesthetic point of view, was the venture productive? Did their individual contributions influence each other's choreographic choices from that time onward?

When questioned about her experience of sharing styles within a balletic framework, Graham's answers were judicious rather than evaluative: "It widened my audience . . . I felt highly privileged to be part of an existing organization so closely identified with the general public."

Though gallant in every way throughout the association and afterward, Balanchine was similarly noncommittal. When Martha needed additional music, he immediately responded by presenting her with the *Six Pieces*, which he was at the moment choreographing for two of his dancers. In his revised edition of *Complete Stories of the Great Ballets*, he graciously but vaguely remarked, "Miss Graham's part of *Episodes* has unfortunately not been seen for some years. It is our hope that one day it will be danced again."

(The New York City Ballet maintained *Episodes II* in its repertoire, calling it simply *Episodes*, and omitting Paul Taylor's unique solo as choreographed by Balanchine. Graham, however, never performed her section again until 1980, when she revised it with significant changes, some to the production's advantage, some distinctly detrimental. Using the same scaffold-like décor by David Hays, she devised a brilliant opening scene to set the solemn mood for "the last moments in the life of Mary, Queen of Scots, when the memories flood back of the episodes which determined her destiny." Courtiers and ladies, sumptuously dressed in Halston-designed jet-black costumes, entered from the wings with formal, elegant gestures. Their entrance was all the more effective for having been heralded by the ceremonious playing of a single bagpiper. But the symbolic tennis game played between Elizabeth and the Scottish queen lacked animation, as if all the strokes had been previously determined. Without Graham's and Wilson's personal portrayals of the rival queens, the new *Episodes* seemed but a shadow of the original.)

That Balanchine was "influenced" by Graham—as stated by certain critics, who presumed that they detected telltale use of her stylistic vocabulary in his later works—is a moot point, just as the reverse is questionable. Both artists were true to themselves: Martha to her own theatrical instincts (even when applied with some misgiving to music already composed), and Balanchine to his personal movement choices, even when choreographing for a Graham dancer. His "furiously contorted solo variation" for Taylor might have appeared to be a strange concoction, but its musical fidelity to what Lincoln Kirstein imaginatively called Webern's "fractured glass-snake noises" was typically Balanchinesque.

Perhaps the truest interchange in the nonsynchronous "collaboration" lay in the exceptional adaptability of the two young dancers who were "on loan" from their respective companies. Sallie Wilson and Paul Taylor could well have been the pivotal reasons why *Episodes I* and *Episodes II* turned out to be a felicitous liaison, if not a lasting marriage, between ballet and modern dance.

———— ··· ————

If, according to one critic, Martha was "beginning to slow down" in 1947 at the age of fifty-three, how can one account for the staggering achievements of the subsequent two decades? Between 1947 and 1969, the year that Martha retired (unwillingly) from the stage as a dancer, she gained increasing mastery as a scenarist of her unique form of dance-drama.

"Slow down"? Scarcely. In 1947 Martha had only hoisted sail on her Greek voyage—a voyage that was surveyed, as we know, with bewildered concern by the immortal gods and goddesses who reside on Mount Olympus. Their watchful eyes, alerted to her every move from the moment she transformed the Medea legend into *Cave of the Heart* in 1946, would be following her for more than twenty years until she would conclude her momentous Hellenic expedition with *Cortege of Eagles,* the last Greek work in which she would perform herself.

The year 1947 was on the contrary a rich beginning: it was the year that Martha opened her own Pandora's Box, from which sprang a Psyche in modern dress. No mere abstraction of the human soul, this twentieth-century Psyche would henceforth serve as the Supreme Questioner of Motivations. Psyche would become Martha's co-protagonist, even when the dancer would switch allegiance from the ancient Greeks to medieval and Biblical characters. With Psyche at her side, Martha would enter the minds and hearts of no less than thirteen personalities, whose inner dramas would keep her dancing to the age of seventy-five! Psyche provided not only the motivating force behind Martha's many-layered interpretations of myths, historical fact, and folk legends, but she also offered the clue to Martha's personal compulsion to perform. The need to perform was basic to her nature. The physical act itself was bound up with sensations that gave her a sense of power over others and over herself—bringing to mind Ruth St. Denis's statement, "I feel when I dance before great audiences that I am delivering a wordless message of immortality."

Martha would not relinquish this power willingly. Choreographing for others, as will be seen when she unwillingly gave the coveted role of Circe to Mary Hinkson, never took the place of dancing herself. Then there was the stalwart Graham pride: the determination to prove to the world that she could still dance. And dance she would, until the day when the world would face her with the fact that her body was no longer hers to command.

Granted that from 1958 on she began to limit her movements to motions within the range of her dwindling technical resources (although the role of Clytemnestra made exorbitant demands upon her, which she fulfilled supremely well in the first two years after its 1960 revival); granted that she drew principally upon acting gifts that could project the smallest gesture or the most subtle expression of body and face to the furthest corner of the theater; granted, also, that her health from her mid-sixties to her early seventies was being undermined by a period of excessive drinking—a habit that could easily have drained the forces of a less sturdy constitution. (Brought on doubtlessly by the very fear of losing her performing capacities, it may have temporarily given her the sense of power that she craved.)

Granted all these personal and professional considerations, what other dancer could dominate the stage as Martha did? With the power that was hers alone, she had but to be within view, or partially within view, to become the center of interest. Younger company dancers fulfilled their roles gloriously, but who kept the story moving toward its climax? Albeit more statuesque than dynamic, Martha was the magnet—the cynosure of all eyes. She would have it no other way.

And so another door was opened for Martha's never-slumbering imagination. The flashback technique begun in *Deaths and Entrances* would continue to yield riches that sustained the long, long view: memory's immemorial images. Out of the haze of the telescoped past would emerge "the young Clytemnestra," "the young Judith," "the young Héloise"—each one represented by a lissome company member. And Martha, standing at the stage's edge, or high upon a platform, would watch her youthful self dancing with lusty abandon as though she herself were experiencing the movements. The choreographic device (one might call it a choreographic ruse) was absolutely convincing. It gave double focus, and, at the same time, double meaning to the plot while allowing Martha to act out her role instead of fully dancing it.

Eschewing this expediency temporarily in the spring of 1960, Martha indulged in two aesthetic escapades which had nothing to do with memory, but which, while conserving her energy, justified her always-effective onstage presence: the delectably humorous *Acrobats of God* and the lyrical spectacle *Alcestis.*

Tantalizingly elusive as to choreographic intention, *Acrobats of God* had all the critics hopping. Walter Terry could not help wondering (as did Winthrop Sargeant of *The New Yorker*) if *Acrobats of God* weren't a spoof on ballet, born from Martha's previous year's experience with George Balanchine. The plethora of multiple turns and high lifts executed with balleticized showmanship in tights and leotards (albeit lavender instead of Balanchinesque black and white) might have suggested as much. Others presumed quite logically that Martha was spoofing herself in the role of an indecisive, overworked choreographer.

And there were still others, the dancers in the piece, who insisted that *Acrobats* was envisioned as deadly serious, and that when the first-night audience started laughing, Martha picked up the cue and began to "ham it up."

Actually, all three impressions have some points of credence. In her notes on *Acrobats,* Martha writes of "3 little swans"—most likely the famous trio in *Swan Lake*—and certainly the use of a barre and the exercises performed on it indicate a spoof on ballet. But could not Martha have taken satirical aim at her old experiences with Denishawn as much as at her recent association with the New York City Ballet? There is another telltale notebook reference: "Javanese steps," a term right out of Miss Ruth's Oriental vocabulary.

And why not poke fun at herself? All those moments of indecision, of frustration, of feeling pressed into service when she hadn't the least desire to stir herself—did they not add up to a portrait that could be stretched to cartoon proportions? Martha did have her moments of humorous self-perception; we know this from her admission that in the early days Louis often insisted on her practicing when she would have much preferred to eat ice cream or go to the movies.

As far as responding to her audience's reactions, this was par for the course. On the stage (and when was she not onstage?) Martha had a sixth sense for theatrical effect. Laughter would only stimulate the natural comedienne within her to try to evoke more laughter.

Whatever gleam was in Martha's eye when she created *Acrobats,* its premiere was highly successful. Enchanted and relieved to be able to relax at a Graham performance, the audience immediately seized the rare opportunity to laugh at and with their suddenly, unexpectedly, charming dancer-choreographer. Those who remembered Martha's early solos—*Petulance* and *Remorse* from *Four Insincerities* and *Comedy* from *Fragments,* or the farcical ballet *Every Soul Is a Circus*—could bask once more in the warm feeling that Martha had not turned her back on the imp within her.

Acrobats of God was, of course, a full company dance, its title taken from the Latin *athletae Dei,* those early churchmen, "athletes of God," who subjected themselves to the disciplines of the desert. In essence, the ballet served as testimony to Martha's lifelong homage to the human body as a thing of wonder: a miracle of gross muscles and small bones set in action by an exemplary nervous system. Programmed as a "fanfare for dance as an art," the work glowed with the conviction that practice is a holy rite, leading to perfection. That the path to such perfection is strewn with "tribulations, disciplines and denials" gave *Acrobats* an air of being at times a hilarious obstacle race, especially for the leading character, who was wryly dealing with the whims and fancies (and sluggishness) of her own choreographic compulsions.

The dilemma of trying to fill the needs of both her dancers and her ballet master—a devil of a fellow with a relentless whip—provided the so-called narrative theme. Goaded by the demands of those for whom she manufactured countless "works of art," the besieged choreographer struggled with an unwilling imagination; and trying to forget the whole business, she sought peace and oblivion on the side of the stage behind a postage stamp of a screen that just about covered her face when she occasionally sat down behind it in frustration. But neither the performers nor the ballet master permitted her the luxury of rest or solitude. Like the incoming tide, the dancers kept leaping in, gung-ho for practicing multiple pirouettes, slithering falls, and tricky, spectacular lifts; while the ballet master, at his wit's end, tried to lasso his recalcitrant choreographer with his whip. Cooly and disdainfully, with a gesture of queenly elegance, Martha merely untied the noose, letting it fall ignominiously at her feet.

217

Acrobats of God derived much of its sheer theatrical fun from Noguchi's whimsical set and Carlos Surinach's sparkling Iberian-esque music, which was played by an orchestra plus three onstage mandolinsts. In addition to being a rollicking accompaniment for the mock waltzes, minuets, and typical dance class routines, Surinach's rhythms had the kind of nonstop vitality that kept Martha on her choreographic toes.

Noguchi's high, curved, red-surfaced barre—an amusing combination of a gymnastic prop and a real barre—served as the central prop. At one moment four girls alighted upon its slanted surface and executed deep knee-bends while their male partners, standing on their hands directly below, mirrored their pliés upside-down. Martha's little niche at stage left with its yellow screen was neatly counterbalanced by three colorfully designed music stands in front of the three mandolinists at stage right who sat and played their portion of the score with solemn equanimity despite the wild goings-on around them. Divining the spirit of Martha's spoken or unspoken intentions, Noguchi impishly utilized space in all directions with his decorative hanging contraptions.

The crowning touch, however, came from Martha herself. Yards of orange silk taffeta, broken by wide horizontal bands of dark brown, seductively enclosed her body with the slinky sureness of a cocoon. The lush fabric had been in her possession for years . . . saved for such a moment when wit and style would require unparalleled elegance. The sight of a svelte Martha Graham advancing toward the audience, her shining black hair piled high on her head, her hands pressed and fluttering together in mock distress, was unforgettable. And so was the impact of *Acrobats of God*.

———

"All of them, men and women alike, are beautiful to look at; all of them are trained to the state of ease in energy; all of them have an underlying dramatic awareness of what is going on about them; and all of them move as if they were sentient branches of Martha Graham herself," wrote John Martin in the *New York Times* on the closing Sunday fo the 1960 season, which included the premieres of *Acrobats of God* and *Alcestis*.

No wonder Martha was proud of her dancers. They were the life-blood of her creative self. Now she relied not only upon Bert, Helen, Ethel, Paul, Linda, Gene, and David, whose choreographic ingenuity played no small part in the realization of *Acrobats* and *Alcestis*, but also upon the dancing talents of new company members such as Mary Hinkson, Richard Kuch, Richard Gain, Dan Wagoner, Robert Powell, and young Akiko Kanda to pull off the ambitious repertoire that included *Clytemnestra*, *Night Journey*, *Seraphic Dialogue*, *Embattled Garden*, and *Diversion of Angels*, plus the two new works.

Martha would be the first to admit her dependence on these exquisitely trained, resourceful, and, yes, brave souls who manned her vessel during those tempestuous times when doubt assailed her frequently, pulling her down into its murky depths. According to one company member, *Alcestis*—that radiant "rite of spring," as it was called on the program—began in those depths of personal suffering. Martha declared as much to her cast, averring that she, like Alcestis, had to go down into hell before she could come back.

A quite plausible explanation, if we accept the supposition that a work of art is a direct translation of the artist's personality; that by studying the creative product we can probe the conflicts and harmonies of the creator's inner life.

In deference to this popular theory, let us first look at the myth of Alcestis, as dramatized by Euripides: Alcestis, wife of King Admetus of Thessaly, offers to die in her husband's stead to appease the gods, who have decreed his death. She descends into the grave, but is heroically rescued by the demigod Hercules, who has come as a guest to the palace of Admetus on the day of the funeral. Her resurrection is hailed as a miracle.

Clearly, Alcestis is willing to die; she even seeks death, admittedly for altruistic reasons. In Martha's *Alcestis*, death is represented by the character Thanatos (who does not appear in Euripides' play), and the main action—one could say, the only dramatic action—consists of the battle between Thanatos and Hercules for the possession of Alcestis's soul. This leads us to believe, if we follow this supposition faithfully, that life, as symbolized by Hercules, triumphed and that health returned to Alcestis in the form of her resurrection.

So far, we seem to be succeeding in linking Martha's nature to that of Alcestis, for we know that her moods were unpredictable, deeply disturbing, and sometimes at the point of facing a dead end. But if we pursue such a view, we would have to consider the character of Alcestis to be a portrait of Martha, and, accordingly, the role could be analyzed to the extent of revealing to the world "the true" Martha Graham. Now, resemblances might exist, and certainly identification with the characters of her ballets afforded the necessary bond between Martha (as it would for any actor or actress) and the personality she would portray; but it would be false to conclude that an artist's products literally describe the artist's mind.

As we have already discovered with *Errand into the Maze,* a work of art is an objectification of ideas and feelings. To analyze Martha's personality in terms of a specific production would be a grave mistake, even admitting that her dances were "deep songs" reverberating from the rich world of her imagination. Indeed, it is their very depth—as products of the unconscious—that gives us the clue as to their ultimate meaning on a universal humanistic scale.

In his wisdom, Carl Jung states: "Whenever the creative force predominates, human life is ruled and moulded by the unconscious as against the active will, and the conscious ego is swept along on a subterranean current, being nothing more than a helpless observer of events."

No, it is not necessary to have entered hell consciously to be able to depict it in a ballet on the stage. That is the task for the creative imagination; with the aid of choreographic skills it renders hell visible for all to see. The torment that Martha repeatedly experienced in her emotional life can be more fully explained again by one of Jung's observations: "The artist is not a person endowed with free will who seeks his own ends, but one who allows art to realize its purposes through him. As a human being, he may have moods and a will and personal aims, but as an artist, he is man in a higher sense—he is collective man—one who carries and shapes the unconscious, psychic life of mankind."

In Martha's personal life, emotional extremes supplied the complex fiber of most of her relationships. On the surface, heaven and hell seemed to rule her. However, to confuse personal emotions with those projected in a work of art would be to discredit the act of creation, which transcends individual feeling. When it came to her work, Martha appeared to have heaven and hell at her command.

Alcestis contained both. Its theme—the struggle between forces of destruction and forces of reconstruction—was by no means new, either to Martha or to her Denishawn parents, who had created their own dances of rebirth (*Egyptian Nights, Ishtar of the Seven Gates,* and others). Contrary, however, to *Clytemnestra,* where the theme of rebirth involved complex psychological significance, *Alcestis* remained a ritual, a resplendent albeit impersonal ritual. Actually, it turned out to be more of an allegory than the dance-drama that Martha had originally intended.

It was a curious switch. In the script that she sent to the composer of her choice, Vivian Fine, with whom she had successfully collaborated at Louis's suggestion in the thirties, Martha laid out the action with clues that revealed her true source of inspiration: not the classic drama by Euripides, but the short modern play by the poet Theodore Morrison entitled *The Dream of Alcestis*. In the latter, the relationship between the queen and Hercules, the life-giver, is symbolically developed.

Once again, a figure at an emotional crossroads takes precedence in Martha's creative imagination. Her Alcestis would have to make the metaphoric choice between succumbing to unproductivity and forgetfulness (death), as portrayed by Thanatos, or rising regeneratively to the acceptance of life's pain and risks, as portrayed by Hercules.

Struck by T. S. Eliot's phrase "circular desert," from his probing verse-play *The Family Reunion*, Martha visualized Alcestis's ambivalence as a traversing back and forth within a circumscribed place where indecision is the emotional protagonist. Unable to commit herself to action, Alcestis inhabits a colorless no-man's-land, in which all shadows are obliterated by a noonday sun. Eliot's play, in critic Russell Kirk's words, is "about visions of terror." Likewise, Martha's response to the lines, "In and out, in an endless drift/Of shrieking forms in a circular desert," suggests that her portrait of Alcestis would have the potential of a banked fire, one that could break into flames from gusts of wayward feeling.

But no such portrait emerged. Martha's danced interpretation of Alcestis metamorphosized into something static and remote, more statuesque than human. By contrast, Thanatos and Hercules, as portrayed by Bertram Ross and Paul Taylor, respectively, were spectacularly dramatic. Onstage, ironically, Martha's "circular desert" image became a reality.

Obviously, she was reaching for a form of suspended drama—a drama of internalized conflict, more in the realm of poetry or opera than dance. She even had in mind to use some pieces of décor designed by Noguchi for her Berlin performance of the solo *Judith* in 1957. Planned to conceal the onstage orchestra and to provide a background for the dance, the scenery consisted of free-standing iron frames, each enclosing a stretched and decorated fish-net that could be placed where they best served the action. Colorless and transparent, they signified for Martha Alcestis's undefined state of mind.

But when production took over, the stage of *Alcestis* was anything but colorless. As almost always, Martha's original conceptions underwent drastic revisions in the course of choreographic realization. The set for *Alcestis* was anything but transparent. By Noguchi, yes. Not his *Judith,* but pieces from the film version of *Night Journey,* created in 1960, provided the décor. There were two monumental structures with simulated granite exteriors: a right-angled corner of a huge square; and enormous wheel resembling a massive stone with a small opening in the center as for an axis. In addition, Noguchi would supply a slanted platform, like a ramp, that could serve as a bed for Alcestis. This last was, perhaps, the only piece that conformed in part to Martha's original idea (as described to Vivian Fine) of Alcestis being suspended physically.

Whereas in the film, Noguchi's huge cornerstone and wheel gave the impression of distantly seen fragments strewn across an endless horizon, on the stage of the 54th St. Theatre the mammoth pieces were jammed together leaving little or no dancing space. No hint of this, however, was given during rehearsals in the big studio at the school. According to David Wood, the set worked beautifully; the enormous wheel was tumbled from place to place and the cornerstone easily turned at different angles. But on the day before the premiere, when the sets were brought to the theater for the first run-through with costumes, orchestra, and lights, it was "utter chaos."

Already in their third day of the season, the company's nerves were on edge. When, in the course of the action, the dancers tried to move the pieces there were either collisions or no space was left for passage between them. The musical cues, so well defined in the studio, were no longer recognizable within the complex orchestration. The last straw seemed to come at the very end when the women dancers, whose costumes had strips of velcro for fastening at the shoulders, raised their arms only to find themselves bare to the waist! Martha was in tears. The need for another full rehearsal was obvious, but to do so after the performance that night would have meant overtime for musicians and stagehands—an unthinkable expense. It was finally decided to call a 9:00 A.M. rehearsal for the dancers and stagehands, with a final run-through with the orchestra at 1:00 P.M.

When morning came, everyone was there...except Martha. When waiting became both intolerable and impractical, David took charge and started making necessary alterations in the choreography as well as rearranging the sets. Placing himself and another dancer who was also not performing throughout the ballet in opposite wings, he was able to give instructions to the cast as they moved the scenery from place to place. In this way, with the help of Bert and Helen when the stagehands left for lunch, the last details were worked out.

At one o'clock Martha showed up.

Approaching her somewhat tentatively, David said, "I've changed a few things, Martha. I just wonder if it's all right."

Obviously nettled and embarrassed by her tardiness, Martha retorted, "How do I know? We haven't gone through it yet."

The atmosphere was charged with nervous tension as the rehearsal began. But everything—music, props, costuming, movement —went smoothly from beginning to end. When the stagehands came to David to determine if the set should be "spiked" for that night's performance, he turned to Martha for her approval. "Is this all right? As you see, I've changed things."

"Of course, it's all right!" Martha ejaculated fiercely. "Why shouldn't it be all right?" And she abruptly left the theater.

Stunned by Martha's rebuff and lack of acknowledgment of his work, Wood sat down dejectedly in the rear of the semidark auditorium. A moment later he saw a curly head turn toward him, and he heard the friendly voice of Jean Rosenthal.

"That's all right, David," said the lighting designer, who had heard the conversation from her workstand midway up the aisle. "Can't you understand...part of Martha's genius is to be able to recognize people's abilities and to rely upon them and let them do their job. She has such an ego herself that she thinks everybody else has that same ego, so if they can do the job they will do it to the very best of their ability. And she is right."

"Yes," David thought in retrospect, "that's Martha's great secret. She knows her dancers, she knows how to use her dancers, and how to rely upon them. Sure, I made the physical thing in *Alcestis* work; but I was doing a part of the job that was part of the total concept of what Martha meant...and still, *it's all hers.*"

Ambiguous as Martha might be in daily life, onstage as the allegorical Alcestis she transcended humanness. The scenario, as usual, was also "all hers," neither Euripides nor Morrison, but a unified

223

Graham conception. And whatever her technical problems with Noguchi's stunning sets, *Alcestis* emerged, according to John Martin, as "one of her most ravishing creations." In itself, Vivian Fine's tone-rich score was a matching declaration of faith in the restorative elements in life—as symbolized by the healthy, natural personality of Hercules.

Martha's personal suffering in the early sixties must have been unbearable; notwithstanding, she created the brightly joyous *Acrobats of God* and *Alcestis*. Once again, Carl Jung has the answer: "Human passion falls within the sphere of conscious experience, while the subject of vision lies beyond it."

Chapter Eleven

Lady of the Labyrinth

By 1962, Martha had harvested more than one hundred and thirty-five dances, among them works that were comparable to historic landmarks of choreography conceived by the greatest of ballet innovators: Petipa, Fokine, Nijinsky, Balanchine. When critics triumphantly proclaimed her the finest living modern dance choreographer and labeled certain compositions "masterpieces," did Martha glow inwardly and look back with pride? Or did she view her work with realistic candor, judging it with the same severity as the ever-critical Louis was wont to do?

The truth was that Martha never looked back willingly. A prisoner in a labyrinth of her own devising and desiring, her compulsion was to conquer each day anew the Minotaur of encroaching time. Her private "errand into the maze" was a continual search for new roles, new visions, new proof of her sustaining powers. Only the future contained the challenge that she needed to prove those powers.

When it was suggested that she reconstruct *Primitive Mysteries*, that perfect synthesis of Hispanic-Indian culture and early modern dance, she produced objections that were convincing enough. First, it would look dated to contemporary audiences used to virtuosity and slick staging. Second, today's dancers would find its weighted, earthbound movement, cast as it was in monolithic design, beyond their aesthetic comprehension, trained as most of them were in a ballet-dominated technique (this had already been proved in the 1947 revival, in which the new-style modern dancers were accused of lacking "the full-blooded vigor of the concert group of the mid-thirties"). Third, it was a shocking fact that *Primitive Mysteries*—as with so many of the old works—no longer existed. Unnotated, unfilmed, it remained but a tattered memory.

Behind these arguments was the supreme unspoken one: Her solos and her solo roles were her most intimate possessions. Each one was a "deep song"; each one was "a graph of the heart." One did not cut one's heart into remnants. It would take a cataclysmic event for her to perform that surgery. But in less than two years, such an event would come to pass. . . .

True, in 1947 she had consented to give to Pearl Lang her triple role of the Virgin Mary, Mary Magdalene, and the Madonna in *El Penitente,* and to Ethel Winter the lyrical solo, *Salem Shore.* Painful as it might have been to relinquish these roles, the exigency of replacing Merce Cunningham in that all-important New York season (the second under the managerial hand of Sol Hurok) required nothing less radical. Then, too, she had to save herself for the premiere of *Errand into the Maze* and for the technically demanding *Cave of the Heart* and *Dark Meadow.* And in the near distance was *Night Journey,* due to open within three months in Cambridge, Massachusetts.

Despite her avowal to continue to perform "in the dignity of my time," Martha still wanted at the age of sixty-seven to project the stuff of dance proper: passion. And why not? In the early nineteen-sixties, she was actually more attractive than she ever had been. No longer gaunt of face and square-boned, she had grown more feminine. The piercing intensity was still there, but a softness had set in with age. For years already, her long black hair had been piled high on her head, lending stature to her spine-straight frame. Held there Japanese-style with pins or ornamental headdresses when she danced, it emphasized the shapely modeling of her cheekbones and brow. The striking classicism of her features and her magisterial way of holding herself made her queens—Jocasta, Clytemnestra, Mary Stuart, Alcestis—vividly credible. The voice that once was small and high-pitched had become low and resonant. According to Martha's purposes (and how diversely calculated they could be!), its low-key intonations could be authoritative, persuasive, or warmly sensuous. And when she spoke in public or tried to evoke emotional responses in her dancers, metaphysical symbols ignited the air around her, making her seem poetically luminous, infinitely wise, mysteriously awesome.

Drama was her personal domain. Whether its use was intentional or a manifestation of her innate personality, the dramatic innuendo—stated vocally or visually—became as dazzling as a jewel, as sharp as a knife.

But there was the other side of Martha's nature: the realist in matters of theatrical horse-sense. All those years with Ted Shawn, who knew the theater inside out and who could design and run a tour that made exorbitant demands on his dancers and on himself—all those "thousand and one night" stands had honed her into a tough-minded trouper, who, on one occasion, could watch a broad-stroked, tasteless parody of her own technique by a foreign dance company and coolly condone the so-called ballet as "a good opener." All those years of learning the craft of composition under the uncompromising Louis Horst, who would not hesitate to put her down or let her fly into a rage and burn herself out—these subsequent experiences, too, tested her professionalism in down-to-earth terms.

The same hard-nosed knowledge would, in time, allow her to take Louis himself with a grain of salt, recognizing that his preference for sparseness and the nonromantic theme would have—if followed —excised all her instinctual identification with dramaturgy and historic event. Her sense of humor, likewise, in its alertness to the absurd in a situation, had a commedia dell'arte ring, as when a desperate husband, anxiously questioning his wife's whereabouts from the star herself as she issued from the stage door after a soul-stirring performance, received the shattering reply, "She stood you up, boy!"

Nor was Martha oblivious to her own misjudgments. In the Biblically based *Visionary Recital,* her role of Delilah had failed as a theatrical conception. In a strange, untypical reversal of emphasis, she had made Delilah secondary to Samson, thereby creating an imbalance that she could not overcome. Guided by sounder reasoning, she retitled the work *Samson Agonistes* and gave Bertram Ross the stature he was entitled to as Samson; and to Mary Hinkson, who was to become increasingly important in the company, she turned over the part of Delilah as The Awakener of Samson's powers.

With or without Martha, however, the work never reached the creative level of any of the preceding year's compositions. Yet *Visionary Recital* was important. It marked the first of future, albeit separate, collaborative ventures with two highly gifted artists: the stage designer Rouben Ter-Arutunian and the musician-composer Robert Starer.

Ter-Arutunian responded to Martha's idea of a protagonist "who was caught in his inner world and was in conflict with the outer world" by creating a stunning set that consisted of a double screen of vertically hung metallic cables across the width of the stage. Combined with a similar series of cables strung in a circular cluster down-stage, the total impression was that of mysterious passages which seemed to trap the dancers within shining tube-like forms. (In 1968 the Russian-born designer would create the décor for the Abé-lard–Héloise drama *A Time of Snow,* set to Norman Dello Joio's music.)

Starer, who was to provide Martha with three more scores in ad-dition to *Visionary Recital,* considered that a "total theatrical entity" should be the all-important result of a successful collaboration. Together they would achieve that aim with the following year's *Phaedra,* a work that was perfectly suited to Martha's purpose of prolonging her dancing career at this time of her life. The title role, already famous in the annals of dramatic literature as an acting vehicle (Euripides' *Hippolytus,* Racine's *Phaedra*), would furnish her with the dynamic motivation she craved. The Starer–Graham col-laboration combined with Noguchi's daring set for *Phaedra* was to become a sensational success.

Based on the Greek legend of the Cretan princess Phaedra, wife of the aging Theseus, the ballet would depart from Martha's use of in-trospection as a main choreographic device and develop its tragic theme almost exclusively in the form of straight narrative. Laden with ironies of a sophisticated nature, the action would center on Phaedra's illicit passion for her husband's young son, Hippolytus. Thwarted when he coldly rejects her, she resorts to duplicity and revenge.

Calling Phaedra's dilemma "tragic and eternal," Martha en-visioned scenes in which Phaedra's wild imaginings would carry the story line. The portrait she drew of an older woman who sought the amorous, rejuvenating powers of a younger man was startlingly con-vincing. The role was to become the Indian summer triumph of Martha's last performing years. Compared to her almost wholly pan-tomimic renderings of the five remaining roles before her retirement in 1969—Judith, Hecuba, the Witch of Endor, Héloise, and The Lady of the House of Sleep—Phaedra contained the unforgettable vi-brancy of the "old" Martha, which is to say, the young Martha of *Let-ter to the World* and *Deaths and Entrances.*

In commissioning the score from Starer, Martha eschewed her usual procedure of drafting a scenario (as she had done for *Visionary Recital*) and invited the composer to discuss the ballet with her one weekend in a house that she had rented for the summer of 1961 at

Shelter Island within the prong-like tip of Long Island's northeastern shore. The weekend proved to be a revelation for the musician. Though he had studied Euripides' *Hippolytus* and Racine's *Phaedra*, he soon discovered that Martha's *Phaedra* would be entirely her own, woven of typical Grahamesque identification with the psychic background of her character; in this instance, the "Phantasmagoria of Desire" that represented Phaedra's infatuation.

"When she talked to me, I began to hear the music as I listened," recounted the composer. "She had a wonderful way of getting one all excited . . . I don't know of anyone else who has. . . ."

Inspired, Starer composed a richly orchestrated score that colorfully conveyed the restless, primitive urgings within the Cretan princess and the debacle that ensued as a result of her uncontrollable passion.

"*Phaedra* was a high point in my work," Starer said. "Martha showed me new things about my music . . . more than anybody else. In *Phaedra* we had this close proximity. We worked after each session was finished. I brought it to her and we talked, and then I went on and described what I wanted. . . .

"The only time she asked me to change anything, she did it very tactfully: 'I'd like you to come to a rehearsal,' she said one day. That was very surprising. She had never asked me to attend choreographic rehearsals. 'Would you like me in the room when you are composing?' We both laughed. But she wanted me to see what needed to be done. The section was too short . . . obviously, if the section is too short you cannot do what you have planned.

"Sometimes, she used my music directly for support, and then she would work deliberately against it in counterpoint. If there was one thing I learned from her it was that the most dramatic things were done in silence."

More than a story of conflictual emotions, the legend of Phaedra is a tale of Olympian rivalry as devastating on a small scale as the epic disasters of the Trojan War. Engaging once more in a contest for supremacy, the goddesses Artemis (who demanded the sacrifice of Iphigenia at Aulis) and Aphrodite (who incited Paris to abduct Helen) play out their antagonisms through the actions of human beings. Always victorious in affairs of the heart, Aphrodite is vexed that the young Hippolytus is indifferent to her charms and devotes himself instead to the chaste Artemis, at whose shrine he worships as he pursues his beloved sport of hunting. The scheme Aphrodite concocts is as intricate as the one she jointly conceived with Hera to plant love in Medea's heart so that Jason would be able to procure the Golden Fleece. That love, as we know, turned to hate, and wrought a fate for Jason that remains to this day the most ghastly revenge ever perpetuated by a woman on a man.

But the stakes for Hippolytus are even higher than for Jason. It is a member of the Olympian family who seeks revenge. Aphrodite's pride has been touched to the quick. The goddess of love must never be thwarted—especially by a young, handsome athlete.

How cleverly she weaves her net! Choosing the younger daughter of King Minos, whom Theseus took a fancy to in preference to Ariadne (he soon found Ariadne's passion tiresome after she helped him slay the Minotaur), Aphrodite plants the most subtle poison of all in Phaedra's unsuspecting heart: insatiable desire. Hardly more than a blossoming girl when she married the heroic Theseus, Phaedra has served her husband dutifully and tended their children conscientiously.

Her stepson Hippolytus, conceived by the Amazon, Antiope, on one of Theseus's early exploits, has grown manly just at the time when Phaedra is reaching the prime of her sexuality. Scandalized by the lustful sensations coursing through her at the sight of Hippolytus, she feels morally guilty; and not realizing that she is the victim of a goddess's revenge, she vacillates between licentious desire and shame. But so vicious is Aphrodite's revenge that she plots Hippolytus's death by means of a double subterfuge that will trap Phaedra as well: the love she has implanted in the young queen will turn into hate when rejected by Hippolytus; losing all sense of reason, Phaedra will seek revenge by lying to Theseus that Hippolytus violated her in his absence. Thus will Aphrodite succeed in setting the king against his own son and bringing to pass the boy's death.

Seen in its true perspective, the legend of Phaedra, whether turned into a play by Euripides or Racine or rewritten in dance form by Martha, is an indictment of unruly passion. In Martha's hands, the myth goes one step further. As with her other Greek works, the legend takes on modern psychological meaning. Among the dream images projected by Phaedra is a nightmarish scene that serves to augment the young queen's corroding sense of guilt: borne in on the shoulders of four men, Queen Pasiphaë, Phaedra's mother, writhes with the same lust that possesses her daughter. This ghoulish vision suggests that Phaedra's passion is a congenital inheritance from her mother, who is said to have consorted with a bull. As the old queen is carried offstage, her black veil falls on the shoulders of her daughter. Symbolically, the veil will become the young queen's shroud when she commits suicide.

The most original innovation, however, takes place in the hair-raising "lie" scene. Whereas in Euripides, Phaedra writes the incriminating letter about Hippolytus's "rape" to her husband, attaching it to her wrist so that he would read it *after* her death, in the Graham version Phaedra reenacts the lie for the benefit of the enraged Theseus. A tour de force of histrionics that sets the spectator's nerves on edge, the lie serves a double purpose: as it stirs up uncontrollable fury in Theseus, it permits Phaedra to live out—as in a wishful dream—the sexual gratification she so desires.

The casting of the vicious role of Aphrodite had begun seven years earlier in Indonesia, when the company was on its Far Eastern tour. The circumstances were somewhat unusual. In a performance of *Ardent Song*, the cast was struggling with a suffocating heat on an outdoor stage that was merely an unshaded platform. At one moment, when her dancing part had just begun, Ethel Winter, who performed the role of Dawn, was lifted high above the heads of the other dancers and placed on top of an outstretched Donald McKayle, the male lead. Within a few minutes she found herself soaked to the bone by Donald's heavily perspiring body. Then, just before her exit, when she was supposed to spin into a network of streamers held tightly by offstage assistants, no one was there to maintain the tension, and she found herself entangled with the streamers wrapped around her feet.

"I came off so mad," remembered Winter, "that I forgot that we were all in the same dressing room—a tent with a dirt floor. I ripped that costume off, stamped on it, and swore. And right next to me was Martha!"

"Good girl, Ethel," said Martha in low, approving tones.

Surprised and embarrassed, Winter realized that Martha had never suspected that "I had that rage within me."

Until she danced the role of Aphrodite, Ethel Winter had mostly been performing lyrical roles. Technically she was brilliant, with marvelous speed and balance, as was seen in her interpretation of the Girl in Red in *Diversion of Angels*; but her delicate features, gentle manners, and easy grace conveyed a certain softness, which was more suitable for *Salem Shore* or the luminous Joan of *Seraphic Dialogue*.

As Aphrodite she became incisive, vindictive. Her legs shot out like spears when she was suspended in the double shell that Noguchi had designed for the goddess's habitat. The double shell, which was a heart-shaped prop, was itself suspended, but it had apertures for Winter to grasp for her midair erotic position.

"Actually," remarked Ethel, "Aphrodite was one of the easier roles for me . . . much easier as communication than all the 'nice' parts. I always had my eye on Phaedra . . . I was the one who was leading her to her destruction."

There were problems with the set, however—typical problems associated with Martha's disinclination to specify to Noguchi exactly what she needed or wanted. Humorous repercussions were to follow. When the sculptor first brought in the shell-like form, everybody gasped. He had intended it for Artemis's shrine, but its interior was lined with foam rubber and painted a "shrieking red," a far too realistic reproduction of female reproductive organs! Shocked, the shy Paul Taylor, who played Theseus, shook his head and murmured, "Noguchi was *very* naughty." It was the sculptor's idea that Hippolytus, portrayed by Bertram Ross, would open the form (the shell's sides closed like little doors) and take the chaste Artemis out, as if lifting her from a womb.

Without a word, Martha sent the prop right back, and in time Noguchi converted Artemis's shrine to Aphrodite's heart-shaped abode by removing the padded interior and providing supports for her aerial maneuvers.

But he did get his way with the prop that he designed for Hippolytus. Following Martha's instructions to build a shoji screen, he created a shrine with segmented apertures at different levels. Each segment had a door of its own which would be opened one at a time by the wily Aphrodite for the express purpose of tantalizing Phaedra. First she revealed the queen's stepson's torso; then his legs; then his pelvis. Gradually, like a striptease act, the entire male figure was disclosed.

The prop that was the most eccentric, however, was Phaedra's bed. The slope of its angular tilt made it almost impossible for one human being to recline on it much less a pair of lovers, as implied in the lie scene.

Yet, in spite of its erotic extravagances, *Phaedra* was essentially moral. In the last analysis, it was the gods who sinned against the humans: out of jealousy and revenge, Aphrodite stooped to murder; the heart-pure Artemis, who was supposed to be "the protectress of dewy youth," permitted a terrible fate to overtake the innocent, worshipful Hippolytus. And the noble Theseus was deaf to his own son's pleas for mercy. Phaedra, the victim, is the one who came close to being blameless. Hating herself for incestuous desires, she took her own life.

———————

The international fame that Martha had acquired during her first State Department tour in 1955–1956 was to receive fresh momentum in the fall of 1962, when the company visited the Middle East, Turkey, Greece, Rumania, Yugoslavia, Poland, Finland, Stockholm, Norway, Germany, and Holland.

As a gesture to Bethsabée de Rothschild, Martha decided to premiere a work in Tel Aviv, a work for which the scenic designer and composer would be Israeli. It was a daring thing to do, for the set would be waiting for the company to rehearse in only when they arrived in Israel. It was daring in another way, as well, for Martha was attempting a second version of a previously successful work: the solo *Judith*. This time she would dance an aged Judith who would look back upon her life as a widow and relive her mission as the savior of her people. Again the theme of introspection as recall would serve to project an epic tale—only this time there would be no self-judgmental conclusion, as in *Clytemnestra*. Surrounded and acclaimed by the victorious Israelites, Judith would receive due honor in her old age.

Legend of Judith was one of the most spectacular of Martha's later ballets, and her acting was just as spectacular as the dancing of her company. The murder of Holofernes, following Judith's entry into the general's tent and her seductive temptation of him with wine, turned out to be the most sensational moment of all: covered by a silver lamé cape with a slit in it through which his decapitated head jutted out, Holofernes was rolled offstage. Conceived by Bertram

Ross as the solution to his macabre exit as Holofernes, the scene took on a terrifying reality.

The tour with its company of twenty and an orchestra picked up in London required two Constellation aircraft: one for the musicians, dancers, and crew; the other for baggage and scenery. And there was no merciful period of rest anywhere until Cologne, Germany, when Martha had a single day to herself. Their performances were sold out everywhere, except in Munich.

The stop in Zagreb, Yugoslavia, had been as thrilling as the first tour's premiere in Tokyo: flowers, curtain call after curtain call, wild enthusiasm. For Martha, the only disappointments during the tour were not to be able to see Greek dancing in Greece and the native folk dances of Eastern Europe, or to have time off to go to museums or theaters. But she did have an opportunity for a brief telephone conversation with Mary Wigman, who, unfortunately, was not well.

Martha had seen Wigman perform in the early thirties when the great German dancer gave a series of concerts in New York, while the latter had seen Martha dance in Berlin in 1957 when she had been invited there for the opening of the new Philharmonic Hall and had presented the solo *Judith.* At that time Wigman was seventy-one years old, and had lived through the grim war years when bombing and Nazi persecution had deprived her of her long-established school in Dresden; she had lost everything and was forced to move to Leipzig, where she taught "pale, worn-out young factory workers who looked like gangsters" the simplest of movements in an effort to rehabilitate their emaciated bodies. Now settled in Berlin, where she had been invited by the "Senate of Culture" to head a large dance department, she was choreographing large-scale works such as *Le Sacre du Printemps.*

Wigman and Martha had more in common than might have been presumed from their divergent styles. As artists they had struggled against the devastating odds of poverty, antagonism, apathy, and misunderstanding. Both women had come to their profession late, commencing their studies in their twenties and giving their first independent concerts when they were over thirty (Martha thirty-one; Wigman, thirty-three). Innovators of unique techniques, searchers, realists, and philosophers, they shared a fundamental awareness of the all-inclusive demands of art. Compare all that Martha believed and experienced with Wigman's analysis of creativity: "the will to act whipped up to a point of obsession."

Only eight years older than Martha, Wigman had already given

Jane Dudley, Yuriko, Helen McGehee, and Pearl Lang as One Who Speaks in
Letter to the World, 1954. COURTESY PEARL LANG.

Mary Hinkson in *Diversion of Angels*, c. 1966. PHOTOGRAPH BY MARTHA SWOPE.

Ethel Winter (Joan), Bertram Ross (St. Michael), Carol Payne (St. Catherine), and Ellen Graff (St. Margaret) in *Seraphic Dialogue*, 1960. PHOTOGRAPH BY MARTHA SWOPE.

Martha Graham in her dressing room, c. 1960s. PHOTOGRAPH BY ARTHUR TODD.
ARTHUR TODD COLLECTION.

Bertram Ross, Martha Graham, and Richard Gain in *Clytemnestra* (The Murder of Agamemnon), c. 1963. PHOTOGRAPH BY MARTHA SWOPE.

Martha Graham and David Wood in *Clytemnestra*, c. 1963. Photograph by Martha Swope.

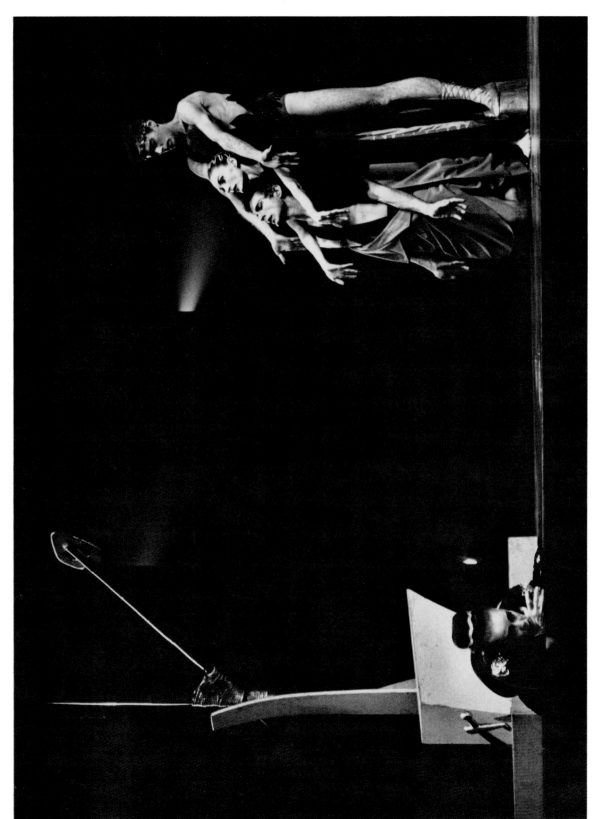

Martha Graham, Bertram Ross, Helen McGehee, and Gene McDonald in *Clytemnestra* (Family Portrait), c. 1963. Photograph by Martha Swope.

Martha Graham (Mary), Sallie Wilson (Elizabeth), Kenneth Petersen (Executioner), and William Carter and Paul Nickel (Heralds) in *Episodes I*, 1959. PHOTOGRAPH BY MARTHA SWOPE.

Paul Taylor in *Episodes II*, 1959. PHOTOGRAPH BY MARTHA SWOPE.

David Wood, Bertram Ross, Ethel Winter, and Martha Graham in *Acrobats of God*, 1960.
PHOTOGRAPH BY MARTHA SWOPE.

Bertram Ross, Martha Graham, and Paul Taylor in *Alcestis*, 1960. Photograph by Martha Swope.

Paul Taylor and Martha Graham in *Phaedra*, 1962. PHOTOGRAPH BY MARTHA SWOPE.

Helen McGehee, Bertram Ross, Martha Graham, and Ethel Winter in *Phaedra*, 1960. PHOTOGRAPH BY MARTHA SWOPE.

Martha Graham taking a bow after *Legend of Judith*. PHOTOGRAPH BY ARTHUR TODD.
ARTHUR TODD COLLECTION.

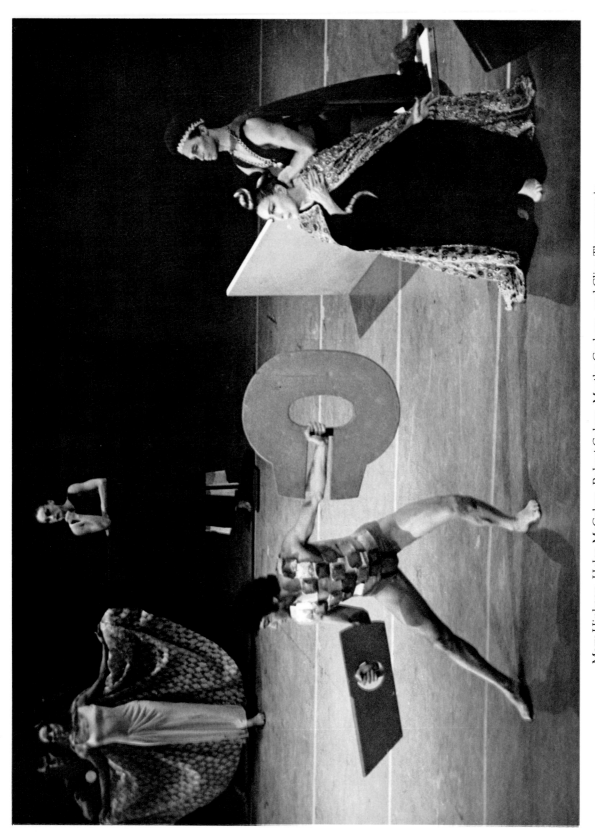

Mary Hinkson, Helen McGehee, Robert Cohan, Martha Graham, and Clive Thompson in *Cortege of Eagles*, 1967. PHOTOGRAPH BY MARTHA SWOPE.

Pearl Lang as One Who Dances in *Letter to the World*, 1970. PHOTOGRAPH BY
MARTHA SWOPE.

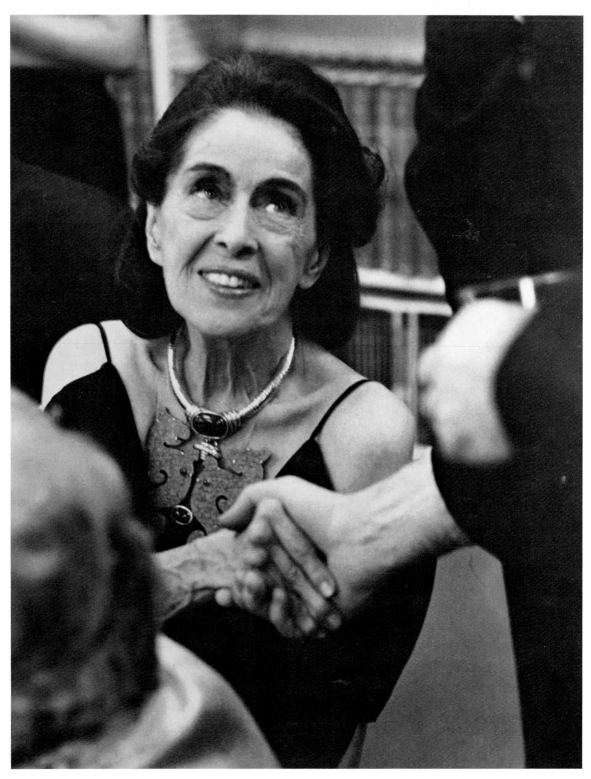

Martha Graham at a party given in her honor at the Dance Collection, New York Public Library, Lincoln Center, 1974. Photograph by Gjon Mili. Courtesy Dance Collection, New York Public Library.

up performing in 1942, when she was fifty-six years old. For Martha, it would take seven more years after *Legend of Judith* to relinquish the stage at the age of seventy-five! In this respect she showed the tenacity exhibited by her first inspiration, Ruth St. Denis, who kept performing well into her eighties. But then, St. Denis was mystically absorbed in the dance as religious experience. She never pretended to be a dancer of technical prowess; she felt that her art was a communication of spiritual truths; and as she grew older it became imperative for her to fulfill her premise that "the great mission of the dancer is to contribute to the betterment of mankind."

Martha, on the other hand, could not emotionally withdraw from the stage. Nor did it seem imperative yet, for she was able to maintain a performing schedule that would have devastated a younger woman. As a result of her highly successful State Department tour of Europe and the Mideast, she was invited, through the efforts of Francis Mason, cultural attaché in London and writer on dance, to appear in the 1963 Edinburgh Festival. She would be performing not only the new *Legend of Judith,* but also *Night Journey,* an even more demanding role. Wisely, the new ballet that she was working on, *Circe,* though originally intended for herself, was now given to Mary Hinkson. Not ready yet for Edinburgh, it would be premiered in London at the Prince of Wales Theatre at the beginning of September in a two-week season made possible through the resourceful efforts of an enthusiastic Englishman named Robin Howard. (Howard was subsequently instrumental with the assistance of Robert Cohan of the Graham Company in the establishment of The Place, a center for contemporary dance in London.)

Even with the best intentions, Martha could not willingly give up the role of Circe, the goddess who bewitched men, turning them into animals. Her reluctance was apparent when she first approached Mary with the tentative words, "I have something in mind for you . . . but I'm not sure I can get it out of you."

Mary, of course, was the perfect choice for Circe. The slender, aristocratic-looking girl who had taken over Martha's role in *Samson Agonistes* and who was also memorable as the Girl in White in *Diversion of Angels,* was exceptionally sensitive. Martha knew in her heart that she would be right. At one time rehearsing *Diversion* with Mary and Bertram Ross, Martha went so far as to say, "You two were born knowing."

Yet, in spite of all that she knew and felt about Hinkson's acting and dancing potential, Martha so closely identified with the role of

Circe that during one of the choreographic rehearsals in the studio, when the men were having difficulty lowering Mary from the "cloud" (a high arch on which she was lying), Martha impulsively shouted, "Get me down! Get me down!"

Nevertheless, she worked with typical objectivity on the piece, casting with that special intuitive awareness of the individual characteristics of her dancers. Commanding in stature, Bertram Ross would act the role of Ulysses; the young, stalwart Clive Thompson, his Helmsman; and the four men who would be transformed by the island goddess into animals were succinctly chosen: tall, tawny, curly-haired Richard Gain became Lion; sinewy, long-limbed Gene McDonald, Deer; compact, lithe Peter Randazzo, Goat; and sinuous, quicksilver Robert Powell, Snake.

Edinburgh had the dazzling experience of seeing *Legend of Judith* with its magnificent Hebraic atmosphere created by Dani Karavan's large-scale props and massive central setting suggestive of a promontory in the wilderness, Mordecai Seter's resonant score, and Martha's brilliantly conceived costumes, cloaks, and headdresses. This time Martha's Judith was surrounded by a large cast, and the very spirit of the Old Testament filled the stage as three Archangel-Messengers wearing heavy winglike sleeves swung boldly around the stonelike form representing the widow Judith's retreat from the world and later the tent where she killed Holofernes.

"To encounter her work for the first time is one of the most stunning experiences the theater has to offer," reported the husband-wife team of dance critics known as "Alexander Bland" in *The Observer Weekend Review of London*. The subsequent Prince of Wales Theatre season was equally triumphant—a far cry from what the response to Martha's London appearances had been in 1954.

New York, too, was warmly enthusiastic when the company returned to premiere *Legend of Judith* and *Circe* in October. Yet there was a note of skepticism in more than one review concerning Martha's lessening dance powers. Admitting "truthfully" that *Legend of Judith* was "more drama than dance," Walter Terry added judiciously: "To remind those who might have doubted that she is still the dancer, she underscored passages of gestural eloquence with the kicks and ear-high sweeping leg movements for which she has long been famous." Other more candid criticism pointed out Martha's lack of fluency.

Staunch admirers like Ben Belitt were incensed. "Why can't people accept what she is doing?" remonstrated the poet in a conversation with Bertram Ross. "She is brilliant. She is like light now. She makes you see what you're supposed to see."

He was right. Her presence, her phrasing, her attack, even when modified by the physical restriction of a woman of sixty-nine, were still amazing. But despite the force of Martha's personality and theatrical showmanship, it was becoming obvious that the light she shed onstage was beginning to dim. It would not be long before the major issue of her work's survival would have to be faced. Could she let go? Could she even decide to let go? In her heart she knew that if her choreography were to endure—in the way that operas and plays outlast their original interpreters—she would have to yield her roles to the younger dancers. She recognized this fact but could not accept it, although it had been proved possible with the transfer of *El Penitente* to Pearl Lang in the late forties. And only recently, in March of the current year, she had had to deal with the recasting of *Herodiade*, when the Juilliard School of Music had approached her and José Limón in regard to a series of presentations honoring the music of Paul Hindemith.

José's choice was *The Demon*; Martha's, reluctantly, *Herodiade*. Ethel Winter would portray the woman; Linda Hodes, her attendant. Eugene Lester, who was listed on the program as assistant and musical advisor to Martha Graham, was involved in the analysis of the score in relation to the dance, a complicated task made easier by the fact that Lester had studied with Hindemith at Yale.

Martha had not come to any of the preliminary rehearsals, only to those just before the performance on opening night. When the curtain went up on *Herodiade*, a strange occurrence took place backstage. As soon as the music started, Graham, who was presumably standing in the wings to watch the dance, suddenly went into action. While Ethel was performing her role onstage, she was dancing it offstage, unseen, of course, by the audience.

Herodiade must have meant more to her than she would willingly admit.

But in less than a year, she would lose a more precious possession than a dance.

———————

The big studio at 316 East Sixty-third Street was completely transformed. Instead of the usual double doors (which ordinarily would have a piece of red jersey wound around the knobs if Martha was inside and didn't wish to be disturbed), multiple strings of beads constituted a hanging curtain, Middle Eastern style. Upon closer examination one discovered that the "beads" were both fragrant and sticky. Lifesavers and gumdrops of all flavors and hues had been threaded through straws to hang vertically: a tour de force of culinary sew-manship executed by Bertram Ross, who was also responsible for other delectable decorations within the studio itself.

To the right as one entered was an assembly of small platforms over which fluffy, tasseled pillows and yards of colorful material had been lavishly draped. In the center a high-backed armchair stood on top of a small Oriental rug decorated with a border of lollipops, all glistening in their transparent wrappers. The occupant of the throne-like chair did not wear a turban, nor did he have flashy rings upon his fingers, but with the self-possession that was always his, Louis Horst did convey the corpulent majesty of a Turkish sultan; and he was willing—evidently more than willing—to play the role that Martha and her company had cast him in upon the momentous occasion of his eightieth birthday, January 12, 1964. (Louis once confessed that he had actually been born on January 13, but that his mother, being superstitious, had reworded her son's birth record to read the previous day!)

As guests entered, Louis would stand up and greet them with a wry twinkle in his sharp blue eyes. His height still impressive, his movements still graceful, he announced to one set of celebrants, "I am the Grand *Im*potentate!"

The large mirrors on the long side of the room reflected other transformations. No leotards and tights but elegant evening attire clothed the familiar bodies of the Graham dancers, while Martha herself—looking like the sultan's favorite in a clinging gown—was surrounded by admirers.

It was a party to remember. Potentates from all fields of art were assembled to pay homage to "Mr. University," whose high respect for practitioners in his own profession—Norman Lloyd, Henry Cowell, William Schuman, and Robert Starer, among others—and for contemporary American painters and sculptors, such as Moses Soyer and Raphael Soyer, was evident in his most recent book, *Modern Dance Forms in Relation to the Other Modern Arts*. Among the prominent non-Graham dancers present were José Limón, who had just returned from a highly successful Far Eastern tour, and whose birthday coincided with Louis's, and ballet luminaries Antony Tudor and Alicia Markova.

It was a party to remember for reasons other than the purely social. Besides being a birthday party, the gathering was celebrating the fact the Louis had received, the previous month, an honorary degree from Wayne State University. No one outside of Louis's personal friends and colleagues could possibly have known how much it meant to the "Father of Modern Choreography" to be so honored. For weeks after the occasion the hood with its richly colored Doctor of Humanities band and the tasseled cap he had worn lay on a chair in Louis's apartment for all visitors to see and admire. The man who had never gone to high school, who built his own education book by book during the years of early adulthood, had merited academe's highest honor! It seemed that Louis himself could hardly believe it. But as with all things that had been connected with his life in the dance world, especially with Martha, the occasion of his receiving that much-coveted honor had been fraught with drama.

Sunday, December 15, was the day of Wayne State University's commencement in the year 1963. Anxious to be there in good time prior to the event, and obliged to travel by train (because of a heart ailment), Louis had planned to arrive in Detroit on Saturday. However, fate and Martha would have it otherwise. Also to receive an honorary degree in the same ceremonies, Martha was to accompany Louis, and, in a sense, take care of him; but she preferred to leave Saturday night. Unfortunately, her lateness in picking him up caused them to miss the night train, and their only recourse was a Chicago-bound express that did not have a scheduled stop at Detroit. It would, however, be stopping briefly at Toledo, Ohio, approximately sixty miles away from the university.

When the information came through that Martha and Louis were on the Chicago train, consternation set in at Wayne. To get off in Toledo, they would have to be in the one carriage that let passengers descend at that station, a fact they might not be aware of. An attempt to warn them by telegram was thwarted because of a blizzard that was raging in upper New York state. Nevertheless, a limousine was dispatched to meet the train. Timing was now crucial.

Professor of Dance Ruth Murray, who was to present the honorary degree to Louis personally, was already on the stage of Cobo Hall, where the commencement exercises were taking place. Looking across the vast audience of assembled parents, students, graduates, and professors, she searched in vain for some sign of Louis's and Martha's arrival. President Clarence Hilberry was just finishing his speech, which he had graciously offered to give in advance of the conferring of honorary degrees to gain a little time. On this occasion, Wayne State University had chosen to bestow honorary degrees on American artists in poetry, literature, music, and dance. Among those to be honored were the poet John Ciardi; Charles Feinberg, a Detroit collector of Walt Whitman manuscripts; and the playwright-novelist Thornton Wilder.

Just before he was about to proceed with the formalitites, the president turned to Ruth Murray and asked *sotto voce,* "Are they here yet?" At that moment, Dean of Students Harold Stewart, who had been stationed at the rear of the huge auditorium, held up his hand reassuringly. Close to the entrance doors two elderly individuals were being bustled into one of the electric carts used for conveying people the length of the hall. As the vehicle neared the stage, its occupants became more visible: a very impressive looking white-haired gentleman and a woman who held herself like a queen. Climbing onto the platform, they had the air of feeling completely at home on a stage.

Not one minute too early, and miraculously not one minute late, they settled themselves as inconspicuously as possible in their conspicuous places and listened with rapt attention as the citations were bestowed in alphabetical order.

When the time came, Louis stood up pridefully. Clear-eyed and quietly self-assured, he listened to Professor Murray's unostentatious reading of a citation that began with the words:

> As musician, artistic advisor, teacher, editor, critic and author, Louis Horst has influenced immeasurably the careers of leading modern dancers who have set out on new paths of creativeness in this age-old art. . . .

The honorary degree was to be the crowning experience of Louis's life. But even before the January issue of his magazine, *Dance Observer,* had come out with its self-congratulatory editorial on the thirty years of its existence—and its mention that Ruth St. Denis had reached her eighty-sixth year and George Balanchine was beginning the sixth decade of his life—Louis was in the hospital battling with pneumonia.

Distraught, Martha rallied to his side. Her role, however, was not that of nurse or sisterly comforter. Each day she would appear, a miracle of youth and animation. Instinctively willing that Louis should relive those wonderful years of their early companionship, she dressed her prettiest and assumed the role of the young Martha Graham, who had been his "first and best student." Meticulously groomed and glowing with memories of a past that constituted the organic foundation of her creative life, Martha would sweep into the room, bringing flowers and gifts to the man who meant more to her than anyone else in her long career. Her very presence, resonant with profound attachment, was proof of her love and gratitude.

Also at Louis's side was Nina Fonaroff, whom he personally cherished and whose choreographic abilities he had encouraged.

On January 23, the inevitable came to pass. No one could have been less sentimental about death than Louis Horst. He had even said to David and Marnie Wood (with just a touch of wistfulness in his voice), upon the occasion of their second child's birth, "Now you have two little girls. I guess I won't be around to teach them. . . ."

Louis's wife, Betty, with whom he had always kept in touch, and his sister, May Forbes, were duly notified.

Early that spring, Martha left for Israel. The loss would always be with her.

———

In his *Idylls of the King*, Alfred Tennyson writes of the "many-corridored complexities of Arthur's palace": a description that could be applied metaphorically to the many-faceted complexities of Martha's personality.

When she was genuinely moved, Martha could be very simple; but most of the time, she seemed to be playing a role. And the roles changed according to the nature of her audience. As a result, she represented "so many different things to different people." Among company members there was a general consensus that Martha was often "playing at playing," which meant that no one ever knew the direction her thoughts were really taking, or for what underlying personal or professional reasons she might be "using" those dancers whom she seemed to trap in an incomprehensible network of insinuations. A rebel against complacency ("The casual . . . to me it's a menace!"), she felt compelled to keep her dancers in a state of nervous tension, the ultimate purpose probably being to produce high-voltage performances that would match hers or vice-versa. While such temperamental maneuvers most always succeeded in keeping the company's nervous energy at a pitch, on the whole, they were emotionally damaging.

In the many corridors of Martha's personality, there was one that led directly, without deviation or manipulation, to Louis Horst. With Louis she never played any games. She may not have always agreed with him, but she deferred to him. She knew he knew what constituted good choreography. He alone could tell her where she had gone wrong. He alone could assuage her self-doubts.

Louis's death deprived her of the one truly intimate friend she had had throughout her career; the one person she had always respected and trusted; the one person she could never bend to her will. In fact, Louis Horst was the only person in the world, besides her father, who could bend Martha Graham to *his* will.

With his aging and his debilitating heart condition, Louis's paternal instincts regarding Martha receded before her maternal concerns. It was at her insistence that he moved uptown to be within the radius of her daily activities—a questionable change in the opinion of those who knew of Louis's longtime affinity for the Village. His apartment at 55 West Eleventh Street had been the meeting place for more than twenty-five years for countless dancers, writers, musicians, artists. It was there that he made up the copy month after month of his *Dance Observer*. He was a familiar figure in neighborhood restaurants and grocery stores.

In the modernized setting of a large, newly built apartment house on the edge of a semi-isolated (as far as restaurants and convivial gathering places were concerned) section of York Avenue near the Queensboro Bridge, Louis was no longer king of his environment. None of his friends lived around the corner. He seemed to lose the driving intensity that used to electrify his students. He was no longer the man who whipped dancers into shape, as when he would take over one of Martha's rehearsals in the old days and insist upon absolute precision. "In *Heretic,* he was a demon," recalled Sophie Maslow. "If we were on a diagonal, every foot had to line up. We would have to do it over and over again until we hit it exactly right. And he did that kind of rehearsing for *Primitive Mysteries,* too."

Primitive Mysteries, Celebration, Frontier, El Penitente: Louis's scores, Martha's choreography. Classic examples of kindred talents working in perfect unison. It was a collaboration that could be likened to the creative rapport that existed between Petipa and Tchaikovsky, between early Stravinsky and Fokine, between late Stravinsky and Balanchine—a collaboration that would shake up history and make the art of the dance and its musical accompaniment travel in hitherto unknown directions.

Shortly after Louis's death, the modern dance community went into action. Theodora Wiesner, director of the Connecticut College Summer School of Dance, set in motion plans to present a Memorial Concert in Horst's name for the following summer's American Dance Festival on the campus in New London. Martha was approached. Would she consider reviving *El Penitente, Frontier,* and *Primitive Mysteries* for the occasion?

Ambivalence set in. *El Penitente* had already been given away, but *Frontier, Primitive Mysteries*? The old problem of facing her declining performing abilities had Martha in its grip all over again. Could she tear those dances out of her personal past and relinquish them to other dancers? For years *Frontier* had been her "signature piece"; *Primitive Mysteries* was uniquely meaningful, an intrinsic part of those early years of deep identification with the Southwest. As before, the struggle became acutely painful, magnified this time by a sense of debt to Louis, who had opened her eyes to the creative potential of Spanish-Indian rituals.

Reluctantly, Martha acceded to *Frontier* being danced by Ethel Winter, knowing that there was a black and white film produced in the late thirties without sound that could be studied. She would not have to be involved personally. But as to *Primitive Mysteries,* since there were no records whatsoever (even from later revivals of the work), it would have to be reconstructed completely with a whole new set of dancers trained rigorously in the old style. She shrank at the idea. A host of practical reasons for not doing it sprang to mind. On the other hand, she could not refuse outright. On the eve of departing for Tel Aviv to work with the Batsheva Dance Company, she left a typically ambiguous message with David Wood, her rehearsal director: *If* the dance could be put together, *if* it could be recalled sufficiently, *if* it could be performed well enough, and *if* she would approve of it, then she would give her consent to have it included on the program in New London.

The outlook was bleak. In charge of affairs at the Graham school, Craig Barton and Leroy Leatherman decided to start with *Frontier*.

——— ··· ———

Over and over again the film would be run. While Ethel Winter tried to pick out the movements, Eugene Lester sat at the piano with Louis's score in front of him. A few notes about the movement had been written here and there over some bars of the music by Helen Lanfer, Martha's longtime personal accompanist; but the main problem was the film. It was so old and jerky that the dancer's movements were hard to read. In addition, it was a silent work film, designed solely for use as a record.

It took hours of study to decipher phrases, not only because there was no accompaniment, but also because the frame speed made it impossible to count the movement metrically, although there was a knob that could be utilized for occasional speed changes. Each time Ethel Winter would run the film she would attempt to find out where a phrase began and when it ended. Lester, on his part, would try to analyze the musical phrasing in relation to the dance. Grueling work. Every once in a while they had to stop, rest their eyes, and talk about something else to relieve the tension.

Gradually the dance took shape, and the music, written in Louis's hand, with its *Allegro con spirito* and *fortissimo* markings for the opening bars, began to punctuate the silence with high, resonant chords that matched the exuberance of the dancer's broad-sweeping gestures. "Louis' scores," wrote music and dance critic Robert Sabin, "with . . . their incisive, free rhythms, their biting dissonance and economy of style, sprang from the same spirit as Graham's dances."

Lester's long experience of working with Martha since the mid-forties gave him the necessary insight into the rhythmic relationships that existed between the dynamics of her phrasing and the musical line. Throughout the fifties and much of the sixties, it was Martha's custom to rehearse with Lester two hours daily on her solo roles for weeks prior to performances. In the process of working together on *Dark Meadow* one day, Lester called attention to the fact

244

that she was not making a specific gesture come out on a certain beat as had been her wont. Appreciating his Horstian-like preciseness, Martha remarked approvingly, "You must hold me to it!" She willingly made the change.

Working in tandem with infinite patience—Ethel peering into the film, Lester increasing the speed of his playing to coincide with the movements—they succeeded in reconstructing the solo without Martha's assistance.

"Then," recalled Ethel, "Martha came in, and we worked about twenty minutes or so.... It's amazing what she can do in a few minutes, what she gives you, what her images are."

Nevertheless, the old reluctance was still there in addition to doubts that couldn't be disregarded: *Frontier* might look as dated as *Primitive Mysteries*, which was four years its senior. Releasing either dance was difficult, but with *Primitive Mysteries* there was a greater risk. By comparison with today's more elaborate choreography (including her own), it might look simplistic, even crude. Again, the labyrinth of doubt enclosed her....

It was David Wood who succeeded in making the impossible happen: the re-creation of a dance whose only record lay in the memories of those who performed it more than thirty years previously, or in a few photographs selectively shot not onstage but in a studio.

Wood's call to the members of Martha's group in the late twenties and early thirties struck resonant responses. Glowing with the memories of having danced in the ground-breaking *Primitive Mysteries*, many came, some from as far away as Canada and Utah, others from close by, but all of them recharged with the old devotion of dancing with Martha, an unforgettable part of their lives. As Ethel Butler, who in the meantime had become one of Washington, D.C.'s foremost teachers and choreographers, remembered, "We dedicated our whole lives to the Graham company, and when you are that dedicated you find strength where you don't think it's possible to find it."

It was a motley group of youngish-looking middle-aged women who still, for the most part, practiced their profession with the same vitality and idealism of former years. In addition to Ethel Butler, former company members who had participated in the successful 1936 Guild Theatre performance of *Primitive Mysteries* included Dorothy Bird (now teaching at the Neighborhood Playhouse School of the Theatre), Nina Fonaroff, Elizabeth Halprin, Marie Mar-

245

chowsky, Sophie Maslow, Marjorie Mazia, May O'Donnell (Maslow and O'Donnell were already established choreographers with companies of their own), Helen Priest Rogers of Mt. Holyoke College, and Gertrude Shurr, who taught Graham technique during the winter at the New York High School of the Performing Arts and during the summer at Utah State University. Sitting on the sidelines, but ready to help if she could, was Ailes Gilmour, Noguchi's sister, who had been in the premiere.

Some of the women were already in practice clothes; a few had merely taken off their shoes. At first, no one knew where or how to start. The only artifact remaining of *Primitive Mysteries* was the worn score that was propped on the piano rack in front of Eugene Lester. Unlike the score of *Frontier,* there were no written-in directions concerning the movements in the dance, a customary habit of Louis's when accompanying dancers. Nor were there any tempo markings. All that could be discovered were some faintly penciled instructions regarding the music—no doubt, Louis Horst's self-directed reminders.

Then Lester began to play the music. The stark simplicity of the melodic line, the clarity of the phrasing, and the rhythmic cadence of the first bars of the Hymn to the Virgin soon began to detonate impulses, so to speak, in the bodies of the listening dancers. That mysterious fibrous substance called muscular memory made itself felt, and a quiver went through the stationary group. One dancer after another would recall personal fragments of the composition: on which side of the stage she was located at the moment of that particular note or chord . . . where Martha was . . . what the others might be doing at the same time; not details but the general design. Questions flew back and forth. "Where were you when I was here?" "Which arm did I make that movement with? Right? Left?" Then, turning to another dancer, the speaker would add something like, "Now I remember: Lillian Shapero was standing right next to me . . . I used to feel her right arm pressing against my left arm as we pointed our elbows toward Martha!"

Strand by strand, piece by piece . . . and in those utterly blank moments when recollections stood still, the women would turn to Barbara Morgan's stencil-clear photographs, where the fervor of the 1936 cast of *Primitive Mysteries* shone through bodies, faces, and gestures; then, another break-through would occur, accompanied by a cry of recognition and a rapid scurrying to memories. Sophie Maslow, to whom Martha had once said, "I'd like you to learn my part" (though she taught it to Lillian Shapero and not to her), was able to re-create the Virgin's role because she had studied Martha's every move. But there still remained some blank spaces here and there that perplexed everyone. Taking the initiative as the rehearsal director, Maslow choreographed the connecting movements in the spirit of the dance.

After three or four intensive rehearsals, the revitalized *Primitive Mysteries* was ready to be transferred to the bodies and minds of the young dancers who had been sitting on the sidelines attentively following the intricate patterns of a work that had been premiered years before most of them were born. Would they be able to capture the special earthbound character of the movement? Martha's doubts were not unfounded. By the mid-1960s, modern dancers had become too facile, too easily airborne, and though they often flexed their feet (as did Balanchine's ballerinas) they no longer recognized the potential of that gesture as revelatory of total body force.

Ethel Butler took charge of teaching the new girls the "old technique," and Sophie Maslow set up a tight rehearsal schedule that would make it possible for them to finish learning the dance before Martha's return. The lovely Yuriko, a current member of the company since the early fifties, would perform the role of the Virgin. She would supply the luminous mystical quality that enveloped the young girl who was chosen from all other girls in the New Mexican village to represent the Virgin Mary at the time of the reenactment of the religious rites. For *Primitive Mysteries* was, like *El Penitente*, a simple folk-like rendering of a three-act passion play, in which the Virgin Mary, surrounded by acolytes, relived the tragedy of her Son's crucifixion and the ecstasy of His resurrection.

"Martha was one of us," recalled Dorothy Bird; "that walk . . . such absolute unity . . . the things we did made her appear to rise in the air."

Yuriko could capture the quality of the original vision; but the new girls had to be trained relentlessly. "I rehearsed that dance longer than I rehearsed anything else—ever," said Maslow.

When the former members of the cast were to meet for the last time, David Wood telephoned Martha, who by then had returned from Israel, to ask her to come to the final rehearsal to speak with them. She refused.

Wood pleaded with her: "You have a responsibility to them. They have done this for you. They love you."

The rehearsal was to end at ten o'clock; at nine forty-five the front door opened and there was Martha. She went directly to her dressing room, but at David's request she came into the studio. "I didn't want to. But I will."

The dancers were standing around the piano. There was an awkward silence. Martha approached them uncertainly, seemed to be at a loss for what to say, murmured a few words, and then quickly left. So deep was the anguish of seeing *Primitive Mysteries* again that there seemed to be no way for her to communicate with them. Mercifully, she had concealed her feelings.

Nevertheless, she was able to come back from time to time, watch Maslow's rehearsals (though often she left abruptly in the middle of them), and even contribute some of her illuminating insights. When the time for the performances at Connecticut College neared, she was present at every rehearsal, determined to make the revivals a success. She took a fresh interest in the costumes of the three dances, adapting, as was her wont, material and designs to fit the new interpreters. In working with Marnie Thomas on her triple role in *El Penitente,* she realized that the cape and hood (a prop-like headdress) weren't quite right for the delicate-looking young woman, so she changed the costume and its accessories to frame the dancer's face more harmoniously. For *Primitive Mysteries,* she added a long ruffled white petticoat that emerged below the hem of the dancers' dark blue dresses. While it disturbed many diehards who came to the Memorial Concerts, it added a certain emphasis to the stroke of the leg, and, of course, white ruffles were typically Mexican. In later revivals the ruffles were dyed a pale blue and brought to a point at the center of the hemline. Such costume changes—though not always to the advantage of a reconstructed work—were obviously part of Martha's need to add contemporaneous touches that she felt would keep her revivals from looking "dated."

The Louis Horst Memorial Concerts brought the modern dance world together on a grand scale. From all over the country, dancers, choreographers, teachers, writers—all those who had been touched (or seared!) by Louis's wisdom (and criticism)—came to pay homage to the "Father of Modern Choreography." Quite suitably, the work of another great modern dance pioneer, a colleague of Horst's, was presented on the same program: the late Doris Humphrey's *Lament for Ignacio Sanchez Meijas,* a composition that revealed the choreographic skills of a woman who was often called the "Architect of Modern Dance."

Looking radiant in her white summer dress, with the manly José Limón at her side when the curtain rose, Martha set the tone of the memorial tributes. They would not be lugubrious. The occasion would henceforth be known as a "Celebration" of Louis's life. There were to be no tears, only gratitude for the manifold gifts of a musician-teacher-critic who dedicated himself to the art of the dance.

Thus did the Lady of the Labyrinth turn the public eye away from her private grief.

———— • ••• • ————

Honor after honor had been bestowed upon Martha by colleges, universities, and national institutions in the form of academic degrees and citations. The list was long and impressive. Like diplomas, the citations were framed and hung on the office walls of the Martha Graham Center of Contemporary Dance on Sixty-third Street. Then came an honor that could be considered similar to the international recognition afforded a winner of the Nobel prize. The Aspen Institute for Humanistic Studies chose Martha Graham from a group of more than one hundred living artists, writers, scholars, philosophers, and statesmen as being "the individual anywhere in the world to have made the greatest contribution to the advancement of the humanities."

The award ceremony took place in a huge amphitheater tent whose orange and blue flaps rippled in the gentle summer wind of a late July afternoon in the mountain resort town of Aspen, Colorado. In the front row on a wide podium profusely decorated with flowers sat dignitaries of the American Philosophical Society, the Ford Foundation, and the Aspen Institute, and between them Martha Graham, attired in a simple white dress with a red scarf thrown over one shoulder. Also in the front row but to the side were Georgia Graham, Martha Hill, Craig Barton, and Nik Krevitsky, a former editor of *Dance Observer*. Behind the group was a full orchestra scheduled to play, when all speeches had been made and recorded, Aaron Copland's score for *Appalachian Spring*.

For nearly half an hour, Martha sat immovable listening to speeches made in her honor, and when she arose to take her place beside Dr. Alvin C. Eurich, president of the Aspen Institute, and to receive from him the coveted award, she seemed to be the very embodiment of the disciplined art of the dance, so straight did she stand and with such ease did she turn to the large audience to deliver her acceptance speech, which, in her usual way, was an impromptu delivery of irregularly threaded philosophical and psychological observations. The silence in the tent was awesome. Once again, Martha was onstage. Once again—this time with words at her command—she ignited the air around her. Drawing the audience into the ineffable world of the imagination, she extolled the miracle of the human body as a dancing instrument and the role of the creative artist as an image-maker. She spoke of the "cultivation of the being," from which come those images which are not "dehumanized things but . . . great figures." And she conjured up Clytemnestra, "that angry, wild, wicked woman," who eventually came to terms with her rebellious spirit.

In speaking of her own commitment to her profession, she added, "It cost me a great deal of effort and a great deal of time, but every minute has been cherished."

But when she sat down and the music for *Appalachian Spring* resounded through the amphitheater, Martha's face mirrored no corresponding emotions as Copland's exuberant melodies and rhythms played out scene after scene of a ballet in which so much joy and hope had been released. Did the music remind Martha of a time when personal life and artistic aims were ambivalently locked together? Or was she already embarked on another Hellenic journey where she would encounter another great figure, a truly noble woman who would become the victim of all that is base in human nature?

The latter seemed more likely, for within a year and a half Martha would create a role for herself that would be the signature piece of her last dancing days: the old Queen Hecuba of Troy, wife of assassinated King Priam, mother of Paris who abducted Helen, of Hector who was slain by Achilles, of Polyxenia who was sacrificed on the tomb of Achilles, of Cassandra who was enslaved as concubine to Agamemnon, of Polydorus who was murdered for a bag of gold by the king of Thrace. A funeral procession of great figures. The title would indeed be apt: *Cortege of Eagles*.

Chapter Twelve
Deaths and Reentrances

If Martha was no longer at the peak of her performing powers in February 1967, when *Cortege of Eagles* was premiered, it mattered little. Whenever she dealt with the high drama of mythological Greece, she created masterworks. *Cortege of Eagles* was no exception. The last of her personal attempts to identify with a character of heroic proportions, the role of the tragic Hecuba would become one of her most impressive acting, not dancing, feats.

Smaller in scope than the monumental *Clytemnestra*, less intimate than the Freudian *Night Journey*, more realistically concerned with good and evil than *Cave of the Heart, Cortege of Eagles* contained the same high-tension sequence of inevitably doomed events. And Hecuba, like Jocasta, like Clytemnestra, was also ''a soul that can feel greatly.'' Certainly, the depth of her suffering—if one can measure suffering in rational terms—was even greater, for Hecuba had lost *everything*.

The moralistic pride that Jocasta clung to when she committed suicide can be regarded as the ego's last admission of acknowledged sin. Clytemnestra's hard-won understanding and self-forgiveness can be traced to a protesting, unrelenting ego brought face to face with its own evil image. Medea's savage fight for a woman's rights denied her by the Greek state was corroded with bitterness. But Hecuba stands clear of sin, unless she could be accused of being guilty of the birth of Paris, and thereby of the war itself—an unwitting complicity, to be sure. Or, unless one can point an accusing finger at her revengeful blinding of Polymnestor, the murderer of her son, Polydor. Seen humanistically, as no doubt Euripides intended in his *Hecabe*, the queen's ruthless act is the first sign of a dementia brought about by events that have proved too much for her. No, Hecuba is a symbol of total pity. She is the sum of all human agony.

Martha Graham's *Cortege of Eagles* is not, however, just a portrait of a tragic figure. It is panoramic in its humanitarian outlook. Inspired by both *Hecabe* and *The Trojan Women*, Euripides' great antiwar plays, *Cortege of Eagles* is Martha's own indictment of "man's inhumanity to man." Aligned with Euripides, who, in the opinion of Edith Hamilton, "alone of all the classic world [had] a sense of the value of each individual human being," Martha chose once more to reveal—in contrapuntal characterizations—the bestial and the sublime in human nature.

On the one side were the victors, the Greek warriors, who hypocritically justified unconscionable acts of cruelty in the name of religious or military necessity. On the other side were the Trojans, whose moral resources gave them the strength to endure dismemberment of their families, destruction of their city, and enslavement; and, in the case of the noble Polyxenia, the courage to submit almost willingly to the primitive rite of human sacrifice. Only the aged Hecuba breaks under the relentless siege of misfortune; only Hecuba, victimized beyond endurance, succumbs to madness, proving thereby that life is frail and when disasters multiply, the human mind can snap.

Compassion resounds on every page of *Hecabe* and *The Trojan Women;* compassion continually sweeps across the stage in *Cortege of Eagles;* but when Euripides' and Martha's curtains descend, only devastation and desolation remain . . . the entrails of war.

No message of redemption rises to console the suffering mind. Even the triumphant Greeks are doomed. For the entire ancient world has gone mad. Poseidon foretold such total destruction when he declared in the opening scene of *The Trojan Women:* "The mortal is mad who sacks cities and desolates temples and tombs, the holy places of the dead; his own doom is only delayed."

No message of rebirth rises out of the mutually destructive war. The only resurrection that could possibly take place would be the return of sanity to the world at large. But this, too, seems remote. For even the gods appear to have lost their reason. Having started the war out of vanity, they joined it, splitting up and taking sides, protecting their favorites, driving spears fiendishly into the bodies of their foes—in short, behaving as badly as or worse than the combatants themselves. But their greatest sin was that they let Helen—the cause—survive the war with all her beauty and insolence shockingly intact.

Is it any surprise that Hecuba, whose son was drawn into the goddesses' silly plot, whose realm and entire family were destroyed by their intrigues, knows not where or to whom to direct her prayers? When at last Menelaus comes to take his wife back to Greece, Hecuba is beside herself with the fear that Helen will go unpunished. "O power who mounts the world...," she beseeches wildly, "O mystery of man's knowledge, whosoever you be, Zeus named, nature's necessity or mortal mind, I call upon you ... bring all human action back to right at last."

There is no assurance anywhere that she has been heard; only Menelaus's perplexed remark, "How strange a way to call on gods."

No wonder Hecuba chooses to punish Polymnestor herself and not rely on the gods whether they be "nature's necessity or mortal mind"—two possibilities daringly named by near-atheistic Euripides. If the gods function as nature functions, then their ways are incomprehensible. Zeus might send lightning bolts across the sky, Poseidon might arouse storms and flood the land, Ceres might cause a drought to spread over the earth with famine as a result, but their purposes are as mysterious as those of nature itself. But if the gods are a creation of mortal mind, then they simply do not exist, either malevolently or benevolently. Euripides the skeptic, the most modern of all the ancient poets, lets loose these implications. If either one be true, then it is mankind, and mankind alone, which is the author of the "pain and cruel compulsion" that surround human life "in an unbreakable ring" when war takes over.

If Martha was acting more than dancing in *Cortege of Eagles,* it was in perfect keeping with the role of Hecuba. In superb histrionic control, she could convey by the most subtle means the breakdown of a queen who maintained her dignity despite the ravaging forces within her and the accumulative pressures around her. Her calm exterior portends unimaginable fury. We see it slowly manifesting itself when the corpse of the murdered Polydorus is brought to her. We see it hardening into a premeditated act when Polymnestor stealthily enters and detaches the gold purse from the dead boy's neck. Then comes her final appeal to the gods before giving way to animalistic revenge: seated, she stretches her hand imploringly to heaven, then ritualistically passes it down the full length of her body, touches the ground, and resumes the gesture, stretching and bending in mute despair. As if in final retrospect before the decisive act, family memories form a ghostly procession: Priam, Hector, Astyanax (Andromache's murdered son), Polyxenia, Polydorus. Behind her stands Charon, Ferryman of the Dead, mounted on a throne. He is stiff as a corpse, and his face is covered by a featureless mask. Polymnestor reenters and bows obsequiously to the queen. She remains unmoved but her hand drifts unconsciously to the sharp-pointed brooch on her bosom. With royal grace she invites him into the cave where she now lives and where, she slyly informs him, more gold is hidden. Tempted by the same avarice that made him kill her son, he obeys. Within seconds, a hooded chorus of five women envelops him. Before he realizes it, the hoods have become a sheath and he is being bent backward against his will. Coldly, deliberately, the queen removes her brooch and plunges it into his eyes. As he falls, her fingers close in on the pin; with infinite tenderness she clasps it in both hands and brings it gently back to her breast. It is all that she has now. She cradles it as if it were a living child.

But there is still more revenge to wreak upon the guilty Polymnestor. She takes the wounded king's hand and leads the stricken, blinded man slowly to the body of Polydorus, forcing him to identify the boy he murdered. One touch and he flies in terror.

The eerie sound of a series of five-octave descending notes played successively by a flute, oboe, clarinet, and bassoon accompany the queen as she staggers insensate to her throne. The unearthly cries of the wind instruments seem to spell out the terrible fate that awaits the demented woman. Her last gesture—a sudden covering of her face with a mask of hideously clawing fingers—is accompanied by a shattering, explosive note struck *fortissimo* by the timpani, bass, drum, and piano, plus pizzicato strings "f possible" ("as loudly as possible"). The effect is that of a barrage of guns. (Legend has it that following her savage avenging of her son's murder, the noble queen is transformed into a dog, and in a state of frenzy she climbs the masthead of Odysseus's ship, on which she is being conveyed to Ithaca as the Greek hero's slave, and losing balance she falls to a watery grave off the coast of Gallipoli near a promontory that would henceforth be called Cynossems, "the Dog's Tomb.")

Cortege of Eagles offers no message of rebirth; but certain philosophical insights emerge to reassure us that nobility of spirit does not die with death. Hecuba's daughter, Polyxenia, represents all that is magnanimous in human nature. The pagan rite she submits to—a sacrifical martyrdom on the tomb of Achilles to appease the gods—honors the heroic in mankind. Though Martha has her kill herself in *Cortege of Eagles* rather than be slain by the Greek soldiers, as in Euripides' *Hecabe,* her death in both instances becomes a symbol of ultimate courage.

It did not matter that Martha hardly danced in *Cortege of Eagles.* Her company—the cream of years of close association—danced for her with unforgettable passion. Prime among them were Helen McGehee as Polyxenia, David Wood as Charon, Robert Cohan as Hector, and Bertram Ross as Achilles and Polymnestor. It did not matter that Martha was more the playwright and actress than dancer in *Cortege of Eagles.* Her ever-resourceful scenic designer, Isamu Noguchi, created a functioning world of demonically whirling shields, kite-like forms, and strange masks around her. Her devoted lighting designer, Jean Rosenthal, pitted shadows against illuminations to re-create the tense atmosphere of an ancient continent peopled by gods and humans alike. And Eugene Lester's powerful score—its clangorous battle scenes contrasting with silence interspersed by arpeggios that sounded like cries of human anguish—served to carry Martha's choreographic conception to epic heights.

———— ··· ————

The Minotaur of Time was waiting patiently in his favorite hedged-in corner of the labyrinth. Looking down his furry nose every now and then, he could see Martha scurrying from corridor to corridor, quite obviously avoiding the path that would lead directly to his lair. Every once in a while, however, she would look hastily and fearfully over her shoulder. He chuckled to himself. Surely, she was not presuming that *he* was running after *her*? With a smug shrug of his massive shoulders, he settled down for another yearlong nap.

Such self-indulgence was not to be, even for an everlasting Minotaur. Without a word of warning, a front-page headline was brought to his attention, making him sit bolt upright.

Upon closer examination, he saw that a drawing, over which was imprinted the word "Berkshire," depicted an eagle with wings spread holding a cluster of spears in one claw and a multi-leafed olive branch in the other. The significance of this symbolic rendering of conquest and rebirth was not lost upon the Minotaur, who at first

Quiet Retirement

Martha Graham, 76,
Dances Her Finale

© New York Times News Service

NEW YORK — Martha Graham will not dance tonight when her company opens its season, nor does she intend to dance again company at the end of her performing career. By leaving the stage and remaining as choreographer, she gives the company the best possible chance to carry on. mixed words and dancing in a 60-minute work that boldly pursued one of her paramount aims, "to make visible the interior landscape."

Though she had won rec-

glance at the headline, shook his head skeptically. Then his eye caught the verifying evidence: in small print, just above the text, was a copyright sign and the words "New York Times News Service." Then it *had to* be true. He quickly scanned the labyrinth. Martha was nowhere to be seen. Knowing her ways, he grew apprehensive. But there was nothing to do but wait. And he was good at that.

Actually, Martha was sitting in a hedged-in corner of her own, thinking out a livid reply to the reporter who stole the rug from under her dancing feet. Not quite sure of exactly what she would say, she tussled with her feelings. While she had once admitted publicly, "It is a bitter thing with me not to be able to dance again," at this moment it seemed of no importance. What mattered was the pain itself. Once again the tug of war began between her lifelong need to perform and her honesty with herself. The performing instinct began to get the upper hand. She moved surreptitiously to another corridor, one from which she knew she could make a quick getaway to Brooklyn. That night she was to be honored with the Handel Medallion, New York City's highest award for cultural achievement, at the Brooklyn Academy Opera House, where her company *without her* was opening a weeklong season.

Two words in the headline rankled her: "Quiet Retirement." *Quiet Retirement!* It had been forced upon her by her new Board of Directors and the reigning company members. Without realizing it, she reverted to the spirit that had possessed her in the late twenties (as described by herself): "In those days I was an arrogant, willful dancer, and I'd take no back talk from anybody."

A few hours later, a very self-assured Martha Graham slipped between the sumptuous red curtains of the Opera House just as Dore Schary, the Commissioner for Cultural Affairs who was to bestow the Medallion upon her, had concluded his introductory speech. Elegantly dressed in black and gold with her hair caught up in a matching turban, she took command of the situation and in her most engaging stage manner launched immediately (after tumultuous applause) into a denunciation of the reporter who had dared to presume that she would retire. When she finally left the stage after further illuminating impromptu remarks about her career, Louis Horst's influence, and the benefits of longevity due to the modern use of vitamins, she had virtually promised that she would appear once more in a new work the following spring.

But the die had been cast. And not by the reporter of the incriminating news release. The company itself had settled the question that had already been in the minds of the Graham devotees who had been witnessing Martha's declining powers over the last few years. Right or wrong, they felt that if the theatrical integrity of the works could be maintained, then the compositions, even without Martha, would endure on their own aesthetic merits. Her roles in the hands of her most experienced women dancers—Helen McGehee, Mary Hinkson, Phyllis Gutelius, Yuriko (who had proved the point in *Primitive Mysteries*), and Patricia Birch—would not, of course, be the same as originally performed by the "irreplacable" Martha Graham, but the truly great dances, like the works of great composers, would survive.

The company's Brooklyn Academy season of 1970 did more than survive. A transformation took place with the glowing presence of three members from years long past. Now billed as Guest Artists, Jane Dudley, Jean Erdman, and Pearl Lang returned to dance in a ballet they once had graced: the eloquent Emily Dickinson–inspired *Letter to the World*. Dudley and Erdman assumed their respective roles as the Ancestress and the One Who Speaks, while Lang, who had interpreted every principal role in previous productions (except that of the dancing Emily), was now to perform Martha's unforgettable portrait of the poetess, the One Who Dances.

Watching as was her wont from the wings, where a chair would be placed for her, Martha could not help but see what was happening. The company was dancing with marvelous energy. Whether she recognized it or not, their performing carried the vigor that had always possessed her. They were indeed her offsprings. And the old works that she had personally avoided involvement with as reconstructions were now pulsating with fresh life. The most revelatory of them all—in fact, the most painful, because it had never been performed without her—undoubtedly was *Letter to the World.*

The second oldest of the six revivals,* *Letter to the World* had been restaged jointly by Lang, Dudley, and Erdman from a work film made years previously at the Henry Street Playhouse. There had been one almost insurmountable problem, however. Due to the cold in the Henry Street theater, plus the fact that the company had just finished a long, arduous season, Martha had stopped short of performing her last tragic solos after nearly five days of filming. These were the obvious conditions for the omission, but there could well have been more subtle reasons. Lang, sensitive to the pitch of Martha's emotional drives, offered her own hypothesis, a convincing one: "The solos are so personal. There is a trepidation . . . one does not want to give away one's inner self."

Working from memory, Lang proceeded to reconstruct the dances she was to perform. When details and transitions would elude her, Jane Dudley would come to the rescue. "Jane's wonderful eye for movement and dramatic weight" enabled the younger dancer to translate Martha's "special simplicity" into a language of her own. She succeeded to such an extent that Walter Terry considered that "she discovered her own dramatic line, retained her own identity, and brought to *Letter to the World* a priceless ingredient I can describe only as 'truth,' for Emily, as renewed for our times by Miss Graham's nerve-deep choreography." And critic Doris Hering, who had seen almost all of Graham's repertoire throughout the years, pronounced Lang "glorious" in the role.

Erdman, who had been given considerable choreographic leeway in her original construction of the part of the One Who Speaks, found herself slipping easily into the character of the articulate Emily. Her gift for reading poetry (an ability clearly evident in her own production of the Joycean-based *The Coach With The Six Insides* of 1962) once more shed its iridescence through the poignant Dickinson lines.

To these two fine interpretations was added Jane Dudley's starkly

---

Every Soul Is a Circus (1939), *Letter to the World* (1940), *El Penitente* (1940), *Deaths and Entrances* (1943), *Appalachian Spring* (1944), *Cave of the Heart* (1946).

acted Ancestress. Tall, gaunt, Victorian in her severity, the dramatically powerful dancer recreated her original role of The Postponeless Creature, Dickinson's embodiment of death.

As for Martha's role in *Deaths and Entrances,* Mary Hinkson's interpretation of the neurotic, willful Emily Brontë proved her stature as "a commanding dance-actress." Commenting on the achievements of the season as a whole, and the company's prospective national tour, John O'Connor of the *Wall St. Journal* remarked that Hinkson alone should ensure its success.

Though limited in personnel and repertoire compared to former years, the Martha Graham Dance Company—now committed to performing independently—went on tour . . . without Martha Graham.

The battle within still raged. More devastating than the humiliation of not heading and steering her own company in her own dances was the tragic recognition that her works no longer belonged to her. Sealed off, self-complete in others' hands, they had become separate organisms. It was not their loss, however, that dug the trench of desolation that she felt; it was a sense of barrenness that drove her downward. The pain/joy of creating out of necessity seemed to have abandoned her.

When had she last composed a work that bore the stamp of her former inexhaustible creative energy? *A Time of Snow,* her poignant tale of Héloise and Abélard, had proved all too clearly that "the dignity of her time" was closing in on her in 1968. Bertram Ross's fine performance as Abélard and Rouben Ter-Arutunian's shining, spiky center-of-the-stage protrusions, though difficult to dance around, sustained the image of thwarted love in medieval France; but these positive virtues, as well as Naomi Lapzeson's moving portrayal of the young Héloise, could not save a work that was only gesturally evocative when it came to Martha's own interpretation.

In the same season was *The Lady of the House of Sleep,* another virtually static rendition of a tale of emotional turmoil. In it she had tried to describe the hero-adventurer's encounters with his most dangerous foes as he sought the Sleeping Beauty of his lifetime dreams. Was the hero's struggle too close to the bone for her to be able to objectify her theme, as she had always succeeded in doing? More than that, *The Lady of the House of Sleep* lacked the magic of intuitive choreographic choices that had always been hers to siphon up from the subconscious.

As her spirits sank, Martha's body seemed drained of reserves. Physically weakened by years of indifference to her own health, emotionally unstable because she knew she was judged "an embarrassment to her company," she no longer had the energy to fight the Minotaur of Time. A strange, disturbing passivity set in, and those friends who visited her in the hospital or saw her bedridden at home with various illnesses were shocked and frightened.

And they were right to be frightened. For Martha had descended, to use a phrase from Campbell's book on the hero, into "the belly of the whale." Her own journey as hero-adventurer was approaching its severest, most formidable task.

"And so it happens [writes Campbell] that if anyone—in whatever society—undertakes for himself the perilous journey into the darkness by descending, either intentionally or unintentionally, into the crooked lanes of his own spiritual labyrinth, he soon finds himself in a landscape of symbolical figures (any one of which may swallow him)."

Sunk in the interior of her own demoralized ego, Martha was facing the crisis of her life: the loss, possibly the death, of her creative will. Such a loss would amount to self-dismemberment (a psychological act akin to the ancient rites in honor of Cybele, goddess of caverns, who is sometimes represented as holding a whip decorated with knucklebones, with which priests flagellated themselves). For Martha's identification with her creative will constituted the very fabric of her personality.

No longer on the threshold of the unknown, she was now deep within it, facing the void of noncommitment, an anathema to her nature. The cost of survival would have to be nothing less than spiritual regeneration. Without creativity, there would be no living of life. Those were her terms from the beginning.

"The psyche has many secrets in reserve," writes Joseph Campbell, "and these are not disclosed unless required."

Between 1971 and 1973, Martha Graham fought her way out of the belly of the whale. Psychologically speaking, her reemergence can be viewed as one of the greatest creative acts of her life.

She returned to her school, resumed leadership as its chief director, took charge of her company, and obeyed once more the imperative of her life: to project ideas and feelings in the form of theatrical entities. A procession of dances choreographed on the bodies of others—with their creative collaboration—would consume her. The cost, "not less than everything," had been paid.

A radically different photograph of Martha Graham appeared on all publicity material: a silhouetted profile of the artist seated on a rehearsal stool and looking out, so it seemed, on a host of invisible dancers. No longer in action, but still formidably in command, the new Martha Graham held herself with the same awe-inspiring dignity. The photograph was the work of a perceptive young man named Ron Protas, who had become the new Executive Director of the Martha Graham School of Contemporary Dance, Inc. A freshly picked Board of Directors, headed by Francis Mason, stood by encouragingly.

In the spring of 1973, a two-week season was offered to a public made up of skeptics and loyal followers. Two world premieres and revivals of some of the finest works in the Graham repertoire would either reinstate the artist as choreographer and director of a brilliant company or write the death verdict on a career that had lasted more than fifty years. Once more, Martha was about to traverse "the high wire of circumstances" from which she, of all people, would "not choose to fall."

With her inborn theatrical sagacity, she chose the very subject that had been her downfall with which to make her comeback. As spectacular as it was daring, it broke through the veil of diffidence that had enclosed her work of the past five years. One eminent critic went so far as to say: "In the spring of 1973 . . . Martha Graham was reborn not simply for herself, but for us."

Inspired by St.-John Perse's sonorous, life-affirming poem *Chronique,* she created *Mendicants of Evening,* a lavishly mounted ballet replete with a painted set and electronic music (new departures) and a text spoken by an actress (Marian Seldes), whom she taught to move like a dancer. *Mendicants of Evening,* like St.-John Perse's poem, was a paean of praise to the "Divine turbulence" of passionately lived experience seen from the heights of advancing age. The dancing surged with vitality . . . the vitality of radiant memories. For the Nobel prize–winning French poet had written of life at evening-tide when the mature mind was open to the beauty of an "ever widening sky." Four lyrically intense love-duets brought the

261

Epilogue

"Acts of Light"

As dancer, choreographer, actress, playwright, costume designer, and the inventor of a unique technique, Martha Graham has made an indelible mark on the dance of the twentieth century.

Her early solos—*Fragments* (*Tragedy, Comedy*), *Dance, Adolescence, Lamentation*—were the first manifestations of a revolutionary mind whose ideas were couched in equally revolutionary movement. In her early ensemble works—*Heretic, Primitive Mysteries, American Provincials*—she used the concerto form as a dramatic or lyric idiom to convey insights into the sociocultural history of her country. In *Letter to the World, Deaths and Entrances,* and her entire Greek cycle, she developed a theatrical form distinctly her own: the introspective dance-drama, a distillation of complex emotional motivations projected through the stream of consciousness of the central character.

In addition, there is her influence on the artists who collaborated with her and on those who were drawn toward or into her creative path: musicians, stage designers, painters, sculptors, writers, poets. Not only are dancers and choreographers performing and composing differently today because of Martha Graham, but audiences are viewing the dance with fresh eyes as a result of her creativity. Her achievements—like acts of light—have encircled the globe, cutting across time zones like meridians, furnishing invisible lines of symbolic association through the timeless, zoneless medium of dance.

To remember Martha Graham the soloist is to relive visions of overwhelming but mystifying impact: the taut, strong torso with its deep contractions and spasmodic breath releases, the whipping arms and legs, the scampering sideways motions, the angular foot-flexed jump, the kick that stabbed the air, the monolithic fall and its swift

---

The chapter title, taken from a letter of Emily Dickinson, is the title of an ensemble work composed in 1980 by Martha Graham.

recovery—mysteriously appealing movements that directly affected one's nervous system.

Conventional standards of grace, beauty, rhythm, and linear design were swept aside when the small, dark-haired, intense-looking woman with the enormous personality took possession of the stage. Nothing she did was even faintly familiar. Severity of line replaced ordinary concepts of gracefulness; beauty shed its decorative outer garments, leaving structural body lines exposed, as it were. Rhythm in accepted terms of measured punctuation was simply bypassed. An irregularly timed phrasing constituted instead the fabric of the dancer's movement. Gestural clarity became less and less important as visceral responses and feelings too vague to be analyzed but too emphatic to be disregarded seized the viewer. Pulled into the orbit of the performer's compulsions, the audience experienced a mesmerizing, undefinable elation.

As Martha Graham, the soloist, was gradually transformed into Martha Graham, the protagonist of compelling dance-dramas, there was no slackening of bewitchment. The labyrinthian course of her imagination might have been obscure at times, and her subject matter a strange amalgam of ancient lore and modern psychology, but the woman's powerful personality and the complexity of her thought processes remained absorbing. Again, one was pulled into the orbit of an indescribable dynamism.

Then, the inevitable. The works themselves had to survive the loss of their creator's onstage presence. Could the performer who felt that she was more dancer than choreographer stand aside and see her compositions live in the bodies of others? For the public, the value of her works was confirmed with every revival, with every reconstruction, with almost every new choreographic effort. But to Martha Graham, whose life had consisted of being in the center of the tumultuous experience of performing her own creations, the cost of standing aside was "not less than everything," the exorbitant price of loss.

As always, extremes. From the beginning, the totality of experience must and would be her lot. Insights of almost unbearable awareness would be accompanied by ideas of shattering newness and actions of incredible daring, in which a consuming ecstasy played no small part. Then, intercepting all, a series of obstacles, seemingly insurmountable, would lead to black discouragement and the emptiness of feeling fallow. At the last moment of engulfing despair, "a door would open," and a new work would force its way into her mind; a work that would reveal the "amazing human power and sense of human knowledge" that poet-critic Edwin Denby found in *Herodiade*.

Is it any wonder that the theme of psychological rebirth obsessed Martha Graham? Is it any wonder that darkness stood for the obliterating shadow of the nether side of life, as in *Night Journey*, as in *Dark Meadow*, as in Clytemnestra's Underworld? Such darkness has its counterpart in light, the luminous world of self-knowledge, of understanding, of renewed identification with nature and its forces.

In *"Acts of Light,"* the noblest, most significant creation of her later, nondancing years, the choreographer sings a paean of praise to the sun. Nothing could be more revealing of the fighting spirit of Martha Graham. Out of darkness, light; out of light, rebirth . . . the cyclical dance of the universe, the psychical dance of Martha Graham, issuing from the depths of a song uniquely hers.

Notes

Prologue/Before Yesterday

The author wishes to acknowledge her debt for information and reminiscences in the Prologue to Martha Graham, Georgia Graham Sargeant, Mrs. Mary H. Bear, known as "Auntie Re" (sister of Mrs. George Graham), Marcella De Marco of Pittsburgh, Helen Lowe and Marguerite Andrus Fuller, high school acquaintances of Martha Graham, and Callie Brennan of Santa Barbara.

Page

2 "Man!...," Auntie Re, interview with author.

2 "Martha, you're not telling me...," Graham, reporting her father's words in conversation with author.

3 "I am Lizzie...," Auntie Re, interview with author.

4 "Out of emotion...," Martha Graham, quoted in Merle Armitage, *Martha Graham* (Brooklyn: Dance Horizons, 1966; republication of 1937 edition), p. 97.

4 "You are in competition...," Leroy Leatherman, *Martha Graham: Portrait of the Lady as an Artist* (New York: Alfred A. Knopf, 1966), p. 46.

4 "When the teacher enters...," Martha Graham interview with Marian Horosko. Broadcast in 1962 by WRVR (Riverside Radio), New York City.

5 "She had a remarkable...," Auntie Re, interview with author.

5 "was chosen," Martha Graham, "How I Became a Dancer," *Saturday Review*, August 28, 1965, p. 54.

6 "I was elected," Graham, Marian Horosko interview.

6 "favorite book," Graham, conversation with author.

6 Auntie Re quoting Dr. Graham, interview with author.

7 "Freedom! I ran...," Graham, conversation with author.

8 "shy, retiring girl," Helen Lowe, conversation with author.

8 "modest girlishness," Marguerite Andrus Fuller, conversation with author.

8 "had a mind...," Auntie Re, interview with author.

8 "Everyone is destined...," Ibid.

10 "or be forever thwarted," Graham, conversation with author.

12 "I'll be your maid...," Auntie Re, interview with author.

13 "There was something about her...," Ibid.

15 "idealized," Marguerite Andrus Fuller, interview with author.

Page

15 "I am not interested...," Graham, reporting her father's words in conversation with author.

16 "I was anything but...," Graham, quoted in *Santa Barbara News Press*, Nov. 3, 1966.

17 "There is only...," Graham, interview with Marian Horosko.

Chapter 1/Denishawn

The author wishes to acknowledge her debt for information and reminiscences in Chapter 1 to Martha Graham, Anne Douglas, Louis Horst, Ted Shawn, Charles Weidman, and Ruth Jentzer.

Page

19 "exceedingly shy...," Ruth St. Denis, *An Unfinished Life* (New York: Harper & Bros., 1939), p. 187.

19 "diagnosis lessons," Ibid., p. 175.

20 The story of Martha's first meeting with Ruth St. Denis was told in conversation with the author.

20 "We seek by every possible...," Ruth St. Denis, "The Education of The Dancer," *Vogue*, April 1, 1917.

21 "all-round practical...," Ibid.

21 "temple of the holy spirit," St. Denis, "Dance as Spiritual Expression," in Frederick Rand Rogers (ed.), *Dance: A Basic Educational Technique* (New York: Macmillan, 1941), p. 104.

21 "To me there is only...," St. Denis, *Life*, p. 241.

21 "*Radha* was...," Ibid.

21 "My final use...," Ibid., pp. 241–42.

22 "We touch...," Graham, quoted in *New York Times*, August 4, 1968.

22 "the frenzy which animates...," Martha Graham's Foreword to Charlotte Trowbridge, *Dance Drawings of Martha Graham* (New York: Dance Observer, 1945), n.p.

22 "anything else...," St. Denis, *Life*, p. 244.

23 "We wanted the school...," Ibid.

23 "The whole articulation...," Ibid., p. 175.

23 "vital importance...," Kay Bardsley, "Isadora Duncan's First School: The First Generation Founders of the Tradition," in Patricia A. Rowe and Ernestine Stodelle (eds.), *Dance Research Collage* (New York: CORD, 1979), p. 220.

24 "all the arts...," St. Denis, *Life*, p. 175.

Page

24 "period in which...," Suzanne Shelton, *Divine Dancer: A Biography of Ruth St. Denis* (Garden City, NY: Doubleday & Co., 1981), p. 21.

24 "Until Isadora Duncan appeared...," Unspecified reviewer quoted in Victor Seroff, *The Real Isadora* (New York: Dial Press, 1971), p. 35.

24 "grace and elegance...," *The Works of Lucian,* translated by H. W. Fowler and F. G. Fowler (Oxford: Clarendon Press, 1905), vol. 2, p. 246.

24 "display of mind," *The Works of Lucian,* translated by A. M. Harmon (London: Heinemann, and New York: Macmillan, 1913–1961), vol. 5, p. 273.

25 "We should regard...," St. Denis, in Rogers, *Dance: A Basic Educational Technique,* p. 103.

25 "I believe that dance...," Ted Shawn, *Credo* (privately published, n.d.), n.p.

25 "I see America dancing," Isadora Duncan, *The Art of the Dance* (New York: Theatre Art Books, 1969; republication of 1928 edition), p. 49.

25 "living leap of the child," Ibid., p. 47.

26 "You seem to know instinctively...," Ted Shawn, conversation with author at Jacob's Pillow.

27 "Most of the time...," St. Denis, *Life,* p. 187.

27 "I was never a good teacher," Ibid., p. 188.

27 "But I can inspire like hell," St. Denis, quoted after her death in *New York Times,* July 22, 1968.

28 "the idea of one...," Martha Graham, "A Modern Dancer's Primer for Action," in Rogers, *Dance: A Basic Educational Technique,* p. 183

28 "Now see how beautiful...," Ruth Jentzer, interview with author.

31 "black-panther ferocity," Jane Sherman, *The Drama of Denishawn Dance* (Middletown, CT: Wesleyan University Press, 1971), p. 60.

31 "would take out...," Anne Douglas, letter to author.

31 "A brilliant young dancer," *Tacoma New Tribune,* September 18, 1920.

32 "So far the only value...," *Santa Barbara News,* October 2, 1920.

Chapter 2/The Immortal Blow

The author wishes to acknowledge her debt for information and reminiscences in Chapter 2 to Martha Graham, Louis Horst, Charles Weidman, May Forbes, Anne Douglas, and Sachio Ito.

Page

34 "Keep it...," May Forbes, conversation with author.

Page

35 "had to keep track of him...," Anne Douglas, conversation with author.

35 "There is no justice...," Louis Horst, conversation with author.

35 "I know it hurts...," Louis Horst and Carroll Russell, *Modern Dance Forms* (San Francisco: Impulse Publications, 1961), p. 88.

36 "free style," Anne Douglas, conversation with author.

36 "esoteric," Louis Horst, conversation with author.

37 "The act of will...," Arthur Schopenhauer, quoted in Will Durant, *The Story of Philosophy* (Garden City, NY: Garden City Publishing Co., 1926), p. 341.

37 "The whole nervous...," Ibid., p. 341.

37 "Philosophy purifies...," Ibid., pp. 360–61.

37 "The classic remark...," Graham, Arthur Todd Collection (privately owned).

37 "With regard to...," Durant, p. 365.

38 "the glorious power...," Friedrich Nietzche, *The Birth of Tragedy and The Genealogy of Morals,* translated by Francis Golffing (Garden City, NY: Doubleday and Co., Anchor Books, 1956), p. 63.

38 "I did not choose...," Martha Graham, "How I Became a Dancer," *Saturday Review,* August 28, 1965, p. 54.

38 "High Priestess...," Suzanne Shelton, *Divine Dancer: A Biography of Ruth St. Denis* (Garden City, NY: Doubleday & Co., 1981), p. 159

38 "I owe all that I am...," Graham, quoted in W. Adolphe Roberts, "The Fervid Art of Martha Graham," *Dance Magazine,* New York, August 1928.

38 "I owe it all to you," Graham, postcard to Louis Horst, shown to author by Louis Horst.

39 "That's the way...," Charles Weidman, conversation with author.

40 "consisted of...," Louis Horst, *Dance Perspectives,* no. 16, "Composer/Choreographer," p. 6.

40 "a clear understanding...," St. Denis, *Life,* p. 244.

41 "music visualizations," Christena L. Schlundt, *The Professional Appearances of Ruth St. Denis and Ted Shawn: A Chronology and an Index of Dances 1906-1932* (New York: New York Public Library, 1962), p. 38.

41 "isolated phenomenon...," Horst and Russell, *Modern Dance Forms,* p. 16.

41 "vague formlessness," Ibid.

44 "divine dissatisfaction," Agnes de Mille, *Dance to the Piper* (Boston: Little, Brown & Co., 1952), p. 335.

45 "...So, when they wanted...," story quoted in Joel Shapiro, "Martha Graham at the Eastman School," *Dance Magazine,* July 1974, p. 56.

Page

47 "handmaiden," Louis Horst, *Dance Perspectives*, no. 16, "Choreographer/Composer," p. 6.

47 "dry, pedagogical," Horst, letter to Ruth St. Denis, Vienna, June 21, 1926.

47 "I was not trying...," Ibid.

48 "My first original...," Emily Coleman, "Martha Graham Still Leaps Forward," *New York Times Magazine*, April 9, 1961, p. 50.

48 "to go I know not whither to fetch I know not what," Aleksandr Afanas (ed.), *Russian Fairy Tales* (New York: Pantheon, 1982; reprint of 1945 edition). Title translation, Theodore Komisarjevsky.

49 "a double matriarch," Graham, quoted in *Dance Observer*, March 1960, p. 38.

50 "Now you work...," "You can't give up...," Louis Horst, conversation with author.

50 The story of the slap is based on the author's conversations with Louis Horst and Martha Graham.

Chapter 3/Revolt in the Dance

The author wishes to acknowledge her debt for information and reminiscences in Chapter 3 to Martha Graham and Bessie Schoenberg.

Page

51 "as if she dared...," Martha Hill, quoted by Bessie Schoenberg in a letter to author.

52 "My dancing is just dancing...." Armitage, *Martha Graham*, pp. 102–03.

53 "A new vitality...," Ibid., p. 84.

53 "No art can...," Ibid.

54 "America's great gift...," Ibid., p. 99.

55 "the cultivation of the being," Martha Graham, "How I Became a Dancer," *Saturday Review*, August 28, 1965, p. 54.

56 "Movement in the modern dance...," Armitage, p. 104.

56 "Your training only...," Ibid., p. 102.

56 "a dynamo of energy...," Graham, in Rogers, *Dance: A Basic Educational Technique*, p. 178.

57 "Come down into the earth...," Horst and Russell, *Modern Dance Forms*, p. 61.

57 "perfect timing to the Now," Graham, in Rogers, p. 179.

60 "Will people never rebel against artificialities...," Helen Tamiris program for January 29, 1928, contained in the Louis Horst Scrapbooks (v. 3), 1926–1929. New York Public Library Dance Collection (MGZRS).

Page

60 "Art is international...," Ibid.

61 "I believe in getting along...," Doris Humphrey, letter to her mother, Julia Humphrey, February 1, 1929.

62 "Moving the body stirs...," Manuscript from the Doris Humphrey Collection at the NYPL Dance Collection (S M62MG Res.3-M37-1).

62 "Out of emotion comes form," Armitage, p. 97.

62 "I remember being taken...," Graham, conversation with author.

62 "who, for me...," Graham, conversation with author.

63 "My dance is an art...," Doris Humphrey, "My Approach to the Modern Dance," in Rogers, p. 188.

64 "the pantomime and dancing...," Louis Horst, "Bars and Steps—the New Allies," *Dance Magazine*, December 1929, p. 17.

Chapter 4/"I Am a Dancer"

The author wishes to acknowledge her debt for information and reminiscences in Chapter 4 to Martha Graham, Louis Horst, Bessie Schoenberg, Gertrude Shurr, Marian Van Tuyl, Dorothy Bird, and Sophie Maslow.

Page

65 "interior landscape," used in the plural by Graham, Arthur Todd Collection (privately owned), February 15, 1952.

65 "thrilling wonder...," Graham, in Rogers, *Dance: A Basic Educational Technique*, p. 178.

65 "shaped, disciplined...," Martha Graham, "God's Athlete," in Edward R. Murrow, *This I Believe*, edited by Thomas P. Morgan (New York: Simon & Schuster, 1952–1954), p. 58.

65 "costing not less...," T. S. Eliot, "Little Gidding," in *Four Quartets* (New York: Harcourt, Brace & Co., 1943), p. 39.

65 "In a dancer...," Graham, in Murrow, p. 59.

65 "clean, precise," Ibid.

65 "The answer is not control...," Martha Graham, *The Notebooks of Martha Graham* (New York: Harcourt Brace Jovanovich, 1973), p. 325.

65 "I am a dancer," Graham, in Rogers, p. 178; in Murrow, p. 59.

66 "Movement never lies...," Martha Graham, "Martha Graham Speaks," *Dance Observer*, April 1963, p. 53.

66 "out of whole cloth," Bessie Schoenberg, conversation with author.

68 "Grace is your relationship...," Armitage, *Martha Graham*, p. 101.

68 "My dancing...," Armitage, pp. 102–03.

70 "a typical Massine production...," Lydia Sokolova, *Dancing for Diaghilev*, edited by Richard Buckle (New York: Macmillan Co., 1961), p. 162.

Page

70 "crossed swords," Oliver Daniel, "Rite of Spring, First Staging in America: Stokowski—Massine—Graham," *Ballet Review*, Summer 1982, p. 69.

70 "You will be a failure...," Graham, conversation with author.

71 "exactly as...," Daniel, "Rite of Spring," *Ballet Review*, Summer 1982, p. 70.

71 "a great turning point," Ibid.

71 "*Sacre* is a ritual...," Graham, Arthur Todd Collection (privately owned), undated.

72 "You're putting out...," Louis Horst, conversation with author.

72 "You have great talent...," Natalie Harris, interview with author.

73 "I abominate...," Graham, interview with Ben Washer, *New York City Telegram*, April 18, 1932.

73 "A strong feeling...," Winthrop Sargeant, "Martha Graham," *Dance Observer*, May 1934, p. 41.

74 "back to the primitive...," Horst and Russell, *Modern Dance Forms*, p. 56.

74 "A truly primitive..." Ibid., p. 57.

76 "a feeling of suspension...," Sophie Maslow, interview with author.

79 "long woolens," Emily Coleman, "Martha Graham Still Leaps Forward," *New York Times Magazine*, April 9, 1961, p. 52.

79 "the subtle being...," Robert Horan, "The Recent Theatre of Martha Graham," *Dance Index*, January 1947, p. 4.

80 "giants of mankind...," Max Eastman, Foreword, in Arnold Genthe, *Isadora Duncan* (New York and London: Mitchell Kennerley, 1929), n.p.

81 "It's not my job...," Dorothy Bird, Dance Critics Association Conference, June 1982.

81 "Grab the floor...," "Putting shoes on is like...," Ibid.

81 "life-changing," Marian Van Tuyl, interview with author.

84 "Why not try Jean...," Horst, conversation with author.

85 "Audiences who come...," John Martin, *New York Times*, in 1929, quoted by Armitage, p. 8.

85 "The cerebral...," Mary F. Watkins, "Five Facets of the Dance," *Theatre Arts Monthly*, February 1934, p. 135.

85 "complete focus...," Martha Graham, Foreword to Barbara Morgan, *Martha Graham: Sixteen Dances in Photographs* (New York: Duell, Sloan & Pearce, 1941), p. 9.

85 "Dancing...," Graham, quoted in *New York City Telegram*, April 18, 1932.

85 "I do not compose ideologically," Horan, "The Recent Theatre of Martha Graham," *Dance Index*, January 1947, p. 4.

Page

85 "Martha Graham demonstrated...," unknown critic, *Philadelphia Public Ledger,* November 16, 1932.

85 "thunder of bravos," Russell Rhodes, *New York Telegraph,* November 22, 1932.

86 "the force of the personality...," "nucleus of comprehension...," Lincoln Kirstein, quoted in Armitage, p. 26.

86 "fanatical prophetess," Michel Fokine, *Memoirs of a Ballet Master,* translated by Vitale Fokine, edited by Anatole Chujoy (Boston: Little, Brown & Co., 1961), p. 250.

88 The story of the Fokine–Graham controversy has been taken from Fokine's memoirs and from a letter written by Frances Hawkins, personal representative for Martha Graham, dated May 3, 1933.

Chapter 5/The View From Vermont

The author wishes to acknowledge her debt for information and reminiscences in Chapter 5 to Martha Hill, Louis Horst, Bonnie Bird, Bessie Schoenberg, Gertrude Shurr, Sophie Maslow, Ben Belitt, Evelyn Lohoefer, May Forbes, Natalie Harris, Nina Fonaroff, Jean Erdman, Joseph Campbell, Patricia A. Rowe, and Edith White.

Page

91 "had a great talent...," Bessie Schoenberg, speaking at Early Years Conference, April 1981.

91 "We should do something...," Sali Ann Kriegsman, *Modern Dance in America: The Bennington Years* (Boston: G. K. Hall & Co., 1981), p. 250.

92 "The fellowship was...," Ibid., p. 264.

93 "open and spacious...," Horst, *Dance Perspectives,* no. 16, "Composer/Choreographer," p. 6.

93 "To compose...," Horst and Russell, *Modern Dance Forms,* p. 23.

94 "Don't behave as if...," Evelyn Lohoefer, correspondance with author, c. fall 1981.

94 "Do the impossible...," Horst in class, observed by author.

94 "Move with audacity...," Ibid.

94 "Tear it...," Ibid.

94 "used any and all...," Gertrude Lippincott, "A Quiet Genius Himself—Louis Horst," *Focus on Dance V, Composition* (Washington: American Association for Health, Physical Education, and Recreation, 1969), p. 5.

94 "Now bring in...," Horst observed in class by author.

94 "Come on in...," Horst observed in class.

Page

94 "the magic of his imagination...," Martha Graham, Foreword to Horst and Russell, p. 11.

95 "even spatial design," Gertrude Shurr, interview with author.

95 "Without Martha Graham...," Kriegsman, *Modern Dance in America*, p. 27.

96 "caught the emotion...," Norman Lloyd, "Composing for the Dance," *Juilliard Review*, Spring 1961, p. 7.

97 "At the beginning...," Ibid.

98 "She has developed...," Paul Love, "Dance Reviews," *Dance Observer*, March 1934, p. 17.

98 Conversation on the ferry described by May Forbes, interview with author.

99 "Man's inhumanity...," Robert Burns, "Man Was Made to Mourn," stanza 7.

99 "The fierce, fighting...," George Beiswanger, "New Images in Dance, Martha Graham and Agnes de Mille," *Theatre Arts Monthly*, October 1944, p. 610.

100 "Every dance...," Horan, "The Recent Theatre of Martha Graham," *Dance Index*, January 1947, p. 4.

100 "aid Spanish democracy," *Dance Herald*, January 1938, p. 3.

100 "art with vital content," "intellectually learned doctrine," Dane Rudhyar, "Art and Propaganda," *Dance Observer*, December 1936, p. 109.

100 "The greater an artist...," Theodore Komisarjevsky, *The Theatre and a Changing Civilization* (London: John Lane, The Bodley Head, 1935), p. 2.

101 "the fundamental process of...," Otto Rank, *Art and Artist*, translated by Charles Francis Atkinson (New York: Agathon Press, 1968; reprint of 1932 edition), p. 64.

101 "constructive victory," Ibid.

102 "official photographer," Kriegsman, p. 306.

102 "sweat and strain...," Ibid.

104 "avant-garde," Ibid., p. 132.

104 "a zone of inexhaustible...," Ibid., p. 274.

104 "unequipped for her simplicity," Lincoln Kirstein, quoted in Armitage, p. 26.

105 "the physical principles...," Armitage, *Martha Graham*, p. 98.

105 "My quarrel...," Martha Graham, "Martha Graham Speaks," *Dance Observer*, April 1963, p. 54.

107 "modernists who...," *Time*, January 10, 1938.

107 "In Broadway theatres...," Ibid.

107 "her own most appreciative...," Graham, describing *Every Soul Is a Circus*, in Morgan, *Martha Graham*, p. 15.

Page

108 "True theatricality...," Graham, in Rogers, *Dance: A Basic Educational Technique*, p. 183.

110 "You must follow your destiny," Natalie Harris, interview with author.

111 "wonderful, wonderful performance," Emily Coleman, "Martha Graham Still Leaps Forward," *New York Times Magazine*, April 9, 1961, p. 57.

111 "You cannot lead...," Natalie Harris, interview with author.

112 "Come to my room...," Ibid.

112 "As the School of the Dance...," Mary Jo Shelly, "The New Plan at Bennington," *Dance Observer*, April 1940, p. 48.

114 "in themselves a form of dance," Elizabeth McCausland, "Martha Graham and *Letter to the World*," *Dance Observer*, August–September 1940, p. 97.

114 "Better let it sleep...," Martha's remembrance of John Martin's review, Kriegsman, p. 210.

115 "rich and lovely," John Martin, *New York Times*, August 18, 1940.

115 "Sometimes a dance takes...," Graham, "Martha Graham Speaks," *Dance Observer*, April 1963, p. 54.

115 "a great part...," John Martin, *New York Times*, January 21, 1941.

116 "I'm Nobody...," Emily Dickinson, *The Poems of Emily Dickinson*, 3 vols., edited by Thomas H. Johnson (Cambridge, MA: Harvard University Press, Belknap Press, 1955), p. 206.

116 "It's Coming, the postponeless creature...," Ibid., p. 307.

116 "Looking at Death...," from "'Tis so appalling—it exhilerates...," Ibid., p. 201.

116 "Gay, Ghastly holiday...," from "'Tis so appalling—it exhilerates...,' Ibid., p. 201.

116 "Inebriate of Air...," Ibid., p. 149.

117 "[Hope is] the thing with feathers...," Ibid., p. 182.

117 "I'm wife...," Ibid., p. 142.

117 "Of Course I prayed...," Ibid., p. 299.

117 "This is my letter to the World," Ibid., p. 340.

118 "Split the Lark," Ibid., p. 644.

Chapter 6/The View From Within

The author wishes to acknowledge her debt for information and reminiscences in Chapter 6 to May Forbes, Ben Belitt, Erick Hawkins, May O'Donnell, Eric Walther, and Susan Au.

Page

119 "You do not realize...," caption under a newspaper photo, n.d., in ref-

Page

erence to a lecture, presumably given October 23, 1938. New York Public Library Dance Collection.

120 "image-maker," Graham, "How I Became a Dancer," *Saturday Review,* August 28, 1965, p. 54.

121 "made his light dance...," Ben Belitt, "Words for Dancers, Perhaps," originally printed in *Bennington Review,* April 1980; reprinted in *Ballet Review,* November 1980, p. 220.

121 "For he who recollects...," Graham, *The Notebooks of Martha Graham* (New York: Harcourt Brace Jovanovich, 1973), p. 30.

122 "In a dancer's body...," Graham, in Rogers, *Dance: A Basic Educational Technique,* p. 178.

122 "darkest," Graham, conversation with author.

122 "The complex inner...," Horst and Russell, *Modern Dance Forms,* p. 90.

122 "Martha Graham's...," Ibid., p. 92

122 "A symbol is...," Suzanne K. Langer, *Feeling and Form* (New York: Scribner, 1953), p. xi.

123 "doom-eager," Graham, "Martha Graham Speaks," *Dance Observer,* April 1963, p. 53.

123 "still as death," Emily Brontë, *Wuthering Heights* (New York: Random House, 1943), p. 58.

123 "Tonight in *Deaths*...," Graham, *Notebooks,* p. 87.

124 "Nothing Martha Graham...," John Martin, *New York Times,* November 2, 1944.

125 "My brother died...," Graham, interview with Walter Terry, November 16, 1952.

125 "When spring came...," Ibid.

125 "poignant stories," Ibid.

125 "the coming of...," Ibid.

125 "The scenery...," Graham, "Martha Graham Speaks," *Dance Observer,* April 1963, p. 54.

126 "I never have hysterics," Erick Hawkins, interview with author.

126 "anti-life," Ibid.

126 "When one is quiet...," Ibid.

126 "It's just that...," Graham, interview with Walter Terry, November 16, 1952.

127 "A role must fit one...," Ibid.

127 "You transform yourself...," Ibid.

127 "a trusting of one's nature," Ibid.

127 "I am a thief...," Graham, *Notebooks,* pp. xi, 303.

128 "the instant...," Rogers, p. 180.

128 "Yes. Come to see...," Hawkins, interview with author.

Page

128 "I would compose...," Erick Hawkins, "Pure Poetry," in Selma Jeanne Cohen (ed.), *The Modern Dance: Seven Statements of Belief* (Middletown, CT: Wesleyan University Press, 1965), p. 50.

129 "has not produced...," Horst, quoted in Morgan, *Martha Graham*, p. 153.

130 "Nowhere in...," John Martin, *New York Times*, November 5, 1944.

130 "I do not see...," Daijaka Horiguchi.

131 The English translation of Mallarmé's poem *Hérodiade* used here was given to the author by May O'Donnell.

131 "When you look...," Graham, "Martha Graham Speaks," *Dance Observer*, April 1963, p. 54.

131 "as a metaphor to define...," Isamu Noguchi, *A Sculptor's World* (New York: Harper and Row, 1968), p. 38.

132 "Where is the mirror...," as quoted by Martin Friedman, *Noguchi's Imaginary Landscapes* [Minneapolis] Walker Art Center [1978], p. 29.

134 "She works blindly...," Ben Belitt, "Words for Dancers, Perhaps," *Ballet Review*, November 1980, pp. 238–39.

134 "The errand into the maze...," Ben Belitt, "Dance Piece," *Wilderness Stair* (New York: Grove Press, 1955), p. 13.

135 "the big sound," Belitt, interview with author.

135 "deceptively accessible...," "it was this kind...," Belitt, "Words for Dancers, Perhaps," *Ballet Review*, November 1980, p. 229.

136 "suppliant hands...," Noguchi, *A Sculptor's World*, p. 126.

137 "Martha Graham completed my triptych...," Sol Hurok, *S. Hurok Presents* (New York: Hermitage House, 1953), p. 65.

137 "she has chosen...," Ibid.

138 "There are times...," Graham, "God's Athlete," in Murrow, *This I Believe*, p. 58.

138 "If you do...," Graham, "Martha Graham Speaks," *Dance Observer*, April 1963, p. 54.

138 "complete focus...," Graham, in Morgan, *Martha Graham: Sixteen Dances in Photographs*, p. 9.

139 "Practice means...," Graham, in Murrow, p. 58.

139 "The Dark Meadow of Ate," program note, June 1982.

140 "I have been ere now...," Empedocles, fragment used as program note for *Dark Meadow*.

Chapter 7/The View From Olympus

The author wishes to acknowledge her debt for information and reminiscences in Chapter 7 to Martha Graham, May O'Donnell, Sachio Ito, and Isamu Noguchi.

Page

142 "reflect not only man's human form...," Jane Ellen Harrison, *Prolegomena to a Study of the Greek Religion* (Cambridge: University Press, 1903), p. 260.

142 "But if I wished...," Edith Hamilton, *Mythology* (Boston: Little, Brown & Co., 1940), p. 25.

143 "snake solo," "hip crawls," "knee crawls," "eaten," "spit out," Graham, *The Notebooks of Martha Graham*, pp. 162–63.

143 "This is a dance...," program note for the first performance of *Medea*.

143 "Thou living hate...," Gilbert Murray (ed.), *Ten Greek Plays* (New York: Oxford University Press, 1953), p. 355. This translation of *Medea* was also done by Murray.

144 "Cave turn," Graham, *Notebooks*, p. 157.

146 "Tragedy's one essential...," Edith Hamilton, *The Greek Way* (New York: W. W. Norton & Co., 1930 and 1943), p. 234.

147 "is enthroned...," Ibid.

147 "Must I not fear...," "This wedlock...," Sophocles, *Oedipus the King*, in *Four Famous Greek Plays*, edited by Paul Landis (New York: Modern Library, 1929), pp. 113–114.

147 "O woe is thee...," Sophocles, in Landis, p. 120.

148 "instant of agony," program note for *Night Journey*.

148 "why stung with...," Sophocles, in Landis, p. 121.

148 "sees with double insight...," program note for *Night Journey*.

148 "tricksy beggar-priest...," Sophocles, in Landis, p. 84.

148 "Thou hast eyes...," Ibid., p. 85.

150 "The very dreams...," Joseph Campbell, *The Hero with a Thousand Faces* (Princeton: Princeton University Press, Bollingen Series XVII, 1949), p. 3.

150 "Call to adventure," Ibid., p. 58.

150 "dangerous crises...," Ibid., p. 9.

150 "the world's symbolic carriers," Ibid., p. 36.

151 "graph of the heart," Horan, "The Recent Theatre of Martha Graham," *Dance Index*, January 1947, p. 4.

151 "labyrinth...," Campbell, *Hero*, p. 23.

151 "not less than everything," Eliot, "Little Gidding," in *Four Quartets*, p. 39.

151 "I did not choose...," Graham, "How I Became a Dancer," *Saturday Review*, August 28, 1965, p. 54.

151 "Contrary to opinion...," Graham, in Rogers, *Dance: A Basic Educational Technique*, p. 183.

151 "The hero is...," Campbell, *Hero*, p. 16.

152 "the everlastingly recurrent...," Ibid., p. 22.

152 "the man or woman...," Ibid., p. 19.

Page

152 "As a result. . . ," Noguchi, *A Sculptor's World,* p. 12.

153 "I am deeply Asian. . . ," Graham, conversation with author.

153 "more complimentary," Noguchi, interview with author, December 1979.

153 "evolving. . . ," Noguchi, interview with author.

153 "I respected. . . ," Graham, conversation with author.

153 "We worked together. . . ," Noguchi, interview with author.

155 "*Frontier* was. . . ," Noguchi, *A Sculptor's World,* p. 125.

155 "the life of Joan of Arc. . . ," Ibid.

155 "I do my sculpture. . . ," Noguchi, interview with author.

156 "The 'doorway' is like. . . ," Noguchi, *A Sculptor's World,* quoting Graham, p. 126.

156 "The visual conception. . . ," Friedman, quoting Graham, p. 30.

157 "I'd like to think. . . ," Graham, conversation with author.

157 "seeking identity. . . ," Noguchi, interview with author.

157 "In my work. . . ," Noguchi, *A Sculptor's World,* p. 21.

157 "to find a way of sculpture. . . ," Ibid., p. 219.

157 "Art should disappear," Noguchi, interview with author.

158 "magic with. . . ," Lincoln Kirstein, *Thirty Years: The New York City Ballet* (New York: Alfred A. Knopf, 1978), p. 111.

158 "had one particular. . . ," Jean Rosenthal and Lael Wertenbaker, *The Magic of Light* (Boston and Toronto: Little, Brown & Co., 1972), p. 129.

158 "intense sensuality. . . ," Ibid., p. 14.

158 "silent collaboration. . . ," Ibid., p. 129.

159 "dedication to as near perfection. . . ," Ibid.

159 "the theatre is a place. . . ," Ibid.

159 "The lighting came. . . ," Ibid., p. 129.

159 "Designing for the dance. . . ," Ibid., p. 117.

160 "To do one. . . ," Ibid., p. 131.

Chapter 8/A Lyrical Lull on Olympus

The author wishes to acknowledge her debt for information and reminiscences in Chapter 8 to Louis Horst, Pearl Lang, Ben Belitt, and Eugene Lester.

Page

161 "monstrous vital rhythms. . . ," Martha Graham, "Seeking an American Art of the Dance," in Oliver Sayler (ed.), *Revolt in the Arts* (New York: Brentano's, 1930), p. 250.

Page

161 "the intensity of self-penetration," Graham, in Sayler, p. 252.

164 "Saw it once...," Louis Horst, conversation with author.

164 "may well be the richest...," John Martin, *New York Times,* May 5, 1955, quoted in James Roose-Evans, *Experimental Theatre from Stanislavsky to Today* (New York: Universe Books, 1970), p. 133.

165 "gay and outward...," Norman Dello Joio, *Dance Perspectives,* no. 16, "Composer/Choreographer," p. 19.

165 "she may have been...," Ibid.

165 "wanted to see...," Ibid.

166 "the ecstasy of the contraction," Pearl Lang, interview with author.

167 "It is the place...," Belitt quote, appearing on the program of the original performance in 1948.

168 "a woman who does not...," Graham, Arthur Todd Collection (privately owned), lecture demonstration, YM–YWHA, March 25, 1951.

168 "I gave William Schuman...," Graham, Arthur Todd Collection (privately owned), February 15, 1952.

169 "I never work...," Ibid.

169 "Her essential quality of movement...," John Martin, *New York Times,* April 3, 1944.

169 "I dressed myself...," Graham, quoted in Friedman, *Noguchi's Imaginary Landscapes,* p. 33.

170 "When a woman...," Ibid., p. 30.

170 "Lear's mind," Graham, *The Notebooks of Martha Graham,* p. 47.

170 "Storm and madness...," Ibid., p. 51.

172 "dark ladies," Graham, lecture demonstration at 92nd Street YM–YWHA, New York, 1951.

172 "It was Norman...," Graham, Arthur Todd Collection (privately owned), February 15, 1952.

172 "I was not happy...," Graham, interview with Walter Terry, November 16, 1952.

173 "Joan of Arc...," Graham, conversation with author.

174 "in praise of the Earth...," program note to *Canticle for Innocent Comedians.*

174 "Who bear belief...," Belitt, "Canticle for Innocent Comedians," *Wilderness Stair* (New York: Grove Press, 1955), p. 38.

174 "I did not want to be...," Graham, in Rogers, *Dance: A Basic Educational Technique,* p. 178.

174 "the miracle...," Ibid.

175 "life-enhancing qualities," Richard Buckle, *The Observer* (London), March 7, 1954.

175 "is one of the great creators...," Ibid.

Page

176 "packed with standees," "News Items from the Martha Graham ANTA Tour," *Dance Observer*, February 1956, p. 24.

176 "the beauty...," Ibid.

177 "Martha Graham, through her art...," "More News Items from the Martha Graham ANTA Tour," *Dance Observer*, March 1956, p. 41.

177 "massive and unrestrained," Graham Souvenir Program 1954–1960.

177 "in the streets...," Ibid.

177 "I do not know...," "More News Items from the Martha Graham ANTA Tour," *Dance Observer*, March 1956, p. 41.

177 "insight that the world...," Plato, *The Collected Dialogues*, Introduction, p. xvii.

178 "The theatre dressing room...," script from the film *A Dancer's World*, commissioned by WQED in Pittsburgh.

178 "You make up your face...," Ibid.

178 "And then...," Ibid.

178 "It is here...," Ibid.

179 "When a dancer...," Ibid.

179 "instant when she recognizes...," Ibid.

179 "bringing the art...," "the greatest single ambassador...," Paul Grey Hoffman, director of UN Special Fund, in 1957 presentation speech for the *Dance Magazine* Awards to Martha Graham and Agnes de Mille; quoted by Sabin in a souvenir program.

180 "her own way," Graham, interview with Marian Horosko, 1962.

180 "But I didn't find...," Ibid.

180 "You make the reverence...," Ibid.

180 "I do not make...," Graham, conversation with author.

180 "deep sense of family tragedy...," Ibid.

180 "Greece is not so different...," Ibid.

Chapter 9/The Darkest Lady

The author wishes to acknowledge her debt for information and reminiscences in Chapter 9 to Bertram Ross, Paul Taylor, Ethel Winter, Ellen Graff, Deirdre Murphy, and David Wood.

Page

184 "You'd never...," Robinson Jeffers, "The Tower Beyond Tragedy," *The Selected Poetry of Robinson Jeffers* (New York: Random House, 1959), p. 89.

184 "angry, wild, wicked woman," Graham, "How I Became a Dancer," *Saturday Review*, August 28, 1965, p. 54.

Page

184 "Gorgon shapes throng up...," Aeschylus, *The Libation Bearers*, in *The House of Atreus*, translated by E. D. A. Morshead (London: Macmillan and Co., 1923), p. 129.

185 "my flower of pain," program note, 1960 season.

185 "Modern literature is devoted...," Campbell, *The Hero with a Thousand Faces*, p. 27.

185 "that most deep...," program note, *Clytemnestra*.

186 "wisdom and...," Ibid.

186 "As though by the will...," Ibid.

189 "a piece of goods...," Jeffers, p. 89.

191 "fierce-lipped," Jeffers, p. 89.

192 "works like a sort of bacillus...," Harrison, *Prolegomena*, p. 218.

193 "puts an end...," program note.

194 "miracle of greatness," John Martin, *New York Times*, April 27, 1960.

194 "*Clytemnestra* would not...," Graham, conversation with author after a performance.

195 "How did you get...," Ethel Winter, interview with author.

195 "I never...," Winter, interview with author.

196 "Aegisthus is *bad*," Paul Taylor, interview with author.

196 "fit me...," Ibid.

196 "dance of triumph," Ibid.

197 "I think I'm...," Bertram Ross, quoting Martha Graham, interview with author.

197 "you see what I...," Ibid.

197 "the most completely...," *Helen McGehee, Dancer* (New York: Alfonso Umana, Editions Heraclita, 1974), n.p.

Chapter 10/Back to Brightness

The author wishes to acknowledge her debt for information and reminiscences in Chapter 10 to Marnie Thomas, David Wood, Sallie Wilson, and Vivian Fine.

Page

201 "I do not theorize...," Graham, conversation with author, Connecticut College, 1963.

202 "We were all superconscious...," Marnie Thomas, interview with author.

202 "I want to become...," Graham, conversation with author. Statement made in the past tense.

Page

202 "Posture is...," Graham, in Rogers, *Dance: A Basic Educational Technique,* p. 181.

202 "There is only...," Ibid., p. 182.

203 "a wonderfully satiric...," Walter Terry, *New York Herald Tribune,* May 8, 1960.

204 "tragic," Horst, conversation with author.

205 "We have all walked...," Graham, in Murrow, *This I Believe,* p. 59.

205 "not give up," Graham, conversation with author, January 1981.

205 "Collaboration was...," Graham, Arthur Todd Collection (privately owned), June 17, 1959.

206 "an evening's spectacle...," Lincoln Kirstein, *Thirty Years: The New York City Ballet* (New York: Alfred A. Knopf, 1978), p. 54.

206 "key characters...," Ibid., p. 149.

206 "essence of...," Ibid.

206 "It is five...," Graham, conversation with author. The story is repeated also in *The Notebooks of Martha Graham,* p. 304.

206 "The work as a whole was...," John Martin, *New York Times,* June 7, 1959.

206 "Fate had decreed...," Stefan Zweig, *Mary Queen of Scotland and the Isles,* translated by Eden and Cedar Paul (New York: Viking Press, 1935), p. 60.

206 "active and lean," George Balanchine, *Balanchine's New Complete Stories of the Great Ballets* (Garden City, NY: Doubleday & Co., 1968), p. 135.

206 "air like molecules," Ibid., p. 134.

206 "super-mechancial nonhumanity," John Martin, *New York Times,* June 7, 1959.

207 "without the...," Ibid.

207 "played it...," Graham, Arthur Todd Collection (privately owned), June 17, 1959.

207 "But I moved...," Ibid.

207 "It was from these two...," Ibid.

207 "In my beginning...," T. S. Eliot, "East Coker," *Four Quartets* (New York: Harcourt, Brace and Co., 1943), p. 11.

207 "In order to possess...," Ibid., p. 15.

207 "This daughter...," Zweig, p. 18.

207 "Mary prepared for...," Ibid., p. 345.

208 "dark turbulence...," Graham, Arthur Todd Collection (privately owned), June 17, 1959.

208 "dear cousin's," Zweig, p. 84.

210 "And what you own...," "East Coker," p. 15.

210 "Come with me...," Sallie Wilson, interview with author.

Page

210 "I must tell...," Ibid.

211 "Sallie Wilson is a beautiful...," Graham, Arthur Todd Collection, (privately owned), June 17, 1959.

211 "Each movement...," Wilson, interview with author.

211 "Now do some of the movements," Ibid.

212 "What shall we do?" Ibid.

212 "Let's pray," Ibid.

212 "14-carat sheen," Ibid.

212 "as delicate as air," Ibid.

212 "Karinska was...," Graham, Arthur Todd Collection (privately owned), June 17, 1959.

213 "It widened...," Ibid.

213 "Miss Graham's part...," Balanchine, *Stories*, p. 133.

213 "the last moments...," program note, *Episodes I*.

214 "furiously contorted solo...," Kirstein, *Thirty Years*, p. 152.

214 "fractured glass-snake...," Ibid.

214 "beginning to slow down," Don McDonagh, *Martha Graham* (New York: Praeger, 1973), p. 197.

215 "I feel when I dance...," Ruth St. Denis, *An Unfinished Life*, p. 242.

216 "3 little swans," Graham, *Notebooks*, p. 363.

216 "Javanese steps," Ibid., p. 361.

217 "fanfare for dance...," program note for *Acrobats of God*.

217 "tribulations, disciplines and denials," program note for *Acrobats of God*, 1960 season.

218 "All of them...," John Martin, *New York Times*, May 8, 1960.

219 "rite of spring," program note for *Alcestis*, 1960 season. Martha compared herself to Alcestis as told by David Wood, interview with author.

220 "Whenever the creative force...," C. G. Jung, *Modern Man in Search of a Soul*, translated by W. S. Dell and Cary F. Baynes (New York: Harcourt Brace Jovanovich, Harvest/HBJ Book, n.d.; originally published 1933), p. 170.

220 "The artist is not a person...," Ibid., p. 169.

221 "circular desert," T. S. Eliot, *The Complete Poems and Plays, 1909–1950* (New York: Harcourt Brace Jovanovich, 1971), p. 277.

221 "about visions of terror," Russel Kirk, author of *T. S. Eliot and His Age*, conversation with author.

222 "utter chaos," David Wood, interview with author. This interview supplies the details recounted here.

224 "one of her most ravishing creations," John Martin, *New York Times*, April 30, 1960.

224 "Human passion...," Jung, p. 162.

Chapter 11/Lady of the Labyrinth

The author wishes to acknowledge her debt for information and reminiscences in Chapter 11 to Robert Starer, Ethel Winter, Mary Hinkson, Bertram Ross, Ruth L. Murray, David Wood, Marnie Thomas, Joseph Campbell, Arthur Todd, Eugene Lester, Sophie Maslow, Jane Dudley, and Nina Fonaroff.

Page

225 "the full-blooded vigor...," Margaret Lloyd, *The Borzoi Book of Modern Dance* (New York: Alfred A. Knopf, 1949), p. 53.

226 "in the dignity of my time," Walter Terry, "Martha Graham Takes a Candid Look Ahead," *New York Herald Tribune*, April 26, 1964, p. 31.

227 "a good opener," Graham, conversation with author.

227 "She stood you up...," Graham, conversation with author's husband.

227 "who was caught...," Rouben Ter Arutunian, *Dance Perspectives*, no. 28, "In Search of Design," winter 1966.

228 "total theatrical entity," Robert Starer, *Dance Perspectives*, no. 16, "Composer/Choreographer," p. 17.

228 "tragic and eternal," Graham, *The Notebooks of Martha Graham*, p. 81.

229 "Phantasmagoria of Desire," Ibid.

229 "When she talked to me...," Robert Starer, interview with author.

229 "*Phaedra* was a high point...," Ibid.

229 "The only time...," Ibid.

229 "Sometimes...," Ibid.

231 "I came off so mad...," Ethel Winter, interview with author.

232 "Actually, Aphrodite was...," Ibid.

233 "protectress of dewy youth," Edith Hamilton, *Mythology*, p. 31.

234 "pale, worn-out...," Arthur Todd Collection, tape of Mary Wigman and Ruth St. Denis, made in Hollywood, April 1958.

234 "the will to act...," Mary Wigman, *The Language of Dance*, translated by Walter Sorell (Middletown, CT: Wesleyan University Press, 1966), p. 12.

235 "The great mission of the dancer...," Ruth St. Denis, "Religious Manifestations in the Dance," in Walter Sorell (ed.), *The Dance Has Many Faces* (Cleveland and New York: World Publishing Co., 1951), p. 14.

235 "I have something...," Mary Hinkson, interview with author.

235 "You two were born knowing," Bertram Ross, Dance Critics Association Conference, June 1982.

236 "Get me down! Get me down!" Mary Hinkson, interview with author.

236 "To encounter...," Alexander Bland, *The Observer Weekend Review of London*, September 1, 1963.

236 "truthfully... more drama...," Walter Terry, *New York Herald Tribune*, October 14, 1963.

Page

236 "To remind those...," Ibid.

236 "Why can't people...," Bertram Ross, interview with author.

238 "I am the Grand...," reminiscences of author, who attended the party.

239 "Father of Modern Choreography," Ernestine Stodelle, *The First Frontier: The Story of Louis Horst and the American Dance* (Cheshire, CT: privately published, 1964), p. 4.

241 "first and best student," Horst, conversation with author.

241 "Now you have two...," David Wood, interview with author.

241 "many-corridored complexities...," Alfred Tennyson, *Idylls of the King*, edited by Elizabeth Nitchie (New York: Macmillan Co., 1928), p. 178.

241 "so many different things...," Marnie Thomas, interview with author.

241 "playing at playing," Ibid.

241 "using," Ibid.

242 "The casual... to me it's a menace," Graham, interview with Marian Horosko.

244 "In *Heretic* he was...," Sophie Maslow, interview with author.

244 "Louis' scores...," Robert Sabin, Graham Company Souvenir Program.

245 "You must...," Eugene Lester, interview with author.

245 "Then, Martha came in...," Winter, interview with author.

245 "We dedicated...," Kriegsman, *Modern Dance in America*, p. 269.

247 "Martha was one of us...," Dorothy Bird, speaking at Dance Critics Association Conference, June 1982.

247 "I rehearsed...," Maslow, interview with author.

247 "You have a responsibility...," Wood, interview with author.

248 "I didn't want to...," Wood, quoting Martha Graham, interview with author.

248 "Father of Modern Choreography," Stodelle, p. 4.

249 "Celebration," Graham's statement, Connecticut College, 1965.

250 "cultivation of the being," Graham, "How I Became a Dancer," *Saturday Review*, August 28, 1965, p. 54.

250 "dehumanized things but... great figures," Ibid.

250 "that angry, wild, wicked woman," Ibid.

250 "It cost me...," Ibid.

Chapter 12/Deaths and Reentrances

The author wishes to acknowledge her debt for information and reminiscences in Chapter 12 to Pearl Lang, Jean Erdman, Jane Dudley, Nina Fonaroff, Eugene Lester, and Isamu Noguchi.

Page

251 "a soul that can feel greatly," Hamilton, *Greek Way*, p. 234.

252 "man's inhumanity to man," Robert Burns, "Man Was Made to Mourn," stanza 7.

252 "alone of all...," Hamilton, *Greek Way*, p. 272.

252 "The mortal is mad who sacks...," Euripides, *The Trojan Women*, in *Ten Plays by Euripides*, translated by Moses Hadas and John McLean (Toronto: Bantam Classic, 1981), p. 177 (first Bantam printing 1960).

253 "O power...," Euripides, *The Trojan Women*, in *Greek Plays in Modern Translation*, edited by Dudley Fitts, translated by Richmond Lattimore (New York: Dial Press, 1947), p. 179.

253 "How strange a way to call on gods," Ibid.

253 "pain and cruel compulsion," Euripides, *Hecabe* in *Medea and Other Plays*, translated by Philip Vellacott (Harmondsworth, Great Britain: Penguin Books [Penguin Classics], 1963), p. 82.

253 "in in unbreakable ring" Euripides, Ibid.

256 "It is a bitter thing...," Graham, *New York Times* interview, October 2, 1970; also *Berkshire Eagle*, October 2, 1970.

257 "In those days...," Graham, *New York Times* interview, October 2, 1970.

258 "The solos are...," Pearl Lang, interview with author.

258 "Jane's wonderful...," Ibid.

258 "special simplicity," Ibid.

258 "she discovered her own dramatic line...," Walter Terry, "Martha Graham, Past, Present and Future," *Saturday Review of Literature*, October 24, 1970, p. 62.

258 "glorious," Doris Hering, "And Tomorrow? What Did the Martha Graham Dance Company—Without Miss Graham—Tell Us about Her Art and Its Future?" *Dance Magazine*, December 1970, p. 26.

259 "a commanding dance-actress," Ibid., p. 27.

260 "an embarrassment...," Vaught, "Notes on Martha Graham," NYU Final Paper.

260 "the belly of the whale," Campbell, *The Hero with a Thousand Faces*, p. 90.

260 "And so it happens...," Ibid., p. 101.

260 *New Larousse Encyclopedia of Mythology* (New York: The Hamlyn Publishers, Prometheus Press, 1959), p. 150.

260 "The psyche has...," Campbell, *Hero*, p. 64.

261 "the high wire...," Graham, in Murrow, *This I Believe*, p. 59.

261 "In the spring of...," Walter Terry, *Saturday Review*, July 3, 1973.

261 "Divine turbulence...," St.-Jean Perse, *Chronique*, translated by Robert Fitzgerald (New York: Pantheon Books, Bollingen Series LXIX, 1961), p. 29.

Page

261 "ever widening sky," Ibid., p. 27.

262 "Great Age, behold us . . . " Ibid., p. 48.

262 "those bleeding ruptures. . . ," Ibid., p. 28.

Epilogue/"Acts of Light"

Page

263 "Acts of Light," Emily Dickinson, *The Letters of Emily Dickinson*, vol. 3, edited by Thomas E. Johnson and Theodore Ward (Cambridge, MA: Harvard University Press, Belknap Press, 1958), p. 850. Full quote: To Mrs. J. Howard Sweetser, late autumn 1884, "Thank you for all the Acts of Light which beautified a Summer now past to it's reward [sic]."

264 "a door would open," Martha Graham, conversation with author.

265 "amazing human power. . . ," Edwin Denby, *New York Herald Tribune*, May 16, 1945.

Bibliography

AESCHYLUS. *The House of Atreus.* Translated by E. D. A. Morshead. London: Macmillan & Co., 1923.

AFANAS, ALEKSANDR (ED.) *Russian Fairy Tales.* Translated by Norbert Guterman. New York: Pantheon, 1982. Reprint of 1945 edition.

ARMITAGE, MERLE. *Martha Graham.* Brooklyn: Dance Horizons, 1966. Republication of 1937 edition.

BALANCHINE, GEORGE. *Balanchine's New Complete Stories of the Great Ballets.* Garden City, NY: Doubleday & Co., 1968.

BEAUMONT, CYRIL W. *Michel Fokine: His Ballets.* London: C. W. Beaumont, 1935.

BELITT, BEN. *Five-Fold Mesh.* New York: Alfred A. Knopf, 1938.

———. *Wilderness Stair.* New York: Grove Press, 1955.

BRONTË, EMILY. *Wuthering Heights.* New York: Random House, 1943.

CAMPBELL, JOSEPH. *The Hero with a Thousand Faces.* Princeton, NJ: Princeton University Press (Bollingen Series XVII), 1949.

———. *The Masks of God.* Vol. 1, *Primitive Mythology.* New York: Viking Press, 1959.

———. *The Masks of God.* Vol. 3, *Occidental Mythology.* New York: Penguin Books, 1964.

———. *The Masks of God.* Vol. 4, *Creative Mythology.* New York: Penguin Books, 1968.

COHEN, SELMA JEANNE. *Doris Humphrey: An Artist First.* Middletown, CT: Wesleyan University Press, 1972.

———. *The Modern Dance: Seven Statements of Belief.* Middletown, CT: Wesleyan University Press, 1965.

COLEMAN, EMILY. "Martha Graham Still Leaps Forward." *New York Times Magazine,* April 9, 1961.

CRANE, HART. *The Bridge.* New York: Horace Liveright, 1930.

CROCE, ARLENE. *Going to the Dance.* New York: Alfred A. Knopf, 1982.

CUNNINGHAM, MERCE. *Changes: Notes on Choreography.* Edited by Frances Starr. New York: Something Else Press, 1968.

DE MILLE, AGNES. *Dance to the Piper.* Boston: Little, Brown & Co. (an Atlantic Monthly Book), 1959.

DENBY, EDWIN. *Looking at the Dance.* New York: Horizon Press, 1968.

DICKINSON, EMILY. *The Poems of Emily Dickinson,* 3 vols. Edited by Thomas H. Johnson. Cambridge, MA: Harvard University Press (Belknap Press), 1955.

DUNCAN, ISADORA. *The Art of the Dance.* New York: Theatre Arts Books, 1969. Republication of 1928 edition.

DURANT, WILL. *The Story of Philosophy*. Garden City, NY: Garden City Publishing Co., 1926.

ELIOT, T. S. *Four Quartets*. New York: Harcourt, Brace & Co., 1943.

———. *The Complete Poems and Plays, 1909–1950*. New York: Harcourt Brace Jovanovich, 1971.

EURIPIDES. *Euripides I: (Alcestis; The Medea; The Heracleidae; Hippolytus)*. Edited by David Grene and Richmond Lattimore. Chicago: University of Chicago Press, 1955.

———. *Medea and Other Plays*. Translated by Philip Vellacott. Harmondsworth, Great Britain: Penguin Books (Penguin Classics), 1963.

———. *Ten Plays by Euripides*. Translated by Moses Hadas and John McLean. Toronto: Bantam Classic, 1981.

EWEN, DAVID. *The Complete Book of the American Musical Theatre*. New York: Henry Holt & Co., 1958.

FITTS, DUDLEY (ED.). *Greek Plays in Modern Translation*. New York: Dial Press, 1947.

FOKINE, MICHEL. *Memoirs of a Ballet Master*. Translated by Vitale Fokine, edited by Anatole Chujoy. Boston: Little, Brown & Co., 1961.

FRAZER, JAMES. *The Golden Bough*. New York: Macmillan Co., 1930.

FRIEDMAN, MARTIN. *Noguchi's Imaginary Landscapes*. [Minneapolis] Walker Art Center [ca. 1978].

GENTHE, ARNOLD. *Isadora Duncan*. New York and London: Mitchell Kennerley, 1929.

GIDE, ANDRÉ. *Two Legends: Oedipus and Theseus*. Translated by John Russell. New York: Random House (Vintage Books), 1958.

GRAHAM, MARTHA. *The Notebooks of Martha Graham*. Introduction by Nancy Wilson Ross. New York: Harcourt Brace Jovanovich, 1973.

———. "God's Athlete," in Edward R. Murrow, *This I Believe*. Edited by Thomas P. Morgan. New York: Simon & Schuster, 1952–1954.

———. "How I Became a Dancer," *Saturday Review*, August 28, 1965.

———. "A Modern Dancer's Primer for Action," in Frederick Rand Rogers (ed.), *Dance: A Basic Educational Technique*. New York: Macmillan Co., 1941.

———. "Martha Graham Speaks," *Dance Observer*, April 1963.

———. "Seeking an American Art of the Dance," in Oliver Sayler (ed.), *Revolt in the Arts*. New York: Brentano's, 1930.

HAMILTON, EDITH. *The Greek Way*. New York: W. W. Norton & Co., 1943.

———. *Mythology*. Boston: Little, Brown & Co., 1942.

HARRISON, JANE ELLEN. *Ancient Art and Ritual*. New York: Greenwood Press, 1968. Reprint of 1951 edition.

———. *Epilegomena to the Study of Greek Religion* and *Themis: A Study of the Social Origins of Greek Religion*. New Hyde Park, NY: University Books, 1966.

———. *Prolegomena to the Study of Greek Religion*. Cambridge: University Press, 1903.

HERING, DORIS (ED.). *25 Years of American Dance*. New York: Rudolf Orthwine, 1951.

HORAN, ROBERT. "The Recent Theatre of Martha Graham," *Dance Index*, January 1947.

HORST, LOUIS. *Pre-Classic Dance Forms.* New York: The Dance Observer, 1937.

HORST, LOUIS, AND RUSSELL, CARROLL. *Modern Dance Forms in Relation to the Other Modern Arts.* San Francisco: Impulse Publications, 1961.

HUROK, SOL. *S. Hurok Presents.* New York: Hermitage House, 1953.

JEFFERS, ROBINSON. *The Selected Poetry of Robinson Jeffers.* New York: Random House, 1959.

JUNG, C. G. *Modern Man in Search of a Soul.* New York: Harcourt Brace Jovanovich (Harvest/HBJ Book), n.d. Originally published 1933.

KENDALL, ELIZABETH. *Where She Danced.* New York: Alfred A. Knopf, 1979.

KING, ELEANOR. *Transformations.* Brooklyn: Dance Horizons, 1978.

KIRK, RUSSELL. *Eliot and His Age.* New York: Random House, 1972.

KIRSTEIN, LINCOLN. *Movement and Metaphor.* New York: Praeger, 1970.

———. *Nijinsky Dancing.* New York: Alfred A. Knopf, 1975.

———. *Thirty Years: The New York City Ballet.* New York: Alfred A. Knopf, 1978.

———. *Three Pamphlets Collected.* Brooklyn: Dance Horizons, 1967. Republication.

KOMISARJEVSKY, THEODORE. *The Theatre and a Changing Civilization.* London: John Lane, The Bodley Head, 1935.

KRIEGSMAN, SALI ANN. *Modern Dance in America: The Bennington Years.* Boston: G. K. Hall & Co., 1981.

LANDIS, PAUL (ED.). *Four Famous Greek Plays.* New York: Random House (Modern Library), 1929.

———. *Six Plays by Corneille and Racine.* New York: Random House (Modern Library), 1931.

LEATHERMAN, LEROY. *Martha Graham: Portrait of the Lady as an Artist.* New York: Alfred A. Knopf, 1966.

LIEVEN, PRINCE PETER. *The Birth of the Ballets-Russes.* Translated by L. Zarine. New York: Dover Publications, 1973.

LLOYD, MARGARET. *The Borzoi Book of Modern Dance.* New York: Alfred A. Knopf, 1949.

LOVE, PAUL. *Modern Dance Terminology.* New York: Kamin Dance Publishers, 1953.

LUCIAN. *The Works of Lucian.* Translated by H. W. Fowler and F. G. Fowler. Oxford: Clarendon Press, 1905.

———. *The Works of Lucian.* Translated by A. M. Harmon. London: Heinemann, and New York: Macmillan, 1913–1961.

McDONAGH, DON. *Martha Graham.* New York: Praeger, 1973.

MacDONALD, NESTA. *Diaghilev Observed.* New York: Dance Horizons, 1975. London: Dance Books, 1975.

McGEHEE, HELEN. *Helen McGehee.* New York: Editions Heraclita, 1974.

MARTIN, JOHN. *America Dancing.* New York: Dodge Publishing Co., 1936.

———. *Introduction to the Dance.* Brooklyn: Dance Horizons, 1965.

———. *The Modern Dance.* Brooklyn: Dance Horizons, 1965.

MOORE, LILLIAN. *Artists of the Dance.* New York: Thomas Y. Crowell Co., 1938.

MORGAN, BARBARA. *Barbara Morgan*. Hastings-on-Hudson, NY: Morgan & Morgan, 1972.

———. *Martha Graham: Sixteen Dances in Photographs*. New York: Duell, Sloan & Pearce, 1941.

———. *Martha Graham: Sixteen Dances in Photographs*. Dobbs Ferry, NY: Morgan & Morgan, 1980. Revised edition.

MORRISON, THEODORE. *The Dream of Alcestis*. New York: Viking Press, 1950.

MORSHEAD, E. D. A. (TRANS.). *The House of Atreus*. London: Macmillan & Co., 1923.

MURRAY, GILBERT (ED.). *Ten Greek Plays*. New York: Oxford University Press, 1930.

MURROW, EDWARD R. *This I Believe*. Edited by Thomas P. Morgan. New York: Simon & Schuster, 1952–54.

New Larousse Encyclopedia of Mythology. Introduction by Robert Graves. New York: The Hamlyn Publishing Group (Prometheus Press), 1959.

NIETZSCHE, FRIEDRICH. *The Birth of Tragedy* and *The Genealogy of Morals*. Translated by Francis Golffing. Garden City, NY: Doubleday & Co. (Doubleday Anchor Books), 1956.

NOGUCHI, ISAMU. *A Sculptor's World*. New York: Harper & Row, 1968.

PERSE, ST.-JEAN. *Collected Poems*. Translated by W. H. Auden et al. Princeton, NJ: Princeton University Press (Bollingen Series LXXXVII), 1971.

———. *Chronique*. Translated by Robert Fitzgerald. New York: Pantheon Books (Bollingen Series LXIX), 1961.

———. *Éloges and Other Poems*. Translated by Louise Varèse. New York: W. W. Norton & Co., 1944.

———. *Exile and Other Poems*. Translated by Denis Devlin. New York: Pantheon (Bollingen Series XV), 1949.

PLATO. *The Dialogues of Plato*. Edited by Edith Hamilton and Huntington Cairns. Princeton, NJ: Princeton University Press (Bollingen Series LXXI), 1961.

PROPERT, W. A. *The Russian Ballet 1921–1929*. London: John Lane, The Bodley Head, 1931.

RAMBERT, MARIE. *Quicksilver*. London: Macmillan & Co., 1972.

RANK, OTTO. *Art and Artist*. Translated by Charles Francis Atkinson. New York: Agathon Press, 1968. Reprint of 1932 edition published by Alfred A. Knopf.

ROGERS, FREDERICK RAND (ED.). *Dance: A Basic Educational Technique*. New York: Macmillan Co., 1941.

ROOSE-EVANS, JAMES. *Experimental Theatre from Stanislavsky to Today*. New York: Universe Books, 1970.

ROSENTHAL, JEAN, AND WERTENBAKER, LAEL. *The Magic of Light*. Boston and Toronto: Little, Brown & Co., 1972.

SAYLER, OLIVER (ED.). *Revolt in the Arts*. New York: Brentano's, 1930.

SCHLUNDT, CHRISTENA L. *The Professional Appearances of Ruth St. Denis and Ted Shawn: A Chronology and an Index of Dances 1906–1932*. New York: The New York Public Library, 1962.

———. *The Professional Appearances of Ted Shawn and His Men Dancers:*

A Chronology and an Index of Dances 1933–1940. New York: The New York Public Library, 1967.

SEROFF, VICTOR. *The Real Isadora.* New York: Dial Press, 1971.

SEWALL, RICHARD. *The Life of Emily Dickinson,* 2 vols. New York: Farrar, Straus & Giroux, 1974.

SHAWN, TED. *Credo.* Privately published, no publisher, no date.

———. *Thirty-three Years of American Dance.* Pittsfield, MA: The Eagle Printing & Binding Co., 1959.

SHELTON, SUZANNE. *Divine Dancer: A Biography of Ruth St. Denis.* Garden City, NY: Doubleday & Co., 1981.

SHERMAN, JANE. *The Drama of Denishawn Dance.* Middletown, CT: Wesleyan University Press, 1979.

SOKOLOVA, LYDIA. *Dancing for Diaghilev: The Memoirs of Lydia Sokolova.* Edited by Richard Buckle. New York: Macmillan Co., 1961.

SORELL, WALTER (ED.). *The Dance Has Many Faces.* Cleveland and New York: World Publishing Co., 1951.

———. *Hanya Holm: The Biography of an Artist.* Middletown, CT: Wesleyan University Press, 1969.

ST. DENIS, RUTH. "Dance as Spiritual Expression," in Frederick Rand Rogers (ed.), *Dance: A Basic Educational Technique.* New York: Macmillan Co., 1941.

———. "Religious Manifestations in the Dance," in Walter Sorell, (ed.), *The Dance Has Many Faces.* Cleveland and New York: World Publishing Co., 1951.

———. *An Unfinished Life.* New York: Harper & Bros., 1939.

STEWART, JOHN A. *The Myths of Plato.* Carbondale, IND: Carbondale University Press, 1960.

STODELLE, ERNESTINE. *The First Frontier: The Story of Louis Horst and the American Dance.* Cheshire, CT: privately published, 1964.

TAPER, BERNARD. *Balanchine: A Biography.* New York: Macmillan Co. (Collier Books), 1960.

TENNYSON, ALFRED. *Idylls of the King.* Edited by Elizabeth Nitchie. New York: Macmillan Co., 1928.

TERRY, WALTER. *I Was There.* New York: Marcel Dekker, 1978.

TROWBRIDGE, CHARLOTTE. *Dance Drawings of Martha Graham.* Foreword by Martha Graham. New York: Dance Observer, 1945.

WIGMAN, MARY. *The Language of Dance.* Translated by Walter Sorell. Middletown, CT: Wesleyan University Press, 1966.

YOURCENAR, MARGUERITE. *Fires.* New York: Farrar, Straus & Giroux, 1981.

ZWEIG, STEFAN. *Mary Queen of Scotland and the Isles.* Translated by Eden and Cedar Paul. New York: Viking Press, 1935.

Personal Interviews

See Acknowledgments.

General Sources

New York Public Library Dance Collection.

Arthur Todd Collection (correspondence, scripts, interviews with the press).

Clipping files of the *New York Times* and *New York Herald Tribune*.

Magazines, such as *Ballet Review, Dance and Dancers* (London), *Dance Index, Dance Magazine, Dance Notes, Dance Observer, Dance Perspectives, Dance-scope,* and *The New Yorker.*

Souvenir programs.

Unpublished course papers done by students at New York University: Sachiyo Ito, paper on Michio Ito; and Susan Kennard Vaught, Notes on Martha Graham and Expressiveness in Dance.

Tapes:

-Martha Graham interview with Marian Horosko, Arthur Todd Collection (privately owned), made in 1962.

-Martha Graham interview with Walter Terry, November 16, 1952. New York Public Library Dance Collection.

-Tape of conversation between Mary Wigman and Ruth St. Denis, Arthur Todd Collection (privately owned), made in 1958.

-Tape of Martha Graham with Tony Merrill of the U.S. State Department, Arthur Todd Collection (privately owned).

Chronology of Works

Martha Graham and Concert Group (also programmed as Martha Graham and Dance Group)

Title	Date, Place of Premiere	Composer	Décor	Costumes	Lighting
1. *Chorale* (Martha Graham and trio)	Apr. 18, 1926 48th St. Theatre, N.Y.	César Franck		Martha Graham (M.G.)	Martha Graham (M.G.)
2. *Novelette* (solo, Martha Graham)	Apr. 18, 1926 48th St. Theatre, N.Y.	Robert Schumann		M.G.	M.G.
3. *Tanze* (trio)	Apr. 18, 1926 48th St. Theatre, N.Y.	Franz Schubert		M.G.	M.G.
4. *Intermezzo* (solo, Martha Graham)	Apr. 18, 1926 48th St. Theatre, N.Y.	Johannes Brahms		M.G.	M.G.
5. *Maid with the Flaxen Hair* (solo, Martha Graham)	Apr. 18, 1926 48th St. Theatre, N.Y.	Claude Debussy		M.G.	M.G.
6. *Arabesque No. 1* (trio)	Apr. 18, 1926 48th St. Theatre, N.Y.	Claude Debussy		M.G.	M.G.
7. *Clair de Lune* (Martha Graham and trio)	Apr. 18, 1926 48th St. Theatre, N.Y.	Claude Debussy		M.G.	M.G.
8. *Danse Languide* (trio)	Apr. 18, 1926 48th St. Theatre, N.Y.	Alexander Scriabin		M.G.	M.G.
9. *Désir* (solo, Martha Graham)	Apr. 18, 1926 48th St. Theatre, N.Y.	Alexander Scriabin		M.G.	M.G.

No. / Title	Date / Place	Composer		
10. *Deux Valses Sentimentales* (solo, Martha Graham)	Apr. 18, 1926 48th St. Theatre, N.Y.	Maurice Ravel	M.G.	M.G.
11. *Masques* (solo, Martha Graham)	Apr. 18, 1926 48th St. Theatre, N.Y.	Louis Horst	M.G.	M.G.
12. *Trois Gnossiennes: Gnossienne, Frieze, Tanagra* (Martha Graham and trio)	Apr. 18, 1926 48th St. Theatre, N.Y.	Erik Satie	M.G.	M.G.
13. *From a XIIth-Century Tapestry*, later retitled *A Florentine Madonna* (solo, Martha Graham)	Apr. 18, 1926 48th St. Theatre, N.Y.	Sergei Rachmaninoff	Earle Franke	M.G.
14. *A Study in Lacquer* (solo, Martha Graham)	Apr. 18, 1926 48th St. Theatre, N.Y.	Marcel Bernheim	M.G.	M.G.
15. *The Three Gopi Maidens* (trio) Excerpted from "The Flute of Krishna"	Apr. 18, 1926 48th St. Theatre, N.Y.	Cyril Scott	Norman Edwards	M.G.
16. *Danse Rococo* (solo, Martha Graham)	Apr. 18, 1926 48th St. Theatre, N.Y.	Maurice Ravel	Earle Franke	M.G.
17. *The Marionette Show* (solo, Martha Graham)	Apr. 18, 1926 48th St. Theatre, N.Y.	Eugene Goossens	M.G.	M.G.
18. *Portrait–After Beltram–Masses*, later retitled *Gypsy Portrait* (solo, Martha Graham)	Apr. 18, 1926 48th St. Theatre, N.Y.	Manuel de Falla	M.G.	M.G.

Title	Date, Place of Premiere	Composer	Décor	Costumes	Lighting
19. *The Flute of Krishna* (dance and film)	May 1926, Rochester, N.Y. Kilbourn Hall, Eastman-Kodak Studio	Cyril Scott		Norman Edwards	M.G.
20. *Prelude from "Alceste"* (Martha Graham and trio)	May 27, 1926 Kilbourn Hall, Rochester, N.Y.	C. W. von Gluck		Norman Edwards	M.G.
21. *Scéne Javanaise* (Martha Graham and trio)	May 27, 1926 Kilbourn Hall, Rochester, N.Y.	Louis Horst		Norman Edwards	M.G.
22. *Danza Degli Angeli* (trio)	May 27, 1926 Kilbourn Hall, Rochester, N.Y.	Ermanno Wolf-Ferrari		Norman Edwards	M.G.
23. *Bas Relief* (trio)	May 27, 1926 Kilbourn Hall, Rochester, N.Y.	Cyril Scott		Norman Edwards	M.G.
24. *Ribands* (duet, Evelyn Sabin and Betty MacDonald)	Aug. 20, 1926 Mariarden, Peterboro, N.H.	Frédéric Chopin		Norman Edwards	M.G.
25. *Scherzo* (trio)	Nov. 28, 1926 Klaw Theatre, N.Y.	Felix Mendelssohn		M.G.	M.G.
26. *Baal Shem* (Martha Graham and trio)	Nov. 28, 1926 Klaw Theatre, N.Y.	Ernest Bloch		M.G.	M.G.
27. *La Soirée Dans Grenade* (solo, Martha Graham)	Nov. 28, 1926 Klaw Theatre, N.Y.	Claude Debussy		M.G.	M.G.

#	Title	Date / Place	Composer		
28.	Alt-Wien (duet, Evelyn Sabin and Betty MacDonald)	Nov. 28, 1926 Klaw Theatre, N.Y.	Leopold Godowsky (arr. by Louis Horst)	M.G.	M.G.
29.	Three Poems of the East (Martha Graham and trio)	Nov. 28, 1926 Klaw Theatre, N.Y.	Louis Horst	M.G.	M.G.
30.	Peasant Sketches (solo, Martha Graham)	Feb. 27, 1927 Guild Theatre, N.Y.	Vladimir Rebikov, Alexandre Tansman, P. I. Tchaikovsky	M.G.	M.G.
31.	Tunisia (solo, Martha Graham)	Feb. 27, 1927 Guild Theatre, N.Y.	Eduard Poldini	M.G.	M.G.
32.	Lucrezia (solo, Martha Graham)	Feb. 27, 1927 Guild Theatre, N.Y.	Claude Debussy	M.G.	M.G.
33.	La Canción (solo, Martha Graham)	Feb. 27, 1927 Guild Theatre, N.Y.	René Defossez	M.G.	M.G.
34.	Arabesque No. 1, revised (group)	Aug. 2, 1927 Anderson-Milton School, N.Y.	Claude Debussy	M.G.	M.G.
35.	Valse Caprice (solo, Louise Gotto)	Aug. 2, 1927 Anderson-Milton School, N.Y.	Cyril Scott	M.G.	M.G.
36.	Spires (trio)	Oct. 16, 1927 The Little Theatre, N.Y.	J. S. Bach	M.G.	M.G.
37.	Adagio (solo, Martha Graham)	Oct. 16, 1927 The Little Theatre, N.Y.	G. F. Handel	M.G.	M.G.

	TITLE	DATE, PLACE OF PREMIERE	COMPOSER	DÉCOR	COSTUMES	LIGHTING
38.	*Fragilité* (solo, Martha Graham)	Oct. 16, 1927 The Little Theatre, N.Y.	Alexander Scriabin		M.G.	M.G.
39.	*Lugubre* (trio)	Oct. 16, 1927 The Little Theatre, N.Y.	Alexander Scriabin		M.G.	M.G.
40.	*Poème Ailé* (solo, Martha Graham)	Oct. 16, 1927 The Little Theatre, N.Y.	Alexander Scriabin		M.G.	M.G.
41.	*Tanzstück* (trio)	Oct. 16, 1927 The Little Theatre, N.Y.	Paul Hindemith		M.G.	M.G.
42.	*Revolt* (solo, Martha Graham)	Oct. 16, 1927 The Little Theatre, N.Y.	Arthur Honegger		M.G.	M.G.
43.	*Esquisse Antique* (trio)	Oct. 16, 1927 The Little Theatre, N.Y.	Désiré-Emile Inghelbrecht		M.G.	M.G.
44.	*Ronde* (trio)	Oct. 16, 1927 The Little Theatre, N.Y.	Rhené-Baton		M.G.	M.G.
45.	*Scherza* (solo, Martha Graham)	Dec. 10, 1927 Cornell University, Ithaca, N.Y.	Robert Schumann		M.G.	M.G.
46.	*Chinese Poem* (solo, Martha Graham)	Feb. 12, 1928 Civic Repertory Theatre, N.Y.	Louis Horst		M.G.	M.G.

47. *Trouvères* (solo, Martha Graham)	Apr. 22, 1928 The Little Theatre, N.Y.	Charles Koechlin	M.G.	M.G.
48. *Immigrant: Steerage, Strike* (solo, Martha Graham)	Apr. 22, 1928 The Little Theatre, N.Y.	Josip Slavenski	M.G.	M.G.
49. *Poems of 1917: Song Behind the Lines, Dance of Death* (solo, Martha Graham)	Apr. 22, 1928 The Little Theatre, N.Y.	Leo Ornstein	M.G.	M.G.
50. *Fragments: Tragedy, Comedy* (solo, Martha Graham)	Apr. 22, 1928 The Little Theatre, N.Y.	Louis Horst	M.G.	M.G.
51. *Resonances: Matins, Gamelin, Tocsin* (solo, Martha Graham)	Apr. 22, 1928 The Little Theatre, N.Y.	Gian Francesco Malipiero	M.G.	M.G.
52. *Dance* (solo, Martha Graham) "Strong Free Joyous Action": Nietzsche	Jan. 20, 1929 Booth Theatre, N.Y.	Arthur Honegger	M.G.	
53. *Three Florentine Verses* (solo, Martha Graham)	Jan. 20, 1929 Booth Theatre, N.Y.	Domenico Zipoli	M.G.	M.G.
54. *Four Insincerities: Petulance, Remorse, Politeness, Vivacity* (solo, Martha Graham)	Jan. 20, 1929 Booth Theatre, N.Y.	Sergei Prokofiev	M.G.	M.G.
55. *Cants Magics: Farewell, Greeting* (solo, Martha Graham)	Jan. 20, 1929 Booth Theatre, N.Y.	Fedérico Mompou	M.G.	M.G.

Title	Date, Place of Premiere	Composer	Décor	Costumes	Lighting
56. *Two Variations: Country Lane, City Street* (solo, Martha Graham)	Jan. 20, 1929 Booth Theatre, N.Y.	Alexander Gretchaninoff		M.G.	M.G.
57. *Figure of a Saint* (solo, Martha Graham)	Jan. 24, 1929 Millbrook, N.Y.	G. F. Handel		M.G.	M.G.
58. *Resurrection* (solo, Martha Graham)	March 3, 1929 Booth Theatre, N.Y.	Tibor Harsányi		M.G.	M.G.
59. *Adolescence* (solo, Martha Graham)	March 3, 1929 Booth Theatre, N.Y.	Paul Hindemith		M.G.	M.G.
60. *Danza* (solo, Martha Graham)	March 3, 1929 Booth Theatre, N.Y.	Darius Milhaud		M.G.	M.G.
Martha Graham and Dance Group					
61. *Vision of the Apocalypse: Theme and Variations* (group)	Apr. 14, 1929 Booth Theatre, N.Y.	Herman Reutter		M.G.	M.G.
62. *Moment Rustica* (group)	Apr. 14, 1929 Booth Theatre, N.Y.	Francis Poulenc		M.G.	M.G.
63. *Sketches from the People: Monotony, Supplication, Requiem* (group)	Apr. 14, 1929 Booth Theatre, N.Y.	Julien Krein		M.G.	M.G.
64. *Heretic* (Martha Graham and group)	Apr. 14, 1929 Booth Theatre, N.Y.	Old Breton Song—de Sivry		M.G.	M.G.

No.	Title	Date / Place	Composer		
65.	*Prelude to a Dance,* retitled *Salutation* (group)	Jan. 8, 1930 Maxine Elliott's Theatre, N.Y.	Arthur Honegger	M.G.	M.G.
66.	*Two Chants: Futility, Ecstatic Song* (solo, Martha Graham)	Jan. 8, 1930 Maxine Elliott's Theatre, N.Y.	Ernst Krenek	M.G.	M.G.
67.	*Lamentation* (solo, Martha Graham)	Jan. 8, 1930 Maxine Elliott's Theatre, N.Y.	Zoltan Kodaly	M.G.	M.G.
68.	*Project in Movement for a Divine Comedy* (Martha Graham and group)	Jan. 8, 1930 Maxine Elliott's Theatre, N.Y.	Silence	M.G.	M.G.
69.	*Harlequinade* (solo, Martha Graham)	Jan. 8, 1930 Maxine Elliott's Theatre, N.Y.	Ernst Toch	M.G.	M.G.
70.	*Two Primitive Canticles* (solo, Martha Graham)	Feb. 2, 1931 Craig Theatre, N.Y.	Heitor Villa-Lobos	M.G.	M.G.
71.	*Primitive Mysteries: Hymn to the Virgin, Crucifixus, Hosanna* (Martha Graham and group)	Feb. 2, 1931 Craig Theatre, N.Y.	Louis Horst	M.G.	M.G.
72.	*Rhapsodics: Song, Interlude, Dance* (solo, Martha Graham)	Feb. 2, 1931 Craig Theatre, N.Y.	Bela Bartok	M.G.	M.G.
73.	*Bacchanale* (Martha Graham and group)	Feb. 2, 1931 Craig Theatre, N.Y.	Wallingford Riegger	M.G.	M.G.
74.	*Dolorosa* (solo, Martha Graham)	Feb. 2, 1931 Craig Theatre, N.Y.	Heitor Villa-Lobos	M.G.	M.G.

Title	Date, Place of Premiere	Composer	Décor	Costumes	Lighting
75. *Dithyrambic* (solo, Martha Graham)	Dec. 6, 1931 Martin Beck Theatre, N.Y.	Aaron Copland		M.G.	M.G.
76. *Serenade* (solo, Martha Graham)	Dec. 6, 1931 Martin Beck Theatre, N.Y.	Arnold Schönberg		M.G.	M.G.
77. *Incantation* (Martha Graham and group)	Dec. 6, 1931 Martin Beck Theatre, N.Y.	Heitor Villa-Lobos		M.G.	M.G.
78. *Ceremonials* (Martha Graham and group)	Feb. 28, 1932 Guild Theatre, N.Y.	Lehman Engel		M.G.	M.G.
79. *Offering* (solo, Martha Graham)	June 2, 1932 Lydia Mendelssohn Theatre, Ann Arbor, Mich.	Heitor Villa-Lobos		M.G.	M.G.
80. *Ecstatic Dance* (solo, Martha Graham)	June 2, 1932 Lydia Mendelssohn Theatre, Ann Arbor, Mich.	Tibor Harsányi		M.G.	M.G.
81. *Bacchanale No. 2* (solo, Martha Graham)	June 2, 1932 Lydia Mendelssohn Theatre, Ann Arbor, Mich.	Wallingford Riegger		M.G.	M.G.
82. *Prelude* (solo, Martha Graham)	Nov. 20, 1932 Guild Theatre, N.Y.	Carlos Chavez		M.G.	M.G.
83. *Dance Songs* (solo, Martha Graham)	Nov. 20, 1932 Guild Theatre, N.Y.	Imre Weisshaus		M.G.	M.G.

84.	*Chorus of Youth—Companions* (group)	Nov. 20, 1932 Guild Theatre, N.Y.	Louis Horst	M.G.
85.	*Tragic Patterns* (Martha Graham and group)	Feb. 20, 1933 Fuld Hall, Newark, N.J.	Louis Horst	M.G.
86.	*Elegiac* (solo, Martha Graham)	May 4, 1933 Guild Theatre, N.Y.	Paul Hindemith	M.G.
87.	*Ekstasis* (solo, Martha Graham)	May 4, 1933 Guild Theatre, N.Y.	Lehman Engel	M.G.
88.	*Dance Prelude* (solo, Martha Graham)	Nov. 19, 1933 Guild Theatre, N.Y.	Nikolas Lopatnikoff	M.G.
89.	*Frenetic Rhythms* (solo, Martha Graham)	Nov. 19, 1933 Guild Theatre, N.Y.	Wallingford Riegger	M.G.
90.	*Transitions* (solo, Martha Graham)	Feb. 18, 1934 Guild Theatre, N.Y.	Lehman Engel	M.G.
91.	*Phantasy: Prelude, Musette, Gavotte* (solo, Martha Graham)	Feb. 18, 1934 Guild Theatre, N.Y.	Arnold Schönberg	M.G.
92.	*Celebration* (group)	Feb. 25, 1934 Guild Theatre, N.Y.	Louis Horst	M.G.
93.	*Four Casual Developments* (group)	Feb. 25, 1934 Guild Theatre, N.Y.	Henry Cowell	M.G.
94.	*Integrales* (group)	Apr. 22, 1934 Alvin Theatre, N.Y.	Edgard Varèse	M.G.
95.	*Dance in Four Parts: Quest, Derision, Dream, Sportive Tragedy* (solo, Martha Graham)	Nov. 11, 1934 Guild Theatre, N.Y.	George Antheil	M.G.

Title	Date, Place of Premiere	Composer	Décor	Costumes	Lighting
96. American Provincials: Act of Piety, Act of Judgment (Martha Graham and group)	Nov. 11, 1934 Guild Theatre, N.Y.	Louis Horst		M.G.	M.G.
97. Praeludium (solo, Martha Graham)	Feb. 10, 1935 Guild Theatre, N.Y.	Paul Nordoff		M.G. costumes redesigned in 1938 by Edythe Gilfond	M.G.
98. Course (Martha Graham and group)	Feb. 10, 1935 Guild Theatre, N.Y.	George Antheil		M.G.	M.G.
99. Perspectives: 1. Frontier (solo, Martha Graham); 2. Marching Song (Martha Graham and group)	Apr. 28, 1935 Guild Theatre, N.Y.	Louis Horst	Isamu Noguchi	M.G.	M.G.
100. Panorama (Martha Graham and group)	Aug. 14, 1935 Vermont State Armory, Bennington, Vt.	Norman Lloyd	Arch Lauterer Alexander Calder (mobiles)	M.G.	Arch Lauterer
101. Formal Dance, subsequently retitled Praeludium No. 2 (solo, Martha Graham)	Nov. 10, 1935 Guild Theatre, N.Y.	David Diamond		M.G.	M.G.
102. Imperial Gesture (solo, Martha Graham)	Nov. 10, 1935 Guild Theatre, N.Y.	Lehman Engel		M.G.	M.G.
103. Horizons (Martha Graham and group)	Feb. 23, 1936 Guild Theatre, N.Y.	Louis Horst	Alexander Calder	M.G.	M.G.

	Music	Set	Costumes	Lighting
104. *Salutation* (solo, Martha Graham) Apr. 7, 1936 Philharmonic Auditorium, Los Angeles, Ca.	Lehman Engel		M.G.	M.G.
105. *Chronicle* (Martha Graham and group) Dec. 20, 1936 Guild Theatre, N.Y.	Wallingford Riegger	Isamu Noguchi	M.G.	M.G.
106. *Opening Dance* (solo, Martha Graham) July 30, 1937 Vermont State Armory, Bennington, Vt.	Norman Lloyd		M.G.	Arch Lauterer
107. *Immediate Tragedy* (solo, Martha Graham) July 30, 1937 Vermont State Armory, Bennington, Vt.	Henry Cowell		M.G.	Arch Lauterer
108. *Deep Song* (solo, Martha Graham) Dec. 19, 1937 Guild Theatre, N.Y.	Henry Cowell		Edythe Gilfond	M.G.
109. *American Lyric* (Martha Graham and group) Dec. 26, 1937 Guild Theatre, N.Y.	Alex North		Edythe Gilfond	M.G.
110. *American Document* (Martha Graham, Erick Hawkins, and group) Aug. 6, 1938 Vermont State Armory, Bennington, Vt.	Ray Green	Arch Lauterer	Edythe Gilfond	Arch Lauterer
111. *Columbiad* (solo, Martha Graham) Dec. 27, 1939 St. James Theatre, N.Y.	Louis Horst	Philip Stapp	Edythe Gilfond	Philip Stapp
112. *Every Soul Is a Circus* (Martha Graham and group) Title: Vachel Lindsay Dec. 27, 1939 St. James Theatre, N.Y.	Paul Nordoff	Philip Stapp	Edythe Gilfond	Philip Stapp
113. *El Penitente* (Martha Graham, Erick Hawkins and Merce Cunningham) Aug. 11, 1940 Bennington College Theatre, Bennington, Vt.	Louis Horst	Arch Lauterer (subsequently redesigned by Isamu Noguchi)	Edythe Gilfond	Arch Lauterer

Title	Date, Place of Premiere	Composer	Décor	Costumes	Lighting
114. *Letter to the World* (Martha Graham and group) Title: Emily Dickinson	Aug. 11, 1940 Bennington College Theatre, Bennington, Vt.	Hunter Johnson		Edythe Gilfond	M.G.
Martha Graham and Company					
115. *Punch and the Judy* (Martha Graham and Company)	Aug. 10, 1941 Bennington College Theatre, Bennington, Vt.	Robert McBride	Arch Lauterer	Charlotte Trowbridge	Arch Lauterer
116. *Land Be Bright* (Martha Graham and Company)	Mar. 14, 1942 Chicago Civic Opera House, Chicago, Ill.	Arthur Kreutz	Charlotte Trowbridge	Charlotte Trowbridge	Arch Lauterer
117. *Salem Shore* (solo, Martha Graham)	Dec. 26, 1943 46th Street Theatre, N.Y.	Paul Nordoff	Arch Lauterer	Edythe Gilfond	Jean Rosenthal
118. *Deaths and Entrances* (Martha Graham and Company) Title: Dylan Thomas	Dec. 26, 1943 46th Street Theatre, N.Y.	Hunter Johnson	Arch Lauterer	Edythe Gilfond	Jean Rosenthal
119. *Imagined Wing* (Company)	Oct. 30, 1944 Library of Congress, Washington, D.C.	Darius Milhaud	Isamu Noguchi	Edythe Gilfond	Jean Rosenthal

No.	Work	Date/Place	Composer	Set	Costume	Lighting
120.	*Herodiade* (Martha Graham and May O'Donnell) Title: Stéphane Mallarmé (originally titled *Mirror before Me*)	Oct. 30, 1944 Library of Congress, Washington, D.C.	Paul Hindemith	Isamu Noguchi	Edythe Gilfond	Jean Rosenthal
121.	*Appalachian Spring* (Martha Graham and Company) Title: Hart Crane	Oct. 30, 1944 Library of Congress, Washington, D.C.	Aaron Copland	Isamu Noguchi	Edythe Gilfond	Jean Rosenthal
122.	*Dark Meadow* (Martha Graham and Company)	Jan. 23, 1946 Plymouth Theatre, N.Y.	Carlos Chavez	Isamu Noguchi	Edythe Gilfond	Jean Rosenthal
123.	*Cave of the Heart*, (Martha Graham and Company) originally titled *Serpent Heart*	May 10, 1946 McMillin Theatre, Columbia Univ., N.Y.	Samuel Barber	Isamu Noguchi	Edythe Gilfond	Jean Rosenthal
124.	*Errand into the Maze* (Martha Graham and Mark Ryder) Title: Ben Belitt	Feb. 27, 1947 Ziegfeld Theater, N.Y.	Gian-Carlo Menotti	Isamu Noguchi	M.G.	Jean Rosenthal
125.	*Night Journey* (Martha Graham and Company)	May 3, 1947 Cambridge High and Latin School, Cambridge, Mass.	William Schuman	Isamu Noguchi	M.G.	Jean Rosenthal
126.	*Diversion of Angels* (Company) Title: Ben Belitt (titled—at first performance only, *Wilderness Stair*)	Aug. 13, 1948 Palmer Aud., Connecticut College, New London, Conn.	Norman Dello Joio	Isamu Noguchi	M.G.	Jean Rosenthal

Title	Date, Place of Premiere	Composer	Décor	Costumes	Lighting
127. *Judith* (solo, Martha Graham)	Jan. 4, 1950 Columbia Auditorium, Louisville, Ky.	William Schuman	Isamu Noguchi	M.G.	Jean Rosenthal
128. *Eye of Anguish* (Erick Hawkins and Company)	Jan. 22, 1950 46th St. Theatre, N.Y.	Vincent Persichetti	Henry Kurth	Fred Cunning	Jean Rosenthal
129. *Gospel of Eve* (solo, Martha Graham)	Jan. 22, 1950 46th St. Theatre, N.Y.	Paul Nordoff	Oliver Smith	Miles White	Jean Rosenthal
130. *The Triumph of St. Joan* (solo, Martha Graham)	Dec. 5, 1951 Columbia Auditorium, Louisville, Ky.	Norman Dello Joio	Frederick Kiesler	M.G.	Jean Rosenthal
131. *Canticle for Innocent Comedians* (group) Title: Ben Belitt	Apr. 22, 1952 Juilliard School of Music, N.Y.	Thomas Ribbink	Frederick Kiesler	M.G.	Jean Rosenthal
132. *Voyage* (Martha Graham and Company)	May 17, 1953 Alvin Theatre, N.Y.	William Schuman	Isamu Noguchi	Edythe Gilfond	Jean Rosenthal
133. *Ardent Song* (Company)	Mar. 18, 1954 Saville Theatre, London	Alan Hovhaness		M.G.	Jean Rosenthal
134. *Seraphic Dialogue* (Company)	May 8, 1955 ANTA Theatre, N.Y.	Norman Dello Joio	Isamu Noguchi	M.G.	Jean Rosenthal
135. *A Dancer's World* (film)	1957	Cameron McCosh	Producer: Nathan Kroll Director, Camera: Peter Glushanok		

No. / Title	Date / Place	Composer	Set	Costume	Lighting
136. Clytemnestra (Martha Graham and Company)	Apr. 1, 1958 Adelphi Theatre, N.Y.	Halim El-Dabh	Isamu Noguchi	M.G., Helen McGehee	Jean Rosenthal
137. Embattled Garden (Company)	Apr. 3, 1958 Adelphi Theatre, N.Y.	Carlos Surinach	Isamu Noguchi	M.G.	Jean Rosenthal
138. Episodes: Part I (Martha Graham, Sallie Wilson, and Company)	May 14, 1959 New York City Center, N.Y.	Anton Webern	David Hays	Barbara Karinska, Cecil Beaton	David Hays
139. Appalachian Spring (film) (Martha Graham and Dance Company)	1959	Aaron Copland	Isamu Noguchi	Producer: Nathan Kroll Director, Camera: Peter Glushanok	
140. Night Journey (film) (Martha Graham and Dance Company)	1960	William Schuman	Isamu Noguchi	Producer: Nathan Kroll Director: Alexander Hemmid	Photographer: Stanley Meredith
141. Acrobats of God (Martha Graham and Dance Company)	Apr. 27, 1960 54th St. Theatre, N.Y.	Carlos Surinach	Isamu Noguchi	M.G.	Jean Rosenthal
142. Alcestis (Martha Graham and Dance Company)	Apr. 29, 1960 54th St. Theatre, N.Y.	Vivian Fine	Isamu Noguchi	M.G.	Jean Rosenthal
143. Visionary Recital (Martha Graham and Dance Company; revised as Samson Agoniste without Martha Graham, 1962	Apr. 16, 1961 54th St. Theatre, N.Y.	Robert Starer	Rouben Ter-Arutunian	M.G.	Rouben Ter-Arutunian

Title	Date, Place of Premiere	Composer	Décor	Costumes	Lighting
144. *One More Gaudy Night* (Company) Title: William Shakespeare	Apr. 20, 1961 54th St. Theatre, N.Y.	Halim El-Dabh	Jean Rosenthal	M.G.	Jean Rosenthal
145. *Phaedra* (Martha Graham and Dance Company)	March 5, 1962 Broadway Theatre, N.Y.	Robert Starer	Isamu Noguchi	M.G.	Jean Rosenthal
146. *A Look at Lightning* (Company) Title: Ben Belitt	March 5, 1962 Broadway Theatre, N.Y.	Halim El-Dabh	Ming Cho Lee	M.G.	Jean Rosenthal
147. *Secular Games* (Company)	Aug. 17, 1962 Palmer Aud., Connecticut College, New London, Conn.	Robert Starer	Marion Kinsella	M.G.	Jean Rosenthal
148. *Legend of Judith* (Martha Graham and Dance Company)	Oct. 25, 1962 Habima Theatre, Tel Aviv, Israel	Mordecai Seter	Dani Karavan	M.G.	Jean Rosenthal
149. *Circe* (Company)	Sept. 6, 1963 Prince of Wales Theatre, London	Alan Hovhaness	Isamu Noguchi	M.G.	Jean Rosenthal
150. *The Witch of Endor* (Martha Graham and Company)	Nov. 2, 1965 54th St. Theatre, N.Y.	William Schuman	Ming Cho Lee	M.G.	Jean Rosenthal
151. *Part Real—Part Dream* (Company)	Nov. 3, 1965 54th St. Theatre, N.Y.	Mordecai Seter	Dani Karavan	M.G.	Jean Rosenthal

No.	Title	Date / Place	Composer	Scenic Designer		Lighting
152.	Cortege of Eagles (Martha Graham and Dance Company)	Feb. 21, 1967 Mark Hellinger Theatre, N.Y.	Eugene Lester	Isamu Noguchi	M.G.	Jean Rosenthal
153.	Dancing—Ground (Company)	Feb. 24, 1967 Mark Hellinger Theatre, N.Y.	Ned Rorem	Jean Rosenthal	M.G.	Jean Rosenthal
154.	A Time of Snow (Martha Graham and Dance Company)	May 25, 1968 George Abbott Theatre, N.Y.	Norman Dello Joio	Rouben Ter-Arutunian	M.G.	Rouben Ter-Arutunian
155.	The Plain of Prayer (Company)	May 29, 1968 George Abbott Theatre, N.Y.	Eugene Lester	Jean Rosenthal	M.G.	Jean Rosenthal
156.	The Lady of the House of Sleep (Martha Graham and Dance Company)	May 30, 1968 George Abbott Theatre, N.Y.	Robert Starer	Ming Cho Lee	M.G.	Jean Rosenthal
157.	The Archaic Hours (Company)	Apr. 11, 1969 New York City Center, N.Y.	Eugene Lester	Marion Kinsella	M.G.	Jean Rosenthal

Martha Graham Dance Company

No.	Title	Date / Place	Composer	Scenic Designer		Lighting
158.	Mendicants of Evening (Company) Title: St.-John Perse	May 2, 1973 Alvin Theatre, N.Y.	David Walker	Fangor	M.G.	William H. Batchelder
159.	Myth of a Voyage (Company)	May 3, 1973 Alvin Theatre, N.Y.	Alan Hovhaness	Ming Cho Lee (Associate Designer: Patricia Woodbridge)	M.G.	William H. Batchelder

Title	Date, Place of Premiere	Composer	Décor	Costumes	Lighting
160. Holy Jungle (Company)	Apr. 30, 1974 Mark Hellinger Theatre, N.Y.	Robert Starer	Dani Karavan	M.G.	William H. Batchelder
161. Jacob's Dream (Company)	July, 1974 Jerusalem, Israel	Mordecai Seter	Dani Karavan	M.G.	
162. Lucifer (Margot Fonteyn, Rudolph Nureyev and Martha Graham Dance Company)	June 19, 1975 Uris Theatre, N.Y.	Halim El-Dabh	Leandro Locsin	Halston	Ronald Bates
163. Adorations (Company)	Dec. 8, 1975 Mark Hellinger Theatre, N.Y.	Donald Frost	Leandro Locsin	Halston	Ronald Bates
164. Point of Crossing (Company) Based on "Jacob's Dream"	Dec. 8, 1975 Mark Hellinger Theatre, N.Y.	Mordecai Seter	Leandro Locsin	M.G.	Ronald Bates
165. The Scarlet Letter (Company) Title: Nathaniel Hawthorne	Dec. 22, 1975 Mark Hellinger Theatre, N.Y.	Hunter Johnson	Marisol	Halston	Ronald Bates
166. O Thou Desire Who Art About to Sing (duet) Title: St.-John Perse	May 17, 1977 Lunt-Fontanne Theatre, N.Y.	Meyer Kupferman	Marisol	M.G.	Nicholas Cernovitch
167. Shadows (Company)	May 24, 1977 Lunt-Fontanne Theatre, N.Y.	Gian-Carlo Menotti	Frederick Kiesler	Halston	Nicholas Cernovitch
168. The Owl and the Pussycat (Company) Title: Edward Lear	June 26, 1978 Metropolitan Opera House, N.Y.	Carlos Surinach	Ming Cho Lee	Halston	Gilbert Hemsley, Jr.

No. / Title	Date / Location	Composer	Set Designer	Costume	Lighting
169. *Ecuatorial* (Company)	June 27, 1978 Metropolitan Opera House, N.Y.	Edgard Varèse	Marisol	Marisol, Halston	Gilbert Hemsley, Jr.
170. *Flute of Pan* (Company)	June 28, 1978 Metropolitan Opera House, N.Y.	Traditional	Leandro Locsin	Halston	Gilbert Hemsley, Jr.
171. *Frescoes* (Company)	December 9, 1979 Metropolitan Museum of Art, N.Y.	Samuel Barber			
172. *Episodes,* reconstructed, reworked (Company)	July 24, 1979 Covent Garden, London, England	Anton Webern	David Hays	Halston	
173. *Frescoes* (Company)	Apr. 22, 1980 Metropolitan Opera House, N.Y.	Samuel Barber		Halston	Gilbert Hemsley, Jr.
174. *Judith* reworked (Company)	Apr. 29, 1980 Metropolitan Opera House, N.Y.	Edgard Varèse	Isamu Noguchi	Halston	
175. *"Acts of Light"* (Company) Title: Emily Dickinson	Feb. 26, 1981 City Center, N.Y.	Carl Nielsen		Halston	Beverly Emmons
176. *Dances of the Golden Hall* (Company)	June 9, 1982 City Center, N.Y.	Andrzej Panufnik		Halston	Beverly Emmons
177. *Andromache's Lament* (Company)	June 23, 1982 City Center, N.Y.	Samuel Barber		Halston	Beverly Emmons
178. *Phaedra's Dream* (Company)	July 1, 1983 Herod Atticus Theatre, Athens, Greece	George Crumb	Isamu Noguchi	Halston	
179. *The Rite of Spring* (Company)	Feb. 28, 1984 State Theater, N.Y.	Igor Stravinsky	Ron Protas	Halston	Tom Skelton

Index